PRAISE FOR *THE BATTLE FOR GOTHAM*

"In her engaging new book, *The Battle for Gotham*, the journalist and urbanist Roberta Brandes Gratz chronicles Moses's reign and the unlikely resistance it sparked from the writer and activist Jane Jacobs."
—*Reason*

"Just as the ideas of Jane Jacobs bridged the Left/Right divide, a good deal of Gratz's book appeals not just to the Left (it's published by Nation Books, after all), but also to Reason-style libertarians . . . [*The Battle for Gotham*] is worth reading." —*National Review*

"[A] profoundly personal account of Moses's bulldozer diplomacy and its consequences for today . . . [Gratz] writes eloquently of her childhood in Greenwich Village, and then proves her point . . . Readers might not share her conclusions, but can't help being impressed with her reporting." —*New York Times*

"Gratz's book is invaluable at demonstrating how a slow accumulation of bitter, contentious struggles eventually gained some traction against Moses's model of clear-cut urban-renewal schemes. Still more important, though, is to remember how precarious those fights were and are, how close New York and other cities came to losing what are today some of their most prized spaces. She is utterly convincing about how vigilant we need to be so as not to lose any more."
—*Boston Review*

"[*The Battle for Gotham*] provides food for thought fo[r . . .] sis." —*New York Post*

"Gratz's essential recommendations—an adherence to principles of considered, context-driven design—still stand, shored convincingly by a half-century of history, public and personal. The result could seem like several books combined into one, but with adroit narration it avoids feeling claustrophobic. *The Battle for Gotham* is an account of the past crafted to support a claim about the future; an homage to a friend who, when it comes to cities, happened to be one of the most influential thinkers of the past century; and a cogent argument for revisiting her ideas and adapting them to a different time and, inevitably, a different New York." —*Metropolis Magazine*

"Though Gratz covers a number of key battlegrounds—Soho, Washington Square Park, the proposed Lower Manhattan Expressway—her account is less a blow-by-blow of such confrontations than it is a study of competing philosophies of urbanism, and a reminder that the legacies of Moses and Jacobs persist in today's fights over tax abatements, public transit funding, and expensive new stadiums." —*Booklist*

"Gratz offers some cogent critiques of contemporary urban planning (while also embracing a few [ideas], like urban farming)." —*Publishers Weekly*

"The spirit of Robert Moses has climbed from its crypt and again stalks the city. Roberta Brandes Gratz—channeling her friend Jane Jacobs—is determined to re-inter him, not with stake or silver bullet, but with a rigorous accounting of the true historical costs of Moses-style development, and the under-appreciated benefits of citizen-led, bottom-up regeneration. Its paean to urban complexity, coupled with its practical policy prescriptions, make the feisty *Battle for Gotham* a compelling and inspiring read." —Mike Wallace, author, *Gotham: A History of New York City to 1898* and director, Gotham Center for New York City History

"*The Battle for Gotham* is a brilliant account of the struggle between Robert Moses and Jane Jacobs—a struggle for how New York would develop in the twentieth century. A meticulous researcher, Roberta Gratz makes every fact resonate; she has made this story matter for our own time, and for people who are not New Yorkers. Anyone who cares about cities should read this book."
—Richard Sennett, author, *The Conscience of the Eye: The Design and Social Life of Cities* and *The Craftsman*

"For close to fifty years, Roberta Brandes Gratz has—with tenacity, acuity, and brio—been fighting the good fight for humane and sustainable cities. Her latest report from the trenches is filled with tales of villainy but, more importantly, with an unshakeable and persuasive hope for a better future. Like those of her great mentor, Jane Jacobs, her prescriptions are both logical and personal, precise and visionary. This is a book that springs from deep feeling of love."
—Michael Sorkin, author, *Twenty Minutes in Manhattan* and Distinguished Professor of Architecture and Director of the Graduate Program in Urban Design at the City College of New York

"Roberta Gratz poignantly weaves her own life story of urbanistic exploration together with the story of the battle of ideas between Robert Moses and Jane Jacobs to give the reader a palpable sense of complex urbanism. The result is an elucidation of how to make a better city."
—Jonathan Rose, president, Jonathan Rose Companies

THE BATTLE
FOR GOTHAM

ALSO BY ROBERTA BRANDES GRATZ

The Living City: Thinking Small in a Big Way (1989)

Cities Back from the Edge: New Life for Downtown (1998)

A Frog, A Wooden House, A Stream and A Trail:
Ten Years of Community Revitalization in Central Europe (2001)

THE BATTLE FOR GOTHAM

New York in the Shadow of
ROBERT MOSES
— AND —
JANE JACOBS

ROBERTA BRANDES GRATZ

NATION
BOOKS
New York

Published by Nation Books,
A Member of the Perseus Books Group

Nation Books is a co-publishing venture of the Nation Institute and the Perseus
Books Group.

Books published by Nation Books are available at special discounts for bulk
purchases in the United States by corporations, institutions, and other
organizations. For more information, please contact the Special Markets
Department at the Perseus Books Group, 2300 Chestnut Street, Suite 200,
Philadelphia, PA 19103, or call (800) 810-4145, ext. 5000, or e-mail
special.markets@perseusbooks.com.

Some of the images in this book have been reprinted with permission: photograph
of my apartment building, reprinted with permission of New York University
Archives; "Ford to City: Drop Dead" reprinted by permission of the *New York
Daily News*; "Mugged: A Victim's Story," reprinted by permission of the *New
York Post Daily Magazine*; "Here II" reprinted with permission of the Barnett
Newman Foundation; "How Westway Will Destroy New York" reprinted by
permission of *New York Magazine*; "Hurricane Katrina" reprinted with
permission of Ricardo Levins Morales.

Designed by Brent Wilcox

Library of Congress Cataloging-in-Publication Data
Gratz, Roberta Brandes.
  The battle for Gotham : New York in the shadow of Robert Moses and Jane
Jacobs / Roberta Brandes Gratz.
    p. cm.
  Includes bibliographical references and index.
  HC ISBN 978-1-56858-438-6 (alk. paper)
  PB ISBN 978-1-56858-678-6
  EB ISBN 978-1-56858-646-5
  1. Urban renewal—New York (State)—New York.   2. City planning—New
York (State)—New York.   3. Urbanization—New York (State)—New York.
4. Moses, Robert, 1888-1981.   5. Jacobs, Jane, 1916-2006.   I. Title.
  HT177.N5G73 2010
  307.3'41609747—dc22

First paperback edition 2011   2009047501

10 9 8 7 6 5 4 3 2 1

For Jane

> Never underestimate the power of a city to regenerate.
>
> JANE JACOBS

Contents

List of Figures

Acknowledgments

I have always relied on various urban thinkers and observers to inform and challenge my own observations and ideas. For this book, I am similarly indebted to a wonderfully patient and generous group who enriched the substance of this book.

Until her death, Jane Jacobs was a critical sounding board. Ron Shiffman and Richard Rabinowitz have been key in both of my earlier books as well as this one. Mary Rowe has both challenged and encouraged the details of this book in the best tradition of Jane Jacobs. Anthony Mancini has been my first reader and essential critic for this, as well as the two prior books, often saving me from myself. Thomas Schwarz, another reader of both prior works, challenged an early iteration of this one that helped me rethink its direction. Victor Navasky, as well, offered insights at an early point that clarified and changed the direction I needed to follow.

Nancy Milford, Nancy Charney, Laurie Beckelman, Stephen Goldsmith, Sandra Morris, and Margie Ziedler have been nurturing friends critical to the writing process. I am indebted to Robert Caro for opening my eyes and the world's eyes to the overarching power of Robert Moses.

I am enormously appreciative of Hamilton Fish, president of Nation Books, for being so ready and eager to publish this book and for turning me over to an extraordinary editor, Carl Bromley. Carl exemplifies the best qualities of an interested, caring, insightful, and nurturing editor whose comments and observations about all aspects of this text were most useful and constructive. I am similarly indebted to Basic Books publisher John Sherer for understanding what I planned to do and for being so interested in publishing this book. Annette Wenda, the copyeditor, Sandra Beris, the production editor, and Brent Wilcox, the compositor, artfully steered this manuscript to life.

Kent Barwick, Eddie Bautista, Marcy Benstock, Mary Beth Betts, Maya Borgenicht, John Bowles, Al Butzel, Joan Byron, Sarah Carroll, Majora Carter, Carol Clark, Joan Davidson, Mort Downey, Coco Eisman, Alexi Torres Flemming, Adam Friedman, Charles Gandee, Michael Gerrard, Francis Golden, Dennis Grubb, Bill Gratz, Isabel Hill, Abbie Hurlbutt, Lynda Kaplan, Jared Knowles, Lex Lalli, Peter Laurence, Corey Mintz, Norman Mintz, Forrest Myers, William Moody, Greg O'Connell, Marianne Percival, Bruce Rosen, Michael Rosen, David Rosencrans, Gene Russianoff, Don Rypkema, James Sanders, David Sweeny, Calvin Trillin, Joshua Velez, Mike Wallace, Anthony Wood, Elizabeth Yampierre. Others are mentioned throughout the book.

Sadly, my husband, Donald Stephen Gratz, did not live to see this publication. His ideas and influence, however, are woven throughout this text. I learned from him daily for many years and always appreciated his encouragement of my efforts. The legacy of his talent is reflected herein in the story of Gratz Industries.

My daughters—Laura Beth and Rebecca Susan—fabulous mothers, teachers, environmentalists, and preservationists—have always been most important in my life and now their children—Halina, Frank, Stella, Isaac, and Danielle—are a source of great pride and joy. I have no doubt they will all grow to be caring, productive citizens. My son-in-law, Jon Piasecki, an innovative landscape architect and committed environmentalist, is an additional source of pride.

Many people have let me know the value of my first two books and, I hope, they will find similar value here. They are the ones who will initiate the regeneration process wherever they live and work.

Preface

I was born and for the first decade of my life lived in Greenwich Village, the iconic urban neighborhood of crooked streets, historic buildings, diverse residents, and the occasional leafy, cobblestone street.

When I walked to school each day, played in Washington Square Park in the afternoon, visited my father in his dry-cleaning store, bought candy at a nearby newsstand, ran an errand for my mom, and came in from Washington Square Park for dinner when she called me from the sixth-floor window of our apartment house, my life was a page out of urbanist, author, and advocate Jane Jacobs's *Death and Life of Great American Cities*.

When my father's main store on West Third Street, where all garments were cleaned and pressed, was condemned to make way for an urban renewal housing project, when our apartment house on the south side of Washington Square also was condemned for another urban renewal project, this one for a New York University library, when my father was pushed to relocate his business and the family moved to a Connecticut suburb, my life was a page from the book of master planner and builder Robert Moses, who transformed New York City and State through the twelve appointed positions he held over forty years, from the 1930s to 1970s.

Mine was a classic city childhood of the 1940s and 1950s. New York street life was robust and vibrant, offering a feeling of total safety. I rode the double-decker bus up and down Fifth Avenue to dance class, shopping, and an occasional outing to Central Park. I took the subway to visit friends and, somewhat foolishly, went all the way to Coney Island with two friends and no adult at the age of eight. Washington Square Park was the primary arena for play, hanging out, or roller skating, with a daily stop to say hi to my grandfather on his favorite bench.

Our move to the suburbs was a distressing one. I had trouble fitting in. The difference between city and country was dramatic back then, and it was reflected in my classmates. I stood out like a sore thumb until I caught on to fitting in. The upstate girls' college I started at was much the same, and I eagerly returned to New York midstream to complete my undergraduate studies at New York University. Even then, New York still offered a rich experience with endless choices, including city and national politics during John Kennedy's election campaign,[1] until I embarked on a newspaper career at the *New York Post*.

I reveled in covering city life and couldn't believe I was getting paid to learn something new every day. Marriage, children, and brownstone living on the Upper West Side came later, and that too revealed aspects of city life that informed my reporting. This was the 1960s and 1970s: New York was changing, incrementally, I thought, but in retrospect quite dramatically. I was part of and witness to a sea change in city life. On one level, I was oblivious to the major forces driving it. With the hindsight and experience of forty years, I understand those forces now and share that understanding in the pages that follow.

I grew up in the shadow of Robert Moses and Jane Jacobs. Their clashing urban visions shaped postwar New York both directly and indirectly. In turn, that clash of visions helped shape the nation.

But I knew of neither of these overarching New York figures until adulthood and then only vaguely until well into my career as a newspaper reporter. Most New Yorkers were and still are similarly oblivious to either Moses or Jacobs. Yet these two giants of urban philosophy had enormous influence on the shape of American cities in general and New York City in particular.

The Moses-Jacobs Lens

To look at recent New York City history through the lens of the conflicting urban views of Moses and Jacobs is to gain a new understanding of the city today. This lens provides a small measure by which to evaluate the kind of big and modest projects outlined in this book. I did not have that lens either growing up or as a reporter for the *New York Post* from the mid-1960s until late in the 1970s covering city development issues. Eventually, I understood that in my writing I was immersing myself in the web of challenges personified in the conflict between the urban perspectives of Moses and Jacobs.

Two things helped develop that lens for me: reading Robert Caro's book *The Power Broker: Robert Moses and the Fall of New York* when it was published in 1974 and reading, meeting, and developing a lasting friendship with Jane Jacobs in 1978. My own urban vision had been shaped earlier during my fifteen years as a reporter, meeting and learning from people all over the city and watching positive and negative city policies unfold. But that urban vision was deepened and added to by that Moses-Jacobs lens and was expressed in my first book, *The Living City: Thinking Small in a Big Way*, first published by Simon and Schuster in 1989. *Urban Husbandry* was the term I coined in that book to describe a regeneration approach that reinvigorates and builds on assets already in place, adding to instead of replacing long-evolving strengths.

From the mid-1960s to the late 1970s, I reported for the *New York Post* on the impact of the great social and economic dislocations in the city. There were the urban renewal projects in Greenwich Village and the Upper West Side and, most dramatically, the opening of Co-op City that vacuumed out so many residents from the Grand Concourse and accelerated the decay of the South Bronx. I covered school decentralization battles in Ocean Hill and Brownsville and urban renewal on the Lower East Side, and I learned the fascinating evolution of Washington Heights while working on an in-depth series about newly appointed secretary of state Henry Kissinger, whose family settled there after fleeing Germany in 1938. There were public housing conflicts, landlord scandals in Times Square and on the Upper West Side, and middle-income apartment shortages. New urban renewal projects and battles to save landmarks all got my attention. But I had no knowledge of the role of Robert Moses in shaping urban renewal policies, locally and nationally, until Caro's extraordinarily well-researched and thorough opus.[2]

I had heard a little about Jane Jacobs's activism in Greenwich Village, particularly fighting the West Village Urban Renewal and the Lower Manhattan Expressway projects, but I had not read *The Death and Life of Great American Cities*. When I finally did read it, just before I was heading to Toronto to meet her, I discovered a way of understanding the city that I could relate to, a way that I had instinctively come to believe during years of reporting on community-based stories, an understanding that Jane believed all keen observers are capable of developing on their own. Over the years she challenged me, broadened my thinking, and encouraged me to look, observe, and understand beyond what I had already learned.

This book now looks back on the city as I first experienced it growing up and then wrote about it as a reporter. By using the Moses-Jacobs lens to examine some of the issues I wrote about in the late 1960s and 1970s, I come to a different conclusion from many experts on how the city reached the ultrasuccessful and constantly adapting condition of today—even if suddenly tempered by a colossal national economic meltdown.

The perspective of time is very useful. My time as a reporter was a trying period for the city. Bankruptcy loomed. Crime hit its peak. The infrastructure was crumbling. Vast swaths of neighborhoods lay abandoned. People were leaving. Fear was pervasive.

PAST IS PROLOGUE

For many, the memory of the depth of the city's troubles back then has dimmed over time. Through the lens of a newspaper reporter I observed this period firsthand. Many of the stories I wrote reflected both the trends of the day and hints of the future. Some directly mirrored my personal experience.

As a native New Yorker, my life and the life of the city are one. I have watched the changes in the Greenwich Village of my birth, lived the ascent of the Upper West Side with my husband and children, felt the impact of dubious city economic policies through the ups and downs of my husband's family-owned manufacturing business. All these experiences informed my observations and reporting and add focus to today's debates. Many of the issues I covered were of the moment—historic preservation, planning, community rebirth, the Westway fight. Most people have forgotten our recent history; some have never learned it. Looking back offers an interesting picture of the period and helps recapture that lost memory. I draw from those stories herein, in part, to look at where we were and how we evolved from that negative era, how New York City "repaired" itself, to borrow Jane Jacobs's word.

We know the past informs and shapes the present. But the past is not often defined as the recent past. The city's recent past, as revealed in this book, will surprise many. It is my contention that the Moses policies were largely responsible for the torn-apart, fallen city that brought the city to its worst condition in the 1970s;[3] Moses's fall from power and the end of his policies—both because of his excesses and because of the drying up of federal funding—brought the city back from the depths of urban despair.

It is also my contention that the modern city of today, which some would give Moses credit for, evolved despite the damage he wrought.

It is ridiculous to think that we could not have built roads, constructed public housing, or created parks without Moses. Europe rebuilt whole cities after World War II without destroying the urbanism that had been bombed away. Alternatives to Moses's plans were always available that did not erase neighborhoods, undermine social capital, and wipe out long-standing economic investment. Once he was gone, alternative options had a chance. For good reasons, the rebound of the city as a magnet for talent and improved neighborhoods all occurred after Moses's departure.

Observation tells us that the most successful areas of the city today are those Moses didn't eviscerate; the most troublesome are the ones he did. I am not ready to let the rehabilitation of Robert Moses go unchallenged. The worst of his legacy lives on.

The fall of Moses allowed the city to meaningfully regenerate. And while I don't think the urban philosophy of Jane Jacobs has prevailed to the degree many observers contend, I do recognize it as the driving force— the foundation, if you will—of the opposition to favored, repetitive Moses-style development policies. It is also the defining force—articulated as such or not—of some of the most innovative current citizen-based initiatives. Fortunately for the city, for all cities in fact, the Jacobs legacy lives on.

This book tells the tale of two cities reflected in two very different and competing urban views, as represented by Moses and Jacobs. Moses's view was antiurban; the city needed to be reshaped, thinned out, controlled. Jacobs's view was the opposite; she found in the city a dynamic energy, a vitality from the absence of control, the ability of so many positive things made possible exactly because of people's ability to self-organize for civic, economic, or social purposes.

I lived, observed, and wrote about things shaped by both of those city views. No single vision can guide a city; by its very nature, a city embodies multiple visions. This book explores their world and mine and, in the process, offers another particular view of what can be seen.

INTRODUCTION

A Clash of Visions—Then and Now

> Cities have the capability of providing something for everybody only because and only when they are created by everybody.
>
> JANE JACOBS

Robert Moses started in the 1920s, Jane Jacobs in the late 1950s and early '60s. While they were of different periods, they overlapped in the 1960s, and their clashing visions have had unending impacts from then to now.

Moses's influence came through the nearly unlimited power he exercised in the administrations of six governors and five mayors; Jacobs's came through the insightful and popular observations of urban life that she penned in seven books, starting with *The Death and Life of Great American Cities* in 1961 and her leadership in New York battles against Moses projects during the 1960s.[1] Moses also directly helped shape projects in other cities; Jacobs inspired resistance to them. The impact of both personalities stretched across the country and beyond.

Moses started in state government in the 1920s as a reformer, but by the end of World War II, he held several positions in New York City that put him in charge of almost all public housing, public works projects, and highway construction. He learned to use the system he helped to reform in order to amass power on a scale never seen before or since. Eventually, his autocratic approach to massive highway building, park creation, and

large-scale public housing construction led to urban policies that were elit-
ist, top down, efficiency based, expert dependent, technocratic, and anti-
democratic. The policies Moses initiated were totally dependent on large
government subsidies under national and local programs he helped create.

Moses and Jacobs were not really adversaries, as is too often suggested,
although she directly and successfully opposed specific projects he promoted.
Adversaries implies equal status. In fact, Jacobs was not a peer of Moses,
and she was often either dismissed or berated as "just a housewife." Make no
mistake: Moses had unlimited power "to get things done"; Jacobs had none.

Moses, as the urban renewal and highway building czar, by way of his
vision of how he thought things *should* be, shaped the physical city and in
consequence the social and economic life of its inhabitants. Jacobs, however,
the activist and urbanist, paid attention to how cities work on the ground,
what a city actually *is* and how it functions. In the process of paying attention to how things work, she framed vehement opposition to Moses's and
other big sweeping projects, advocated on behalf of an organic process of
how a city truly evolves, and helped give voice to a strong civic sentiment.

Moses came out of the Progressive reform tradition. Antagonistic to
politics, he learned to use the embedded patronage tradition of the powerful Democratic Party to advance his agenda and assume more control.
Jacobs came out of a community-based radical sensibility, antagonistic to
both patronage and centralized control, and directly confronted elected
officials supportive of Moses.

Moses's vision derived from the popular urban design theory of the day
promoted by French architect Le Corbusier in his 1925 Plan Voisin for
Paris.[2] Le Corbusier's Plan called for both the demolition of the historic
core of Paris and its replacement by high-rise towers-in-the-park. As urban
design professor Robert Fishman notes, the Plan "announced modernism's
ruthless attitude toward the past and its demand for a revolutionary redesign of the city."[3]

COMPETING VIEWPOINTS

Jacobs saw value and logic in the sometimes messy traditional neighborhoods where work, play, residence, industry, retail, and education lived
cheek by jowl in a variety of building styles, ages, and scale—what she
termed "mixed use." Moses, however, saw sprawling chaos that needed
replacement with functions spatially separated from each other.

He was about ideology, she about observation. He posited; she watched. He was power; she was common sense. Moses saw static form; she saw process.

Jacobs celebrated the complexity of the urban fabric, recognizing it as a web of interconnections and interdependencies; Moses called for cleaning it up and imposing efficiency and order.

Jacobs advocated interventions in scale with what exists; Moses planned interventions as replacements for that time-woven fabric.

Jacobs saw wisdom in the observations and proposals for change from the local residents and businesspeople whom Moses disdained.

The pedestrian was central in Jacobs's view, the car in Moses's.

Jacobs saw regenerative potential in well-worn, solid neighborhoods; Moses saw blight and prospects for clearance and new projects.

Jacobs viewed social and economic problems as needing social and economic solutions, identifying what positive elements could be added to alter the negative dynamic; Moses promulgated the illusion that spending money on the physical plant solves social and economic problems.

Jacobs defined economic development as new work added to older work; Moses defined it as building new buildings for economic activity not yet identified. "You can't build the ovens and expect the loaves to jump in," Jacobs said of Moses's definition of economic development, a definition that is officially still with us today. Jacobs focused on the yeast and loaves, Moses on the ovens.

Moses advocated an efficiency of scale; Jacobs said small is not necessarily beautiful but economies of scale are a myth.

Moses's projects depended on big government financing of one sort or another; Jacobs abhorred big government underwriting. "Loans, grants, and subsidies are golden eggs which, being only gold, don't hatch goslings."

Such intellectual overlays to public policy and events take a long time to articulate. And although the 1950s and '60s were when some of the specific project battles took place, the penetration of the broader society and public discussion seemed to come to a head in the late 1960s and 1970s.

CONVENTIONAL THINKING CHALLENGED

The Jacobs ethos emerged, even before her name was attached to it, in reaction to the Moses philosophy and policies. Resistance to massive clearance, appreciation of street-level neighborhood life, suspicion of expertise, advocacy of investment in mass transit equal to highway building, oppo-sition to large-scale displacement, and recognition of the physical and so-cial strengths of existing low-income neighborhoods too easily designated slums were all present before Jacobs's first book and her emergence as a spokesman for the anti-Moses viewpoint. But her writing and activism validated and expanded that civic energy and provided the vocabulary for coming civic battles. Before I knew of Jacobs or had read her works, I was drawn to the stories in the city reflecting that resistance. They formed the core of my reporting at the *New York Post*.

Moses's power collapsed in the late 1960s due to his own overreach-ing and the intensity of the growing opposition to his projects.[4] He couldn't sustain such a monopoly on power. The physical and human cost of the massive dislocation of residents and businesses all over the city became too high. So while he fell due to political overreaching, the Jacobs voice gained strength because it was populist, antipolitical (or at least antiparty politics), citizen based instead of "expert" reliant.

Both shortly before and after the Moses-Jacobs clash in the larger arena of intellectual life, assorted voices challenged prevailing authority. The humane world challenged the machine world, a biological view of the built environment versus a physical one, human ecology versus the machine. The primacy of the physical sciences was giving way to the rise of the social sciences.

Marine biologist Rachel Carson would soon jump-start the environ-mental conservation movement with *Silent Spring* (1962).[5] Carson's cri-tique was broad in specifics and impact because she brought attention to "the interconnectedness and fragility of the natural world," whether on land or sea, threats posed by the "quest for profits, government policies and by reckless human intervention." She saw the threats to urban oases, parks, and nature by six-lane highways, the threat to nature of suburban development, and then the threats to the whole environment posed by pesticides and herbicides. She saw the "destruction of beauty and the sup-pression of human identity in the hundreds of suburban real estate devel-opments where the first action is to cut down all the trees and next to build infinitude of little houses, each like its neighbor."[6] Carson brought attention to the wholeness of nature the way Jacobs focused on the web of connections that add up to an urban organism. The concept of interde-pendency contradicted the idea that elements of nature or the world could be studied and understood separately.

Not long before Jacobs's rise to prominence, in the late 1950s humanist psychologist Abraham Maslow focused on real people and real lives over statistical analyses and scientific tests. Psychologist Rollo May also emphasized the humanist reality over conventional techniques, a view resonating in the 1960s when people tired of the mechanistic measurements and methods of the behaviorists. Margaret Mead, of course, had brought a whole new human dimension to the study of culture through her pathbreaking observations of primitive peoples, challenging accepted thought about gender, race, and habitat. Canadian educator and communications theorist Marshall McLuhan had already been stirring the media field with his prediction of the emerging "global village," the term he coined for the coming electronic age.[7] And Betty Friedan's *Feminine Mystique*, published in 1963, launched the women's movement.

Sociologists, journalists, and other nonacademics in the 1950s and '60s were challenging the conventional wisdom dominated by academics in different fields, questioning prevailing theories and societal behavior, exposing wrongdoings and injustice. They challenged the status quo and wrote books that were accessible, not abstract or scholarly. Those books set the terms of national public discussion, shaped movements, and gave birth to policy modifications.

David Riesman opened the 1950s with an examination of the American character with *The Lonely Crowd: A Study of the Changing American Character* (with Nathan Glazer and Reuel Denney). William H. Whyte's *Organization Man* (1956) defined corporate conformity in white-collar suburbs and observed the loss of individualism. Vance Packard's *Hidden Persuaders* (1957) critically dissected the advertising profession and its manipulation of consumers. John Kenneth Galbraith's *Affluent Society* (1958) challenged conventional thought, addressing economic inequality and coining the terms *affluent society* and *conventional wisdom*. Galbraith demystified economics by treating it as an aspect of society and culture rather than an arcane discipline and forced the country to reexamine its values, labeling America a "democracy of the fortunate." Ralph Nader took aim at the automobile industry, the backbone of the country's postwar back-to-work economy, first in a 1959 article in the *Nation*, "The Safe Car You Can't Buy," and then in 1965 in his book *Unsafe at Any Speed*. Michael Harrington exposed the country's deep poverty in *The Other America: Poverty in the U.S.* (1962). These were transformative books of immense power and resonance that defined a moment. Perhaps most or all of these books gave the public license to reject the prevailing dogmas in any field, and to think for itself, surely a basic Jacobs theme.

Another dimension must be studied as well. What is considered the conventional thinking of the postwar era evolved logically. World War II proved the effectiveness of large-scale planning and the role of expertise. The war built the prestige of a certain kind of mindset of thinking big and the effective role of government in a top-down command economy. During the war, neighborhoods and downtowns deteriorated with no new investment. After the war, the industrial model was applied to domestic and environmental challenges. The cost of dislocation was not of great concern. After all, that industrial model gave rise to the agribusiness food industry we wrestle with today. The quantity of people that could now be fed amazed everyone. This is what Carson was reacting to.

Moses had the prestige to apply this model to the problems of cities. Liberal support was strong for big government programs to address various problems. The prestige of government was strong. The authorities who had done miracles in many areas earned the public's respect. Opposition was minimal.

NEW WAYS OF SEEING

An echo of all this was found in the design and planning fields, where new voices were being heard. *The Exploding Metropolis* (1958), written mostly by editors of *Fortune* and edited by William H. Whyte Jr., directly challenged the idea of the Le Corbusier "skyscraper city" and the growing dominance of the car. Jacobs contributed a chapter, "Downtown Is for People," while Whyte, in his introduction to the book, extolled the virtues of the vitality of "messy," complex urban districts versus the sterility of efficiently planned ones.

Housing advocate Charles Abrams published *Forbidden Neighbors: A Study of Prejudice in Housing* (1956), calling attention to discrimination in public housing and the social upheaval of slum clearance. Herb Gans would publish *The Urban Villagers* (1962) a year after Jacobs's *Death and Life*, rebutting prevailing notions of what was a slum by focusing on the destruction of an Italian community in the West End of Boston. Gans's book resonates as much today as it did then in its depiction of community ties and networks that provide social and economic strength.

Architectural critic Lewis Mumford had already published in 1953 *The Highway and the City*, lambasting the impact that new highways were having on still-viable cities. Mumford was also a sharp critic of the public housing towers, although his solution—in contrast to Jacobs—was a low-density, quasi-suburban form of Garden City, bringing more country into the city. And while Mumford encouraged Jacobs to write *Death and Life* (they had met in 1958 at a Harvard symposium), he was horrified at its final publication with its contrast to his own views of urban life and wrote a scathing review of her book for the *New Yorker*. "Mother Jacobs' Home Remedies" was the headline, reflecting the condescending tone of his review.[8]

Paul Davidoff's 1965 article "Advocacy and Pluralism in Planning," following shortly after Jacobs's book, accelerated the emergence of the advocacy planning movement. Advocacy planning takes a totally different approach to planning than most of the profession. Advocacy planners listen and hear what people on the ground have to say, recognizing that people in the neighborhoods and in area businesses are better able to understand conditions and contribute solutions. Advocacy planners learn what the real problems are, take seriously locally promulgated solutions, and provide technical expertise to the implementation of locally developed plans. Advocacy planning grew out of both civil rights and urban renewal struggles. Davidoff, considered the father of the advocacy planning movement, was greatly influenced by Jacobs.

This was an intellectually rich era "when book publishers sought books that could change thinking and the political agenda," observes University of Massachusetts history professor Daniel Horowitz.[9] This broad group of authors gave the public license to come to their own conclusions and to be skeptical about institutions.

BOOKS CAN CHANGE THE WORLD

Thus, challenges to the highly planned, mechanistic strategies of building that Moses epitomized were in the air. Jacobs's writing paralleled this humanistic trend. The city was not a machine for living, as architect Le Corbusier had pronounced. Urban life could not be reduced to engineering models for traffic, housing, entertainment, and employment, Jacobs argued. Ultimately, the world is too complicated for such simplistic approaches to the complex web of urban issues.

Jane Jacobs challenged the emperor's new clothes when she said quite simply that things don't happen the way the experts say they do or should; observation proves otherwise. She exposed the falsehood of expert predictions: If you move people out of tenements into high-rise housing blocks, crime will drop. If you build more roads, traffic will ease. If you direct the arts into cultural islands, the arts will be enriched. If you wipe out the messy mix of small and large companies, incubators and corporations, the city will grow. If you provide efficient new facilities in separate districts, the economy will improve. Jacobs's observations of real city life showed these predictions were not true. Crime doesn't decrease if you move people out of tenements. Traffic doesn't get better if you build more roads. Artistic life isn't richer if you create malls for the arts. The economy doesn't improve by separating uses, trying to make the city efficient and wiping out the organically evolved diversity of businesses.

Jacobs challenged economists to think in new ways and to observe how things really work, not project how they should. She understood early the issues of urbanism and sustainability in both economic and environmental terms, but not until her later books did she focus directly on them. The complex underpinnings of society defied reengineering by experts, she argued. Universities and other intellectual institutions deceive the public into thinking urban issues are distinct and separate. Observe, observe, observe, and listen, Jacobs challenged the experts with the publication of her first book.

On the ground, people were doing what she wrote about. They were doing it intuitively, and she observed and learned from them, distilling the essence of what they did and validating both their observations and their strategies. Early in the introduction to *Death and Life*, for example, Jacobs cites her visits to public housing projects in East Harlem where Union Settlement social workers Ed Kirk and Ellen Lurie opened her eyes to the failures of public housing design and development. She listened to them, observed what they were seeing, and learned from them. The extraordinary impact on her thinking is clear. This excerpt about East Harlem speaks volumes:

> There is a housing project with a conspicuous rectangular lawn which became an object of hatred to the project tenants. A social worker frequently at the project was astonished by how often the subject of the lawn came up, usually gratuitously . . . and how much the tenants de-

spised it and urged that it be done away with. When she asked why, the usual answer was, "What good is it?" or "Who wants it?" Finally a tenant more articulate than the others made this pronouncement: "Nobody cared what we wanted when they built this place. They threw our houses down and pushed us here and pushed our friends somewhere else. We don't have a place around here to get a cup of coffee or a newspaper even, or borrow fifty cents. Nobody cared what we need. But the big men come and look at that grass and say, 'Isn't it wonderful! Now the poor have everything.'"[10]

On the one hand, Jacobs gave voice to popular sentiments. On the other hand, she was too sophisticated and complicated a thinker to be just a voice. Even today, her teachings are the stuff of lively intellectual discourse, often invoked inappropriately to gain acceptance of a new development proposal.

Recent New York history is incomprehensible without some awareness and understanding of the clashing visions of these two seminal figures. Through the Moses-Jacobs lens, one recognizes the distinctions between genuine examples of regeneration and those that are only label deep. Genuine regeneration's critical value to the city's economy and social and physical framework becomes clear. Equally important, the wrongheadedness of some current Moses-style projects reveals itself as well.

EXAMINING THE PAST AND THE PRESENT

The Moses-Jacobs lens is as helpful in assessing what is happening today as it is relevant to understanding broad urban change in the second half of the last century in New York and other cities. The scale of clearance and displacement may be less than the heyday of urban renewal, but the destructive worship of bigness is no less now than it was then. What Jacobs identified as "the belief in bigness as a solution" is still central to official planning and development policies in New York City and elsewhere. But as Jacobs also observed, "More is not more if it is not right. People have been corrupted into thinking that the most important thing about anything is its size instead of the substance of what is happening."[11] When you hear the oft-repeated quote of Daniel Burnham, "Make no little plans," you know something big and probably too big is about to be unveiled.[12]

Scale, however, is not the only issue today through which the Moses-Jacobs lens is useful. Considerable development is overplanned based on a simplistic interpretation of mixed use. Mixed use is much more complex than a combination of residential, commercial, and retail. The spontaneity and innovation of a true urban place can be just as stifled in a development of this combination as in a single-use project. The authentic urban fabric cannot be replicated whole cloth. As Jacobs shows, an all-new mixed-use project attracts only a limited variety of users, users suited to expensive new space. The real diversity of users in a vibrant city requires a mix of old and new buildings of different styles and scale, an authentic urban mix.

The impact and philosophies of Moses and Jacobs permeate New York controversies surrounding such recent and current city projects as Westway, the defeated proposal to expand and rebuild the West Side Highway along the Hudson River; the excessive investments of public funds in stadia instead of more critical city needs; and the upzoning (increasing what developers can build) of more than one hundred areas, including industrial and waterfront neighborhoods. Upzoning has had an enormous impact, pricing out middle-income tenants, new creative enterprises, and small manufacturing, all vital components of the city's economy.[13]

Enormous projects are promoted as beneficial for the city's future, while businesses and residents are pushed out of the targeted gritty, mixed-use districts. These megaprojects struggle even in good economic times due to their own internal weaknesses, and they undermine the creative resident community and local manufacturing that offer enduring social and economic value to the city. Worse, such projects erase early precursors of regeneration that, if allowed to evolve, can bring authentic, positive urban change, and they require enormous public funding.

The big projects never fulfill expectations; small ones always exceed theirs.

BIG IS EVEN BIGGER

The four-billion-dollar Atlantic Yards in Brooklyn, in a twenty-two-acre campuslike setting, has stumbled along since 2003 and has already sacrificed a viable taxpaying community, productive jobs, occupied residences, and worthy historic buildings. This follows a long-discredited Moses tradition, as will be shown later in this book.

Columbia University pushes forward aggressively its new seventeen-acre campus in Harlem, displacing 400 families, 1,600 jobs, and countless businesses, home owners, and property owners, whereas a worthy expansion of Columbia could have been accommodated without this sacrifice. This, too, will be shown to be a Moses clone.

Willets Point, sixty-one highway-encircled, pothole-filled acres in Queens adjacent to Shea Stadium (now Citi Field), with its 250 known businesses—and more than 1,500 workers—is the target for total demolition in order to build yet another massive copycat mixed-use development. This area has never had sanitation, sewers, streetlights, or paved roads but survived a Moses scheme with the help of a young unknown Queens lawyer and future governor, Mario Cuomo. Now, it is a Moses vision revived. Willets Point is a dramatic example, as will be detailed later, of how to do the wrong thing, Moses style, with massive public subsidy. And here again the city is prepared to confiscate the land of staunch resisters under eminent domain at great expense and then turn it over to new private owners with tax breaks and other incentives.

These are only a few Moses-style projects being promoted as the next best "regenerative" plan (as discussed in the conclusion). These projects rely heavily on the strength of the real estate market, adding a vulnerability that over the years has seen much cleared land sit untouched and unproductive for decades after clearance is completed. The promise is always of jobs, taxes, and, these days, affordable housing, but no one calculates the jobs, taxes, and affordable commercial and residential units lost in the process. Demolition sweeps away uncalculated numbers of jobs, housing units, and other uses in a diverse urban district.

Moses relied on real estate and government funding; Jacobs looked to the energy, innovation, and commitment of citizens. For too long, developers and corporations either threaten to leave or promise Oz-like goodies will come of their projects. New York's long-standing policy of giving them subsidies and tax incentives is unrelenting.

Enduring Change Starts Smaller

At the same time that these big projects are promoted and fought, escalate in costs, and, for the most part, fail, modest but meaningful things are actually happening, bringing positive change and showing the ongoing potential of big change achieved incrementally. The opportunity to nurture

and build on such successes is lost because they are officially undervalued, sometimes hardly recognized, and too often stymied. Small upgrades
are happening in every conceivable neighborhood, not because of any
helpful official policy but because the appeal of urban life has accelerated
in recent years and the opportunities to enjoy city life have expanded. In
fact, independent of public policies, new areas of economic activity are
occurring where civic resourcefulness, ingenuity, and improvisation are
not interrupted. Occasionally, smart public policy follows these bottom-
up initiatives.

The immigrant-filled neighborhoods that had been experiencing high
vacancy rates not long ago bring new entrepreneurs and local vitality.
New industries—food preparation, custom furniture, movie production,
green products, and renovation and restoration services—have emerged
just when the available industrial space is shrinking owing to upzoning
and overdevelopment. Artfully converted empty buildings have been salvaged and upgraded with new creative uses in neighborhoods long declared dead by "experts" who have no real understanding of the
authentic urban process.

As Matias Echanove and Rahul Srivastava have noted:

> Fifty years after Jane Jacobs' advocacy work in Manhattan, policy-
> makers and planning departments have yet to acknowledge what local
> knowledge and expertise can contribute to the planning process. Ignor-
> ing local actors comes at a high cost, accompanied as it is by strong op-
> positions, and more often than not resulting in inadequate urban
> development. It is only with a paradigm shift in the way we conceive of
> cities that we can actually tap into local intelligence and its productive
> capacity. In an age of "information" where billions of people are ex-
> changing bits and data across platforms and boundaries, we should no
> longer rely on the master-planner's map and the one-way PowerPoint
> presentations that pass off for community involvement.[14]

Individual catalysts have altered whole neighborhoods. The diversity
of those catalysts is as rich as the work they do and illustrates, once again,
how big change comes in varying ways dispersed around the city. Beat
cop–turned-developer Gregory O'Connell, for example, has transformed
Brooklyn's Red Hook in the fifteen years since he started converting Civil
War warehouses on the waterfront that the city wanted to demolish. He

created space for 150 businesses and 1,200 workers and always has a waiting list for available space. He was the catalyst for the explosion of economic activity in Red Hook.

Common Ground, an organization developing low-income housing in renovated buildings especially for the formerly homeless, exhibits a different creative problem-solving path. Involving future tenants in the design, Roseanne Haggerty has created three thousand units of housing for displaced low-income tenants and the homeless in the fewer than fifteen years since she started Common Ground. Her strategy is to ask potential tenants what they need and build it. Common Ground facilities, mostly restored formerly deteriorated hotels, fit comfortably in their community from West Forty-second Street to Bushwick.

Challenging standard economic assumptions, Jacobs argued that meaningful economic progress always depends on the continued development of new kinds of work replacing or expanding existing forms. In this vein, a new "green" industry is evolving in small steps in various corners of the city. For instance, Omar Freilla's expanding recycling operation, ReBuilders Source, in the Hunts Point section of the Bronx, sells used and overstocked building supplies at deep discounts, almost like a Salvation Army model for home improvement, Freilla says.[15] Freilla believes it to be the first worker-owned cooperative for reused building materials. He got the idea of selling salvaged and donated materials while working for Sustainable South Bronx, or SSBx. That grassroots organization, under the formidable leadership of its founder, Majora Carter, pioneered a green roof project with its own newly created for-profit installation company, Smart Roofs, LLC, and started a "green-collar" job-training program.

In a similar vein, Spec-It-Green is NYIRN's (New York Industrial Retention Network) effort to get city manufacturers to produce green products and get builders to buy them, thereby infusing the whole supply stream with new made-in–New York green products.

David Sweeney, with his Greenpoint Manufacturing Development Corporation, is profitably converting underused industrial buildings into incubators of small businesses and light manufacturers, while city planning policies continue to undermine industrial neighborhoods by upzoning policies that escalate real estate values. His waiting list for space only gets longer as the city loses industrial space. Although he started rescuing old factories through this nonprofit organization, he has since continued to

preserve industrial space in old buildings with the use of private investment money. Venture capital has recognized what official policy denies,
that manufacturing not only has a future in the city but is critical to maintaining diversity in the city economy.

Assorted community-based development groups spread around the
South Bronx led the revival of that borough, starting in the 1970s with the
rescue and renovation of abandoned housing, the building of new infill
housing, and community-based housing management.[16] But in the 1990s,
a new wave of groups—the Point, Sustainable South Bronx, Mothers on
the Move, Youth Ministries for Peace and Justice—emerged there and
around the city, integrating youth, environment, criminal justice, and an-
tiviolence. They have become the true nurturers of what Jacobs described
as "adaptations, ameliorations, and densifications" that add up to enduring, positive change.

The Bronx River Alliance is a public-private partnership of more
than sixty-one grassroots organizations, institutions, and public agencies that first came together as the Bronx River Working Group in the
late 1990s in a real example of community-initiated healing of an area
torn asunder by urban renewal. The alliance, with the help of the city's
Department of Parks, is working to restore the Bronx River, construct
the Bronx River Greenway, build not-so-small parks, initiate boating
programs on the river, and use the river for student and community environmental education. Youth Ministries for Peace and Justice, the
Point, and Sustainable South Bronx were among the founders of the
Bronx River Alliance.

With some overlap in member organizations, the Southern Bronx
River Watershed Alliance is composed of a smaller number of local and
citywide organizations that came together specifically to advocate for the
community plan to eliminate the Sheridan Expressway and redevelop its
footprint for affordable housing, community and commercial space, and
parks.[17] The Sheridan Expressway is a little-used, never-completed 1.25-
mile Moses road that runs parallel to the river and separates a huge community from it. Despite the road's minimum transportation value and
maximum community damage, the State Department of Transportation
has been trying for years to maintain and finish it.[18] The community plan
to demolish it would instead reclaim twenty-eight acres and reconnect existing neighborhoods—West Farms, Longwood, Bronx River, Hunts
Point, and more—to each other and to the Bronx River (and the new

greenway parks).[19] Local streets would be extended to connect the community to the river, wetlands would be restored, and land would be reclaimed on which to build affordable housing.

It is hard to overstate the impact, especially on the Bronx, of the proliferation of citizen efforts since the earliest ones in the 1970s. What occurred between then, when the South Bronx looked like Berlin after World War II, and now, when finding empty land to build on is difficult, is a story with more lessons than experts can absorb. A cleaned-up Bronx River, new parks, youth programs, cultural venues, community-planned new development, environmental improvements, and community events—the list is endless but all part of the regeneration process that evolved from the bottom up to repair the damage of the Moses era. Various agencies under Mayor Bloomberg have been clearly responsive, leading to partnerships that have strengthened and advanced the momentum of positive change. This is the same Bronx that Robert Moses and housing commissioner Roger Starr (Planned Shrinkage)[20] declared hopeless and wanted to only clear and rebuild or landbank.

Private efforts in upscale Manhattan neighborhoods also have had enormous impact. One of the most celebrated, and internationally emulated, new public spaces is the High Line on the Lower West Side, six blocks of hulking elevated rail track once used to carry goods from Hudson River piers to warehouses in Lower Manhattan. The effort to transform it into a linear park, designed by Diller, Scofidio + Renfro, is the result of two citizens, Josh David and Robert Hammond,[21] who fought the demolition plan of former mayor Rudolph Giuliani and found a sympathetic administration with the election of Mayor Michael Bloomberg. The High Line cause paralleled the rising appeal of the neighboring Gansevoort Market Historic District, a once-gritty, truck-filled area now dominated by upscale fashion retailers, art galleries, and restaurants. All of these efforts demonstrate clearly the enormous positive change possible from assorted modest citizen-led initiatives.

Big City Change in Incremental Steps

The city administration as well is making big changes with small strides even while it more aggressively promotes and overvalues controversial large projects. Individuals within the administration have a mandate to find new creative ways to make positive changes, especially in the area of reducing traffic congestion and air pollution. The Housing and Preservation Department under Shawn Donovan, now head of Housing and Urban Development in Washington, D.C., created 81,500 new low-income units scattered around the city, out of a goal of 165,000 over five years, less than they hoped for but considerable nonetheless.[22] The Housing Authority is making possible needed infill development on long-underused and unnecessary open space left from the tower-in-the-park era of misguided development. For years the Housing Authority has been replacing windows, upgrading water-conserving plumbing, and installing low-energy-consuming appliances in public housing, increasing efficiency and lowering energy costs. None of these are individually big projects in one place but are large overall, with positive effects nonetheless.

The Transportation Department, under director Janette Sadik-Khan, is achieving enormous citywide change with small-scale initiatives that wrest traffic lanes from vehicles and expand the bicycle path network. Sadik-Khan created new plazas on street space where cars were once the sole occupants. Tables and chairs proliferate. More than two hundred miles of bike lanes have been added across the city in three years, with more planned. Bus stops are more welcoming. In the process, Sadik-Khan has reminded us of the multiple purposes of city streets. Nibble by nibble she is reclaiming city space eroded during the more-cars era—she calls it the "attrition of automobiles."[23] But she's done something equally significant in demonstrating that a department of transportation has a greater responsibility than just moving traffic and that streets belong as much to pedestrians and bikers as to cars. This is part of the mayor's ambitious vision to reduce pollution and traffic congestion.

PlaNYC is a shrewd planning document that includes many of the big development schemes that would have been included in a traditional master plan. However, this is not a traditional plan. What is unique are dozens of farsighted environmental initiatives that have never been seen in a city plan, including citywide storm-water drainage upgrades, making city buildings energy efficient, eliminating thousands of parking permits for city employees, the planting of 1 million trees (200,000 so far), and providing incentives to get 15 percent of the city's taxi fleet converted to hybrids. This "long-term vision for a sustainable New York City" is based on a somewhat mysterious prediction that by 2030, the city population is expected to rise to 9.1 million, from its current 8.36 million. Such predictions are always tricky, like the one in the 1970s when the City Planning Commission predicted the population would go down to the 5 million range. The PlaNYC prediction, of course, did not anticipate an economic collapse or the exodus of some immigrants returning to their home countries as opportunities in the United States diminished. Futurist predictions are always risky and often wrong. Nevertheless, many of the modest accomplishments of city agencies already mentioned are enumerated worthwhile goals in this plan, regardless of population changes.

It is well known that the city's communities of color and low-income residents carry the heaviest burden in pollution and traffic, from garbage handling, incinerators, and power plants. For years, environmental justice groups had been pushing for equity in the handling of the city's solid waste, both commercial and residential. The goal was to shift waste export to rail and barge from thousands of trucks and to equitably redevelop the city's dormant network of marine waste-transfer stations. Progress here has been made on several fronts. Instead of just building new big power plants, some existing plants have been retrofitted to increase megawatt production, while simultaneously decreasing pollution emissions. Two new marine transfer stations were approved for Manhattan, one on the Upper East Side and one on the Lower West Side, to reduce the truck traffic having a negative impact on the South Bronx, Brooklyn, and Queens. Recycling efforts have increased to reduce the volume of garbage. Again, it's big change in small increments.

Perhaps most significantly, a long-term solid-waste management plan proposed by Mayor Bloomberg and adopted by the New York City Council in 2006 is revolutionizing garbage removal for the city. This plan had been championed by environmental justice activists for a decade. All Bronx residential and municipal waste—about 2,100 tons per day—was shifted from truck to rail. The Staten Island Railroad was reactivated, and household waste in that borough now travels by rail. In 2009, residential waste generated in the North Brooklyn waste shed was shifted to rail from trucks. This Brooklyn operation represents up to 950 tons of waste per day. Eliminated are an estimated forty long-haul tractor trailer trips a day and about thirteen thousand trips a year. Permits to construct new marine transfer stations are also being sought so more containerized waste can be transported by barge to rail loading points or out-of-state receiving sites. Reducing large vehicular traffic on a big scale is no small feat. At present, more than one-third of the city's residential and solid waste is now being transported out of the city by rail.

Mayor Bloomberg not only agreed to the environmental justice civic coalition's longtime proposals but also brought into the administration one of the leaders of that fight. Eddie Bautista was the lead organizer for the Organization of Waterfront Neighborhoods before he was appointed director of the Mayor's Office of City Legislative Affairs to oversee the Bloomberg administration's local legislative agenda. Bautista also continues to work with administration officials on the implementation of the landmark 2006 Solid Waste Management Plan.

The extraordinary success at the three-hundred-acre Brooklyn Navy Yard—between the Manhattan and Williamsburg bridges—under Andrew Kimball is the clearest evidence any city official should need to understand that New York City is still a perfectly viable site for light industry and that not enough space for it exists, as more than one hundred neighborhoods are upzoned, squeezing out existing manufacturing. In five years, the Navy Yard has gone from 3,500 to 5,000 jobs in forty or more buildings. The 230 companies vary remarkably in size, with many having grown exponentially in recent years. New buildings are in construction. The waiting list continues to grow. Only one company failed during the economic collapse, and as soon as one moves out, another moves in, all this while Wall Street, tourism, and retail hemorrhage jobs.

The Parks Department's two-billion-dollar ten-year capital plan to build new and repair old facilities is the largest ever, and its impact is incremental citywide. In 2008 alone, four hundred million dollars was spent, clearly a stimulus package of the best kind. The restoration of the historic Highbridge, a substantial new park in Elmhurst; replacement of gas tanks, an indoor pool, and a skating rink in Flushing Meadow; restoration of McCarren Pool (a beneficial Moses legacy); creation of a huge new park on the former landfill of Staten Island's Fresh Kills; and renovation and upgrades of small parks all over town are significant quality-of-life and neighborhood investments that have nothing to do with real estate or conventional economic development projects. In themselves, however, these investments function as magnets for economic and social improvement of an area, the kind that really works. Most significantly, many of the city's best park investments (Hunts Point, Bronx River, High Line, community gardens) followed grassroots proposals. Responding to local ideas is the highest form of government leadership.

After years of debate and indecision, the mayor also began installing 3,300 bus-stop shelters made in New York City, 20 public toilets, and 330 replacement newsstands; converted more of the city's car fleet to hybrids; and drastically reduced parking privileges for city employees who unnecessarily added to traffic congestion.[24] These are not insignificant quality-of-life and environmental issues, either; they will have citywide social and economic impacts rather than the big-bang impact of one big development project in one place.

All these governmental efforts dovetail nicely with local, private, and nonprofit initiatives. These are big efforts in modest doses spread all over town, adding up to big change. This is building on and adding to existing assets, appropriate in scale and context—Urban Husbandry at its best.

-1-

THE WAY THINGS WERE

I am a creature of the city I was born in. Although my parents contributed, it was the city—with its vibrancy, diversity, challenges, and choices, along with its sights, smells, and sounds—that raised me and shaped my urban sensibility. Our move to a Connecticut suburb shaped me also. It gave me a taste of another way of life, one that sharpened my urban sensibility. Mine is a New York tale, but more than that, my family story parallels that of millions of Americans and illustrates patterns of social change that altered the face of American cities, not just New York.

My parents were both the children of immigrants, both born and raised in Brooklyn, enthralled by the American dream as defined in the early decades of the last century. I was the first of my family to be born in Manhattan, a tremendous achievement for my parents' generation, as moving from Brooklyn to Manhattan was a mark of accomplishment.

My father was in the dry-cleaning business, first learning the business by working for someone else, then opening his own store with money borrowed from the family circle, and expanding that business into a small chain of four stores in Greenwich Village.[1] This pattern of entrepreneurial evolution was typical of new immigrants and their children. It still is. One can observe this happening, particularly in immigrant neighborhoods, in cities everywhere. Borrowing from the "family circle" or "community network" has always been the first step in new immigrant business formations. My family was no exception. Conventional banks are an intimidating, alien experience and not usually welcoming to immigrants.

The main store was on Eighth Street between Fifth and Sixth Avenues, then the primary shopping street of Greenwich Village. The plant, where

1

garments from all four stores were cleaned, was on West Third Street, around the corner from where we lived. When I was very young, my mother worked there with my father while my older sister and I were in school. My mother enrolled in a decorating course at NYU (neither of my parents had been to college) and eventually became a professional interior decorator (today she would be called an "interior designer"). She developed an active career gaining clients through word of mouth.

We lived in a spacious apartment on the sixth floor of a twelve-story building on the south side of Washington Square Park with windows overlooking the park. My mother could keep an eye on me when I played in the park or beckon me if I overstayed my playtime. Roller skating, jumping rope, swinging a leg over a bouncing Spaldeen to the "A My Name Is Alice" game, and trading-card games against walls of buildings were favorite pastimes.[2] Others played stoopball, stickball, curb ball, and many more. The variety of kids' games on the sidewalks and streets of the city is infinite. The vitality that this street activity represented, under the watchful eyes of parents and neighbors, was often misinterpreted as slum conditions.

Television was not yet affordable for my family, but I had a friend on the twelfth floor who enjoyed that luxury. Every Tuesday night, I would visit her to watch Uncle Miltie (Milton Berle). Occasionally, I also got to watch Sid Caesar's *Show of Shows* or, just as exciting, Ed Sullivan. I even saw the show on which he introduced the Beatles.

I walked seven or eight blocks to school; played freely and endlessly in the park; listened to folk singers who gathered regularly at the Circle (the local name for the big circular fountain); traveled uptown to museums, theaters, and modern dance lessons; and shopped Fourteenth Street for inexpensive everyday clothes and Fifth Avenue uptown for the occasional more expensive special purchases.

On Christmas Eve, my parents, my sister, and I would take the Fifth Avenue bus up to Fifty-ninth Street (Fifth Avenue was two-way then) and stroll down to Thirty-fourth Street to enjoy the exuberant Christmas windows of the department stores. While all the department stores competed to produce the most artful window displays, Lord & Taylor always won hands down; Saks Fifth Avenue and B. Altman alternated for second place. Even the few banks and airline offices then on Fifth Avenue put on a good display. Then we would take the bus the rest of the way downtown and join carolers singing at the huge Christmas tree under the Wash-

1.1 My apartment house and block on Washington Square South before condemnation. *NYU Archives*.

1.1a NYU's Bobst Library replaced my block. *Jared Knowles*.

ington Square Arch. It was a great tradition. The city was a delightful place to be in the 1940s and 1950s.

The Push-Pull Effect

Two things led my family to move to Westport, Connecticut, then a paradigm of suburbia. Opportunity beckoned my father. The first strip shopping center, with the area's first branch of a New York City department store, had opened in Westport. Like in so many downtowns across America, this one was a short distance from downtown, enough to draw business away. Across from that, only minutes from Main Street, a second was about to open. The builder of the second center wanted to include a dry-cleaning store. He wanted my father to be the one to do it.

Strip centers across America of that time imitated city shopping streets and actually repackaged in a planned version the successful commercial mix that evolved spontaneously on urban streets. Developers went by a formula that included a mixture of service and specialty stores. Thus, the builder wanted a dry cleaner to locate between the supermarket and the baby-clothes store, with the hardware, carpeting, and other stores and the luncheonette to follow down the line. The offer was a hard-to-resist business opportunity for my father.

My father hungered for the appeal of suburban life, but my mother definitely did not and never settled into it happily. "You pay a stiff price for that blade of grass," she used to say. Nevertheless, opportunity was having an irresistible pulling effect on my father. We made the switch.

My mother resisted the stay-at-home suburban-housewife lifestyle, but she definitely got caught up in the car culture. My father drove a second-hand Chevy station wagon, but my mother's first car was a red Ford convertible with a V8 engine and stick shift. If she had to be in the suburbs, she wanted a fun car. A few years later, her second car was similar but in white. Both cars were guaranteed boy magnets in the parking lot on the very rare occasion that I was permitted to drive her car to school. For after-school activities, most of the time, I hitchhiked or biked to my destination. My mother refused to be a chauffeur.

While opportunity and suburban living were having a pulling effect on my parents, three negative forces intruded on our balanced urban existence and helped push us over the edge. The Third Street building in which my father's main "plant" (I never knew why it was called a plant) was located was condemned as part of a large urban renewal project, devised by Robert Moses. "Urban Renewal" was the federal program that funded the major overhaul of most American cities starting in the 1950s. The plant's Third Street block was part of the sizable chunk of the South Village's multifunctional, economically viable urban fabric that was sacrificed for subsidized middle-income apartment houses set in green plazas, namely, Washington Square Village and south of that the Silver Towers designed by I. M. Pei. This area, just north of Houston and the future SoHo, had a similar mix of cast-iron commercial buildings, tenements, small apartment houses, and a few federal houses.

Through urban renewal, New York University, not yet the dominant force in the neighborhood that it has become, acquired our apartment building and let it be known that all tenants eventually would have to move to make way for university expansion. Urban renewal, then as now, helped educational institutions expand campuses through eminent domain, the taking of private property for a loosely defined public purpose. Bobst Library, a hulking sandstone library designed by Philip Johnson, was built on the site.

As if losing our apartment and my father's plant were not enough, underworld forces were muscling in on small businesses, like my father's on Eighth Street, making it increasingly difficult for business owners like my father to remain independent. The primary site for Larry Brandes Dry

1.2 "L. Brandes Cleaners" was my father's store on Eighth Street, circa 1930s or 1940s, with delivery truck parked in front. *Eighth Street BID.*

Cleaners was centrally located on Eighth Street, at MacDougal. Eighth Street is the Village's equivalent to a Main Street.

PUSHED TO LEAVE

The combination of Robert Moses Urban Renewal and the underworld shakedowns made our departure inevitable. So we moved to Weston, Connecticut, the neighboring town to Westport. My father, having sold what he could of the business in the city, opened in neighboring Westport one of the first cash-and-carry dry-cleaning stores in a Connecticut shopping center. My sister, Paula, was working for a New York advertising agency, and she created a newspaper campaign that started weeks before the opening, playing on the theme of "city to suburb."

No pick-up and home delivery service was offered in the new store, as had been done in the city, but same-day service and on-site shirt laundering were possible that hadn't been in his city stores. The store opened in 1953, and I eagerly worked there after school and Saturdays, starting by assembling hangers and eventually waiting on customers.

"Hand-finishing" (a fancy term for ironing) was a service not usually available in dry-cleaning stores. My father introduced that service in

Westport. Katie, a woman who worked in the West Third Street plant, commuted from Harlem to Westport to continue working for my father. He picked her up every morning at the train station. Amazingly as well, two of the pressers, Al and Phil, who lived in Brooklyn's Bedford-Stuyvesant and also had worked on West Third Street, commuted from the city every day to continue working for my father. They were ardent Brooklyn Dodger fans; my father and I were equally ardent Yankee fans. During games—especially pennants and World Series—the store was wild with cheers and jeers. Customers came second.

I remember being fascinated at how many customers knew my father from the Village. "Are you the same Larry Brandes, dry cleaner, that used to be on Eighth Street?" they would ask. They were former city customers, now new suburbanites seeking the same greener pastures as my father. Greenwich Village residents were moving to Westport. The exodus to the suburbs was gaining momentum. We were witness to and participants in a phenomenon that would change the face of America.

Weston, where we moved to, was a small-town adjunct to the larger, better-known Westport. I went to junior high in Weston but high school in Westport because Weston did not yet have one. My father's store was in Westport.

My father dreamed of building a year-round house. We had the land. Our summer cottage—no heat or winter insulation—was on the site. That tiny two-bedroom house was an expression of family creativity. My father built closets, installed windows where only screens had been, and created a small but efficient kitchen. My sister painted Peter Hunt designs on cabinets and closet doors. My mother sewed slipcovers and curtains. I helped "drip" paint the floors with my mother and sister à la Jackson Pollock. That cottage was demolished to make room for a year-round split-level house, the popular housing design of the 1950s.

Weston, in the heart of Fairfield County, was one of those idyllic communities where comfortable homes were surrounded by woods, streams, and lawns. A Long Island Sound beach was a short drive. Historic white clapboard farmhouses and similarly redolent colonials dominated the landscape until suburban development overran so much open space in the 1950s and '60s. Year-round country living appealed to my father. For a boy who grew up on the streets of Brooklyn, learned to dive off piers in New York Harbor, and played stickball in the street, the lure of the lawn, the rose garden, and the swimming pond was irresistible. He planted an apple tree from seed, and every few years I drive by to assure myself it is still there. Taxes were cheap. The public schools were nationally acclaimed. In those days, New York City was only one hour away by train, an hour and a half by car. Both modes of travel to New York City take longer today due to excruciating vehicular traffic and diminished train service.

SUBURBIA IN FORMATION

Model homes were going up around Westport, a great attraction for city residents. Low-interest, federally guaranteed mortgages, new federally funded modern school construction, low taxes, and the allure of home ownership added appeal. I was oblivious to the suburbanization of America then in full swing. But I do remember when the woods and fields where we went horseback riding were lost to a development of split-level homes.

My mother, by then a well-practiced interior decorator, worked for local new home builders, making the insides of the model homes as appealing as the larger idea of moving to suburbia was. The trick of the trade, she told me, was to furnish the model home with diminutive furniture to make the rooms look bigger—such as cot-size beds instead of twins, a love seat instead of a full-size sofa, small paintings on the walls. Most of what was going up in and around Westport, as with the rest of suburban America in the 1950s, were split-level homes with the single (only sometimes double) garage and unfinished basement. That unfinished basement was the middle-class sweat-equity opportunity to finish yourself. When we in fact built our own new home to replace the summer cottage, it was a "customized" and enlarged version of that split-level model.

In a nutshell, there it was: many of the urban-suburban issues that would dominate development news for the second half of the last century. They shaped my early life and my journalistic interests later.

We were living the "push-pull" effect. People weren't simply fleeing cities for the suburbs. They were being pulled by the opportunities to buy a home, pay low taxes, open a business, or send kids to brand-new schools. The amenities of the suburbs—the roads to get there, the low-interest loans to finance homes, the modern schools, the shopping centers to lure city businesses—were subsidized by the federal and state governments.

No comparable programs were investing in cities. In fact, the reverse was true. Redlining by banks and insurers and blockbusting by realtors precluded the home-ownership dream in most New York neighborhoods and in cities across America. "When I lived in New York," Jane Jacobs told me years later, "we had savings and could borrow from family members to buy a small house in Greenwich Village. We couldn't get any bank loans. Banks had blacklisted or redlined this area. In America, all sorts of cities that were very viable were redlined. People couldn't get a loan. We could have gotten a loan very easily to move to the suburbs. There was a lot of social engineering manifested through where money would be lent and wouldn't be lent, what would be built and wouldn't be built. People weren't told they were being socially engineered like this, but they were."[3]

DEFINING PROGRESS

The push to leave for us and many others was not due to the so-called deteriorating urban conditions popularly blamed for the population shift to the suburbs. We didn't experience or witness serious crime. And even though young, my sister and I moved around Manhattan alone, by bus, subway, or on foot. I didn't know how to go outside Manhattan. I did not experience fear, and, obviously, my parents felt comfortable enough letting me go places on my own.

The dramatic push at that time was the push of urban renewal, massive demolition, and disappearing neighborhoods. Banks stopped giving loans for businesses and properties destined to fall under the urban renewal wrecking ball. Businesses like my father's (and later my husband's) and residents like my family did not move out simply by choice. It is not difficult to observe how the tear in an urban fabric, regardless of its size, weakens the threads around it so further erosion becomes inevitable. The displacement by a highway, or an urban renewal clearance project, was very much the crux of the push.

Many years later, I reflected with Jane Jacobs about this period—when federal funding priorities led to sweeping changes to urban neighborhoods and downtowns. She cautioned me that "there are two kinds of change, and you can symbolize them on the land," she explained. "There's the kind of change in which the topsoil is being built up, and it's being made more fertile and is good husbandry of the land. The land is changing when you do that, but it is positive change. Then there's a kind of change that's just as definitely change—that's erosion. Gullies are being dug in the land, and the topsoil is being carried away and it's being made infertile. The fact that it's changed doesn't mean that it's progress. It's ruin. But people were, for a long time, brainwashed into the idea that every sort of change in a city was progress. 'Well, yes, it's bad, but that's progress.' No, that's erosion. And people didn't want to be thought of as old-fashioned."

THE SHOCK OF THE NEW

The transition to the suburbs was not easy. For me it was traumatic. To transfer from a progressive private school in Greenwich Village, the Little Red Schoolhouse, to a conservative public junior high school, Horace C. Hurlbutt Jr., in Weston was, to say the least, a dramatic shift in education and social lifestyle. The educational philosophies were opposite, one quite progressive, the other traditional. I had only learned to print at Little Red; now I had to learn to write script, almost overnight, to catch up. I had learned to build tables and make birdhouses in shop at Little Red; now I went to "home ec" with only girls and learned to bake cakes and make pudding. "Why don't they teach you to cook a piece of meat?" my mother asked. I was used to wearing blue jeans to school; in Weston, the girls not only wore skirts or dresses but had made their clothes themselves.

Outdoor activities were probably better at Weston. In New York, we were limited to a rooftop play area or an asphalt sports field around the corner. We never felt at all deprived. But in Weston, I played basketball, baseball, and archery and—what shocks my daughters—became a cheerleader (yes, felt skirts with poodles).

At Little Red, we had talked about big social issues, learned things about the human anatomy no public school dared teach, and even studied comparative religion—Christianity, Judaism, and Islam—and visited different houses of worship. I remember reading a powerful book I think was called *One God*. It certainly introduced me to the idea of religious diversity and tolerance at an early age. In Weston, we started the day with not only the Pledge of Allegiance but also the Lord's Prayer, something a private school that believed in separation of church and state would never do.

Our class at Little Red was modestly integrated racially and religiously, but in Weston, very much the Connecticut Yankee suburb, I was the outsider. I was the third Jew in this junior high school, the first from New York City. Most painful was when I had a birthday party that some of my classmates were not allowed to attend because I was Jewish.

Weston didn't have a high school then, so we all attended Staples High School in Westport. Westport was already on the way to being a less provincial, more cosmopolitan town than Weston, and the high school reflected it. I was not the only New York City transplant, and there were a few other Jews.

I missed New York, however, and my mother missed what New York offered the teenager. My best friend and neighbor was the daughter of my mother's closest friend, also city transplants. Both mothers happily gave us permission—in fact, encouraged us—to leave school early on an occasional Wednesday and take the train to the city for a Broadway matinee. Saturday excursions for a museum and show were also a regular routine.

SUBURBS ARE DIFFERENT

Today Westport is well populated with former New Yorkers and home base for a number of substantial businesses, and its main street is chain-store heaven with few of the local stores left. The contrast is dramatic—a condition familiar across America. But in the 1950s and 1960s, Westport was dominated by local merchants with an increasing number of New York writers, artists, and advertising people moving in.

Back then Westport was already considered a highly cosmopolitan New York suburb. With the Westport Country Playhouse, the Famous Artists School ("Famous Writers" was added later), and a diverse professional community and host of celebrities, Westport had cachet. Local stars included Paul and Joanne Newman (my father's customers), Martha Raye, Liza Minelli, Rod Serling (another customer), Kirk Douglas, photographer Milton Greene (with Marilyn Monroe his frequent guest), and writer Hamilton Basso. Westport was often in the spotlight.

Westport's downtown had everything—a library, small park, movie theater, locally owned book and stationery store, YMCA, ice cream parlor, Bill's Smoke Shop selling many magazines and newspapers, and many other local merchants who knew everyone, not unlike downtown in many towns. There was plenty to interest me, and I spent many Saturdays taking advantage of it all. On Saturday night, there was Miss Comers's ballroom dancing classes to which we wore formal dresses and white gloves and the boys wore tuxedos. Formal dresses then were long, full-skirted, often strapless, and made out of organza. This was the center of our social life, although the PTA also organized a more egalitarian Teen Canteen where kids could gather and dance around a pre-DJ jukebox.

In high school, I became an editor on the student newspaper, got involved in whatever clubs were available, and spent most afternoons behind the counter at my father's store. When it came to considering colleges, I had little guidance from my parents, who had not been to college themselves. Mistakenly, I started at what was considered a good upstate girls' college. I soon discovered it felt like a continuation of my suburban life. I hungered to return to the city. I quit in the middle of my sophomore year, got a job as a legal secretary near home, took some courses at a nearby university, and applied to transfer to New York University, right back where I began.

My mother was all too happy to help me find a city apartment where she, too, could stay when she came in weekly for her decorating work. It was a delightful one-bedroom apartment in an unusual five-story apartment house on Central Park West. I took the subway daily to classes. This building was—and remains—a rarity amid the large prewar apartment houses, mostly from the 1920s and '30s, that dominate Central Park West north of Fifty-ninth Street. I had a fire escape that served as a terrace overlooking Central Park. My mother charmingly decorated the apartment mostly in mattress-ticking-covered furniture and thrift-shop bargains. I was thrilled.

BACK TO NEW YORK FOR GOOD

Attending a New York City university had many advantages but none bigger than being back in the great metropolis. For me, it was a homecoming: New York University in the Greenwich Village of my birth. I was stunned by the envy of my New York–born NYU classmates who couldn't imagine suburban life being less than ideal and an out-of-town college being a privilege anyone would give up. They couldn't comprehend negative reports of suburban life and couldn't fathom my transfer from a highly regarded upstate campus school to NYU. As the saying goes: one has to leave home or the city to fully appreciate it. They had never left the city. The city offered me the limitless opportunity to tackle the activities and issues that interested me.

Democratic politics and the early civil rights movement had already captured my interest while I was in high school in Westport and years younger than voting age (then twenty-one). I remember walking around town in 1956 in my Adlai Stevenson straw hat handing out buttons and literature. Westport was staunchly Republican, but I didn't realize how my political activity would anger many of my father's customers. Some threatened to take their business elsewhere. I've always admired his response. He didn't discourage me one bit but asked that I not put a bumper sticker on the car that he sometimes parked in front of the store. He also did not object to my letter to the editor of the Westport paper in the late 1950s applauding the students sitting in at lunch counters down South. That paper criticized the sit-ins in editorials.

My interests found new outlets when I returned to New York. While at NYU, I joined Students for Kennedy (even though I was still too young to vote) and participated in founding meetings of Students for Democratic Society. It was an exciting time. Any student could jump into city politics. The Reform wing of the Democratic Party was in the midst of overthrowing the old-line city machine. For the 1960 election, I served as a poll watcher. That was a joke. I was so intimidated when "dead" people voted—people who came claiming to be someone who was dead, a favorite political-machine ploy—I didn't have the guts to challenge their vote.

Later, I did two student internships with elected officials from the West Side district where I lived: Assemblyman Albert Blumenthal, who would later become a champion of abortion law reform, and State Senator Manfred Ohrenstein, who would later become an articulate opponent of Westway, the four-mile highway along the Hudson River that would become one of the biggest city controversies of my lifetime.

I headed the student club council and joined the campus civil rights groups. I did not have the nerve to join other students on bus rides to the southern sit-ins, but I did jump into the student wing of city Democratic politics, particularly organizing student volunteers for the close races around Manhattan. Emblazoned in my memory is climbing the stairs and knocking on doors in East Harlem tenements in 1961 with activist-writers Jack Newfield and Paul DuBruhl to campaign for Carlos Rios, running for city council against Democratic machine candidate John Merli. Rios won by a small margin.

After NYU, when I joined the *New York Post* as a copy girl, I had to cease all political involvement but continued to hang out with some of the friends I had made while active in citywide politics, including Jack Newfield, who was then an occasional freelancer for the *Village Voice* and eventual staff writer. We spent many a Friday afternoon sitting in *Voice* editor Dan Wolf's office with other regular Friday "drop-ins." The *Voice* had been founded in 1956 by Wolf, Ed Fancher, and Norman Mailer as an alternative weekly focusing on the arts, especially the off-Broadway scene. It evolved into the center of outsider arts and politics, while covering a lot of issues not well covered, if at all, in the mainstream press.

I mostly listened as big news events were debated among regular visitors. Michael Harrington and Nat Hentoff were among them. That is where I first met *Voice* writer Mary Nichols, who became a good friend. Jane Jacobs was an occasional participant, but I don't remember meeting her there. Village Democratic Reform leader, future congressman, and eventual mayor Ed Koch always seemed to be there. Koch was the first politician I met who knew how to laugh at himself. Koch and then mayoral hopeful John Lindsay were among the few politicians whom Wolf supported editorially. City politics was always the hottest topic of debate in these afternoon sessions, especially the campaign to overthrow the long-entrenched Democratic machine. Both Koch and Lindsay were in their ascendancy. Not long out of college, I was in the thick of city life, as I had wanted to be.

THE NEWSPAPER

"Boy!"

That was the call that made me hop to my feet when I started at the *New York Post* in March 1963 as a copy girl. "Boy!" It was a lowly position, equivalent to errand runner. But after the first African American copy boy was hired the next spring, the shout gradually changed to "Copy!"

"Copy!"

"Copy" is what a reporter's story was called, typed on a manual typewriter in triplicate and needing to be picked up from the reporter by a copyboy, carried to the editors' desk, and subsequently carried from the editor out to the composing room where typesetters set it in lead type and makeup men laid out each page before sending it along on the printing process. The term *hard copy*, an actual printed page, remains in use today, even in the age of computers.

That City Room would seem prehistoric today. An assorted collection of wood and metal desks held mechanical typewriters in a sunken center section. Paper and carbons were scattered everywhere. Cigarette butts littered the floor. Paper coffee cups with Greek symbols sat around for days.

Wrappings from drinking straws hung from the ceiling, blown there by impish and bored copyboys. One end of the wrapping was torn off and the other end dipped into the jelly of the donuts. Blowing through the straw would propel the paper to the ceiling, and the jelly would make it stick. The sports department was in one corner, and the fashion and food section took up a smaller space in another corner. The chatter of the Teletype machine of the AP and UPI wire services never ceased.

New York had seven daily newspapers (the *Herald Tribune*, *World Telegram and Sun*, *Daily Mirror*, and *Journal American* no longer exist) when I started at the lowest rung of the City Room ladder, the promised first step to being a reporter, which, it turned out, didn't always happen. Because of a seven-month strike that affected all the city papers, copy boys resigned in droves, leaving precious job openings when the strike ended. I grabbed one. At a salary of $52 a week, I needed my parents' assurance of supplemental support since my monthly rent was $154.

A New York newspaper job fresh out of college with no out-of-town newspaper experience, the prescribed route for landing on a New York paper! Leaving New York again for me was out of the question. It was either get a New York newspaper job or pursue another field. So even the offer of a lowly copy boy position was a coup. This was the city of my birth from which I had been taken unhappily, but I couldn't wait to return. I was back soaking up the excitement of the city and determined never to leave again.

DIVERSITY IN THE CITY ROOM

While my New York City youth was totally Manhattan-centric, my new colleagues at the *Post* came from all over the city and beyond. The City Room overflowed with talent. Pete Hamill. Ted Posten. Oliver Pilat. Gene Grove. Helen Dudar. Fern Marja Eckman. Bill Haddad. Barbara Yuncker. Norman Poirier. Judy Michaelson. Ed Kosner. Don Forst. Nora Ephron. Stan Opotowsky. Just watching them churn out great stories and well-turned phrases was the best possible journalism school.

Jimmy Wechsler was the editorial-page editor. He had been the executive editor, famous for standing up to J. Edgar Hoover and Joseph McCarthy and for breaking the story of the scandal that led candidate Richard Nixon to deliver the tearful Checkers speech on television. Paul Sann was now the skillful executive editor. With his cowboy-booted feet up on the desk and his antique two-part candlestick phone, Sann seemed like the editor after whom Walter Burns of *The Front Page* was fashioned. The *Post* City Room looked like the stage set out of *The Front Page* era. In fact, for a revival of the play, the star, Bert Convey, came to observe and get a "feel" for his role.

The *Post* occupied the first few floors of an early-twentieth-century office building in Lower Manhattan, 75 West Street, only a few blocks south of what would become the World Trade Center. This 1920s building was converted to an upscale condominium in 2003. That district was then a bustling collection of electronics stores with a thriving wholesale produce market just to its north. I watched all that disappear under the bulldozers of so-called progress defined by the extraordinary excavation that made way for the Twin Towers. That excavated dirt became the landfill on which Battery Park City was created, directly across the West Side Highway.

The Hudson River and expanding landfill were the view from our office window until, in 1969, the *Post* moved to the other side of Lower Manhattan, at 210 South Street (former home of the *Journal American*), between the Brooklyn and Manhattan Bridges and just north of the Fulton Fish Market. There, we watched the South Street Seaport Museum and mall fill up the restored historic buildings. Some of the fishmongers stayed in the Fulton Fish Market despite the city's efforts to relocate them up to the Hunts Point Market in the Bronx, but the great fish restaurants— Sweets, Sloppy Louie's—disappeared. By 2004, the fishmongers too had left for either the Bronx or out of town. With their move from the Fulton Market, more of the smaller fish businesses closed, and big ones have gotten bigger.

THE LUCKY BREAK

Within my first year, I moved up from copy boy to editorial assistant, a move hardly worthy of the word *up*. I answered phones and wrote plot lines for TV listings in the feature department, but all around me was the buzz of the real news business and I soaked it up.

In August 1963 I traveled to Washington, D.C., to attend the March on Washington. It was one of the most memorable events of my life. Editorial-page editor James Wechsler, who, like many people, didn't anticipate the significance of the event, asked me many questions about it when I returned. He regretted not going and said, "This is something you will be happy to tell your grandchildren about." He was correct.

Months later, the hot topic in the City Room was all the political jockeying unfolding before the 1964 Democratic National Convention in Atlantic City. I was dying to go. But the *New York Post* management was notoriously tightfisted. The editors were happy to have me work at the convention as editorial assistant if I took vacation time to go, paid my own way to get to Atlantic City, and covered my own expenses. Once there, I was paid my normal salary. Of course, it was worth it. Mostly I ran errands, but it took me to the convention floor among the delegates.

The convention was an emotional one, less than a year after Kennedy's assassination. I watched from the press box as Robert Kennedy addressed the cheering crowd and received a twenty-minute standing ovation before he said his first word. Tears welled in his eyes.

My big editorial break came on the last day of the convention. All staff reporters were off on assignments. I was alone in our makeshift office with managing editor Stan Opotowsky. A press release came in announcing that President Lyndon B. Johnson would celebrate his birthday on the boardwalk with a big cake. Stan sent me up to take notes. The cake was in the shape of the United States. Johnson took his first slice out of the state of Texas. A more obvious story lead could not be handed to the most inexperienced reporter. I came back and instead of typing notes, as Stan had asked, wrote the story, starting with LBJ taking the first slice out of Texas. Stan was caught by surprise, edited the story, and sent it in immediately. It made the front page—no byline—under a photo of Johnson slicing the cake. The word spread around the City Room that it was my story, and many of the reporters cheered. They were now my friends and rooting for me.

Soon after the Atlantic City convention in August 1964, a Young Democrats event was scheduled to take place at Gracie Mansion, the official residence of New York mayors. LBJ was now the presidential nominee, and much was being made in the news about Texas barbecue replacing the elegant French food served in the Kennedy White House. Walter Jetton was Texas's most famous barbecue chef, and he was coming to New York. I was still only an editorial assistant at the *Post*, but I offered Dan Wolf the story for the *Village Voice*. He said yes.

The story depicted Lynda Bird Johnson's New York political debut at this young citizens' event at Gracie Mansion, hosted by Robert Wagner Jr., son of the mayor. The Texas-style barbecue and Texas-sized portions of food marked the abrupt transition experienced by these young sophisticates, many of whom had first been politically energized by the youthful "vigah" and style of the Kennedys, not to mention the dominance of French food and understated elegance.

I don't know if that story in the *Voice* advanced my standing with the *Post* editors, but two months later, I started my three-month "tryout" as a reporter. On my first day, Judy Michaelson, a veteran reporter, advised me, "Take your first assignment, run right out of the office as if you know exactly what you are doing, and then call me from the nearest phone booth." As it turned out, I didn't need to. I was sent to cover a press conference held by proabortion advocate Bill Baird calling for legalization. Only a year or two earlier, I had had an abortion, forced to go to the infamous Women's Hospital in Puerto Rico rather than succumb to the illegal, unsafe backroom procedure available in the United States. I knew more than any reporter—even a new one—needed to know about the subject.

A few years later, abortion would become one of the issues on which I focused as a reporter. I covered efforts to change the law, wrote a six-part series on the issue, and then wrote the cover story for *Ms.* when the *Roe v. Wade* decision was handed down from the U.S. Supreme Court in January 1973. That was the height of the women's movement, and I was as much a part of it as my professional restrictions permitted. When editors allowed me, I wrote stories related to women's issues, not something many editors allowed at other newspapers.

Rape was another topic that I covered in depth in the early 1970s before the laws applying to it were liberalized. There was little talked about and less written about a subject fraught with myth and pain. Susan Brownmiller's *Against Our Will*, published in 1975, changed all that and catapulted the issue into the nation's consciousness. But when I was writing this series a few years earlier, corroboration requirements were so onerous, a "woman's word" so suspect, juries so doubtful, and policemen and district attorneys so unsympathetic that most women didn't even report the crime, and if they did very rarely achieved justice. I wrote a six-part series on rape in 1972, spotlighting the inequity of the law. What I learned over the months of research and interviews for that series angered me greatly. Attitudes ranged from "women should relax and enjoy it" to "they ask for it." Blaming the victim was common. My slowly emerging feminism ratcheted up to full speed.

PROMOTED TO REPORTER

In January 1965 I was promoted to full "general assignment" reporter, byline and all, loving the daily routine of being sent all over the city on whatever news story was unfolding. Murders, press conferences, "daily close-ups" (features on personalities in the news—authors, bank presidents, actors, philanthropists, and so on), and everyday mundane assignments consumed most of my time. But the full luxury of picking issues to write about came after several years of being a reporter.

The '60s art scene, very much a new "scene"—auctions, museum openings, artist personalities—was another reporting focus. Art auctions were now making big news on a regular basis. I had grown up in a household where art was a daily interest. The Whitney Museum, the quintessential institution of the Village and then still on Eighth Street, was a favorite place for my mother, my sister, and me to visit. The Whitney moved uptown in 1954. Young, not yet well-known artists were my parents' friends, including Mark Rothko and his wife, Mel, who lived in our apartment house, and Milton Avery, whose daughter, March, was my sister's classmate and friend. My mother sold art by her friends, then still unknown, to her decorating clients.

And then, in May 1965, I married Donald Gratz, a metal manufacturer peripherally in the art and architecture business. Architecture was a new world for me, and I learned from him. My interest in art and architecture expanded, and I applied it to the reporting assignments I requested.

At the same time, I reported on housing, urban renewal, and community battles for survival, on small successes and large failures, on historic preservation and neighborhood revitalization. I saw government policies repeat the mistakes of the past because vested interests, misguided analyses, and wrongheaded plans stood in the way of appropriate urban change. And I saw neighborhoods rebuild themselves despite government-created impediments. What I learned about the dynamic of cities I learned first in the neighborhoods of New York and from the people who fought to save and renew their turf. Residents and business owners in any place, the essential users, instinctively know what is needed and not needed to keep their community healthy or to make it better.

I covered the fight to build low-income housing in middle-income neighborhoods and wrote with colleagues Anthony Mancini and Pamela Howard a six-part series, "The Great Apartment House Crisis." I worked on another six-part series, this one about the newly opened Co-op City and its impact on the South Bronx, especially the Grand Concourse from which many of the residents had moved. I was stunned to observe such massive relocation out of one neighborhood into another. Later, I investigated shady landlords and cheating nursing home operators, covered hot zoning battles and ongoing urban renewal clearance projects, and investigated Forty-second Street property owners purposely renting to illicit uses to make a case for city condemnation and payout for their properties.

THE APPEAL OF HISTORIC PRESERVATION

Historic preservation grabbed me most of all, probably because so much of the city was threatened by demolition and I was so impressed by the local people I met in the neighborhoods fighting to save their communities and the things that made them special. Sometimes the battle was to save a building, other times to get a traffic light in front of a school or to prevent a rezoning that would permit an out-of-scale new project to intrude on a neighborhood.

Most of these grassroots warriors did not know the difference between architects H. H. Richardson and Philip Johnson, but they knew what the local church, school, library, or firehouse meant as an anchor to their neighborhood. They saw the row houses and modest apartment houses dating from the lost eras of quality and care being replaced by dreary, barrackslike structures or excessive scale, projects that undermined the fragile economic and social ecosystem on which any community rests. They knew what inappropriate new development could do. Planners, city officials, academics, and other experts either dismissed or ignored the common wisdom. Worse, many of them didn't even know how to hear it.

At the same time, some grassroots community rebuilding efforts were mobilizing to reclaim solid but abandoned buildings, trying to create affordable housing for people being displaced by demolition-style rebuilding all over the city. These efforts grew into the significant community-based redevelopment efforts that laid the groundwork for the renewed city, an observable truth ignored or minimized by most contemporary histories of the city. The Cooper Square Committee on the Lower East Side. The People's Firehouse. UHAB (Urban Homesteading Assistance Board) on the Upper West Side. The People's Development Corporation and Banana Kelly in the South Bronx. Bedford-Stuyvesant Restoration in Brooklyn.

These groups didn't oppose development; there was no development to oppose. They created community-based housing organizations and renovated eighty thousand units, setting the stage for the private investment that followed. Collectively, they pushed for changes in the insurance laws that did more to discourage landlord-sponsored arson than any public policies. They developed new ways to finance the rehabilitation of housing, pushed for tenant protection, devised preservation strategies, and developed new and renovated units all over the city that helped stem the tide of abandonment and pave the way for new investment. Over the years, they advanced more redevelopment than for-profit developers did. "More importantly," notes Ron Shiffman, former director of the Pratt Center for Community Development and longtime adviser to many community efforts around the city, "they have enabled many places to retain their genetic footprint, the form that gave the distinctiveness and unique character to that particular community. They helped spawn the environmental justice and industrial retention movements. And they spurred greater attention to sustainable planning practices and green building approachers."

I watched these citizen-based efforts rebuild a city in ways officials despaired to understand. To this day, too many "experts" and public leaders fail to recognize the continued validity of this process, in New York City or elsewhere. These citizens all resisted official plans reflecting how experts said things *should* work and how people *should* live but not reflecting how people actually lived or that added to the vibrancy of urban life. These citizen groups were planning from the bottom up, and step by small step they were slowly adding up to big change. I was fascinated by these groups, and I learned from them. I didn't appreciate then that I was witnessing the precursors of the regeneration of the larger city.

The only way to understand any city or any part of it is to walk the streets, talk to people who live and work in the neighborhoods, look at what works or doesn't work, and ask why, how, who. Direct observation, not theory. Instinct over expertise. That is the journalist's habit or should be. It was not the habit of many professionals who claim to know best the interests of the city.

THE 1960s

In many ways, the city in the 1960s and 1970s seemed no different from the New York of my childhood. But in so many ways it *was* different. The

World Trade Center and Battery Park City were not yet built. Lincoln Center was in construction. The Metropolitan Opera and the McKim, Mead, and White Pennsylvania Station still stood. The New York City Landmarks Law—one of the earliest in the country—did not exist. *New York Magazine* was yet to be born, first as a supplement to the *Herald Tribune*. Passenger liners graced West Side piers. The Twentieth Century Limited still went from Grand Central to Chicago. Yankee Stadium had not been renovated the first time, and Shea Stadium was in construction.

Suburban malls had not yet made an impact. All the department stores were in their rightful places along Fifth Avenue—Bonwit-Teller, Bergdorf-Goodman, Saks, Lord & Taylor, Best & Co. Fifth Avenue was "the Avenue," and Thirty-fourth Street was still the preeminent "pedestrian" shopping street. B. Altman's was at the Fifth Avenue end of Thirty-fourth, Macy's and Gimbels at the Sixth Avenue end. Ohrbach's was in between, along with dozens of small shops, both chains and locals. Soon, malls would vacuum the heart out of many American Main Streets. But while malls killed much of downtown America, they only partially injured New York City. The density of this city guaranteed a less dramatic impact than the shell shocks that crippled so many other cities.

On Forty-second Street, stores sold foreign newspapers, hats, costumes, and a great variety of entertainment-related goods. The sparkling marquees of great first-run movie houses were lined up one after another along that still quintessential street. A mix of low-end entertainment outlets, holdovers from the 1920s, gave the street its seedy feel. A few grind houses could be visited. Hubert's Museum, a Coney Island–style sideshow, had a flea circus, snake charmer, belly dancer, and wild man of Borneo. The pornography was soft core with hard core soon to come in the late 1960s. As newspaper exposés revealed, disreputable property owners welcomed the degenerate uses as tenants to strengthen their push for a publicly funded city renewal scheme and generous bailouts that would handsomely enrich them. Contrived or accelerated deterioration has long been a property owner's excuse for seeking financial concessions from the city. This pattern was common elsewhere in the city but most glaringly at the time on Forty-second Street.

Beneath its glittering gaudiness, the Times Square district overflowed with great original musicals (*Fiddler on the Roof, Funny Girl, Cabaret, Hello, Dolly*) and dramas (*Golden Boy, Tiny Alice, The Subject Was Roses*). The regal Astor Hotel had not yet been replaced by a die-stamped, glass-walled office tower. The Astor replacement was the first of many similarly banal ones that followed.

Until the bulldozer of urban renewal and misguided city-planning policies took their toll, the city's neighborhoods often had their own thriving entertainment centers with at least one movie house, local restaurants, and neighborhood retail to keep many residents happy. Times Square, Broadway theater, and Manhattan nightspots were for the Big Nights on the town and first-run films. By the 1970s, little of that was left, and the days were numbered for what remained. Times Square was New York's epicenter, and even that was in decline, and not an entirely natural decline at that.

The Upper West Side was like the set for the long-running musical *West Side Story* (opened in 1957), and years away from becoming chic.[4] Run-down brownstones, their high quality intact, lined the side streets. Neglected but elegant apartment towers dominated Central Park West. I loved my first one-bedroom apartment in that small building overlooking Central Park, but walking the side streets was something one did quite cautiously. Nighttime crime in the park was a constant.

The Upper East Side was then the enclave of the rich and the famous. And Brooklyn was another world. Visits to Coney Island and relatives were about the limit of my Brooklyn experience until then. When we lived in the Village, my grandfather occasionally came from Brooklyn for Sunday breakfast, bringing pickled herring, white fish, lox, and bagels from Brooklyn's Avenue J. When I returned to New York as an adult, he would meet me at the Horn & Hardart on Forty-second Street for a Sunday meal. He was intimidated by Manhattan and knew only the one subway stop at Forty-second Street from Brooklyn. The Bronx was out of my consciousness—except for the zoo and Botanical Garden—though I used to visit relatives there too as a child. Queens I hardly knew, and Staten Island I don't remember even having visited.

THE 1970S

New York hit bottom in the late 1960s and '70s, and even optimists could not foresee the rebound that has occurred. Crippling events and conditions scarred the decade. Crime, drugs, police corruption, municipal strikes, litter, housing abandonment—anything that could go wrong did. Even a cable on the Brooklyn Bridge snapped in the mid-1970s.

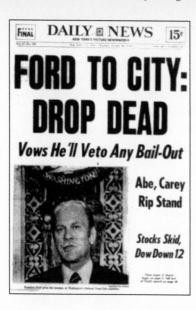

1.3 "Ford to City: Drop Dead" was the *New York Daily News* front page that summed up the state of the city. *New York Daily News*.

The famous headlines are the stuff of legend. "Ford to City: Drop Dead" screamed the front page of the *New York Daily News* on October 30, 1975, when the president refused to help bail out the city's near bankruptcy. A few days later, he reversed the decision and loaned the city $500 million. In 1979, when Chrysler seemed destined for bankruptcy, the federal government easily extended $1.2 billion in loan guarantees. The same benefit had not been offered ailing New York City. The "fiscal crisis," as it was appropriately called, had reached the point when the city could no longer sell the bonds it needed to fund its budget. Sympathy from around the country was nonexistent. In the 1970s, New York was probably the most unloved city in the country.

"There it is, ladies and gentlemen, the Bronx is burning," noted Howard Cosell as he looked up during a game at Yankee Stadium in 1977 and noticed a building on fire. "The Bronx is burning" became the catchphrase of the day. Arson—both landlord and tenant initiated—was rampant in poor neighborhoods, not just in the Bronx. Few saw a bright future for the city. The South Bronx served as the poster child for the collapse of the country's inner cities. The worst conditions were visible there. The movie *Fort Apache*, starring Paul Newman, took place in the South Bronx and highlighted the grim reality of uncontrolled crime. That movie wasn't made until 1981 and kept the worst image alive. Tom Wolf's *Bonfire of the Vanities*, also set in the Bronx at its worst, was published in 1987. A big hit, it, too, kept the worst images alive.

And then there was a whole year of the serial killer Son of Sam, who preyed on young women and couples, increasing the city's unease from anxiety to full-blown fear. The media heyday culminated in "CAUGHT," the *Post*'s dramatic 1977 headline at his capture. And while feeling a sense of relief, the elevated anxiety level of the city did not diminish. Son of Sam seemed to symbolize the crime wave the public feared, a condition common in all American cities in the '70s. High crime rates depressed everything. Revelations of systematic police corruption did not help public confidence in the era of high crime.

Beyond the memorable headlines were the endless psychic wounds underscoring the city's sinking state. In 1972, *The Tonight Show* abandoned Broadway for Burbank, California, as if leaving a sinking ship. The city became a favorite target of late-night talk-show jokes. Mayor John V. Lindsay appeared on the Dick Cavett panel show and in defense of New York said, "It isn't true that people get mugged all the time in Central Park." Replied Cavett: "No. They just get murdered."

That same year revealed an even deeper wound when Mayor Lindsay tried to build needed public housing in the middle-class neighborhood of Forest Hills in the borough of Queens. "Scatter-site" projects—smaller increments of public housing inserted in middle-class communities—were offered as a socially progressive alternative to the postwar urban renewal format of high-rise ghettoes that evolved into new slums. The conflict sparked a virulent debate about race, class, and the post–civil rights era goal of integration. The large-scale project challenged the commitment of the heavily liberal and predominantly Jewish Forest Hills community. Representing the resistant community was a little-known Queens lawyer, Mario Cuomo.[5] Cuomo helped fashion a compromise that downsized the proposed public housing apartment buildings to half the planned size. Celebrated *New York Daily News* columnist Jimmy Breslin turned the spotlight on Cuomo's defense of the average middle class and catapulted him into the political spotlight. Cuomo had successfully represented another fighting Queens neighborhood in 1966. At that time, the city was condemning sixty-six private homes in Corona to build a school. Cuomo challenged the city's plan to take the properties by eminent domain, a right formally expanded by the U.S. Supreme Court in 2005 to allow taking property from one private owner to give to another private owner without the conventional public purpose.

Two years after the Forest Hills project, in 1974, a portion of the West Side Highway collapsed, putting the deteriorated state of the city's infrastructure in the spotlight. Cutbacks in maintenance dated back to the heyday of big new projects and highway building when maintenance and rehabilitation neither scored political points nor provided enviable photo opportunities. A hugely expanded proposed replacement, Westway, became the lightning rod for the debate over the ongoing reshaping of the national landscape for the automobile. Opponents forced recognition of the importance of reinvesting in public transit after years of frenzied highway building at transit's expense. The battle marked the decade. The defeat in the mid-1980s marked a turning point in the regeneration of the city. (See chapter 9.)

In 1976 Mayor Lindsay promised the South Bronx a rejuvenated neighborhood when he committed $25 million to renovate Yankee Stadium—"the centerpiece of another New York City neighborhood renaissance," a city hall announcement boasted. When it was finished in 1977, the cost had escalated to $120 million, but not a penny of the promised $2 million had been spent improving the surrounding neighborhood. One can be sure that with the completion of the new Yankee Stadium, the city and ball club will take full credit for the regeneration of the surrounding neighborhood that occurred long before the stadium's current re-creation. Maybe the public will eventually forget the important local parks taken from the community, the expanded traffic-generating publicly paid-for parking garage given to the Yankees, and the millions in public subsidies for the stadium. Maybe the community will eventually accept the new park on top of a parking garage counted as a partial replacement and a scattering of replacement parks that will take years to deliver.

While the city invested in the stadium in 1976, the South Bronx was losing five thousand housing units yearly in rows of private houses, apartment buildings, and small businesses. Nothing comparable was invested in the renovation of potentially viable but partially abandoned neighborhoods. Arson for profit was the property owner's way out of neighborhoods the city had glaringly given up on. The city cut back on fire services, closing firehouses in the most vulnerable of neighborhoods, as if to say "Let it burn." Community groups, not government, took the initiative to enduringly rebuild Bronx neighborhoods block by block while official city priorities were elsewhere.

FROM BAD TO WORSE

The deep decay of our cities poisoned the decade. Across America, conditions varied only in degree, not in kind. Every social ill imaginable was blamed on the urban condition. None of the big-project bromides meant to rejuvenate cities were working anywhere. St. Louis had demolished its economic heart on the waterfront to build the Saarinen Arch in the 1950s and kept losing economic strength and population. Chicago had erased the dense neighborhoods of the South Side for the parade of dysfunctional public housing high-rises now being torn down and replaced, but that city's decline continued. Pittsburgh had wiped out the vibrant black community of the Hill District made famous by August Wilson to build an arena and arts center (not built), and left vast unused land empty around it for decades. Los Angeles had wiped out its authentically urban downtown when it leveled Bunker Hill. An interstate highway had wiped out Miami's vibrant and historic black community of Overton. Buffalo had wiped out at least half of its downtown to build a highway and then watched the unused cleared land lie fallow as the rest of the city continued to fall apart. Boston had cleared its bustling West End. By the 1970s, urban challenges had gotten worse. All the big visions had mushroomed. All the big visions had made things worse.

The lost neighborhoods had mixtures of working poor, industry, small manufacturers, and strong social networks and institutions that bolstered the difficult lives of their residents. The social upheaval caused by these physical changes was catastrophic. Baltimore, Portland, Seattle, Miami, Indianapolis, you name it, urban renewal or highways demolished large swaths of the urban fabric in almost every city, weakening almost beyond repair the remaining urban threads. Few cities stood firm against the bulldozer like Savannah, which, as one native recalled, "resisted urban renewal as a communist plot." All of the bulldozed neighborhoods, of course, were either predominantly low-income African American and Hispanic or a mix of residents, small businesses, and industries, or both.

Decades of postwar federal investments in highways and suburban developments coupled with decades of financial institutions' abandonment of urban dwellers and their properties had done the trick. The suburban ideal reached its height, the urban alternative its depth. Throughout the 1970s, the bleak condition of urban America was on the front pages of newspapers across the country.

These were turbulent times, to be sure. New York City was at the point of collapse. Over the space of a decade, the city went from bad to worse. Strikes by sanitation and subway workers occurred and even briefly by police and doctors in city hospitals. The blackout of 1965 had brought out the best in everyone. People came through it with grace and dignity. We patted ourselves on the back with the slogan, "When the going gets rough, New Yorkers get going." Everyone was ineffably polite. The riots of the 1960s, both in New York and in other cities, had focused mostly on black rage, racial injustice, and the until then out-of-sight, out-of-mind dire conditions in urban ghettoes. But by the blackout of 1977, looting marked the day, taking the city to the brink of disaster. More than two thousand stores were burned in twenty-four hours. Areas of Brooklyn, the Bronx, Harlem, and the Lower East Side, after years of tumultuous physical and social reengineering, seemed to implode. It was as if the rug had been pulled out from under the city. City planners predicted the population would drop precipitously from just under eight million to five.[6]

The limits—and question of usefulness—to the projections of planners and urban economists come into focus every few years. As *New York Times* columnist Joyce Purnick pointed out in a December 31, 2006, article, "New York, Where the Dreamers Are Asleep," "The city's population has had a way of taking on a life of its own. Zoning consultants in the 1960s advised city officials that New York's population would grow to 8.5 million in 1975—it may well have if not for the fiscal crisis that was at its worst in 1975. Instead, the numbers dropped so sharply—to 7.2 million in 1980 from 8 million in 1970—that some social scientists advocated 'planned shrinkage' in city services." Purnick also noted that by 1990 the city's population was up to 7.6 million, "an increase that was also unanticipated." With that growth came the need for some schools to build annexes in prefabricated trailers to handle the equally unanticipated increase in students. Families with children living in the city—what a concept! How things had changed.

Jim Dwyer reflected in a July 14, 2007, *New York Times* column, "Only the deranged or visionary could have imagined on that summer night in 1977 that New York in 2007 would be fat, happy and standing-room only; perched here in 2007, many would find it hard to believe that 2,000 stores were burned or looted inside of 24 hours."

SMALL STEPS, BIG CHANGE

As despairing as the 1970s were, symbolic events helped boost the city's fragile ego. For example, in 1976, to honor the Bicentennial, the Tall Ships from around the world sailed into New York Harbor on a glorious summer weekend, reminding New Yorkers and the world of the treasure that is the city. The event, along with the decadelong debate over Westway, reminded the city that it had turned its back on the untapped resource of 572 miles of waterfront.

New York Magazine celebrated New York's celebrities throughout the 1970s and coincidentally celebrated the city itself. Aspiring cities across the country spawned similar city-focused publications, fueling the aspirations of the urban boosters.

Exuberant nightlife flourished, personified in John Travolta's performance in *Saturday Night Fever*. Studio 54, the headline-grabbing discotheque, opened in 1977, demonstrating to the world that New York life could be hard, but entertainment and nightlife still thrived. The Bronx, too, was giving birth to a unique music scene, hip-hop, born in the unglamorous first-floor community room in "an otherwise unremarkable high-rise just north of the Cross Bronx and hard along the Major Deegan," wrote David Gonzalez in the *New York Times*. There, in 1973, Clive Campbell, known as DJ Kool Herc, spun together the tunes that spilled out onto nearby streets and parks, eventually spreading worldwide.[7]

In 1978, in the gritty, crime-ridden meatpacking district on the Lower West Side, a Frenchman, Florent Morellet, opened a diner and French-bistro hybrid where longshoreman ate at Formica countertops next to a rising number of well-heeled customers, raising the neighborhood's profile that today is the epitome of chic. The classic diner structure was a centerpiece of this once vibrant food-focused district of low-rise buildings with projecting canopies and cobblestone streets. By 2008, Florent had had enough and closed the restaurant. By then, the Gansevoort Historic District was one of the city's most upscale.

New York had become the center of the international art world in the 1960s but came into full bloom in the 1970s. With the defeat of the Lower Manhattan Expressway, SoHo blossomed into both an arts district and an exemplary reborn industrial neighborhood. SoHo helped change the way the country viewed cities. *New York Magazine* declared SoHo "the most exciting place to live in the city." Loft living became the new chic. Other cities followed suit. Urban resilience was the wave of the future.

SoHo grabbed the headlines, but the real early stirrings of rebirth were totally citizen generated in neighborhoods out of the mainstream consciousness. The Back-to-the-City and Brownstone Movements began slowly in the 1960s all over New York City and in cities across the country. The increasing urban appeal gained strength in the 1970s. Historic architecture, great financial values, and urban lifestyles were the draw. Young middle-class families—called "urban pioneers"—began repopulating run-down neighborhoods around the country. It seems incomprehensible today to think that Georgetown in D.C., the Vieux Carre and Garden Districts in New Orleans, the Victorian Districts in San Francisco and Savannah, Back Bay in Boston, Rittenhouse Square in Philadelphia, and so many other now chic neighborhoods were once deteriorated slums.

And in the either abandoned or half-empty neighborhoods that most pioneers overlooked, new immigrants found shelter and opened new businesses. By the late 1970s, seventy-five thousand immigrants a year were coming to New York, twice the number of New Yorkers leaving for the suburbs. Immigration laws were loosened in 1965, but it wasn't until the 1970s that one could observe the full flowering of these changes.

The enormous positive impact of the new waves of immigrants took a long time for experts to acknowledge. To this day it is a rare expert who acknowledges the long-standing and full positive impact because with that acknowledgment should come recognition of the organic nature of what has occurred, in that it was not developer or government driven.

Early in 2009 during the debate over the size and nature of the congressional stimulus package, Thomas L. Friedman wrote a column, "The Open-Door Bailout," advocating a nonprotectionist bent to the legislation. He pointed out how critical to our past and recent national history have been the waves of immigrants. In the recent context, he cited a study showing that more than half of Silicon Valley start-ups of the last decade were founded by immigrants. Another study showed that increases in patent applications parallel increases in H1-B visas. Friedman quoted the somewhat tongue-in-cheek stimulus advice from Shekhar Gupta, editor of the *Indian Express* newspaper, "All you need to do is grant visas to two million Indians, Chinese and Koreans. We will buy up all the sub-prime homes. We will work 18 hours a day to pay for them. We will immediately improve your savings rate—no Indian bank today has more than 2 percent nonperforming loans because not paying your mortgage is considered shameful here. And we will start new companies to create our own jobs and jobs for more Americans."[8] In effect, that is what happened in New York in the 1970s and '80s with the great immigrant influx.

REBIRTH'S BEGINNINGS

The seeds of recovery were being sown off the conventional radar screens, real even if unseen. Far from the public consciousness and not spotlighted in the press, local groups in the 1970s started forming in the worst of neighborhoods, too. The creativity and innovation that often evolve out of struggle were laying the foundation for the resurgence to come. The renaissance began in a multitude of small ways, all of which would eventually add up to big change. The 1970s allowed for positive measures emanating from the most local level because government was out of ideas and money and desperate for new solutions. When given the opportunity, local citizen-led groups were innovative and productive agents of urban change. Small steps collectively made a big impact.

Urban economist Dr. Saskia Sassen points out that an infusion of young women began making an impact. "In the 1970s, a lot of young people were coming to New York, including many professional women coming for things like publishing," she says. "Women were leading the lives they wanted and not leaving the city after marriage."

Significantly, in 1977, Congress passed the Community Reinvestment Act (CRA) that provided a lifeline for moderate-income home buyers and local housing groups and forced financial institutions to find ways to reinvest in the same neighborhoods they had taken money out of years before. This critical access to capital had been missing from poor neighborhoods for decades. Financial institutions were now required to serve the qualified poor as well as the rich. The CRA was the result of a vigorous national campaign, led by Chicago activist Gale Cincotta, founder of the National People's Action. Banks, following strict standards, were now required to make loans to *qualified* borrowers of all income levels in the neighborhoods from which deposits originate. The act allowed for community challenge of bank policies that negatively affected low-income neighborhoods, forcing many banks to reexamine their former redlining policies that gave them license to use investment dollars earned in cities to build suburbia. Eventually, some bank executives admitted that if the CRA had not forced them into it, they would never have discovered what turned out to be a profitable market of underserved low- to moderate-income home buyers. The CRA made possible a needed in- fusion of resident and business investment in deteriorated neighborhoods.

Former *City Limits* editor Alyssa Katz, looking back in 2006, wrote, "By the summer of 1977, more than 20,000 buildings in New York would be abandoned. At the end of that year, the city owned 6,000 buildings and was poised to foreclose on 25,000 more. Yet pockets of hope took hold in besieged neighborhoods across the city. With the support of com- munity groups, tenants were taking charge of their buildings as the land- lords abandoned them. The earliest of these efforts had won the backing of the administration of Mayor John Lindsay."[9]

Alphabet City on the Lower East Side, Kelly Street in the South Bronx, UHAB on the Upper West Side, Bedford-Stuyvesant in Brooklyn, and many other low-income communities in between all had rejuvenating projects bubbling up. The Cooper Square Committee, Adopt-a-Building, organized in East Harlem to reclaim abandoned buildings and spear- headed other groups on the Lower East Side, then called Loisada, into joining Mobilization for Youth and Pueblo Nuevo Housing and Devel- opment Association, all of them working in small segments that eventually spread over a large area.

The first rooftop windmill, solar panels, composting, and recycling ef- forts were undertaken by some of these groups. On East Eleventh Street a small apartment house was reclaimed and a windmill and solar collectors installed on the roof. This effort was led by the Energy Task Force with the Pratt Center designing the building. The People's Development Cor- poration, Mid-Bronx Desperados and Banana Kelly in the Bronx, the East Harlem Renegades in Harlem—all over the city grassroots efforts were the precursors to the city's future rebirth.

Robert Schur, assistant housing commissioner, left his city position and formed the Association of Neighborhood Housing Developers, a coali- tion advocating on behalf of local groups. This was a unique coming to- gether of grassroots groups and technical capacity provided by advocacy planners mostly associated with the Pratt Center for Community Devel- opment in Brooklyn.[10] These were the people whose homes, businesses, social networks, and family connections had been destroyed under the Moses bulldozer and who had been displaced and relocated one too many times. "Enough," they declared. They dug in their heels where they were and set about rebuilding their lives, their communities, and, eventually, the city itself. Their ingenuity and determination emerged in spite of minimal resources.

This primarily community-based housing movement, with foundation funding, ignited a momentum for change that persuaded conventional developers—and their institutional lenders—to follow their lead with new investment in the very neighborhoods they had previously redlined and declared hopeless. Smart city officials, cajoled by community advocates, responded to proposals for new innovative housing policies that by the end of the century had restored or replaced almost all of the city's once-endless supply of vacant and deteriorated buildings. Eventually, establishment developers and financial institutions followed, building on the foundation of local efforts and, of course, took credit for it all. Their only measure for success was developer investment. Nothing was real to them without developers. But, incontrovertibly, it was the grassroots, citizen-based movement that regenerated the city that developers and Wall Street took over. This organic, diverse, and incremental renewal process, not so-called economic development projects, revived New York and simultaneously took root in many communities across the country.

The precursors of regeneration took many forms and were allowed to evolve fully because there was no money or interest from either government or the private sector to interfere. Even the country's community-garden movement had one of its earliest starts in the most down-and-out neighborhoods of this city. The Green Guerillas tore down barbed-wire fences, cleaned up garbage, and cultivated abandoned lots first on the Lower East Side but eventually all over the city and beyond. The term *guerilla gardening* was born here. This early effort matured into a revival of urban agriculture in low-income neighborhoods around the city.

The Union Square Greenmarket overcame official resistance and the cynicism of the experts to get off the ground in 1976, part of a then small national revival of farmers' markets nationwide that is now a big-time national success. On the West Coast, Alice Waters had opened Chez Panisse in Berkeley, buying from a network of local farmers and ranchers dedicated to sustainable agriculture and beginning a slowly contagious national trend championing locally grown food, small farms, and fresh ingredients. Similarly, new restaurants opened around Union Square, taking advantage of the immediate access to fresh products from regional farmers. The ripple effects were widespread. Now Greenmarkets blanket

1.4 The necklace I never take off. *Sandra Morris.*

the city, giving many low-income communities access to fresh, healthy food direct from farmers.

All of this was part of the renewal process, one that took root in communities across the country, not just New York. One charismatic leader did not make these things happen. Nothing happened quickly. This bottom-up change came out of the city's culture of confrontation, contention, and caring. More important, none of this positive change was about stadia, convention centers, big clearance projects, tourist attractions, or other officially embraced baubles encased in rejuvenation rhetoric.

Preservation was the most visible of the bellwether issues indicating good things to come. For this reason, the next chapter recalls early landmark history to understand preservation as a framework for change. Reporting on landmark preservation revealed my eventual passionate commitment to the issue.

When New York seemed to hit bottom and outsiders derided everything about it, New Yorkers rose up in defense, forming block associations, planting trees and flower boxes, organizing house tours, finding many ways to demonstrate their loyalty. In response to external hostility—particularly the "City Drop Dead" headline—the "I Love New York" campaign took hold. I had always been one of those New York boosters and wrote a little feature story on the things one could buy to flaunt one's New York chauvinism. Not much was available, but I still have and regularly wear the gold necklace I found at B. Altman's with the words "I Love New York." That was all I could find for the story. The "Big Apple" and "I Love New York" campaigns came later, an outgrowth of New Yorkers' shared chauvinism.

Nationally, too, not everything was negative. In September 1975, a National Neighborhood Conservation Conference was held in New York City. Grassroots urban preservation and historic neighborhood repopulation efforts were under way in forty-five cities, including New York. Most historic preservation efforts started in response to the urban renewal clearance projects in each city. Representatives from those efforts came together in New York to compare "war stories" and learn from one another.

The Bicentennial celebration in 1976 unleashed a new interest and pride in ethnic roots and national history, so much of which is urban based. The historic preservation movement grew in popularity as the fight to save Grand Central Terminal scored a dynamic victory in the U.S. Supreme Court in 1978. The appreciation of the authentic city, the fight to protect neighborhoods targeted for "renewal," and the self-help inclination of local people were all visible and gaining momentum in the 1970s.

Jane Jacobs's principles were in their ascendancy. The Moses-style strategies were in a free fall and fiercely resisted. Where they might have continued, the cessation of the federal money flow did the trick. Today, the New York City neighborhoods with the strongest appeal are the ones that reflect best Jacobs's teaching; the ones in need of greatest help are the ones erased and replaced with Moses-style visions.

The world and this city have changed enormously in the intervening years. Change is the constant, unfolding in sometimes dramatic but often subtle ways. Yet as much as things change, the more they stay the same. Many of the kinds of things I wrote about in the 1960s and 1970s still go on today in different guises. In this book, I use some of the earlier New York stories to spotlight the larger issues they illustrate. Useful lessons and parallels can be drawn from many of those stories. Most assuredly, however, the contrast of the city now and then reflects today's stark contrast to the topsy-turvy world of the 1960s and 1970s when a girl could be called a boy and nobody would blink an eye.

LANDMARKS PRESERVATION
Precursor of Positive Change

> Preservationists are the only people in the world who are invariably confirmed in their wisdom after the fact.
>
> DONOVAN RYPKEMA,
> *economist*

For this reporter, community and landmarks preservation battles were always a good story. The little guy versus the big one, a citizen taking on the heartless government and/or greedy developer, the local residents' resistance to inappropriate change. It always added up to good journalistic fodder.

When I first started covering the occasional landmark struggle in the late 1960s, preserving old buildings was considered by many as simply a means of opposing progress or change. People were accused of not wanting change in their backyard or for other so-called illegitimate reasons. However, when I listened carefully to the local voices, this was clearly not the case, as this book argues in many ways. More than physical structures were at stake. The values of memory, human connection, vanishing quality, and public purpose were all wrapped up in architectural beauty.

As I kept writing about preservation, I observed the full spectrum of local issues and incremental change of which preservation was just one part and recognized it as a precursor of genuine positive change, the kind that fertilizes and enriches, not undermines and erodes. In many communities, people weren't just fighting to preserve old buildings. They recognized that the threatened buildings and the varied uses contained in them were important threads in the urban fabric. And they weren't just fighting to save them. They were buying some of them, fixing them up, opening new businesses, committing themselves to their community—all precursors of more good things to come, to be sure.

Of course, many demolition projects were opposed for reasons other than preservation. But, Jane Jacobs observed, "if you listen closely to people at public hearings, you will understand their fears." Most opponents of a demolition and replacement plan were resisting the particular manifestation of change, not change itself; erosion, not progress, as Jacobs articulated. I found their stories compelling.

Urban planning professor Robert Fishman notes, "The city was caught up in this riptide of destruction that seemed to have no end" that combined with "a rolling wave of abandonment and sprawl in the terrible period of the '70s and '80s," challenging some to wonder if cities were viable.[1] So, to me, the great value and real meaning of historic preservation were not just about preserving neighborhoods but about preserving urbanism and the city itself.

New York was not alone. Increasing numbers of civic resisters fought both highway and urban renewal projects across the country. With the 1956 Federal Highway Act, many places were gaining a reputation among citizens for decision making by bulldozer that left a legacy of urban blight and empty cleared land still evident today. Preservationists not only valued what was being lost but recoiled in horror at the ribbons of concrete and barracks of brick that emerged to replace long-established places and communities.

Historic preservation is an indicator of urban change. This is true in all cities. In retrospect, I think it is one of the things that gave me reason for optimism in the 1970s. The resilience of the city and its people was clear in these battles. The city was bleak and, to some, seemingly hopeless. But as I watched the positive personal and communal energy expended on behalf of places around the city, it was clear something creatively new was under way.

THE TIDE TURNED

Early in the new administration of Mayor Michael Bloomberg, a controversy arose over the use of one of the city's premier landmarks, the Tweed

2.1 The Tweed Courthouse today. It was almost torn down in the 1970s. *Jared Knowles.*

Courthouse, an imposing neoclassical building located directly behind City Hall. This was early in 2003 and in itself was an incredible sea change from the mid-1970s when the administration of Mayor Abraham Beame planned to demolish and replace that legendary 1871 building.

Who should get to use this monumental landmark became a high-level, much publicized fight. What a novelty! What a milestone! How far the very concept of historic preservation had come in New York; the fight was now over *how to use* a landmark, not *whether to lose* a landmark.

Nowhere was this extraordinary turnaround noticed—at least publicly during the 2003 controversy. New York had forgotten its recent history. Looking at New York through the prism of changes in historic preservation—its victories, its losses, its laws, public policies, and public attitudes—spotlights some of the differences between the city of the 1970s and now.

Today, the restoration and continued use of such notable buildings as Tweed Courthouse—especially publicly owned ones—are almost taken for granted. This marks a total reversal of conventional thought and public policy of a mere thirty years ago. And while a significant number of real estate developers profiting from the conversion of landmark buildings now extol the virtue of the historic preservation they disdained not that long ago, their appreciation is limited by how much they experience interference with their own development plans.

People no longer assume an old building has outlived its usefulness. New is no longer assumed to be automatically better and more economically viable. That was the convention in the 1960s and '70s. And while today developers with the right political connections can still keep landmark status off their property, they can't change either the preservation experts' or the public's judgment of a building's worthiness for designation. As people witness the need for total renovation of relatively young buildings dating from the 1960s and '70s, they recognize even more the inherent value of the solidly built old. So many buildings built in the 1960s and '70s require more drastic upgrades than buildings twice their age.

A request for approval for demolition of a designated landmark from the Landmarks Preservation Commission is almost unheard of today. How actual landmarks are handled can be a different issue. In fact, now many developers instead request the official landmark designation they need to qualify for lucrative federal preservation tax credits. The weekly calendar of the commission is filled with applications to restore and upgrade landmark buildings of all kinds in every corner of the city. Many developers seek the zoning breaks available with the restoration of a designated landmark. Restoring a landmark is now a prestigious endeavor. For developers, preservation now pays. The record is clear: no designated landmark has shown to be an economic failure *because* of its designation; in fact, most are a financial success.

PRESERVATION ACCELERATES CHANGE

To appreciate where preservation in New York and, in fact, the country, is today, one must understand the progression of the past thirty years. New York set the standard for the country. The rescue, and reuse, of Tweed Courthouse is, in fact, a small measure of how much things have changed from the New York City of the 1970s. Considerable mythology has grown up around the background to passage of the law and the history of landmarks preservation in New York.

Few remember—if they ever knew—that the 1965 Landmarks Preservation Law was almost meaningless in its first iteration. The law's administration was unimpressive for several years after passage, but it lulled the public into assuming significant progress was occurring. Some obvious buildings were being designated landmarks, but important buildings were falling all over town to make way for the postwar definition of progress that only meant new. Amazingly, under the new law, the Landmarks Preservation Commission was allowed to designate for only six months every three years. It is important to fully understand what that meant—six months of designations followed by three years of unstoppable demolition. This became clear to me only, as this chapter will show, while covering what appeared to be a routine protest over a building demolition in the early 1970s.

The actual reasons for passage of the Landmarks Preservation Law in 1965 are misunderstood. It had more to do with Robert Moses than is at all recognized. The common assumption is that it was prompted by the highly publicized loss of Pennsylvania Station in 1963 and was meant to prevent future disastrous losses. This was definitely not the case. In fact, the demolition of Penn Station—universally recognized today as a monumental act of civic destruction—was at the time greeted with limited and polite opposition. The small group of citizens, preservationists, architects, journalists, and historians who picketed in front of the station did not inspire broad protests. Even an eloquent *New York Times* editorial written by Ada Louise Huxtable—"we will be judged not by the buildings we build but by those that we destroy"—had little impact.

When it was all over, when the last of the incomparable Corinthian columns was carted off to a New Jersey landfill, the full measure of the loss began to sink in. Perhaps the questioning of what is meant by "progress" was accelerated but nothing more dramatic than that. If it was true that the landmark law was a reaction to that loss, the administration of Mayor Robert F. Wagner would have seen passed a very different law, a law with teeth. Instead, the 1965 law can be said to have produced a set of baby teeth; a mature set of teeth came almost ten years later.

The further assumption that New York's law immeasurably changed the nature of planning and architecture in the city and the whole country, as many suggest, did not really happen for many years. What actually changed everything was the 1978 U.S. Supreme Court decision that upheld the city's 1965 landmark law in the Grand Central Terminal case. Even the city's fight to save the law might not have happened if city and commission leaders followed their first inclination to give into Penn Central Corporation and remove landmark status from that stellar gateway to the city. Public pressure made them defend it.

New York was early but not first in the preservation game. In the 1930s, due to the advocacy of vigorous women's groups, New Orleans and Charleston, South Carolina, were the first nationwide in preserving historic structures and districts of styles that set them apart from most of the country, especially big cities like New York. Determination to preserve these cities' unique architecture was strong, and protectionist laws were established. In fact, women in Junior Leagues, garden clubs, and similar women's organizations in several other American cities were the real vanguard of the historic preservation movement nationally. From Providence, Rhode Island, to San Antonio, Texas, women led the fights to preserve their cities.

A PROBLEM GROWS IN BROOKLYN

Weak as it was, this first iteration of the law in 1965 for New York City, perhaps late in the game, was an important turning point, psychologically for the public at least. Most important, it addressed a number of prickly political problems faced by Mayor Wagner in the first half of the 1960s. Urban renewal, highway clearance, and a whole host of Robert Moses excesses had stirred up serious public discontent. The battles were fresh in the public's mind. Mayor Wagner needed something to pacify a disgruntled citizenry.

In Brooklyn Heights, a new civic battle was brewing over an urban renewal clearance project adjacent to what was to become the historic district. This activist neighborhood already had a track record of taming Robert Moses. In the 1950s, he wanted to plow the Brooklyn Queens Expressway through the neighborhood. The well-fought battle was resolved brilliantly with the expressway going under the Brooklyn Heights Esplanade that overlooks the New York Harbor.

In Greenwich Village, several fights (to be explored in the next chapter) had given Mayor Wagner a black eye: the plan to drive a road through Washington Square Park (1955–1956), the attempt to demolish most of the far West Village for urban renewal (1961), and the fight against the Lower Manhattan Expressway (mid-1960s)—all projects pushed by Moses and opposed by Jane Jacobs and others in the movement she gave voice to. Jacobs accused Wagner of still operating under Moses's rules, even though in 1961 he promised the Village that no "improvements" would happen that were not in keeping with "physically and aesthetically West Village traditions." And when he said "the bulldozer approach is out," Jacobs dismissed the promise as "pious platitudes."

So it is no coincidence that those two historic areas of the city—Brooklyn Heights and Greenwich Village—were the first to be designated historic districts, a move that mollified at least some of the participants in the emerging grassroots community and historic preservation movements.

Other development battles also plagued the mayor. In 1957 Carnegie Hall was scheduled to be demolished and replaced with a forty-four-story vermilion and gold skyscraper surrounded by a sunken plaza lined with cultural exhibits. An elegant rust-colored brick building, Carnegie Hall is internationally famous more for its acoustics than its Renaissance Revival design of 1891, appealing as that may be. But it is clearly architecturally distinctive as well.

Lincoln Center was meant to *replace* Carnegie Hall and the Metropolitan Opera. The city opera and ballet companies were to share a new home at Lincoln Center, moving them out of City Center on Fifty-fifth Street. A very well-publicized protest against Carnegie's impending loss ensued, led by violinist Isaac Stern, his wife, Vera, philanthropist Jacques Kaplan, and Ray Rubinow, the administrator of Kaplan's foundation. The public hue and cry was deafening and incessant. But only the combination of the fame and determination of Stern et al., backed by a strong public sentiment, could overcome the formidable combined power of Robert Moses, John D. Rockefeller III (chair of the effort to build Lincoln Center), and Mayor Wagner.

In 2003, Carnegie Hall went through a well-publicized, high-quality refurbishment under the guidance of Richard Olcott of the James Polshek Partnership. Polshek had been the architect for renovations and additions since its rescue in the 1960s. Inexplicably, an exhibit at Carnegie Hall about its rescue and restoration paid little attention to this earliest rescue. I subsequently taped an oral history of both Isaac and Vera Stern to record the story for posterity. Unfortunately, Kaplan was already deceased.[2]

MOSES INCREASED MAYOR WAGNER'S PROBLEMS

More high-profile development controversies added to Mayor Wagner's public relations problems. During his administration (1954–1965), huge Upper West Side clearance projects—Lincoln Towers, the Coliseum, Manhattantown (now Park West Village), all Moses projects—saw a lot of historic and reusable urban fabric fall under the wrecker's ball, despite public opposition. And, quite significantly, in 1956, Robert Moses overreached the staunch editorial support he enjoyed from the *New York Times* when he tried to bulldoze a beloved patch of Central Park at Sixty-seventh Street to extend the parking lot for the privately run Tavern-on-the-Green restaurant. This was a favorite park location of a potent group of West Siders, including members of the press, along with theatrical and art-world celebrities.

Angry protesting mothers with baby carriages facing down the bull-dozer made news. A community group sued to stop demolition. But be-fore the court case was decided, Moses, as he had done elsewhere, had the trees torn down and the patch of park cleared in the middle of the night. Despite the loss, the community did not let the battle end and con-tinued its lawsuit. The well-publicized, extended battle continued. Moses experienced a humiliating defeat, forced to give up the parking plan to resolve the litigation. The Adventure Playground was built on that site in-stead. The well-publicized Moses defeat was his first big one. It is consid-ered the beginning of Moses's descent from public hero status.

To add to the administration's public relations woes, *New York Post* investigative reporters Joe Kahn and Bill Haddad had been covering Moses excesses since 1956. They exposed corruption occurring in the West Side clearance project farther uptown, known as Manhattantown (now Park West Village, 97th to 100th Streets). Project sponsors, selected by Moses, did one of two things. They tore down buildings with no effort to move new construction forward and used empty sites as commercial parking lots. Or they let buildings stand, collected rents, but provided ten-ants with no maintenance or basics like heat or hot water. On top of this, only 20 percent of the displaced residents were given relocation assistance. Sponsors were paid handsomely to provide relocation service in full, whether or not those services were performed.

As Norval White and Elliot Willensky say of Park West Village in their *AIA Guide to New York*: "This large and banal housing development was built in the aftermath of the 1957 Manhattantown *urban renewal scandal*. Developers had acquired six blocks of tenements at *a reduced price* from the City under the federal urban renewal program. Instead of developing the site, they sat tight for five years, collecting rents, neglecting repairs, and in-venting ingenious schemes *to exploit their unhappy tenants*. Some say these disclosures marked the beginning of N.Y.C. construction czar Robert Moses' loss of power." Mayor Wagner endured unending political prob-lems from the Moses backlash, adding up to a big public relations prob-lem. For all these troublesome reasons and more, the 1965 landmark law had a broader political purpose for the mayor than a preservation one.

Wagner was known for addressing problems by first appointing a committee. So in 1962, before a law was passed, Mayor Wagner appointed a temporary Landmarks Preservation Commission that came up with a list of twelve hundred buildings and two historic districts worthy of designation. While the law was pending, the flamboyant 1890 Brokaw Mansions, on Fifth Avenue at Seventy-ninth Street, that *New York Times* architecture critic Ada Louise Huxtable so eloquently immortalized, were demolished in 1964. To no avail, pickets protested in front of the chateaulike assemblage of four townhouses built between 1880 and 1912. This debacle, following so closely the demise of Penn Station, pushed final passage.

A Movement Grows

These accumulated political headaches were not at all apparent to me when I was writing about historic preservation for the *New York Post* in the early 1970s. Certainly, the full measure of Robert Moses's impact on the city was not in my consciousness, nor the strong civic resistance to his decades of demolition and rebuild policies. Wagner may have had motives only slightly related to preservation, but what he and others did not count on was what was already unleashed—the grassroots preservation movement. It was a rapidly growing civic force, not yet large in numbers but significant in passion and energy.

Preservationists would not be mollified for long with a tepid toe-in-the-water approach to official preservation policy that the 1965 law represented. Satisfaction had lasted for a few years, however, while some obvious landmarks were officially designated. Then, in 1972, one developer, Peter Kalikow, overstepped the mark on Fifth Avenue across from the Metropolitan Museum of Art, not far from the site of the demolished Brokaw Mansions, a site in a neighborhood bound to gain considerable citywide attention. It became my first major preservation story.

Like many others, I had followed Huxtable's Brokaw articles and thought subsequent passage of the landmarks law was a real solution. And I was certainly not politically astute enough or even aware of the growing impact of the Moses era and the political challenges then facing Wagner. But when I went to cover the story of the newly threatened Fifth Avenue mansions in 1972, I discovered the reality about the landmark law. It was a charade. Whoever heard of a law that functioned for six months and then went into hibernation for three years? I was stunned. I, like so many New Yorkers, thought the truth was different. I simply could not understand how significant buildings could be demolished with the landmark law in place.

An editor had handed me the press release, just another daily story assignment. That release was written by a tall, articulate preservationist, Kent Barwick, who was director of a then little-known citywide group, the Municipal Arts Society (MAS). The press release called attention to the imminent demise of one of the last remaining rows of low-rise Fifth Avenue mansions, despite the existence of the landmark law. Kalikow's intention was to replace almost the whole corner, including a townhouse and small apartment house on Eighty-second Street. The law, the release noted, was powerless to stop the demolition of these historic but undesignated mansions. Two of the Fifth Avenue limestone mansions were already down, but the most ornate of the original five still stood at the corner along with the one around the corner. The bulldozer was on site, ready to keep going. Mimi Levitt, a resident and townhouse owner on Eighty-second Street, was the catalyst of this fight. She was like so many fierce defenders of neighborhoods and historic preservation—mostly women—whom I have encountered on stories around the city and country.

Levitt was not previously a civic activist. But the threat to her neighborhood—including her own house—appropriately aroused her defensive instinct. The neighborhood group of which she was part, aided by Barwick's citywide Municipal Arts Society, invoked a host of legal maneuvers to slow the process in an effort to thwart demolition. The buildings had not had a public hearing at the Landmarks Commission. The commission was on its three-year hiatus, but civic lawsuits stalled the demolition.

The battle continued through the courts for three years when a compromise was struck to resolve the lawsuit. The third mansion went down, but the rest were spared. The ornate mansard-roof Duke Mansion on the corner, built in 1901 for Benjamin N. Duke, director of the American Tobacco Company, was not included in the demolition plan and would have survived alone in the shadow of a banal tower. A conventionally dull twelve-story apartment house with a fake mansard roof went up in 1980 on the cleared site adjacent to the Duke. Actually, the "roof" is just a parapet on top of the facade. As a concession to the protesting public, ordered by the court, the developer had the facade of the new building designed by Philip Johnson with not much noticeable improvement.

For me in September 1972, writing the first of six stories over three years about this fight, it was an eye-opener. The more questions I asked, the more I realized the purposeful inadequacy of the law. The story revealed the major defect in the law as well as a timid attitude on the part of the Landmarks Commission. With my editors' consent, I spent several months investigating the larger picture. Out of that came a series of articles highlighting the continuing and severe threat to the city's historic buildings and parks. Reading those articles today reveals the tenuous state of preservation only thirty-eight years ago.[3] The New York then seems like a different city.

The first of those articles, in January 1973, revealed the flaws in the law and its apparent intentional weaknesses. In the world of historic preservation, this was a bombshell. Most people who thought the landmark law was a great achievement and protective of the city's special buildings had no idea how limited was the commission's power. Most critically and little known was the provision that the commission could designate landmarks after a public hearing; but it could hold those hearings *only every three years*! What did people think would happen during the three years between designation periods? Once designated a landmark, of course, a building could not be torn down or externally altered without commission approval. Vulnerable buildings just didn't get designated and, often, still don't.

A Lot Left Unprotected

The law was interesting for its omissions. For one thing, it did not cover interiors. Thus, if the Grand Central landmark designation, at the time being challenged in the courts, was upheld, Penn Central would still be able to gut the interior so long as it left the facade alone. The law also did not cover scenic landmarks. Thus, Central Park, Prospect Park, and other treasured patches of green were not qualified for landmark protection.

The law was binding only on private owners. A privately owned designated landmark—such as the turn-of-the-century Plaza Hotel—could not be torn down or its exterior altered without commission approval. But the Metropolitan Museum of Art, also an official landmark, could simply ignore—and had—the commission's disapproval of plans for its new Lehman wing. If the administration had decided to tear down City Hall, the commission would have had no power to stand in its way. The commission's judgments on public buildings were not even a matter of public record.

And then there was the commission itself.[4] Some critics went so far as to say that it was the worst enemy of the work it professed to do. Harmon H. Goldstone, an architect and former member of the City Planning Commission, was appointed the commission's first paid chairman in 1968. The chair is the only paid commissioner.

In December 1970, the commission declared a moratorium on landmark designations. Meeting in executive sessions, it decided without formal vote that no more designations would be made except when a building was in immediate jeopardy. Four "historic districts" and 54 individual sites were designated before the moratorium. Five proposals were rejected. The official explanation for the moratorium was the lack of "staff, space and money" that commission chairman Goldstone said was needed to administer 360 individual landmarks and 18 landmark districts already designated.

The unofficial explanation—arrived at after an extensive investigation—seemed to be an extreme reluctance on the part of the commission to designate in the face of even mild opposition, a reluctance to designate properties that might stand in the way of anticipated real estate development, and a reluctance to designate sites where property owners simply threatened a lawsuit. This was 1973, eight years after the law was passed. Many notable structures the public probably already thought were protected by landmark status had not been designated.

PROTECTION CAME SLOWLY

Everyone concerned acknowledged that selecting landmarks to designate was not easy. Many observers noted that this dilemma was just one element in the growing agony of many American urban centers where the quality of the built environment often collided head-on with the demands of real estate development. The heart and soul of historic cities were being erased by more than just real estate development; Moses-style highways and urban renewal projects were tearing the economic, social, and physical heart out of cities, taking down both plain and special old buildings and disrupting thousands of lives and businesses. Even the most ardent preservationist agreed that treasures of the past must sometimes be sacrificed for the needs of the present. At this point in time, the balance was nowhere near being struck, and the unspoken mission of the Landmarks Commission was supposed to be just that.

The Woolworth Building, for example, was the only skyscraper ever even considered for designation in the first seven years of the law. A striking Gothic tower built in 1913, Woolworth was called the Cathedral of Commerce and was for a while the tallest building in the world. Today it is filled with high-priced offices and condos. But, by 1973, Woolworth and such other New York icons as the 1929–1931 Empire State Building and 1930 Chrysler Building and 1932–1940 Rockefeller Center—all owned by very important real estate people—had not yet been considered for landmark designation.

The 1965 law was the first glimmer of hope on the preservation scene, and, considering the intense opposition of banking and real estate interest, it was an achievement that surprised the most cynical preservationists. But it was real estate people who spoke most highly of the results of the law. J. Clarence Davies, real estate commissioner under Mayor Wagner and a member of the commission for its first six years, told me at the time, "Opposition diminished because the commission turned out not to be as much a threat as expected. When people saw what was being preserved and understood the law, they were no longer worried."

What Davies and others also understood is that the commission—by careful avoidance of designation—rarely stood in the way of real estate development, even for worthy buildings. At the same time, most preservation advocates were lulled into complacency. They didn't know what to expect. Those who did complain went unheard. And the snail's pace of action was useful to a cautious commission, as my second article, the next day, indicated.

Commission spokesmen liked to point out that they had lost only one of 360 designated landmarks to the wrecker's ball—the Jerome Mansion, at Twenty-sixth and Madison, the elegant house that was the home of Winston Churchill's grandfather and later the Manhattan Club. Critics argued that this is an empty boast. The Jerome Mansion could have been saved, they claimed, if the commission hadn't been anxious to have that one important loss to prove to the real estate industry how small a threat they were. "It's their only loss," commented Kent Barwick, "because the commission hasn't designated buildings that are in danger of coming down." The old Metropolitan Opera House, the Thirty-fourth Street Armory, the Beaux Arts Singer Building at 149 Broadway, and the old

Ziegfeld Theater at Fifty-fourth Street were among those that were never designated and are now gone.

The Metropolitan Opera may have been outdated. The opera company may have needed more space. But the overriding reason for its demise was the new Metropolitan Opera theater included in Lincoln Center. While great nineteenth-century opera houses all over the world have been renovated and modernized, it was not even considered here. The agenda all flowed from the Robert Moses plan for Lincoln Center (more on this later). A forty-two-story combined office tower and street-level school replaced the Thirty-fourth Street Armory. U.S. Steel's black and glass office tower on Broadway replaced the Singer Building, a masterpiece of renowned architect Ernest Flagg. A fifty-story office building with a new theater adjacent to it replaced the Ziegfeld Theater.

Few people, I noted, were aware of the two-year-old moratorium. One person who actively worked for the 1965 law and knew vaguely about the moratorium noted with a bit of embarrassment: "I think a lot of us felt everything was in good hands after the law passed so we went on to other things. But the fact is, the public doesn't realize just how weak the commission is. So little is known about the law and the commission that people have the impression it is more powerful than it has been."

The late city councilman Carter Burden (D-Man.), formerly on the staff of Senator Robert Kennedy and key in the establishment of the Bedford-Stuyvesant Restoration Corporation, introduced legislation based on a long study by the Municipal Arts Society that would close some of the loopholes in the landmark law—primarily the three-year limitation. That crippling clause had been included after intense, mostly behind-the-scenes real estate opposition to the 1965 legislation. It was the price of passage.

At the time of these articles, many potential landmarks were in imminent danger of loss. There was the row of Fifth Avenue mansions, about to be demolished for a luxury high-rise. A row of nineteenth-century townhouses in the landmark district of Mount Morris Park was left half-demolished by the State Narcotics Control Agency that had once planned to use them. Developers cast an eager eye on the yet unprotected Cast Iron district in SoHo, the largest remaining example of a unique American architectural form. The fate of the Renaissance Revival Police Headquarters on Centre Street was left precariously unresolved as the Police Department prepared to move into its new Pearl Street headquarters.

The Manhattan Focus

In the early years of the landmark law, aside from Brooklyn Heights, the focus of both the Landmarks Commission and the preservation advocacy community was Manhattan. The Flatbush Town Hall, as the next article in the series showed, was an exception, but that was due to a persistent local community organization. Brooklyn didn't have a vigorous landmark advocacy group beyond Brooklyn Heights, and, in fact, the borough still suffered from being overshadowed by Manhattan, an inferiority complex hard to believe considering its popularity today. The Flatbush Town Hall was a small window into rich Brooklyn history.

Built in 1875, it has played a part in Brooklyn life ever since. But it was then to be torn down and replaced by an eighty-car parking lot. The handsome Victorian hall was the center of civic and cultural life for the Town of Flatbush until 1894, when Flatbush was absorbed by the City of Brooklyn and the hall became a police station. It remained a police station until the Sixty-seventh Precinct moved to a new facility three blocks away. In July 1969 it was scheduled for demolition. For almost two years a group of community residents had been appealing to all levels of city government to let the community retain the building for a multiuse community center. The Landmarks Preservation Commission resisted designating because they didn't want to interfere with another agency. By law, of course, the commission had no power to consider designation of the town hall before June 1973, five months after the article was written. Demolition seemed imminent. The city council, at the time, was considering reform legislation that would eliminate that restriction. "Curiously," I wrote further, "the Landmarks Commission appears to be the only interested party not actively lobbying for its passage." Councilman Burden told me, "I very definitely get the feeling that the commission is not anxious to have that power. Any landmarks issue is a nest of vipers because you're dealing with very powerful real estate interests." Goldstone had said unofficially that he wasn't for it because he would have more people wanting designations.

The Flatbush Town Hall is a building of considerable historic interest. It is of the same architectural vintage as the 1876 Jefferson Market Courthouse in Greenwich Village that was rescued through intense and well-organized community pressure before passage of the 1965 preservation law. It was a rare early preservation victory. But Flatbush Avenue merchants

claimed more parking space was desperately needed, and the Traffic Department agreed. As the country became more and more car-centric, downtown merchants everywhere thought more parking was the answer to their
increasingly diminishing customer base. This is often still true today. In
this case, an existing municipal parking lot adjacent to the hall was somehow inadequate, merchants claimed. Teachers at nearby Erasmus High
School were allowed to monopolize it. Parking has long been the most
common excuse to tear down old buildings of all kinds. This continues
today in many cities, towns, and neighborhoods where the actual number
of existing parking spaces and how well they are used are rarely known.
Parking is just the easiest thing on which to blame a downtown's woes
when, in fact, more fundamental things are usually askew.

The Flatbush Town Hall is not only significant as an individual landmark. It is part of a trilogy of history contained on one square Flatbush
block. At the corner of Flatbush and Church Avenues is the 175-year-old
Flatbush Reformed Church, which was granted its charter by Peter
Stuyvesant, New York's last Dutch governor, and has occupied its present
site since 1654. Next to that, in the courtyard of Erasmus High School, is
the 185-year-old Erasmus Hall Academy, a wooden schoolhouse built as a
private academy for the Dutch church that remains one of the oldest in the
country. All three structures—the church, the school, the Hall—had been
named national historic sites by the U.S. Interior Department, making them
eligible for matching state and federal restoration and preservation funds.
But during the first set of public hearings following passage of the 1965
landmark law, the commission heard and later designated only two buildings in the this historic Flatbush triangle—the clapboard schoolhouse and
the church. Eventually, the Town Hall was designated and stands today.

The Landmarks Commission was not just Manhattan-centric, but East
Side Manhattan-centric. The West Side still suffered from the image of
blight, a slum of little value, an image perpetuated energetically by Moses,
however erroneous the slum tag might be. He had declared several West
Side areas ripe for urban renewal. Despite this, a vigorous local community took aim at one of the city's unique landmarks and pushed the Landmarks Commission where it was reluctant to go. The fourth article in this
series told the story of saving the Ansonia at Seventy-second Street and
Broadway, a landmark of incomparable value today. That the effort was
so difficult reflects how little value was ascribed to most of the city's extraordinary historic architecture.

2.2 An old postcard of the Hotel Ansonia. Once threatened with demolition, it's now a magnificently restored upscale apartment co-op.

A WEST SIDE LANDMARK

The curving, turreted Beaux Arts Ansonia—built as a hotel—is one of the city's most obvious landmarks, as well as the heart of its West Side community. Even the local post office is named in its honor—Ansonia Station. The hotel was built in 1904 by William Earl Dodge Stokes, a multimillionaire developer and amateur designer of the Phelps-Dodge family, who was one of the leading developers of Riverside Drive and the brownstone belt of the Upper West Side. It was the biggest and best of its kind, boasting a variety of construction and engineering firsts—including two huge swimming pools, one of them at the time the largest pool in the world. It quickly became a cultural treasure because of its unparalleled facilities for the teaching and practicing of the performing arts.

The seventeen-story chateau with mansard roofs and delicate ironwork is considered one of the most successful marriages of design and function. There are three-feet-thick concrete walls and specially insulated ceilings that allow entire orchestras to practice without letting neighbors hear a sound. A unique method of air circulation made it the first "air-conditioned" structure in New York. Its heyday was the first three decades of the century when just about every great name in music lived or practiced in its elegantly detailed suites—Caruso, Chaliapin, Elman, Pinza, Pons, Stravinsky, Toscanini. Other tenants included Babe Ruth, Theodore Dreiser, and Florenz Ziegfeld. The importance of the Ansonia to performing artists is so international in scope that Italian performers reported that news of the battle to save it was carried on Rome television. In recent years, the building had become more important as an arts center because of its proximity to Lincoln Center—the apparent reason that John D. Rockefeller III, retired chairman of Lincoln Center, had joined the campaign for landmark designation.

The Ansonia's threatened state was a perfect journalistic subject to demonstrate the impotence of the Landmarks Commission, as the fourth article demonstrated. It took seven years, two commission hearings, more than twenty-five thousand petition signatures, a foundation-financed publicity effort, a sing-in protest on the steps of City Hall, support from Senators Javits and Buckley, John D. Rockefeller III, and other luminaries, and—most crucially—a threatened community lawsuit. But finally the Landmarks Preservation Commission declared the Ansonia a landmark . . . just when the owner was talking about tearing it down.

The citizen effort lasted more than a year with no response. Finally, a community group went to see Goldstone. They told him that foundations were interested in buying but that the owner refused to sell. And, they told him, they were prepared to testify at capital budget hearings that the commission had vacillated and therefore didn't deserve full funding. They said too that they were prepared to go to court to prove it was the commission's responsibility under the law to designate the Ansonia. A few weeks later the matter was unanimously approved by the commission.

The Landmarks Commission didn't actually ignore the West Side. But it turned down the designation of some worthy buildings that in later years would be designated:

- The Central Savings Bank across Broadway from the Ansonia—considered one of the city's finest examples of Italian Renaissance architecture—was turned down for landmark status after a hearing in June 1966. The *AIA Guide to New York* describes it as a "a Palladian Palace. Wrought-iron lanterns and window grilles by Samuel Yellin are the finest features of this richly embellished limestone bank." The interior was designated after the law changed to permit interior designations.
- The East River Savings Bank at Ninety-sixth and Amsterdam, which the *AIA Guide* describes as "a classical temple inscribed with exhortations to the thrifty," was also turned down by the commission in 1966 but redesignated years later.

- Pomander Walk at Ninety-fifth and West End Avenue, also rejected in 1966, was described by the *AIA* this way: "Pomander Walk is a tiny street in the London suburb of Chiswick. It came to New York in 1911 as the name of a stage play. This double row of small town houses is modeled after the stage sets used for the New York production."[5]

Big swaths of the Upper West Side had been cleared under urban renewal: Lincoln Center, Lincoln Towers, the Coliseum at Columbus Circle, Park West Village, and the West Side Urban Renewal Area (Eighty-seventh to Ninety-seventh, Central Park West to Amsterdam). The public unrest caused by the sweeping scale of this demolition was part and parcel of the headaches that Mayor Wagner had to deal with.

The first seven years of the new landmark law seemed to be serving the mayor well, giving the public the erroneous impression that landmark protection was in place. "So after 10 years," Evelyn Haynes observed in my final article, "out of 5000 miles of streets in this city we have 360 landmarks. That's not a grain of sand in the desert. What is that, 30 a year? That whole list is as phony at a $3 bill because it's overloaded with public buildings over which the commission has no power and lots of churches which are non-savable anyway if they are unused and falling apart. All you really have is the Good Housekeeping Seal of Approval on some nice buildings."

Eight years after the law was enacted, preservation battles were no longer primarily in fashionable neighborhoods, mostly in Manhattan. The disputes crossed all borough and income levels. "Landmark designation has become one of the most potent forces stabilizing community life," Goldstone noted. "The demand for it far outstrips our potential."

Unquestionably, the preservation movement had already outgrown the expectation of the 1965 landmarks legislation. As long as the economics of land use dictates that high-density new structures, whether commercial or residential, were more valuable than character, quality, and open space, there was little doubt that the movement would continue to grow.

THE LAW CHANGES, BUT THE COMMISSION DOESN'T

For seven years, a complacent, slow-moving Landmarks Commission had not come under fire in any major way, and City Hall was not feeling much heat. Putting the issue in the spotlight of the press, as the *Post* articles did, surprised a relaxed public, accelerating the momentum for reform and providing ammunition for key advocates. Ten months later, in November 1973, the city council amended the law. The changes were significant and form the backbone of the commission's strength today:

- The three-year limitation was eliminated.
- Designation of publicly owned scenic landmarks was permitted.
- Designation of private interior spaces was permitted, if accessible to the public.
- Commission reports on city-owned buildings were no longer to be kept secret and were made binding.

But the commission was still reluctant to change its pace of operation, even with newfound authority. The commission wasn't moving any faster than City Hall under Mayor Wagner would permit. Then came the lawsuit against the city over the fifty-six-story office tower proposed to be built over the 1913 Grand Central Terminal, owned by the Pennsylvania Railway Company. The proposed tower, designed by esteemed modernist Marcel Breuer, was turned down by the commission in 1969. Describing the terminal as "overpowering in its timeless grandeur," the commission noted at the time that "to balance a 56-story office tower above the flamboyant Beaux-Arts facade seems nothing more than an aesthetic joke. Quite simply, the tower would overwhelm the terminal by its sheer mass" and "reduce the landmark itself to the status of a 'curiosity.'"

After that proposal was rejected another was put forth that would demolish the terminal, except for the main concourse. That too was rejected. Penn Central then sued to overturn the landmark designation and to declare the landmark law unconstitutional. The case moved slowly through the courts. Expecting to lose, the commission and other city officials were even more gun-shy, preparing in fact to pull the rug out from under their newly achieved powers.

In November 1974, I wrote an article revealing that the city was considering withdrawing the landmark designation of Grand Central Terminal after receiving indications it may lose a multimillion-dollar lawsuit challenging that designation. Although New York Supreme Court Justice Irving Saypol had not issued a written decision, he had made a number of statements from the bench that indicated he was leaning heavily in favor of the plaintiffs. If, as was then anticipated, the city lost the five-year legal battle, it faced the possibility of paying upwards of sixty million dollars in damages. Judge Saypol appeared to be leaning toward ruling only on the specific application of the law to the Grand Central situation without ruling on the overall constitutionality of the law.

Settlement discussions had been going on for several months between representatives of the plaintiff and the city. And the justice was asked to defer judgment in the hope the case could be settled beforehand. One of the proposals under discussion was a withdrawal of the damage claim if the city were to withdraw the landmark designation. This would have allowed the owner and developer to build the skyscraper the Landmarks Preservation Commission disallowed.

JACKIE KENNEDY ONASSIS MAKES THE DIFFERENCE

Civic groups, led by the Municipal Arts Society, expressed outrage and gathered a delegation to meet with Mayor Abraham Beame, who had succeeded Wagner. That was when Jackie Kennedy Onassis famously stepped in, writing a letter to Mayor Beame, pleading with him to save the terminal.[6] Her letter helped raise the alarm in the city and the nation. Historic preservation was now in the headlines. Jackie, the great arbiter of good taste in fashion, food, and architecture, raised the consciousness of the nation to the importance of historic preservation. The mayor was persuaded to continue the court fight after the first court ruling in Penn Central's favor. The case lasted until 1978, when it reached the U.S. Supreme Court.

In the years following the 1973 law change, under relentless and very public pressure from vocal preservationists, the commission responded to its new authority, gained a series of new chairs with each new administration, went beyond its emphasis on individual landmarks to focus on historic districts, took a stronger interest in all five boroughs, and wrestled with the City Planning Commission to finally take its place as a peer agency instead of being Planning's stepchild. In the early 1990s, as part of a city-charter revision effort, an attempt was made to bring the Landmarks Commission under control of the Planning Commission. It failed. Originally, the Landmarks Commission came under the Parks Department jurisdiction and was considered subservient to the Planning Commission.

Recognizing landmark preservation as an integral part of citywide and neighborhood planning and as a politically attractive issue took time, but it did take hold, even if not always applied consistently. But, more than anything else, it took the U.S. Supreme Court ruling in the Grand Central case in 1978 to gain expanded acceptance of and appreciation for historic preservation. The impact was profound also on planning and architecture in the city and in the whole country, giving the New York landmark law the substance that many people today assume it had when first passed in 1965.

In the five intervening years between the 1973 amendment and the 1978 Grand Central ruling, more significant buildings were threatened and significant landmark battles undertaken. But all of this ensued in a new atmosphere in which the significance of preservation was not dismissed. But even after the Grand Central case and the celebrated participation of Jackie Kennedy Onassis, it was at least another decade or more before widespread public acceptance of preservation took hold.

Significant Landmark Battles Were Many

The 1970s was a decade of continual battles to save important buildings taken for granted today. Pier A (1886), Police Headquarters (1905–1909), Grace Church Houses (1883–1907), SoHo, the Flushing Town Hall (1862–1864), Empire Stores (1869–1885) on the Brooklyn waterfront, the Villard Houses (1884), and Radio City Music Hall (1931–1932), to name a few, were all threatened with demolition. Each one of them could have been lost without battles to stave off the wrecking ball. Pier A, the city's oldest covered pier, still standing regally on the Lower West Side waterfront, has been in limbo ever since its rescue, due to be a restored public space. The grand old Police Headquarters was elegantly renovated into high-end condominiums. Grace Church Houses, due to come down to build a gymnasium for the Grace Church School, instead have that gymnasium on the inside. SoHo is SoHo, the ultimate chic former industrial neighborhood. The Villard Houses provide a grand entrance to an otherwise pedestrian hotel along with a restaurant in one of the city's most extraordinary interior spaces, plus a wing of offices. And Radio City Music Hall? It is still amazing to think the attempt to tear it down really happened, but it did. I covered all these threats and more, believing that the unique historical, cultural, and aesthetic character of the city was under assault. Clearly, it was.

Tweed Courthouse: An Old Controversy

In this context, the fight over what to do with Tweed Courthouse in 2003 seemed like a petty squabble after what had transpired in the 1970s.

Given the state of preservation in the early years of that decade, Tweed's near loss at that time is understandable. I wrote five articles over three years on Tweed's doomed future. The first was June 14, 1974. In that and subsequent articles, I reported on the administration's determination to replace the undesignated landmark building with a redbrick mock-colonial structure. The decision, I wrote, threatened to "turn into the biggest architectural controversy since the demolition of Pennsylvania Station." Civic groups rallied in opposition and called on the administration to restore and reuse all the historic city-owned properties near City Hall. They included:

- The 1846 Sun Building (corner of Broadway and Chambers Street), a subdued five-story Italianate structure built to house A. T. Stewart Dry Goods Store, the first department store in America. The city eventually restored it and occupies the upper floors with retail on the ground floor.
- Next door to the Sun Building, on Chambers, the 1912 Emigrant Industrial Savings Bank, an ornate mixture of Beaux Arts and Art Nouveau built for the bank to serve the city's Irish Catholic immigrant population. It was once America's wealthiest savings bank, according to the *AIA Guide*. The city eventually restored and occupied this too.
- At one point in the 1960s, those two significant landmarks and the old Police Headquarters were due to be replaced by a new civic center.

The 1970s fight over Tweed Courthouse was a pivotal moment. But as then City Club trustee William Hubbard noted, "There's a predisposition in the city toward demolition. . . . There's a lot of rethinking being done in this field but it hasn't yet caught on in municipal construction."

My last report on the eventual rescue of Tweed was the last one I wrote on any preservation issue before leaving the *Post* in 1978. The editors under new owner Rupert Murdoch saw no news value in the issue of landmarks preservation. I wrote that the Tweed Courthouse—described by one architectural historian as "the finest public building in the Italianate style in the country"—was coming back to life.

Under the cunning guidance of city council president Paul O'Dwyer, the high-ceilinged, spacious rooms were gradually being stripped of layers of dirt and rows of old file cabinets to make way for O'Dwyer staff people. Glass doors with graceful etchings of the city's seal were clean and glistening once again, milk-glass fixtures were being rescued from piles of debris and rehung, fireplaces long blocked with cartons now served as elegant ornamentation, and well-carved plasterwork had been stripped and repainted.

Clearly, the determination of O'Dwyer and his staff saved this well-known monument to civic corruption. But the economics of renting office space for city use and the then fiscal crisis were what made using it acceptable to bureaucrats. The 90,000 square feet of Tweed office space was rent free, saving $630,000 yearly. O'Dwyer was an old hand at fighting for preservation of the city's heritage, and he had long advocated making the civic center area around City Hall more of a tourist attraction. O'Dwyer's achievement was to rescue this storied landmark from destruction, to get the roof repaired, the building modestly upgraded, and, most important, get it back into use. It was not designated a landmark until October 16, 1984.

Twenty years later, during the administration of Mayor Rudolph W. Giuliani, under the determined guidance of Landmarks Preservation Commission chair Jennifer Raab, Tweed Courthouse underwent a three-year, $90 million full restoration. Little support existed within the administration for Raab's dogged determination to make this an achievement of her tenure, until, that is, the idea of using it as a relocation site for the Museum of the City of New York. The high-quality restoration job was led by one of New York State's preeminent restoration architects, Jack Waite. Nothing like this quality of restoration would have even been considered thirty years earlier. The current use of this venerable landmark by the Board of Education will be debated among partisans for years to come, but the miracle is that it still stands.

The most compelling argument for use by the museum was that the public should have full access to the extraordinary interior, with its skylighted five-story rotunda and modestly elegant rooms. The most compelling reason for use by the Board of Education was as a signal that Mayor Bloomberg considered public education reform the highest priority of his administration and that bringing the board next door to City Hall underscored his determination to give education major attention and to demand accountability.

As it turns out, something of a combination of the two is the result. Offices of the Board of Education are comfortably ensconced, and some of the small-scale public spaces around the rotunda on the different floors are well used as meeting places. Two kindergarten public schools now occupy space here.[7] And the main floor of the rotunda is used for some public events.

RAISING PRESERVATION AWARENESS AMONG STUDENTS

Bringing public school children to Tweed for any length of time is probably the most significant use of the building. Most public school children live in neighborhoods where the value ascribed to old buildings is almost nonexistent. Little of the reverence for historic buildings so evident in much of Europe and other foreign places is true in New York. Most often, the potential of the historic fabric in many neighborhoods is appreciated primarily by new relocating residents moving in. Many current residents whose landlords are loath to perform more than minimum building maintenance think only new construction should be aspired to. This is often true even if the new is flimsy, as it usually is, compared with the neglected old.

When I was writing the story about Flatbush Town Hall and the trilogy of history of the former village of Flatbush, I discovered a wonderful gem. In the courtyard of Erasmus High School, a Gothic confection typical of many of the city's public schools, is a little-known historic treasure—the 1786 Erasmus Hall Academy, a wooden schoolhouse built as a private academy for the Dutch church that remains, one of the oldest in the country. It's in the courtyard, yet no mention or use of it made its way into the curriculum of the high school surrounding it.

New York City schools, like most public school systems around the country, have been remiss in giving students reason to appreciate their own neighborhoods, especially their historic fabric. Is it any wonder these kids grow up with the idea that upward mobility means moving out to a suburban tract house? Only a new appreciation of where they now live can change that and, in turn, advance the stability of their neighborhoods.

To my mind, then, if use of the Tweed Courthouse by the Board of Education does that for the current generation of public school students, it will be a worthwhile achievement. If they can see the value in something old, they may not be deceived into equating new with better. Equally important is the assurance of the intrinsic and *lasting* value of this stately edifice. The Board of Education will probably not be located there forever, but the building at least exists to accept an unpredicted future use.

The days where buildings like this one could be considered deserving of the garbage dump are over—at least in New York. Many American cities lag far behind New York in this evaluation, even though in New York vulnerable buildings still don't get landmarked if a well-connected real estate owner wants an area of the city redeveloped.

The fundamental dilemma of the Landmarks Preservation Commission is the conflict between preservation and new development in a city where real estate ownership trumps all else in access to power and influence. How well preservation has prevailed over the years from administration to administration often depends on which prominent owner is involved. But when a site does get put on the commission calendar to be considered for designation and when owners seek permission to alter a landmark, the public hearing process is quite admirable. The public is not just heard. People who testify are really listened to by the commissioners. The measure of the commission is not just what gets designated a landmark or a landmark district. The key is what the commission avoids doing.

Opponents continue to argue that preservation is about freezing the city—*embalming* is the favorite word—about stopping change or stopping progress. Facts to the contrary make no difference in the public debate. Notable new buildings exist in many historic districts. An endless array of additions to historic buildings exist all over the city. The historic preservation movement rescued cities from the bulldozer of urban renewal and cataclysmic change, thereby rescuing urbanism itself. Preservationists first fought to preserve not only buildings but the urban fabric itself, all those elements now extolled by mainstream planners and urban designers—importance of density, real mixed-use and mixed-income neighborhoods, walkable streets and community gathering spaces. Through preservation, everything is connected.

For the most part, preservationists are too defensive. Once and for all, the time is now to acknowledge that preservation is about city building in the most expansive way, about enhancing the new by preserving and adaptively reusing the old, about moving forward and looking back at the same time. Preservation is about building anew on assets that exist, about Urban Husbandry at its best.

-3-

GREENWICH VILLAGE
Jacobs, Moses, and Me

> The Village is amorphous; I can shape it into any place. . . . Everything in the Village . . . seems haphazard, accidental. When we first moved there, the old-timers told us the Village had Changed. The Village does not change, not really. The Village—the real Village, the one bounded by Fifth Avenue on the east and the Hudson River on the west—remains an accident.
>
> MARY CANTWELL,
> *"Manhattan When I Was Young"*

I was a four-year reporter in 1969—almost a "veteran"—when I was one of nine *Post* staffers sent to the neighborhoods of their youth to write a series of articles meant to dramatize the changes wrought by time. Anthony Mancini went to the Northeast Bronx, Judith Michaelson to Flatbush, Timothy Lee to Park Slope, Jerry Tallmer to Park Avenue, Lee Dembart to Jackson Heights, John Mullane to Kingsbridge, Carl J. Pelleck to the Lower East Side, Arthur Greenspan to the Grand Concourse, and I to Greenwich Village.

For the most part, except for Park Avenue, the neighborhoods retained their working-class character. The Northeast Bronx, the Grand Concourse, and Kingsbridge, along with Jackson Heights ("the poor man's Forest Hills"), were already on the upward-mobility route. The Northeast Bronx had not lost its rural feel, although the not-so-distant Co-op

City, then in construction, was looming large. Park Avenue had already been transformed into mostly cooperative apartment houses with only twenty rental buildings left. And the Grand Concourse had not yet lost its "insular, isolated existence" primarily for Jews.

In every neighborhood, however, were signs of "city services getting bad, buildings getting shabby . . . and a tension that wasn't there before," as one wrote. The city had not hit the downward spiral that marked the 1970s, but its slow beginning was evident. Every neighborhood, it seemed, was in flux. Dramatic, if slow or subtle, shifts were unfolding, not the normal change of a healthy city. Moses's massive urban renewal and high-way building projects were increasingly causing disruptions that rippled throughout the city and were a primary cause of out-migration.

Too many chroniclers of the exodus from urban America are either unaware, choose to ignore, or downplay the enormous destabilization caused by the massive clearance projects that wiped out whole residential and industrial districts that would today be gentrified hot spots of renewing districts. Few acknowledge the significant impact of the push-pull effect. The riots of the mid-1960s accelerated that migration to the expanding suburbs. And the decade of the 1970s brought us to the brink of the deep abysmal fiscal crisis that marked so much of that decade.

THE STATE OF THE NEIGHBORHOODS

A few themes run through most of the reporters' recollections. As a group, these observations reflect New York as it entered the 1970s. Many older people were still "in the neighborhood," having been in the same residences for decades. People didn't seem to move often. Many of their kids had left, although Jackson Heights, according to Dembart, was still considered by many "the first push to the 'suburbs'" from the Bronx and Brooklyn. Every neighborhood was experiencing a changing ethnic makeup, often making longtime residents nervous. Some noted that each group "stayed to themselves" and didn't "bother with one another." Others were quick to blame creeping downward trends on "them." The "them" varied from neighborhood to neighborhood. Often, the new arrivals were the displaced of the latest "clearance" project elsewhere in the city. Many of those interviewed said the problems were being caused by their own kids, not as well behaved as they used to be.

The ethnic mix of each of these neighborhoods was still predominantly Irish, Italian, and Jewish, in differing proportions. Puerto Ricans, South Americans, Asians, and blacks were adding to the mix in different areas, but the minority numbers were still marginal in contrast to today. On Park Avenue, middle-class West Siders, mostly Jews, were moving over. In the Slope, Timothy Lee reported, "the new people" were the "transplanted Manhattanites who have bought a few score of the attractive brick and brownstone houses over the past 10 years." This was the only mention in any of the stories of the beginning of the great transformative trend that would bring middle-class residents back to so many historic neighborhoods in New York and across the country. Sometimes called "the Brownstone Movement," "the Back-to-the-City Movement," or just "urban pioneers," this early trickle of new, mostly young city investors was the vanguard of what is today one of the clearly recognized trends of urban regeneration. And like most movements of positive change, this one started slowly at a small scale at the grassroots level and was totally unrecognized or underestimated by the Experts.

Gangs had been a factor in almost everyone's childhood, but as Timothy Lee noted about the "predominantly Irish and Italian working class" Park Slope, "For years their sons fought each other in gangs, sometimes to the death. They fought because one gang, the Tigers, was Irish, and the other, the Garfield–South Brooklyn Boys, was Italian. They stopped when pistols became more readily available during the Korean War and the fun was suddenly gone out of the fighting."

Now, though, each neighborhood was experiencing new kinds of trouble—vandalism and crime—which the city would see dramatically increase during the 1970s. In Flatbush, Judith Michaelson observed, the street conflicts had been between "the apartment-house kids and the private-house kids." Carl Pelleck remembered "hanging out with gangs cause it was the thing to do." What I thought I remember as gang fights in Greenwich Village were, according to author Victor Navasky, a classmate of my sister, "culture conflicts between the Italians of the South Village and the private school kids. Fights broke out during school soccer games and sometimes they'd steal our soccer ball. When they taunted us after school, fist fights occasionally broke out." What I witnessed in Washington Square Park was never worse than rough bullying and weapons never more dangerous than sticks. The degree of minimum violence and fear didn't compare to the 1970s.

A DIFFERENT KIND OF CRIME

In all of the neighborhoods, crime had been petty, but by the dawn of the 1970s, in many areas, things were getting rough. The rise in drug abuse was a common complaint, first experienced, Tim Lee noted, during the Korean War. At first, many of the drugged kids were the children of heavy-drinking parents, he added, but, increasingly, new groups were bringing drugs into several of the neighborhoods.

Almost everyone's neighborhood had a busy retail shopping street. John Mullane said of West 231st Street in Kingsbridge: "It was impossible to go more than five steps without meeting another acquaintance." For Kingsbridge, 231st Street was still its "Times Square," and even the RKO Marble Hill was still operating. This onetime common community experience, where the faces of shopkeepers were familiar and cops still walked the beat and were on a first-name basis with kids, seemed to be diminishing everywhere.

Streets had been playgrounds for many of us. "Stickball was the big game," Carl Pelleck noted about the Lower East Side. "You asked a driver to please not park on the base, to drive to the other end of the block to keep the field clear. Most complied." And in Kingsbridge, John Mullane noted, "the curb was reserved exclusively for bouncing pink Spaldeens off it." No more. Stickball and curb ball were now clearly a thing of the past. Complaints now were of too many cars, either double-parked on the street or racing through the community "like the Indianapolis Speedway," as one Bronx resident complained to Anthony Mancini.

On the Grand Concourse, Arthur Greenspan found, displeasure was expressed about what traffic engineers had done to the residents' beloved boulevard. "They've widened the street, ripped out half the trees, built dividing traffic islands of green concrete instead of grass, built yellow-pavement entrances and exits—all the better to use the Concourse to flee elsewhere," Greenspan wrote.

Only one return visitor, Jerry Tallmer, found his neighborhood quite improved: Park Avenue and Eighty-second Street, "the only homogeneous area in the city, with no weak spots, 86th St. down to 60th, between Fifth and Lexington . . . with the swinging scene" concentrated on First, Second, and Third Avenues. And only one returnee, Carl Pelleck, found his neighborhood, the Lower East Side, filled with dramatic poverty, "filth, high crime and total change" . . . but "never considered a fashionable place to live" in the first place.

The following is what I found when I went back to the Village.

"The Old Neighborhood: Greenwich Village"
Post Daily Magazine, December 26, 1969

My apartment house is long gone, replaced by a grotesque monument otherwise known as the NYU Library. Washington Square Park is in a state of bulldozed shambles, a renovation promising some grand, improved design of the park that none of us thought needed improvement. Nathan's is coming to 8th St., Blimpie's is already on the corner of MacDougal and Bleecker, and Rienzi's—the once famed coffee house—is now a boutique.

If there is anything remaining of the Greenwich Village in which I grew up in the '40s and '50s, it is elusive. Many of the brownstone-lined streets remain, their West Village quality intact, but the box-like shadow of intruding apartment houses is never far off the horizon.

Gone is the spirit of the small community, separate and distinct from the rest of New York and the nation. Gone is the feeling that whatever was off-beat in the Village—the people, the dress, the symbols, the issues—was at least its own and not imported.

Gone too is the predominance of small shop-owners—more craftsmen than businessmen—who once thrived in the low-rent store fronts or cold-water lofts.

It is difficult to assess change in Greenwich Village. On the most personal level, nothing is the same. Yet in a larger sense there is still something special about the Village. It is still a geographic area unique to this city in architectural diversity, with a personality all its own. It is still the hub of newness—new movements, new dress, new life styles—even if all these are immediately commercialized. And it is still politically avant-garde, the first to take politics out of the hands of the professionals, the leader in zoning fights and landmark preservation.

What I wrote forty years go almost sounds current. The laments of many Villagers today are very similar, although a lot of specifics are quite different. I also noted that "bit by bit NYU was taking over prime Village real estate to create a campus for itself."

It was an ideal location for a child. The park was my backyard, and there were few park regulars we didn't know. Except for the university students, park people were Villagers and their friends. Strangers were immediately recognizable. Crowds were unusual even on warm weekends, and tourists were few and obviously out of place. Folksingers, artists with their easels, the chess players were always there, but they were just a part of the scene. No one interfered with anyone else. Buses still trafficked through Washington Arch to turn around and start back up Fifth Avenue, but that never stopped the ball games, roller skating, or the biggest sport of all—seeing who could throw the ball to the top of the Arch. Our mothers let us play in the park, unwatched, confident that should a fall or fight occur, some grown-up would take care of it. There was little mischief you could get away with without your parents hearing about it.

Today, forty years later, all of the streets I walked are much improved. The strip clubs are gone from West Third, and the celebrated Blue Note survives. The variety along MacDougal is similar but of a higher quality, a mark of definite economic upgrade but not necessarily lifestyle change. It is truly a mixed bag, with a tattoo parlor here and there.

For after school, the then still uncommercialized coffeehouses—where the espresso was brewed by the elderly Italian proprietor—were the equivalent to everyone else's corner drugstore soda fountain. There were the Italian hero shops, bakeries, vegetable stands, pushcarts with flavored ices. "Some of the South Villagers were pushed out by newcomers, others departed seeking upward mobility," I noted in the article. "Today the Italian enclave is still very much in existence but it is also smaller."

LITTLE ITALY TODAY

The South Village and Little Italy used to be one and the same. Today, Little Italy survives commercially only and covers a smaller area. Most of the resident Italians have moved on, but many of the well-known restaurants and specialty shops remain, some owned and operated by Armenians. The Italian feel is less but endures nonetheless because of the businesses that remain.

The area, like so many others, is undergoing development pressure, and community efforts have been aggressive to have it designated a historic district. Deservedly so, at that. One can assume this sizable area south of the park, with its colorful assortment of cafés and shops, was omitted from the original landmark district designation because in the mid-1960s, working-class districts of tenements and assorted businesses were not considered high architecture worthy of designation. Instead, they were targets of slum clearance. The South Village was more than just the cradle of Italian immigration. It was the epicenter of the beats from the 1920s on and the folk communities of the 1950s and '60s so long identified with the Village.

But in my 1969 article, I focused on the changing assortment of businesses that changed everything as rents escalated: "Most obviously hurt were the small entrepreneurs—the ones who slapped together jewelry, crafted hand-sewn shoes and bags, or created other 'Villagey' merchandise. Then, too, success led some of these craftsmen to the less personal but more lucrative world of Uptown. The small stores were the heart of the Village's life style, one of the things that kept it a community within a city. Their demise has only accelerated the destruction of the neighborhood's character."

On Eighth Street, everything new was offensive: open-front hot-dog stands that were a cheap reflection of Times Square, chainlike clothing stores offering the newest in ugliness and claiming their styles were of the Village. And one stretch of small stores was enclosed in a most incongruous imitation of a colonial-style suburban shopping center, with the pointed roof, redbrick front, white columns. If the new stores throughout the area weren't part of citywide chains, I noted, they looked like they might as well be. This intrusion was perhaps the most distasteful. Whatever used to be in the Village—good or bad—was at least its own.

Another diminishing characteristic of the Village, the article noted, was its rich source of used and rare bookshops. Only a few remained. One bookseller in business since the 1920s observed: "One old brownstone was better for me than a 20-story apartment house. The brownstones had libraries, room for books. Sure, apartment dwellers read, but they have no space. All they want is paperbacks." The concentration of used bookstores that still existed was in the East Village, dominated by the phenomenal Strand Book Store. Renovated in 2007, it remains one of the great stores of that kind in the country.

Then the article spotlighted some of the Village battles, noting the defeat of William Zeckendorf from completely transforming the Village into another Upper East Side. New high-rises were erasing the architectural and economic diversity.

While I was still living there I saw the high-income No. 2 Fifth Avenue replace the "Henry James" houses on Washington Square North. The Strunsky houses on Washington Square South in which, for many years, many artists lived were bulldozed to make way for the imitation Federal-style NYU Law School.

I had made only a quick and meager mention of the Moses defeats, mentioned with the same interest as the demise of Carmine DeSapio as a reigning political power. The Village always seemed to have multiple battles going on at the same time. The combative nature of its citizens was famous. But to me, those battles were just that, a series of citizen battles, and the role of neither Moses nor Jacobs had yet made much of an impression on me. In retrospect, this amazes me.

By the 1950s, I noted in my article, the Village had started to join the rest of New York, and penetration by new groups and outsiders seemed to change it. The beats took over MacDougal, and Washington Square changed from a community to a metropolitan park. The Village still was a place with character, but it seemed to be fighting a rearguard action.

As Much As Things Change . . .

Greenwich Village will probably always be "the Village." Change inevitably brings differences from one era to another. But the essential character endures, reflected in the coffeehouses, artist studios, jazz clubs, railroad flats, walk-up apartments, esoteric bookshops, and artisan-based businesses.

In 1969, the changes I observed seemed a dramatic contrast to the Village of the 1940s and 1950s. In truth, they were. The 1960s were years of great ferment throughout the country. Here, national dramas always played out in the extreme. But more apparent today, somewhat in contrast to my 1969 observations, is how well this historic enclave absorbs those great social and economic shifts while retaining its essence.

The historical distinctions endure within this neighborhood of contrasts within a city of contrasts. More than most neighborhoods, the Village is difficult to categorize. Block by block, the neighborhood changes. Some broad distinctions are discernible. The elegant and luxurious Greek Revival and Federal townhouses of the northern streets remain among the city's most fashionable addresses. The venerable wide assortment of houses and tree-shaded streets of the West Village retain the quiet residential air of the era of Edna St. Vincent Millay, Allen Ginsberg, Jack Kerouac, e. e. cummings, and John Reed, despite the scattered presence of brassy, commercial tourist spots.

The Lion's Head on Sheridan Square, where journalists from the one-time diversified daily press gathered, disappeared as the selection of newspapers dwindled. But the White Horse Tavern, once the meeting place of Dylan Thomas, Norman Mailer, Michael Harrington, Jane Jacobs, and William Styron, survives on Hudson Street. The southern portion of the Village is still where the humbler assortment of tenements mixes in with townhouses and storefronts. Here, where the remnants of Little Italy survive, urban renewal did the most damage. And the enduring rakish and radical character of the East Village, birthplace of the flower-child generation and theatrical innovations like La Mama, is reflected in outlandish and colorful hair and dress styles, New Wave eateries, and entertainment uses.

For post–World War II America, the Village was the cradle of free-spirited, bohemian culture in the city and country. Abstract expressionism of Jackson Pollock and Mark Rothko, the beats, radical politics, sexual freedom, folk-song artists—all manner of countercultures and cutting-edge movements—were born or nurtured there. Greenwich Village once seemed so separate from the rest of the city. Today, it is more integrated and not so far out of the mainstream. The center of the cultural avant-garde shifted long ago and now migrates every few years to the next yet-to-be upscaled city neighborhood, usually with the artists in the vanguard.

STILL A WORLD APART

For many who live there, however, the Village is still a world apart from the rest of the city. And for some, it has the hometown feel they left behind to come to New York years ago. Kansas City–born author Calvin Trillin moved in 1968 with his wife, Alice, to a Federal row house when, he recalls, local stores put pictures of neighbors on their walls and when both rich and poor attended the public school, as did their daughters. Trillin wrote in a *New Yorker* article in June 1982: "I have always believed that my attachment to the Village has to do with what it shares with the Midwest, rather than with what Midwesterners would consider arty or bohemian. Compared to uptown Manhattan, it has always seemed less formal, more neighborly, less densely populated, built closer to human scale, and less dominated by the sort of building that requires walking past a doorman and into an elevator in order to go home—an act that Midwesterners tend to find considerably more unnatural than a drunken poetry-reading in the park." Twenty-eight years later, Trillin says that the fundamental atmosphere is the same. "A lot has been fixed up," he says. "The stores are better and there are more and better restaurants, more places than I can eat at. I never on purpose go to a restaurant I can't walk to."

Even for me, having moved away so long ago, some places feel very familiar, even if considerably changed. The walk I took to school, primarily down MacDougal, has improved since my 1969 look back. But the lackluster assortment of gift shops and restaurants doesn't seem to have much character or appeal. Maybe it never really did.

The school I walked down MacDougal to get to, the Little Red Schoolhouse, remains an educational stronghold in the city and is totally recognizable in its original Bleecker Street location. This simple four-story redbrick schoolhouse has been comfortably expanded into a sensitively restored Federal row house next door. And the school added space in a modest, contemporary way next door to that on Sixth Avenue. The playground we used around the corner at Sixth Avenue and Houston survives due to its ownership by the New York City Parks Department.

Today, this vibrant district remains a great magnet for the unconventional; it is, however, no longer the only one to do so because so much of the city has improved in recent decades, so that now no one area of the city is the favorite locale of the avant-garde, the artist, the off-beat lifestyle. In fact, what is unconventional is not easy to determine these days. Decades ago, a reasonable assumption could be that people dressed in all black were from the Village. Today that black-clad person could just as likely be an internationally known establishment architect from midtown or an uptown restaurateur.

The Village is still the great gathering place it has been historically. The variety of personalities is endless. Weekend users pour in from around the city and out of town, a long-standing phenomenon. In Washington Square Park, until the recent controversial redesign, a varied crowd still hung out around the huge circular water fountain that many people call "the fountain" or "the Circle." The Circle was our summer wading pool. In great numbers on Sundays, folksingers gathered playing guitars, banjos, harmonicas, and handcrafted improvised instruments. They sang all the familiar songs of Woody Guthrie, Pete Seeger, and the unknowns. Many became famous, including Bob Dylan and Joan Baez, but those days are a distant memory. Diverse crowds assemble there now. Groups cluster. But the music is gone. Now it is just one of the city's many magnetic gathering places.

LANDMARK PROTECTION WORKS

The historic grittiness of Greenwich Village remains stable in large part because the complex urban fabric does, still fostering a diversity of uses and people. One hundred square odd-shaped blocks on a crazy quilt of meandering streets, Greenwich Village retains varied elements of historic layers that began with Dutch farmers in the 1700s. Affluent, upwardly mobile downtown merchants and bankers came in the 1800s. Downtowners fleeing cholera and yellow-fever epidemics migrated in the 1900s. In parallel time periods, the rough-and-tumble port activity along the Hudson waterfront spilled out onto Village streets.

Postwar buildings built before the 1965 landmarks law often do not relate well to the Village context. But since designation as a historic district, all alterations to existing structures and designs for new buildings must be reviewed by the Landmarks Preservation Commission. This sustains the Village's unique urban fabric and fundamentally protects its architectural heritage. Absorption of change is, for the most part, deliberative, incremental, and manageable, but change—including many new buildings— there definitely is.

Physical and economic change has not stopped, but cataclysmic change has. In fact, incrementalism is exhibited there in its most effective form with storefront upgrades, historic restorations, conversions of commercial buildings to residential, many modest rooftop and rear yard additions, and new buildings fitting into scattered available sites. Equally significant, the Village remains a hotbed of community activism, easily stirred into forceful action as threats arise from private developers, public officials, or large-scale institutions like St. Vincent's Hospital or NYU. Civic protest movements have been recurrent in the Village for generations. They mounted as the garrets and saloons of bohemia fell under the wrecker's ball, as apartment houses replaced some of the Greek Revival homes of the nineteenth-century wealthy, and as New York University increased its holdings to more than 80 percent of all the real estate on Washington Square.

It was in Greenwich Village that Jane Jacobs and others ignited nationwide resistance to authoritarian planning policies so forcefully shaped by Robert Moses. The legacy of that civic watchfulness endures. From the 1959 closing of Washington Square Park to vehicular traffic and the more recent unsuccessful fight to save the Edgar Allan Poe House on West Third Street from demolition by NYU to an unsuccessful fight to stop St. Vincent's Hospital from a total disregard for the landmarks law and efforts to prevent the controversial transformation of Washington Square Park, the tradition of the engaged and vigilant community shows little sign of abating. Periodic public fights continue to provide the glue that keeps the spirit of community intact.

THE PARK

The commons of the Village, the 8.6-acre (eight square blocks) Washington Square Park, once again, has many young children in its one big playground, a reflection of the increase since the 1970s of young families in the neighborhood. Plenty of old people can be found sitting on park benches, too. Villagers don't move away easily. My grandfather and his friends had a favorite bench. I would run to say hello to him after school each day. I see the elderly on that bench today. And just as was true during my childhood, NYU students use the park well. They guarantee a youthful feel to the park population.

Before even the newest redesign, the drug pushers were considerably diminished in number since the 1970s. One fools oneself to think they are not there at all. Their numbers had increased in the 1980s when Union Square Park at Fourteenth Street was "cleaned up" and relandscaped, following its newfound popularity with the success of the city's first great Greenmarket.[1] When the drug pushers were pushed out of Fourteenth Street, they just moved south to Washington Square. The law-abiding users of both parks are so plentiful that whatever criminal element exists does not feel threatening. Density and diversity of users, like on a street, are the best enforcement tools.

Probably my favorite park feature remains: the chess players. In the southwest corner of the park are eighteen concrete chess tables, a tradition dating back to 1932 under Mayor La Guardia. Clusters of onlookers can always be found watching their favorite game. This is a fascinating group to watch.

The park has been something of a lightning rod for Village protests—"eight acres of sociology," Gay Talese once called it. The 1970s redesign stirred considerable debate but reflected genuine community involvement.[2] The controversy surrounding the current $16 million redesign, unveiled in 2004, reflects both the increased dominance of NYU and a "high-design" mind-set coming from the Parks Department.

The quintessential gathering place, Washington Square Park's appeal was always its casual informality. A true neighborhood park, it was never meant to be a showpiece. Comfortable, safe, user-friendly, offering something for all, this park just happens to work. With its assortment of spaces, all manner of spontaneous activity took place here over the years, from roller skating in my youth to Rollerblading now, from pavement chalk games like hopscotch to impromptu guitar-playing songfests. The studying student, chatting neighbors, playing toddlers, dog-walking residents, and drug-pushing intruders all have claimed their space. I remember as a child being aware of the area where drunks hung out. It was to be avoided.

Showing wear and tear in recent years, this park needed some repair and renovation. But when the city unveiled its in-house design for a more formal, somewhat sanitized, and extremely groomed "greener" park, the community uproar was to be expected. Villagers understandably assumed the design was done with NYU's needs in mind (the school is contributing $1 million to the work but claims to have had no input), especially the change in stage design and ground leveling that make the graduation ceremony more comfortable but is officially to make it handicap accessible. (Wheelchairs, however, have been all over this park for years.)

The loudly opposed initial provision for a fence and gates was withdrawn early on. But the equally controversial moving of the 1856 circular fountain remained. Here was a perfect case of an apparent legitimate need for repair of the pipes and underground infrastructure forming the ludicrous rationale for moving the fountain to make the plaza around it symmetrical and aligning the fountain with the Stanford White Arch to gain the view directly up Fifth Avenue! Symmetrical?! One could already see up Fifth Avenue. Ironically, few people even sit on the edge now during warm seasons because the vertical stream of water in the recalibrated fountain is so high, it blows over the edges that were favorite seating spaces.

Unbeknownst to anyone until a Village resident filed a Freedom of Information Act query, the Tisch family agreed to donate $2.5 million to the fountain work and, in exchange, secured the name, the Tisch Fountain. This occurred before the public review process but was not revealed until that process was over.

3.1 The circle fountain in Washington Square Park has been a favorite gathering place forever.

A nineteenth-century landscape orthodoxy is creeping into this and other park designs. The Parks Department's plan included removal of five of the six much-loved and well-used alcove seating areas, added in the 1970 plan at community urging. Five were to be removed. Local city councilman Alan J. Gerson noted in his strong opposition to this design element: "Informal group seating, chit-chatting, debating, socializing has been an historic part of the Park. The alcoves and their predecessor corner seating areas in the park's previous incarnation have long provided the settings for their activities." The designer excuse for this alteration, besides the supposed advantage of creating more green space, was that seating capacity for the park was actually being increased. This is a sly numbers game. Benches elsewhere had been removed over the years, but now extra benches were to be added to the walkways. This is not about gathering places; this is just about sitting. Numbers don't reflect use. In the end, four alcoves were retained. This park needed repair, not an overhaul.

The recent controversy over this park's redesign reflects several issues common in many cities and other neighborhoods; it is more than just about parks. The conflict between design for design's sake versus design to reflect use patterns, the difference between open communication and collaboration with the community and a manipulated form of community participation, the issue of unknown agendas and private interests, all these issues played out here. In fact, they will continue to play out as the phases of the park's redesign proceed.

THE MOSES ROAD

This is the park—one of the city's most storied—through which then parks commissioner and master road builder Robert Moses wanted to put a road. Fifth Avenue would extend through it, connecting Upper and Lower Manhattan. Until this proposal in 1956, only the Fifth Avenue buses entered the park to turn around and go back up Fifth Avenue. The avenue was two-way then, as were all streets and avenues until traffic engineers made the priority the acceleration of traffic through cities, instead of within them.

A coalition of Village groups formed in 1956 to kill this plan and, in addition, to ban all traffic from the park. Two housewives, Shirley Hayes and Edith Lyons, started this fight. Jane Jacobs joined the coalition and became its most celebrated leader in the battle against Moses. She would later lead the fight against Moses's Lower Manhattan Expressway plan a few blocks south of the park. (See next chapter.) But the two battles were inextricably connected, although no one knew it at the time of the park conflict. "We found out why it was so important to put the road through Washington Square," Jacobs recalled when we discussed the Moses era, "by seeing an artist's rendering of it on the wall of the office of the borough president of Manhattan when we went down for something else. The road through the park was to be one of the ramps for the expressway."[3]

So when the coalition not only wanted to stop the road but ban traffic completely, Moses "had a fit," Jacobs said, because he needed it for his larger expressway plan. "So he came up with all kinds of figures about the amount of additional traffic that was going to go around the square," she said, "if this were done and how congested the streets would be." Undoubtedly, the idea of limiting traffic capacity instead of increasing it was nothing short of heresy in the era of enlarging automobile capacity everywhere and in every way. Jacobs said: "Moses was trying to scare people— and he did scare some who lived on the perimeter of the square. He scared them to death about how much traffic would be there. We knew that was nonsense because there wasn't any room for it. The only way you could get increased traffic was by increasing the road space."

The coalition was very crafty in asking for the park's closure to traffic. They proposed that it be done on a trial basis, to see what would happen. "We knew it was perfectly safe to just ask for a trial basis," Jacobs said. "We knew that if the test were successful, it would become permanent. This was nothing radical really, just a chance to experiment a little." Nevertheless, Moses was adamantly opposed. "Moses and all the city traffic engineers had always opposed doing anything like this anywhere," Jacobs said. "They told us: 'You will be back on your knees begging us to put that roadway back because of the inundation of traffic elsewhere.' We didn't believe that for a minute. We just said, 'We'll try it. This is an experiment.'"

Not only did chaos not happen, but no predicted tie-ups occurred around the park. In fact, Jacobs noted, "there was less traffic. Actual traffic numbers declined where they had been predicted to rise."

TRAFFIC DISAPPEARS

That "experiment" offered a significant lesson that was never learned and only in recent years has been recognized in the sporadic places around the globe where traffic is being "tamed" and measured. In 1997 a U.S. study, "Road Supply and Traffic in California Urban Areas," determined that every 10 percent increase in road capacity was followed by a 9 percent increase in traffic volume within a five-year period.

Cases like this happen all the time with anticipated traffic catastrophes not happening. But this broad insight into traffic behavior came long after the Washington Square road fight. Back then, Jacobs said, "for the first time, people began to understand that the more provision you make for cars in the city, the more cars and more traffic there will be. You don't solve the traffic problem by making more provision for cars, with the potential supply of cars utterly inexhaustible."

TIDE TURNING AGAINST CARS?

At the time of my conversation with Jacobs in 1978, the proponents of expansion of highways and roads seemed, on the surface at least, to have the cards stacked in their favor, or so it seemed in the press. The idea of saying no to expanded automotive accommodation was still alien to most people. If not alien, the concept just didn't occur to many people in the 1970s, let alone the 1950s. After more than twenty years of indoctrination in favor of cars, malls, and the suburban lifestyle, people seemed very accepting of this as the norm of the time.

Jacobs disagreed. "Not really," she said in a comment that turned out to be prescient.

It's running the other way. Time is on our side. There's more doubt about these things. The fights get harder and harder, more and more widespread. Really, Roberta, if you were my age, you would remember back to 1955 and '56. It was unheard of to fight a thing like that, and it was unheard of to talk in the kind of terms that educated people now find it perfectly natural to talk in—whether they agree or disagree about what automobiles do to cities, that they can do harm, and that you would ever stop a road without planning for compensating road space nearby. Those were the terms it was put in: which alternative do you prefer, the road through the park or widening around it? Most people at the time just couldn't imagine any other alternative.

"And it was Edith Lyons and Shirley Hays," Jacobs recalled, "who sat in the park with their little kids and wondered why they should be stuck with either of these options and why you had to have additional roads for traffic around Washington Square at all. And they were considered crazy women who just didn't understand the facts of life. 'Isn't this just like a woman to think that way' was the attitude." They turned it into an enormous community victory. Prominent leaders joined them, like planner Victor Gruen, critic Lewis Mumford, housing advocate Charles Abrams, and Eleanor Roosevelt.

Today, thirty years after our conversation, this understanding is almost commonplace. But another lesson that Jacobs noted has not been learned. Traffic engineers then and many now insist that traffic behaves like water. If you narrow the passage for them, bottlenecks and congestion increase. But, as Jacobs noted, that is a theory that does not hold up under scrutiny. Instead, traffic often disappears, as it did in Washington Square. "They don't learn from observation," Jacobs noted, "and they are not curious enough to study what actually did happen to the traffic.[4] Mysteriously, it disappeared, and much conjecture tries to explain it, but no one has actually studied it."

The number of cases around the world where a similar phenomenon is observable, that is, diminished space and disappearing traffic, is increasing. This is true whether in San Francisco after the earthquake brought down the Embarcadero or in Milwaukee after an elevated portion of the downtown expressway was removed or in Seattle in 2007 with the partial closure of Interstate 5—dubbed "the Big Clog"—when dire traffic predictions proved wrong.

Clark Williams-Derry, reporting in the *Seattle Times* on August 30, 2007, noted that traffic remained "far better than average, despite slowdowns through the construction zone" and that people were finding alternative ways to get to work. "The main lesson from The Clog That Wasn't," he wrote, "is this: The conventional wisdom about traffic just isn't right. We tend to think that Seattle commuters are tied to their cars and can't—or won't—use alternative modes of transportation in large numbers. But that notion was just turned on its head. As it turns out commuters are much more adaptable, flexible and wilier than we give them credit for."

NEW YORK UNIVERSITY

The one big drawback to the park, the city's smallest, is the same as it is for the surrounding district. NYU owns or rents so much of everything around it that this historical heart of Greenwich Village is, for all intents and purposes, the NYU campus. As long ago as 1958, an article in the *New York Times* noted, "The park is now in effect a campus shared with tourists and mothers who sun their infants and watch youngsters roller skate on the park pavement."[5]

"Overbearing" is how one park neighbor described NYU's presence, while ambivalently acknowledging the positive contribution of the students' youthful presence. "The crowd is not the blackstocking crowd of my youth," she says, "but I like their esprit. NYU has made the neighborhood too campuslike, however. They even close the park for graduation." In fact, notes another longtime resident, "NYU is the landlord of so much of the Village that you don't see the same degree of groundswell of resistance to its continued encroachments. That is the hidden side of the neighborhood now. Too many people are beholden to NYU and thus stay silent."

Overbearing is surely the appropriate description for what NYU has become in recent years. Once a good solid commuter school with primarily New York City students, NYU with its fourteen separate schools has now grown to be the largest private university in the country, attracting students from around the world, as much for its top rank as for its New York City locale. After twenty years of expansion and about a dozen new high-rises, NYU owns or occupies one hundred buildings between Sixth and Second Avenues and has become the defining presence. And instead of seeking to develop a secondary campus elsewhere in the city where it might be a welcome, regenerative presence, it continues to expand in place. In 2007, NYU—with forty thousand students and thirty-one hundred faculty—claimed a need for another six million square feet of space over twenty-five years.

Many residents of the Village are, of course, concerned that their historic neighborhood character will be subsumed into NYU's overarching presence. It is not an unfounded concern. In fact, it parallels the concern of many neighborhoods around the city as educational, hospital, and other institutions take advantage of zoning privileges provided "community facilities" to physically expand in all-consuming ways. Cities across the country, from New Haven to Berkeley, wrestle with this dilemma, especially since urban colleges are a prime student choice nationally these days. Many also have wealthy donors who have been all too happy to have their name on a new building.

While the university is somewhat dispersed around the East Village, its most dominating presence is felt around the park. The Greek Revival row houses on the park's north side were once the home of John Dos Passos, Edward Hopper, and the social elite. Their elegant, restrained red-brick fronts with white marble entryways and classic fluted columns framing the front doors are beautifully maintained and guarantee the future for one of the park's most distinctive architectural features. Now most of these designated landmarks house NYU departments. The gracious old apartment houses on the park's west side, where so many of my childhood friends lived, are also owned by NYU and used for faculty and student housing. Eleanor Roosevelt had her apartment on the top floor of number 29 while her husband was president. I vividly remember walking my dog at the same time she walked her Scottie, Fala. She was very friendly and often stopped to talk as our dogs sniffed each other. I was much too young to be in awe of whom I was chatting with.

ENHANCING THE STREET, OR NOT

On the east side of the park, NYU has converted all the onetime factory buildings into classrooms and other uses. This includes the infamous 1911 Triangle Shirt Waist Fire building, a designated landmark. Some of the buildings have never looked better. Unfortunately, however, insufficient *transparent* street-level uses exist in NYU buildings. Ground-floor windows can add or diminish interest where it matters most, on the street. Too many of the university's ground-floor functions are hidden by painted-over or filled-in windows. What could possibly be happening behind the darkened windows that the passerby should not see? Even mechanical equipment is more interesting to look at than a painted-over window.

The scattered visible activity spaces—an attractive reception hall facing the park, a study area, a cafeteria—subtly add to the pedestrian experience. They are too few in number. In the suburbs, this would not be noticeable, nor would it matter, since everyone drives by in a car. But in a city, what happens on the ground floor of every building adds to or subtracts from street life. Relating better to the street is vital to NYU and the city.

Street-level windows are probably the most underappreciated, smallest, and least-considered element of urban life. Yet they are the perfect vehicle to reflect local activity, character, and history.

NYU is not alone in missing the opportunity of street-level spaces. New York street life is being nibbled to death all over town, one store window and one ground-floor space at a time. The federal office building near City Hall has solid green glass. The expanded Museum of Modern Art has turned most of Fifty-fourth Street between Fifth and Sixth Avenues into a solid wall of contemporary, metallic material, deadening the street. Even a few small windowlike openings—originally promised— could make a pedestrian connect to the museum space. This is a prime walking district. Banks, drugstore chains, and assorted uses have dulled the window-gazing experience on many streets.

Ironically, in contrast, one of the best examples of a street-enhancing window use is an NYU one, a few blocks north of Washington Square Park at the corner of Broadway and Ninth Street. "Broadway Windows," a program of the NYU School of Fine Arts, contains rotating exhibits of truly fine student work on the ground floor of a 1920s apartment house. It always grabs my attention. Imagine if windows around the district served as a showcase for student and neighborhood creativity.

The most suburban feature NYU has added in recent years is a truly un-fortunate one—the campus circulating bus. Understandably, many campus universities around the country today have a circulating bus system. On a spread-out, self-contained nonurban campus, this may make sense. But the NYU campus is the city itself. NYU is concentrated in one of the city's most walkable—and bikable!—districts, well served by mass transit. Almost every subway line runs into it. This may not be what out-of-town or sub-urban students are used to. But the advantages of being here should be demonstrated, not circumvented. As an NYU student, I lived on the Upper West Side and commuted to class by subway and by foot, as did and do thousands of city students. Instinctively, some people say, "Students need a quick way to get from one class to the next when distance is a problem." Well, it is doubtful that the bus is where every student needs it to be at the appointive time and going lickety-split, nonstop, to *that* student's next class. In fact, most of the time that I observe this circulating bus, it has only a few passengers. Walking is probably more direct and faster, biking even better.

THE POE HOUSE CONTROVERSY

One of the big Village controversies in recent years was NYU's destruction in 2000 of the 1835 redbrick house in which Edgar Allan Poe lived when he published his poem "The Raven." The unadorned Poe House was lo-cated on the West Third block between Sullivan and Thompson Streets. On the west end was Judson House, originally three separate Greek Re-vival houses that were merged and redesigned in the 1890s by McKim, Mead, and White. Judson House backed up to the landmark Judson Church facing the park, also designed by McKim, Mead, and White, one of the country's most important historic architectural firms.

This unassuming stretch of four- to six-story mustard and redbrick buildings was a quintessential urban block, representing varied building types, styles, and periods built over time. Such physical variety, when not totally occupied by one user, invites assorted economic uses on which a di-verse city economy depends. The loss of this undesignated but landmark-worthy block was yet another clear diminishment of the Village's historic character. The four-story law school replacement is at best an ordinary design with an unmistakable institutional look.

A very public fight arose around NYU's planned demolition of the Poe House. NYU rationalized that it had been heavily altered over time, something that can be said of many restorable landmarks. Yet it still reflected what Henry James described as the "established repose" of the once fashionable Federal and Greek Revival row houses built when the area was first developed in the 1830s. NYU argued that the loss was necessary for its survival. Many institutions make the same argument when, instead, they could be creatively weaving such landmarks into their institutional future, as well as the city's.

In a letter to the editor published in the *New York Times* on July 27, 2000, E. L. Doctorow, who teaches English literature at NYU, wrote, "NYU has consistently recognized and celebrated its connection to the historic literary culture of Greenwich Village. How uncharacteristic of this great university that it now wants to raze this . . . small house that is very suggestive of the writer's perpetually straitened circumstances. I wonder why plans can't be drawn to build the school around, above and behind it. This sort of thing has been done elsewhere when architects have been faced with a historic but inconvenient structure." Also in a letter to the editor, Woody Allen noted that "surely it can be worked out in a way that does not destroy yet another piece of this fast-vanishing area."

The judge who ruled in the university's favor in a lawsuit brought to stop the Poe House demolition nevertheless took the university to task, noting, "As a leading academic institution where Poe's cadences are still heard . . . NYU would seem to be the natural guardian of the Poe House. . . . From a historical, cultural and literary point of view, Poe House should stand."

Subsequently, in negotiations with community and preservation groups, the university agreed to reconstruct the facade of the house as it appeared in the nineteenth century, using salvaged original bricks, lintels, cornices, and other materials. Even this concession was not fulfilled. "There were not enough usable bricks," a spokesman claimed in all seriousness. Instead, a silly rendition in new brick of the historic building was incorporated into the ground floor of the new block-long building, a few doors away from the historic site. This fake is not even worthy of Colonial Williamsburg.

Judson Memorial Church is all that remains of the south side of Washington Square Park. Philip Johnson's hulking red-sandstone Bobst Library built by NYU in 1960 flanks the east end; the mock-colonial law school flanks the west end. In between is NYU's thirteen-story Kimmel Center, built in 2003. Ironically, NYU promotional material still offers the opportunity to live in "Greenwich Village, one of NYC's most creative and energetic communities and a historic mecca for generations of world renowned artists, writers and scholars."

In NYU's favor, it must be said, is its overall respect for the urbanism and the street grid of its locale. NYU and Greenwich Village are woven into each other around the university buildings. This, of course, is ensured because of the Historic District designation regulated by the Landmarks Commission. And even though it has effectively transformed the community in which it resides, NYU never tried to change the street patterns to make it feel like a private enclave. A visitor does not know the extent of NYU's dominance. One feels comfortable coming into it or passing through. The same cannot be said for Columbia University's planned expanded campus, as will be further explored later in this book.

THE WEST VILLAGE

While NYU clearly dominates the east side of Greenwich Village, it has had no visible impact on the West Village. Cross Sixth Avenue and you feel transplanted back into the historical Village of small stores, one-of-a-kind boutiques, walk-up apartments, restaurants, cafés, and unpredictable happenings. The West Village, with its textbook array of historic architecture, misses the aesthetic unity of scores of the city's historic residential and industrial districts. It does, however, have a different sort of unity. Here, the art of architecture is found in the treasured old, not the fashionable new. Housing costs have skyrocketed, but the resident population remains diverse in all ways. The content of the diversity is not the same—no longshoremen, more blacks—but varied nonetheless.

"The West Village has done very well," Jane observed on a visit in 2004. "If other city neighborhoods had done as well there would not be as much trouble in many cities. There are too few neighborhoods as successful right now so that the supply doesn't nearly meet the demand. So they are just gentrifying in the most ridiculous way. They are crowding out everybody except people with exorbitant amounts of money, which is a symptom that demand for such a neighborhood outstrips the supply by far."

One of the most interesting sites is right on the corner of Sixth Avenue and Third Street. Until 1927 Sixth Avenue ran from Central Park West to a short distance north of here at Carmine Street. In that year, the city blasted away tenements to continue Sixth Avenue south. A few little wedge-shaped pieces of empty space remained, such as a small asphalt lot enclosed by a chain-link fence with several handball and basketball courts that daily host some of the most serious competitions in the city. Not just anyone gets to play there, and sport scouts reportedly come by looking for talent. This is one of those serendipitous urban activities that spring up where space just allows it to happen—never organized, never formalized, but eventually institutionalized in its own urban way. A busy subway entrance sits on this corner. I pass there frequently, but I never go by that a large crowd is not gathered to watch.

Throughout the West Village, small change continues to unfold but sometimes with large impacts. The stretch of Bleecker Street west of Seventh Avenue, during the recent economic boom, was transformed into chic and upscale retail. It has long been fashionable, but somehow the presence of national retailers seems to many people to be more dramatic. But nothing has been torn down to make this happen, and the talked-about transformation may be more of a perception than a reality. The large retail chains can't dominate. Landmarks and zoning limits deny demolition of walls between buildings for expansion of the ground floor to create the huge spaces that supersize national chains require. Most important, when each phase passes, as it inevitably does, the historic fabric will house the next wave of retail chic that is always looking for modest, affordable street-level space. Natural urban shifts unfold this way.

For the most part, small businesses—particularly family-owned ones—do well there because the tiny store sizes work well for them and because Village residents are especially appreciative of the convenience of having them and can be very loyal customers.

EIGHTH STREET

Bleecker Street has long been the most interesting and probably best-known commercial street, but Eighth Street, from Sixth Avenue to Fifth Avenue, was the location for more of life's essentials when I was growing up: the grocery store, pharmacy, delicatessen, butcher, and my father's dry-cleaning store. Comfortably mixed in was a second-generation family-owned jeweler, a leather crafter of citywide renown, a jewelry designer, and an art store. Eighth Street was a center as well of Village artistic and intellectual life. The Washington Square Book Shop was a literary beacon. The Eighth Street Playhouse staged cutting-edge plays and later became an art-film house. The Whitney Museum was founded on this street in 1931 and stayed until it moved uptown in 1948. The Studio School with Hans Hoffmann at the helm was also an important art center. Many artists lived above the stores along Eighth Street or nearby. The street was the epicenter for the New York School of artists in the 1950s.

By the 1960s, drugs and fast-paced tourism took their toll. By the 1970s, most of the individually owned stores and cultural sites had closed, and the local character was completely gone. Eighth Street continued to get worse. Cheap shoe stores, head shops, and low-end clothing invaded like locusts and endured right up to the turn of the new century. The Eighth Street Playhouse, its facade gone, is now a cheap dollar store.

A few good things have occurred, however, and indications point to a slow but sure turnaround, especially with new restaurants opening. Barnes & Noble replaced Nathan's fast-food hot-dog chain. A few years ago, a merchant group organized a business improvement district. Store upgrades are concentrated on the east side of Fifth Avenue. But west of Fifth, the sidewalk is widened, traffic is calmed, new historic-style lampposts are installed, and various events promote the positive qualities of the street. The balance between pedestrian and car is better, and people feel less pushed aside. A Belgian sandwich shop with fresh baguettes, pastries, and coffee opened on the west corner of Fifth Avenue, the first new sign that upgrading is moving westward. An upscale restaurant opened next door to my father's former store. Other new and better uses are sure to follow. Ironically, the current economic collapse has shuttered many more of the cheap shoe stores, leaving several vacancies. What will replace them when the economy turns around will be interesting to see.

For me, the Village has mostly been defined by the geography of my own experience growing up there and then attending NYU. And while Washington Square Park is central to all of it and NYU is the overarching presence, the Village is really an assortment of very distinct enclaves with a history and character different from each other.

As Jane Jacobs observed about Greenwich Village years ago in conversation, "It is not small. In fact, it is a pretty big district. Parts were always considered better than others and all different. The South Village was heavily Italian and before that I guess mainly Irish. That area was considered bad. Sullivan Street is considered very chic now, but I remember when it was just teeming with poor children and tenements, so I suppose it was considered bad."

Jacobs had moved to the Village with her sister in 1934, selecting it because "she found so many people walking in such a purposeful way and so many interesting stores and activities to observe." This iconic neighborhood became the incubator for her ideas. It was a study area, a laboratory. She observed the different elements that added up to vibrancy in city life. She recognized the same characteristics in other vibrant neighborhoods, large and small, and assembled them into a web of related precepts. "Of course, the West Village where I lived was considered bad," Jacobs said. "We didn't know it when we moved here, fortunately, but it had been designated a slum to be cleared first way back in the 1930s when Rexford Tugwell, who would become one of Roosevelt's 'brain trusters,' was chairman of the Planning Commission." But one official's slum can be someone's definition of a good neighborhood to live in. And the Village has always drawn a place-proud population.

West Village Houses:
Known As the Jane Jacobs Houses

Parallel to the Hudson along the West Side Highway and a few blocks inland are the West Village Houses built in the mid-1970s. This complex could serve as a national model of everything that was wrong in postwar development policies and everything that is right when community sensibilities prevail. A community fight there defeated the Robert Moses Urban Renewal Plan—apparently, the first defeat nationwide of an urban renewal plan—that would have wiped out the entire fourteen square blocks of historic urban fabric filled with owner-occupied, well-maintained one- and two-family houses, tenements, and individual buildings. All had been restored with private money. But it was designated a "slum," a necessary official step to qualify for urban renewal money. Residents and businesses in the area knew it wasn't a slum. They thought well enough of the area, in fact, even with its service and physical limitations, to remain there, open businesses, and invest money. "The people in the Village had watched urban renewal around the city with its waste and profiteering vandalism," Jacobs recalled.

So much land was being taken, and so much was being lost. The West Village people understood the negative impact all these plans were having on the city.

The sin of the Village was that it had all these mixed uses. All the manufacturing buildings were to be demolished and replaced with high-rises. There would be a little enclave left of all the most expensive and aesthetically appealing houses. The rest would go. Now all those former manufacturing buildings are turned into the most expensive lofts in the city. These people, even the real estate experts, they didn't know from nothing. They were so ignorant, not just about what they were destroying but what people would like.

The term *slum* is very subjective, differing according to who is using it. Poor conditions in an area may be due more to a lack of municipal services than anything else, as we will see throughout this book. A few buildings may be in need of repair or even in danger of imminent collapse. Some may be fire hazards, or abandoned and run-down. None of these individual conditions should qualify an entire area as a slum, especially when renovation and new infill options have not been explored. More than anything else, the terms *slum* or *blight* reflect the motivation of the people using them.[6] All of this was clear in the fight against the West Village Urban Renewal Plan.

A survey of the area, for example, revealed the presence of 1,765 residents, including 710 families, plus warehouses, truck depots, and mom-and-pop businesses. More than 80 businesses employed hundreds of people. In fact, this designation of "slum" was not too different from the designation applied to many other city neighborhoods declared "blighted" and cleared by Moses in the name of slum clearance. "We took Lester Eisner, regional administrator for the Federal Housing and Home Finance Agency, on a tour so he would learn what the community was really made of," recalled Jacobs, who led the resistance.[7] "It convinced him this was not a slum. He was floored, couldn't believe the great range of incomes. He said it was wonderful. But this is the secret he told us: Never tell anyone what you would like. As soon as you do, you will be judged a participating citizen. You're hooked, trapped. They can ignore you. Eisner alerted us to this. People in New York never knew why we were only so negative. Wagner eventually decided the urban slum designation had to be lifted."

One of the brilliant things about Jane but little acknowledged was that she believed in and followed smart tactics that she often learned from observing others. She came across as very confrontational and anticompromise, all of which had a purpose. But in this anecdote she reveals that the

3.2 The Little Red Schoolhouse on Bleecker Street with the expansion into the smaller brick building next door. My elementary school and still a great one.

lesson learned from Eisner was to resist saying what you want until what you don't want is defeated. Jacobs also believed that it was vital to culti- vate your own constituency instead of trying to persuade opponents.

After the defeat of the Moses Urban Renewal Plan, the successful cit- izens group the West Village Committee, led by Jacobs, hired its own ar- chitect and promulgated its own plan and design for new housing. A basic, modest-scale apartment-house configuration was designed to flex- ibly fill in the district's vacant lots, avoiding any demolition or displace- ment. "Not a single person—not a single sparrow—shall be displaced" was their slogan. The result is an assortment of plain redbrick five- and six-story walk-up apartment houses of different shapes and sizes and three different layouts with an occasional corner store on the ground floor.[8]

The planning establishment hated this proposal because it was initi- ated by the community and left intact the organically evolved mixture of residential and commercial uses. "We hired Perkins and Will, not a New York City firm, so they wouldn't be blackballed for working with us as all city architects feared," Jacobs explained. "The West Village Committee was totally self-organized. Anything self-organized is inimical to planners who want control. The city was furious. We had an informant in the Planning Office who told us what was said: 'If we let this neighborhood plan for itself, all will want to do it too.' Planners always pick control over spontaneity. If one believes things can happen spontaneously and work well, it diminishes the importance of planners."

City officials, especially then housing and development administrator Roger Starr, did everything possible to strip the design of appealing amenities. He succeeded, nibbling away at the design in every little way possible. It was twelve years of delays. Costs escalated. The result is bare-bones architecture. Yet a waiting list of potential renters existed from the day it opened. Architecture critic Michael Sorkin has written, "West Village Houses fits unobtrusively within the intimate weave of its surroundings. It's a model piece of urbanism because of this careful integration; because its architectural expression is not treated as a big, determining deal; and because it grew out of the self-organizing impetus to provide new and better housing for people of modest means for whom the market had little empathy."

The West Village Houses are probably the country's first and most significant example of genuine infill housing design. Today, the "infill" description is inappropriately applied to whole blocks of new developments on cleared land inserted into existing neighborhoods, often like an alien species introduced among the natives. Genuine infill is inserted in spaces within a block, not in substitution for a block. However, neither the West Village Houses' infill value nor other innovations were ever spotlighted by critics, professionals, or professors for the lessons they illustrated. Thus, most people are unaware that it was probably the first successful community-designed challenge to the conventional planning and development policies of the day.[9]

West Village Houses started as a moderate-income Mitchell-Lama rental under a program conceived in the 1950s as a solution to a shortage of low- and middle-income apartments. Named after State Senator MacNeil Mitchell and Assemblyman Alfred Lama, the 1955 law offered owners and landlords tax breaks and favorable loan terms in return for keeping rents within the range of low- and middle-income tenants. It also permitted owners to "buy out" of the program by paying off the mortgage and other debts after twenty to forty years, depending on the date and type of project. Once the developments exit the program, they can either go to market rate or go under rent stabilization, unless successfully challenged by owners.

In 2007, the tenants of West Village Houses successfully organized to buy the buildings from the landlord who was planning to opt out of the program. After four years of negotiation with the landlord, the deal struck by the tenants to convert to a cooperative and rental mix guaranteed no evictions for tenants, a twelve-year period of rent restraints (rent stabilized), the right of tenants to buy their apartments at an insider price, the right of the new owner to sell the 10 vacant units out of the total 420 at market rate, and a guarantee new buyers would meet the federal middle-income standard. Other sensible terms were provided, but suffice it to say that this represents a reasonable compromise that affords the owner a fair profit without losing the larger city value as a middle-income enclave.

In recent years, the city has been losing too many Mitchell-Lama middle-income apartments. From 1990 to 2005, the surviving number of rental units developed under this program dropped from 67,000 to 44,000, according to the Community Service Society. And according to the magazine *City Limits*, another 3,691 apartments were lost in 2006 alone.

If its success had been recognized, West Village Houses could have become a model for other Mitchell-Lama projects that were privatized after the legislated thirty- to forty-year period, especially the large-scale ones like Stuyvesant Town, the thirty-five redbrick buildings in typical housing-project style with 8,757 units on East Fourteenth Street and First Avenue that were privatized a few years ago.[10] The privatization of Mitchell-Lama units is one of the significant causes of the recent loss of middle-income housing units all over the city.

FARTHER WEST

Just west of the West Village Houses along the Hudson River waterfront is, perhaps, one of the most interesting districts in the Village and the city. Perhaps I should say "was," since so much has been lost in recent years. Presumably, the far West Village was omitted from the first Greenwich Village historic district in 1969 because of continuing hope among some public officials of pushing through the urban renewal and West Side Highway widening schemes. In a 1963 letter to the Landmarks Commission promoting the inclusion of these westernmost streets, Jacobs noted, "From its beginnings, the old river-landing settlement combined work, residence and transportation, and these activities, while local were not provincial. They all had ties, in part, to the larger settlement of New York.

With truly remarkable integrity and fidelity, this historic land use persists today: work, residence and transportation, with very similar links and the same quality of being local but unprovincial."

Nevertheless, this veritable heart of the city and country's economic beginnings—the locus of activity that shaped the larger Village—was omitted. Not much change occurred, however, in the years in the 1970s and '80s during the fight over Westway, the highway-expansion scheme. Everything was on hold, anticipating the government buyout for the highway. But once that scheme was killed, speculators took a new look and started buying, demolishing, or renovating and slowly rebuilding.

Three highly publicized and aesthetically appealing sixteen-story glass towers designed by architect Richard Meier now sit amid the remaining intimately scaled nineteenth-century houses, stables, and maritime hotels. Yet the Greenwich Village Historic Society, aggressively pushing the Landmarks Commission to expand the historic district, noted that the area still contained fifty-five nineteenth-century buildings as well as dozens of period factories, warehouses, mills, and bakeries. Correctly, the GVHS argued that this area's "gritty and more heterogeneous architecture was mistakenly consigned to the dustbin of preservation history when it was overlooked for inclusion" in the historic district. However, since one of the commission's guidelines devalues areas that have been substantially altered over time, the commission was slow to respond.

JACOBS MAKES THE CASE AGAIN

In 2003, shortly after Mayor Michael Bloomberg took office, I was asked by Deputy Mayor Patti Harris to serve as a commissioner on the Landmarks Preservation Commission. When I went on the commission, Jane was skeptical at first but then agreed it would be a worthwhile thing for me to do. Subsequently, she urged that I promote the designation of this "most interesting and historically illuminating and valuable part of Greenwich Village." In a letter to me for transmittal to the Landmarks Commission, she wrote:

> For many people, like the New Urbanists for instance, the important ideas of mixed uses, functional diversity, and self-organization and organic adaptability are little more than trendy planning and design fashions, susceptible to being used inauthentically and meaninglessly . . .

[but] the far west village . . . is the authentic seed bed and nursery of these qualities in Manhattan, beginning in colonial times and persisting thereafter. It may well be the most important historical area of New York, for that reason. It was the place of origin of many of the city's important industries, such as machine manufacturing, food preserving, publishing and printing, to name a few, and . . . remnants of this history persist there, still appropriately very mixed, along with evidence of trains and adaptations. Even the roots of the meat market district itself were there.

It has been overlooked and undervalued, I think, precisely because it has never been considered trendy, like the meat market district in recent times and the Henry James rowhouses and the bohemian village before the meat market. But it is something better than trendy. It is authentic. It was deeply influential. It will be a great pity if its remaining witness and evidence are wiped away in favor of towers with expensive views, empty of history . . . I beg of you, don't let this happen . . . .

The far West Village was designated a week after Jacobs died in April 2006.

The East Village — Another World

Greenwich Village is a microcosm of the city, an assortment of very different communities in close proximity to one another. The East Village is the most different from the rest of the Village, and it is here that some of the precursors of regeneration were first occurring in the 1970s, as noted earlier regarding the Cooper Square Committee and other citizen-based efforts.

Like the South Bronx in the 1970s, officially no one cared. And no one paid attention to the small things happening in the East Village. No money was available anyway to do a Moses-style renewal on an area best known for high crime and deteriorating housing. Slumlords predominated. City services were almost nonexistent. With a history of Irish, German, East European, and Hispanic immigrants, the East Village defied easy categorizing. Pockets of social and economic energy, however, produced an almost sub-rosa vitality to which mainstream New Yorkers were oblivious, unless, of course, they dared venture forth to dine at vintage East European restaurants or delicatessens or attend a performance at the avant-garde La Mama or one of the offbeat music venues. St. Mark's Place was as far east as most venturers would go, where Yoko Ono performed at the Bridge Theater or Andy Warhol presented the Velvet Underground at the Dom, formerly a Polish entertainment hall. Beats, hippies, punks, and postpunks all settled or passed through here. Artists found studios. Galleries followed. Music venues appeared everywhere.

It is here—in empty lots—that the Green Guerillas launched the community garden movement that is today international in scope. The city under Mayor Giuliani auctioned some off to private developers, but after an intense, contentious battle and the intervention of philanthropists, some of those locally created parks survived and are now overseen by the Parks Department. Squatters took over city-owned abandoned buildings that the city had no program or money to deal with. A variety of community-based efforts evolved and were replicated in derelict neighborhoods around the city, as mentioned in chapter 1.

The tag *East Village* was meant to clearly distinguish the area from the rest of Greenwich Village. So far, except for incursions by NYU, the East Village has been spared much of the march of high-rise development so visible elsewhere in the city. This predominantly tenement district has also been spared an excessive proliferation of mass retailers, primarily due to the small scale of most of its retail spaces and a lower population density than found in areas of large-scale apartment houses. As such, it remains an incubator for fledgling designers of all kinds looking for small and cheap space to test their new offerings. Like the rest of Greenwich Village, this ever-changing enclave has its share of community activists willing to take on the large-scale forces that could bring corrosive, not productive, change.

If history had taken a different turn and the community had been less vigilant, all of Greenwich Village, East and West, would be a completely different place today. Instead, it is both different, reflecting many small changes, and the same, its basic physical, social, and economic fabric intact. The economic and social mix is not as diverse, but this is a citywide phenomenon visible in many neighborhoods, not just a Village issue.

Jane Jacobs is probably most popularly known for writing about the Village, especially Hudson Street, where she lived. Too many people make the mistake of defining her observations there as advocacy for the replication of its small-scale and "quaint" mixtures. This could not be further from the truth. It was not about tall buildings versus short, modernist versus Federalist, loft versus residential, small business versus large. The Village was her laboratory to observe the larger truths about urban life. Hers was not a prescription of what *should* happen but an observation of what *does* happen when certain genuine urban conditions exist. In all her writing, she used specific examples to illustrate observable truths, never intending them to be prescriptive. In her description above about the importance of the undesignated portion of the Village, she referred to "the important ideas of mixed uses, functional diversity, and self-organization and organic adaptability." In this case she was referring to the Village, but she applied those ideas to many urban areas that look nothing like the Village.

Each area of the Village offers lessons applicable elsewhere in the city and beyond. These are lessons from community-based resistance to inappropriate change or from successful community-based solutions to real, not manufactured, challenges and problems. But none of the Village battles or victories compare to the next area in the spotlight, SoHo.

SoHo

A Moses Defeat, a Jacobs Victory

> New York seems to be finally repairing itself after decades of "urban renewal"—wiping out small businesses, dislocating thousands of families, and frittering away its wealth on projects that were supposed to compensate the city's tax return. Consider SoHo; big plans for a highway and urban renewal would have wiped out most of that district's people, buildings, and potential for new and existing businesses. Now that district is one of the richest in the world and a great benefit to the city's tax structure. For thirty years after the war, the city was not behaving like this. It was throwing away its potential.
>
> JANE JACOBS, 2000

The public takes SoHo for granted. Few people are familiar with its near loss. Few today who complain SoHo is overcommercialized are aware of the ruinous fate planned for it decades ago. And, perhaps, even fewer who celebrate its enduring uniqueness know what a hard-won victory it was to get it designated a landmark district after the defeat of the Lower Manhattan Expressway. Furthermore, the enormous impact of SoHo's success on the rest of the country is hardly recognized. SoHo

4.1 SoHo actually has quite a variety of buildings in scale and style. *Jared Knowles.*

marked a turning point on many urban fronts that were not apparent to me when I first covered its changing fate.

In February 1973 I wrote a story noting that almost three years after a public hearing, the Landmarks Preservation Commission still seemed to be a long way from designating SoHo a historic district and formally recognizing the unique character of its mid-nineteenth-century Cast Iron architecture.

SoHo takes its name from its location south of Houston Street and has the largest concentration in the country of Cast Iron architecture, one of the few original American contributions to architectural history. Few people even knew about Cast Iron buildings until the effort to save this substantial collection of them was initiated by a determined local resident, Margot Gayle. Gayle, a longtime Village resident, formed the Friends of Cast Iron to advocate for designation of the twenty-six-block area, circulated petitions, and educated the public unaware of the district's value.

Cast Iron refers as much to a method of construction as an actual architectural style. It was an early form of modular construction and a product of the Industrial Revolution. The facades of buildings—including the Doric,

Ionic, or Corinthian columns and all the intricate ornamental details—were cast in off-site New York foundries and assembled on the building sites, in much the same way prefabricated building is done today.

It was then both economical and efficient for commercial buildings because the extra strength of iron allowed larger window and interior spaces. In the nineteenth century, SoHo was New York's wholesale textile center, with display areas dominating ground floors and storage space above. Boston, Chicago, New Orleans, St. Louis, Baltimore, and a host of other cities followed New York's lead and built Cast Iron buildings in the nineteenth century, but most of these areas outside of New York have been substantially destroyed. Remnants of such districts in cities across the country have since seen a renaissance following SoHo's. Where they survive, their preservation and reuse reflect a national phenomenon.

THE DEATH-THREAT SYNDROME

Robert Moses, the Lower Manhattan Expressway's primary planner and advocate, had the area declared "blighted" in the 1950s. That designation was essential to condemn private property for the highway. *Blight* is as subjective a term as *slum*, as described in the previous chapter. And clearly, one can recognize how hollow was the term as applied to this area when one recognizes the solidity of the buildings since renovated. All of the upgrades now making SoHo so expensive could occur only after the expressway and blight designation were defeated.

The expressway would have wiped out what is now SoHo, even though scores of thriving businesses still filled the buildings that were so functionally flexible. But the designation of blight was the death knell for the neighborhood, a guarantee of accelerated decay. As Jacobs observed in our conversation about the expressway fight:

> Sure, a scheme like that either causes or accelerates deterioration. Businesses leave when they see the handwriting on the wall or don't even try to establish themselves in such a location. Property owners hold out for the lucrative buyout. It's a miracle when a place like the North End in Boston or the West Village keeps on improving and people keep putting money in when a death sentence hangs over it. They can only do it with the courage of knowing that they aren't going to allow that death sentence. Or being totally ignorant that it exists.

4.2 Cast-iron facades distinguish most SoHo buildings and did in the demolished areas as well. *Jared Knowles.*

But the bankers are never ignorant about it and stop giving loans. When there's a death sentence like that on an area, you always have to work around it and get odd bits of money and so forth, which can make a very good area in the end, if it's done.

"Odd bits of money" traditionally meant drawing on family and friends. To make way for the planned ten-lane expressway and housing projects, forty-five acres of five- to six-story factory buildings (no higher than a hook-and-ladder fire truck could reach) were marked for extinction. "Hell's 100 Acres," the area was called by the fire department. Fires were common in the warehouses and small factories, and fire officials labeled the buildings firetraps. However, the activity in those buildings, not the buildings themselves, caused the fires. Code enforcement, not demolition, was called for. Factory floors were often piled with rags, garment scraps, bales of paper, open cans of chemicals, and other flammable objects. But the fire officials' assessments fed right into the general public impression of the area as filled with derelict and discardable buildings.

In the 1960s the area became known as "the Valley" because its vast stock of low-rise industrial buildings lay between the skyscrapers of Wall Street and midtown. From the distance, the Manhattan skyline gives the impression of two separate cities, with a vast empty space between them.

Once the massive clearance projects were unveiled, this until then economically and socially viable district was doomed. This is the *death-threat syndrome*, also known as *planners' blight*. Any residential, commercial, or industrial area begins to die once a new destiny is planned for it. Property owners cease maintenance, anticipating condemnation and demolition. Banks won't lend money, even if property owners are inclined to invest. Businesses move out, not waiting for the battle to play out. In this case, few expected the plans to be canceled. Defeating highway and urban renewal plans was almost unthinkable at the time. Even if an announced plan eventually fails, the announcement alone has already killed a district or catalyzed its decline.

These kinds of plans are like a big billboard with a message to property owners: no future for this area, disinvest, cash out, leave. City services diminish. Activity spirals downward. This happens today, in New York and elsewhere, when big plans for stadia, mixed-use projects, and convention, entertainment, or retail centers and the like are announced. The decline of the targeted neighborhood becomes a self-fulfilling prophesy. This is what happened to the South Houston Industrial Area that became SoHo. The death-threat syndrome killed it, not natural decay. Many experts tried to identify it otherwise. Many still do.

It is contradictory to label as dead or a slum any district where buildings are occupied, businesses function, and an economic ebb and flow exist. Any neighborhood witnessing sustained economic activity and new businesses moving in can't be honestly declared blighted. This defies reason and economic logic. But it is still happening now in New York and elsewhere despite the lessons of the late twentieth century, as shown in different chapters of this book. Unfortunately, the leniency of the law simply allows a municipality to declare an area blighted on very loose standards.

THE EXPRESSWAY FIGHT

The expressway had been planned and talked about since the 1940s, but was formally unveiled in 1959. The 1956 Federal Interstate Highway Act, with its 90 percent federal funding, gave highway planners the opportunity to implement scores of road projects long on the drawing boards. Jacobs got involved in 1962. During the West Village Urban Renewal fight in which she was so engaged, urban renewal and highway hearing dates would occasionally coincide. Thus, Villagers, like Jacobs, would hear informally about the expressway fight. "There was so little in the newspapers that I wouldn't have been aware that it was going on if I hadn't run into people in City Hall," Jacobs recalled. "That's how badly it was being covered. It wasn't regarded really as news."

Although the expressway had been in the planning for years, it really drew attention in the late 1950s or very early '60s. The process accelerated with the expropriation of property, vacating of buildings, and eviction of people. Jacobs got involved when Father LaMountain from the Church of the Most Holy Crucifix on Broome Street in Little Italy called her. "He and his parishioners had been fighting it," she said. "It would wipe out his street, church, parishioners, shops, and more. This was right after our West Village fight, and we'd won it, so he asked me if I would come to a meeting on this in early '62. I was reluctant. I had put in a horrendous year. We didn't get the West Village Urban Renewal designation removed until February '62. It was a whole year." Sleepless nights, skipped family meals, and dining room meetings marked the year. The Jacobs family had a signal to their cohorts: if the porch light was on, neighbors were welcome; if off, privacy requested. "There were meetings going on all the time. Most of the time, everybody was at work. Only in the evening could we do these things, so that's the kind of year the whole family had. And we wouldn't have missed it. I mean, we'd all love to have missed having the problem, but as long as we had it, we wouldn't have missed fighting and winning it. No question about that. But we were pretty tired, and the idea of another fight. . . . So it took some persuasiveness on the part of Father LaMountain to have me just come to the meeting."

That meeting in the spring of 1962 was the first time she realized the expressway was connected with the earlier fight to keep the road out of Washington Square. "We fought that very hard, beginning back in '56," she said. "Now I began to understand that this was connected. And if this expressway came through, our victory in Washington Square was a very Pyrrhic one. The ramps would be coming off, and if they didn't come off through Washington Square, they'd come off damn close and in other places in the Village too. These monsters come back, you know."

The larger citywide agenda of Moses and city officials slowly became visible. They had heard about a map in David Rockefeller's Lower Manhattan Development Office. "It showed all the redone things, combinations of highways and new real estate developments on both sides of Manhattan, all the way up the West Side. So I began to see that these were other facets of the very same fight, that somebody had a great vision of how New York was to be. We kept running into this vision, and it was a monstrous vision. You would see this piece of it and that piece of it, and it wasn't paranoid to think that it was an overall plan that the public really didn't know that much about. It was clear what a disaster it would portend for the Village and other neighborhoods." A built Lower Manhattan Expressway would have relegated the city to neighborhood fragments scattered between and within the clover leafs. His only goal: efficiency for moving automotive traffic. Cities, he believed, should serve traffic. This does not make for a strong city.

It had not been long since *Death and Life* was published in 1961. She had finished it just before the West Village fight. "Thank God," she said with a great sigh. "If I'd had to give that much time to the fight, I'd have had to drop the book. I finished it in January, went back to work at *Architectural Forum*, and in February the West Village fight began. The book was published in October 1961."

The conflict seemed right out of the pages of her book. She agreed. "It was even much worse than I had ever believed or dreamed when I was writing the book. I couldn't believe there would've been this much stupidity about New York."

At Father La Mountain's meeting, everybody said the expressway was inevitable. "All of our elected officials, because they knew how unpopular it was, were always going on record against it," she remembered, "but were never doing a thing to stop it and were always preaching defeatism. Moses was the real promoter, joined by all the traffic and highway people, the Regional Plan Association, the Planning Commission. Mayor Wagner seemed to be for it, but with Wagner, a wonderful thing happened. We had a hearing, and we actually changed the mind, as far as one can tell, of the Board of Estimate." The hearing was a day or two before Christmas, not an uncommon ploy to ensure poor public turnout. "Well, instead we neglected our Christmas. I even feel bitter about that to this day, that they stole one of my Christmases from me. Well, they didn't really. We ended up with a great Christmas present." The issue, she recalled, was probably the expropriation of the land, funds, and authorization for it. "It was one of the big steps," she said. "Once that was okayed, it was the point of no return."

But the public testimony changed the mind of the Board of Estimate. The opposition had been conducting a long, hard fight with every kind of pressure, and more and more people were involved and were showing up in busloads. That seemed to persuade the officials. "It may have been what it seemed like," Jacobs said. "But how does one know behind the scenes what were the operative levers and deciding factors? There was really nobody there who argued for it, except a man from David Rockefeller's downtown association. I think it's important that there weren't many highway people and not much preparation on their side. I think they thought they had a sure thing. And we had so many people, so much preparation, and facts and figures and arguments. I really think that it swayed them; they already knew they had a big and growing fight on their hands."

Opponents testified about jobs that would be destroyed and businesses that would be lost, contrasting lost jobs with the temporary nature and number of jobs that would be achieved. "What we talked about most was how New York would be ruined," she continued, "if you kept trying to supply, first and foremost, roads for automobiles, and letting everything else disintegrate and just fit in the margins. Then the Board of Estimate went into a session, and we waited. It was an hour or two, quite a while. They came out, sat down, and voted against the expressway. Incredible! We'd won. Fantastic!"

The fight died down for a while, but it wasn't the end. It came up again the next year in some form for reconsideration. "Now the fight was not only taken up by the Planning Commission," she said, "but also very vigorously by the State Highway Department, which meant it was taken up very vigorously by Governor Nelson Rockefeller [1959–1973]. The state became our chief opponent."

Gee, this is one reason I hate Nelson Rockefeller. I only saw him face-to-face once and talked to him once in my life, and he told me a lie [laughter]. The only firsthand experience I had with him is one great big lie.

He came down to the San Gennaro Festival when he was running for governor. It was in the area that would be destroyed. We had a bullhorn and kept following him. We kept telling people that this man had a plan that was going to destroy the neighborhood, that this man was supporting the expressway, that this man was going to take their homes away from them. The expressway would've taken the guts right out of Little Italy. We took turns saying, "Governor Rockefeller, why do you want to destroy this neighborhood?" We stuck close to him.

Finally it got on his nerves, evidently. He tried to ignore it for a long time; we just kept at it. So he turned around, and I happened to have the horn in my hand. We were all taking turns. He said that this was a city, not a state, matter. I disputed him on that. I said it was on the state highway map, and we wanted it taken off. He said that he believed in local government, and the state would do whatever the mayor and the Board of Estimate wanted. So I pinned him down. I said, "If the Board of Estimate turns down this plan, will you have the state take it off the highway map?" And he said yes, he would.

I really pinned him down: "You promise that if the Board of Estimate turns this down, that you will take it off the state map?" "I promise I will," he said. "It's your own government that wants this; don't come after me about it. We will do whatever the city wants." Okay, that was the great big lie, because then we got the Board of Estimate to turn it down. We promptly began trips to Albany to get it off the state map. Governor Rockefeller promised this. Thousands of people heard him. He promised it to me!

[But in Albany] we got a great runaround from everybody. Everyone was sympathetic. God, we saw a lot of people. They all would say you have to have the city liaison people . . . and the city liaison people would say that it was up to the people in Albany. What it came down to was that the governor wouldn't allow it to be taken off in spite of this grand public promise before thousands of people. So, that's the only person-to-person communication I ever had with Rockefeller, and all it amounted to was a huge lie. If the only thing somebody ever told you was a lie, would you like him?

After that, in 1964 she thought, it was rescheduled, and this time the opposition lost. Dozens of construction workers showed up, as they often did for big projects (and still do). One can always tell if they're paid; they leave right at five o'clock. The new hearings were on technical aspects of land acquisition, not whether it should or shouldn't happen at all. Many postponements followed for one reason or another. "All kinds of shenanigans were occurring. We kept finding out new things, such as that they were promising a housing project and that it would transgress the new pollution laws soon to be passed." Much was "going on at top speed," she said. "Eventually came the time when they had to change their tune because of those pollution laws."

NEW AMENITIES PROMISED

The pollution laws had a significant impact on the course of this fight, since increased traffic would logically increase pollution. The idea that the speed of the cars diminished the pollution did not prevail. Thus, the proponents changed the argument for the expressway to what was to be built with it. "All of a sudden they were going to have this great, glorious swatch of land right across Manhattan that was going to be full of fountains, gardens, and new buildings of all sorts," Jacobs explained. "That's what they now tried to say the expressway was all about. It wasn't about how many cars it would carry anymore, for heaven's sake."

The new school and park proposal apparently stiffened the resolve of people in Chinatown. They would get enough carbon monoxide at their children's school to do them harm. About this time, Jacobs recalled, it became known that in the apartment houses built over the newly constructed approach to the George Washington Bridge, people couldn't open their windows.[1] "The whole idea of combining housing or schools with expressways, for the first time, was frightening people," Jacobs observed. "People there were complaining they had headaches all the time. The Department of Health, I think it was, warned people not to open their windows. The song and dance about, 'Oh, there's less pollution, because the cars are going fast,' just didn't hold up in real life. There was concentrated pollution there."

So the pollution issue, because of the new laws, was becoming a real problem. The proponents had already given figures about how many cars this expressway would carry.

I think they were inflated for cost-benefit purposes. Using those figures creates the pollution problem. Now all of a sudden they have to argue that they won't have many cars. They never would discuss these two things—cost benefits and pollution—at the same meeting.

So, they tried very hard to change the subject. This is the first time the subject had to be changed, because it was the first time that these things came into conflict—the amount of pollution as against the cost? That was in '67 when they began changing the subject, without much success, because this had gone on for so many years, people understood what an expressway would do. It was something very real to them.

ARREST

One of the great eccentric stories about Jane Jacobs is her arrest during the expressway fight. Many versions are told. Some who say they were with her during the incident even tell a different version from her own. She recounted in detail how it really happened in our conversation of March 1978, some of which is included here.

> The state held a hearing to focus on a new big promotion for all this great land development that was going to occur, all of a sudden soft-pedaling, or ignoring, the number of cars, because now they worried about the pollution factor. The plan for the school had been found out. A committee was researching the pollution impact, and they were very frightened. So now comes a hearing on the grand physical environment that was going to be built around the expressway, downplaying the number of cars. They kept talking about fountains, fountains everywhere, so many beautiful fountains. And gardens and things to appeal to the environmentalists.
>
> People tried asking: if it wasn't going to increase the pollution because there would not be so many cars, then how could the cost be justified? They would say that's not what this hearing is about. It was a great charade.

Then a hearing was scheduled that she knew was meant to pacify the community. According to Frances Goldin of the Cooper Square Committee, Jacobs arranged with a few of them to stage some kind of protest action. When they got to the meeting, something new was happening. Instead of the lectern for speakers from the public facing the stage where officials were supposed to be listening, it was instead facing the audience, as if citizens only needed to address each other. This was like adding salt to a wound. The public already felt the elected leaders were not interested in what they had to say. This was proof.

Jacobs wanted to "send a message" to officialdom. No one of official consequence was on the stage to listen anyway. Her strategy of "sending a message" was to just quietly walk across the stage from one side to the other in protest. She invited anyone who was similarly inclined to follow. As they walked across the stage, an apparently frightened stenotypist grabbed her steno machine, clutched it to her chest, and, in the process, dropped the tape, which began unraveling all over the stage. Protesters apparently helped send it in the air, grabbing it and tossing it around like confetti. At this point, Jacobs declared that the hearing didn't happen because there was no record.[2]

What ensued was quite serious in Jacobs's mind. She didn't like being arrested and charged with inciting to riot, criminal mischief, and obstructing public administration. The community had to hold fund-raisers to pay for her defense. Of course, charges were eventually dropped but not before she was actually booked, charged, and eventually ordered by a judge to pay for damages. She didn't believe for one minute that any damage occurred, but she and her lawyer kept asking the city for receipts of costs of damage in order to fulfill her responsibility. They never received any. The matter simply ended.

In various conversations, Jacobs repeated the point that lawsuits are most useful in these fights just for the benefits of delay, delay, delay. "Some issues you fight with lawsuits and buy time that way," she explained. "With others, you buy time by throwing other kinds of monkey wrenches in. You have to buy time in all these fights. The lawsuit way is the most expensive."

THE IMPACT OF ENVIRONMENTAL LAWS

"We accomplished something with all this mess," she pointed out. "The feds held a hearing, declaring the expressway environmentally unacceptable. Well, well, that verdict *really* changed the subject, you see what I mean? [laughter] So my arrest bought some time, and it was well worth it. That's why I plea-bargained, to buy more time. I would have gone to jail if necessary. But the only point of it was to buy time to continue working in Washington on the environment and get a judgment against the expressway based on figures about that school, for instance, and about the general pollution that it would cause based on their own figures on new traffic to be generated."

By the time the decision was made in D.C. on the environmental questions, the Jacobs family had moved to Toronto in 1968. "It was a little like the West Village fight," she said. "After a while, Washington wanted the West Village thing to end. It was giving the urban renewal program a bad name all over the country. There were editorials in the *Saturday Evening Post* about the West Village. [laughter] There were pictures all over the U.S. of people protesting it with adhesive tape and *x*'s on their glasses. It was a bad image for them, a bad press that they were getting. I think highway people in Washington began to feel the same thing was happening with the expressway, too."

The pollution laws were still new. "It was one of the earliest cases to go this way. And it was an unequivocal thing. You could see how much pollution would occur. The state had used these increased car figures very early to justify spending this much money and doing this amount of destruction because of how much traffic it would accommodate. But now it was over and, eventually, demapped."

Expressway Killed; SoHo Emerged

After years of protracted battles, the expressway was killed by the Lindsay administration.[3] By then, the district was an empty shadow of its former self.

With the expressway out of the way in 1969, the Landmarks Commission held a hearing on the district's designation proposal in 1970, the first historic district in a primarily commercial area. There were then eighteen districts. Also that year, the city legalized the residential use by artists of lofts in commercial buildings. Buildings with artists illegally occupying them had small signs put on the front door, AIR for "artist in residence," to alert the fire department in case of a fire. Occupied buildings were given this designation also to protect people who had fixed up derelict spaces. Art galleries, boutiques, restaurants, and a few artist-entrepreneurs were already sprouting around the area, coexisting comfortably with the more than twenty thousand people who still worked in a variety of light manufacturing industries. No one doubted that industry would probably continue to leave the area.

The significance of SoHo and the critical importance of its preservation for the course of urban development and downtown regeneration nationwide was unclear to most people at the time citizens were vigorously seeking its designation as a historic district. Certainly, it was not yet clear to me. I wrote several stories about the civic campaign, but my focus was on SoHo as an internationally significant architectural district and the fight to gain historic district status for it. My recognition of the multidimensional significance emerged slowly. Eventually, SoHo's profound impact on the course of American urban history became apparent.[4]

The designation of SoHo as a historic district in August 1973 marked a turning point in the evolution of historic preservation in New York and the country. It was the first gritty, working commercial district so designated and thus expanded preservation thinking from the limitations of individual architectural treasures and residential districts with a cohesive style. Its rescue and landmarks designation broadened the understanding of what makes areas historically, culturally, and economically important, not just architecturally significant. Until then, the Georgian, Federal, brownstone, and other period-dominant districts were the convention. Georgetown, Greenwich Village, Rittenhouse Square, Beacon Hill, the French Quarter, and similar revered districts were the favorites.

INDUSTRIAL USES DISPLACED

Manhattan manufacturing during the Depression decreased less than in the rest of the country. During World War II, it increased moderately. The biggest cause of subsequent decline in New York City was the clearance for urban renewal at numerous sites around the city, including the dozen square blocks south of Washington Square Park to Canal Street, where SoHo now starts, and east of City Hall in lower Manhattan for vehicular access to the Brooklyn Bridge. Remember, these businesses were not planning to close. They were forced out. Some survived elsewhere; others closed for good.

In the 1960s decline accelerated considerably, as more neighborhoods were cleared and the new highways made cheap suburban sites readily accessible. It is difficult to recognize even today the viable economic uses in messy, down-at-the-heels working districts. Such areas are rarely pretty, seldom freshly landscaped, and hardly ever located in new, pricey buildings. Trucks proliferate. White-cloth restaurants are a distance away. On the surface, nothing significant seems to be happening. This is very deceptive. Incubation of the new and growth of the established are difficult to detect easily. This is the process Jacobs described as "adding new work to old," the real expansion of economic activity. This definition of growth is quite different from the conventional economic development today.

This Lower Manhattan district had the kind of mix of size, style, and age of buildings that observers today recognize as cradles of diverse and productive activity. This is obvious today because so many districts have followed the SoHo pattern, but when Jacobs et al. were fighting the expressway, few recognized this economic occurrence. "Innovators like to be around people and environments that are friendly to them versus rigid environments," Jacobs observed. "They want the SoHos of the world where they can function in idiosyncratic ways."

A 1963 study of SoHo by Chester Rapkin, an economist and unconventional planner, revealed some fifty categories of industrial activity, including furriers and makers of dolls, rags, belts, pens, wheel hubs, and boxes, among other things. The twelve-block district contained 416 buildings, 2,000 housing units, 800 commercial and industrial businesses, and 12,000 jobs. Most workers were minorities; almost half were women.[5]

Rapkin's report officially changed nothing. "Good planners are powerless," Jane Jacobs observed. The official word remained that the district was dead or dying, a collection of moribund, out-of-date, falling-down buildings. This is always the well-publicized, often-repeated official description of a district for which a new agenda has been written. Probably every rejuvenated district in the country has been, at one time, declared moribund and always "blighted" by the so-called experts, hired to justify the new political or development agenda. SoHo is probably the best known of them.

In this case, the new agenda was Robert Moses's plan for the Lower Manhattan Expressway and his large-scale housing schemes mentioned earlier. Thus, SoHo offers a sharp lens into urban change, Robert Moses style. Here, a highway is central; later, we'll see on the Upper West Side, Lincoln Center and housing developments were central.

Nowhere was the Robert Moses approach to cities more clear. Vast highway networks and urban renewal plans were valued more than organically evolved cities; elaborate schemes gratuitously ripped through neighborhoods, setting a pattern of highway building, centralized planning, and urban annihilation for the country. Robert Moses was the earliest, most visible, and most powerful exponent of this view, as the next chapter demonstrates. From New York, the Moses doctrine took hold all over the country. Ironically, the Lower Manhattan Expressway battle began the shift away from the Moses doctrine to the views expounded by Jacobs.

CHANGING ART

Once the expressway was announced, serious deterioration set in. Vacancies multiplied. Artists grabbed the opportunity of vast, cheap space and pioneered the organic rebirth of the district. They began filling the vacant lofts illegally, creating attractive, functional living and work spaces. Residential use in the industrial area was against the law. But landlords, unable to find business tenants, welcomed the artist-occupant. It was a cash agreement and kept secret until the highway project was killed and the move began to legalize artists' living and work spaces.

Coincidentally, contemporary art experienced a radical shift to large-scale work in the 1960s. Lofts averaged twenty-five hundred square feet of open floor space. (Manufacturers remained longer in the bigger ones.) The large windows of Cast Iron construction flooded each floor with natural light. Freight elevators provided useful access. Rents were affordable. It was a perfect prescription for artists.

Even before the SoHo loft trend took hold, Westbeth, an innovative industrial conversion, had occurred. This complex of thirteen attached buildings was built over twenty years starting in 1880 and served as the research center of the American Bell Telephone Company. In 1965, with critical support and guidance from the J. M. Kaplan Fund and designs by architect Richard Meier, the complex was converted to live-work spaces, the first on a large scale. The media attention it attracted surely helped the loft-conversion momentum.

Elsewhere, urban renewal and market high-rises were demolishing artists' lofts and studios, along with whole neighborhoods, particularly in Greenwich Village, the artists' neighborhood in the 1920s and 1930s. Artist space was at a premium. The destruction in the Village was halted with its designation as a historic district in 1969. The expanding grassroots group pushing the Landmarks Commission for designation counted on the same result for SoHo.

With the defeat of the expressway and gradual occupancy by artists, the transformation of SoHo had begun. City planning, zoning, and landmarking policies just had to catch up.

Not one dime of public investment or developer subsidy made SoHo happen. In fact, the defeat of a big misplanned public investment made SoHo possible. Only in the defeat of the highway did urbanism have a chance. Only in the defeat of excessive, top-down plans did SoHo have a chance. After the defeat, spontaneous regeneration took hold. Individual creativity rescued the beleaguered district planners sought to raze. When not doomed by centrally planned, inappropriate projects, many urban and small-town districts can regenerate productively.

JANE JACOBS VERSUS ROBERT MOSES

This pattern of planned urban destruction parading as renewal, set by Moses and his disciples, led to the sprawling, dysfunctional landscape with which the country now wrestles. Jacobs was Moses's most vigorous and visible opponent.

Jacobs argued that the unplanned mix of uses is what constitutes a healthy urban district and sustains a viable urban economy. Her concept of mixed use is defined here with the complex combination of industrial, commercial, residential, and cultural uses. Additionally, and quite importantly, a mix of building ages and scale is present. Districts like this, she argued, were more valuable to a city's economy than highways. Their value was underappreciated, she believed. Such a sensible and observable reality was heresy when *Death and Life* was published in 1961. She contradicted what the profession of planning was about and threatened power centers everywhere.[6] The "sacking of cities" is how she labeled what was happening at the time. This adds significance to the expressway defeat, a significance that reaches well beyond even the rescue and regeneration of SoHo. Urban districts should not be sacrificed for expensive, wasteful, destructive clearance projects, she argued.

SoHo was the biggest and most obvious battleground of the Moses-Jacobs urban philosophies that first unfolded in Washington Square Park. Grassroots battles against similar wrongheaded plans increased exponentially across the United States, especially highway urban renewal plans, inspired by Jacobs's words and activism. Community-based planning, historic preservation, and the "recycling" of buildings triumphed. Other neighborhoods and cities followed the pattern, stalling the bulldozers of urban renewal and highways in many places.

The lines were drawn dramatically in SoHo. This was a widely publicized and significant grassroots victory over top-down, autocratic planning. The reverberations had national impacts: Other groups were energized to fight harder if they were already embattled or to begin to do so if they weren't.

There were other community leaders around the country leading local fights against highways through cities, as Jane Jacobs did in SoHo. None gained the attention she did, being in the media capital of the country. Until then, only government officials and business leaders made decisions. They usually didn't live in the community and knew nothing of its vitality. If it was old, they just declared it a slum.

Before its designation for a highway, SoHo performed the age-old function of a healthy urban neighborhood that provides an outlet for innovation, gives birth to new businesses, permits established businesses to grow and adapt, adds new substance to the local economy, and exports its people and innovations to the rest of the city and country. "A lot more work than you imagine is occurring in SoHo," Jacobs observed in a 1981 conversation, "especially in artists' studios. Art is work, a very important work for cities, a very important export. Also, a lot of the services to this work, suppliers of various kinds, are there too. This is one of the few up-and-coming areas of New York. There ought to be forty to fifty neighborhoods like that."

SoHo's revival demonstrated that the spontaneous generation that once characterized New York's growth was still possible. In fact, this revival was happening during the 1970s when the economic condition of the city as a whole could not have been bleaker. The impact of SoHo on the larger city of New York is endless. SoHo changed the way we view all cities.

SoHo Broadened the Historic Preservation Movement

Preservationists have long been in the vanguard of opposition to inappropriate change, since historically or culturally important resources are often in the way of misguided plans. Incorrectly, preservationists are often accused of being against all change and for freezing the city. In fact, they oppose the erasure, mutilation, and overwhelming of places of value.

The highway defeat gave heart to urbanists, community defenders, progressive planners, and all other opponents of invasive projects mislabeled as "progress." Thus, SoHo helped slow the automobile-focused development nationwide that has destroyed so many viable neighborhoods, architectural treasures, and cultural resources.

SoHo survived the worst kind of planned impediments and then flourished under strict government limitations imposed first by the Landmarks

Preservation Commission and then the City Planning Commission. Basic rules and regulations have protected the area from excessive and overwhelming change, not from change itself. SoHo buildings are being constantly altered by what Jacobs called "adaptations, ameliorations, and densifications," and new Modernist buildings are replacing nonhistoric structures and filling empty sites. In fact, because SoHo was so successful, it attracted a parade of upscale, innovative contemporary buildings, designed by big-name architects (Jean Nouvel, Gwathmy Siegel, Smith Hawkinson), all enthusiastically approved by the Landmarks Preservation Commission in recent years.

These are the kind of rules that permit, even encourage, change within the context of what already exists. The integrity, scale, and individuality of scores of distinct neighborhoods are similarly protected by historic district designation. SoHo's transformation after the expressway defeat defines productive change: New is added to old; some pieces are replaced, but new does not overwhelm the whole. Some old is renovated and updated for new uses. The layering process of history is continued, not interrupted. Most dramatically, the SoHo Syndrome has done more to retain the middle class in cities and stimulate new economic innovations than any planning or government-supported new development.[7]

Discouragements to conventional development fundamentally helped SoHo's spontaneous metamorphosis. The restrictions were precisely what prevented wholesale alteration of the district, prevented a different development agenda from overwhelming it, and gave it the value property owners enjoy today.

Citizen activists stood ready to defend SoHo turf each step of the way. They lost few battles. No public funding, tax incentives, or zoning bonuses were necessary. The conventionalists who once decried the messy mixture of urban uses in gritty districts now celebrated the "mixed use" that SoHo epitomized.

Conventional economists, Wall Streeters, planners, and city officials undervalue these microeconomies that feed, sustain, and expand the larger city economy, the way the city's economy functioned in its most robust eras. These are the areas where new work is added to old, the kind of new work that authentically grows an urban economy. In recent boom years, misguided upzoning plans have been the constant threat to the continuation and expansion of these microeconomies. The frontiers within the city to which this dynamic energy can move are fewer and fewer due to a wave of upzoning, excessive development schemes, and escalating real estate values. Too many of these people and activities are simply being pushed out of the city limits.

What has happened in recent years can't be called modest anymore. In some ways, this has been a function of a national economy affecting every New York neighborhood and most American cities. What will happen now that this overheated cycle has cooled dramatically is anyone's guess. But only one thing is sure. The variety and flexibility of SoHo's building stock are in a good position to weather future dramatic shifts. The urban constant of change will continue to reshape SoHo and every other neighborhood.

SoHo's Exports Help Rejuvenate Other Places

Change is a constant in SoHo. As it exported its innovations and innovators, new things have taken their place. The complaint today is that SoHo is losing its character as an arts district. As prices escalate, galleries and artists leave, chain stores and restaurants move in, and tourists increase in numbers. This is especially dramatic in the era of a weak dollar, making New York City a foreign shopper's dream. Fortunately, the City Planning Commission followed the lead of a few dissenting commissioners and resisted an attempt in the 1990s to permit larger retail stores that would have accelerated that change and more dramatically undermined SoHo's artistic character and economic value. In this case, however, several fights ensued to prevent the Planning Commission from increasing parking. The protections in place for maintaining mixed use and manufacturing were constantly under attack. Over the years, however, manufacturing uses continued to diminish, but gradually, and conversions to residential continue today. Modest urban change, however, is both inevitable and most often healthy.

Nothing born or created in SoHo has been lost in the last decade of change. Whatever and whoever have left exist elsewhere. Chances are their art or business has expanded. The only losers, actually, are the residential or business renters outpriced by the market. Some of the artists and entrepreneurs who left did so in better condition than when they came. An artist friend of mine, for example, lives in a SoHo loft co-op. He was there fifteen years ago when it went co-op and bought cheap, as did other artists in the building. Several of his neighbors have sold their apartments, gaining financially, moving elsewhere to live more cheaply, using their financial gain productively, leaving town for greener pastures, or making other life changes of their choice.

Is this bad? It could be, if it weakens New York as a creative capital and if New York does not continue to regenerate and incubate new artists. But this incubation is, for the moment, still happening, very much so, in pockets all over the city. Some of the very people leaving SoHo and moving elsewhere are helping the process take hold in emerging SoHo-type districts in other cities. If anything, the recent economic freefall helps them stay. Landlords know better than to try to continue to raise rents excessively and, in fact, have lowered them in many places. Some areas are a convenient train ride or a short drive from the New York City marketplace. Isn't this what healthy urbanism is all about, the nurturing and exporting of innovations and innovative people? Both the incubating and the exporting must be happening at once, however, for the process to be a healthy one.

The piecing back together of the abused and undervalued manufacturing precincts like SoHo is happening across America. But the SoHo Syndrome doesn't work if assets are not there. The places where this process works have context, urban fabric, history, and committed citizens to make it work. It can't work where demolition is overwhelming. At that point, reproducing the urban fabric may be as alien as an enclosed shopping center. Replication is a trap. The result is form, not substance.

One Last Stand on a New York City Controversy

Jacobs actually summed it up quite well in 2005, a year before she died. On my periodic Toronto visits, we always discussed what was going on in New York, and I reported to her the proposed zoning changes for the Greenpoint-Williamsburg neighborhood of Brooklyn. This was a classic gritty, mixed-use neighborhood in the real meaning of mixed use. Single-family homes, small apartment houses, tenements, and small local retailers were scattered among all manner of manufacturing and art and artisan uses, housed in former warehouses and manufacturing buildings. This neighborhood was a classic incubator of new businesses of all kinds.

As gritty as it looked, Greenpoint-Williamsburg had been improving in recent years in a natural pattern of individualized upgraded uses (*unslumming* was the term Jacobs used in *Death and Life*). It had become

4.3 Low-scale Greenpoint-Williamsburg was rezoned and overwhelming high-rises followed—stopped, temporarily only, by the economic collapse. *Ron Shiffman.*

4.4 New upscale towers raised real estate values throughout Greenpoint-Williamsburg, threatening affordable housing and industrial uses. *Ron Shiffman.*

one of the new frontiers for artists and small or start-up manufacturers, as SoHo, Tribeca, and other Lower Manhattan districts became unaffordable. An overscaled rezoning that encouraged new high-rise, high-rent housing would undoubtedly undermine this robust economic and social process. And that was exactly what the city was proposing, without even a required percentage of units at affordable prices or any significant protection to keep industrial properties from conversion to residential. Incentives for developers to provide affordable units were included, but it meant letting them build even more units than permitted under the new zoning. In prior years, developers were required to include a minimum percentage with zoning bonuses only for an increase above the minimum.

Jacobs had seen this scenario unfold too many times, not just in New York. Hesitant to go public anymore on New York issues because of the flood of phone calls that usually followed, in April 2005 she agreed to write a letter in this case:

Dear Mayor Bloomberg:

My name is Jane Jacobs. I am a student of cities, interested in learning why some cities persist in prospering while others persistently decline; why some provide social environments that fulfill the dreams and hopes of ambitious and hardworking immigrants, but others cruelly disappoint the hopes of immigrant parents that they have found an improved life for their children. I am not now a resident of New York although most of what I know about cities I learned in New York during the almost half-century of my life here after I arrived as an immigrant from an impoverished Pennsylvania coal mining city in 1934.

I am pleased and proud to say that dozens of cities, ranging in size from London to Riga in Latvia, have found the vibrant success and vitality of New York to demonstrate useful and helpful lessons for their cities and have realized that failures in New York are worth study as needed cautions.

Let's think first about revitalization successes; they are great and good teachers. They don't result from gigantic plans and show-off projects, in New York or in other cities either. They build up gradually and authentically from diverse human communities; successful city revitalization builds itself on these authentic community foundations, as the community-devised 197-A plan does for Greenpoint.

What the intelligently worked-out plan devised by the community itself does not do is worth noticing. It does not destroy hundreds of manufacturing jobs, desperately needed by New York citizens and by the city's stagnating and stunted manufacturing economy. The community's plan does not cheat the future by neglecting to provide for schools, daycare, recreational outdoor sports, and pleasant facilities for those things. The community's plan does not promote new housing at the expense of both existing housing and imaginative and economical new shelter that residents can afford. The community's plan does not violate the existing scale of the community, nor does it insult the visual and economic advantages of neighborhoods that are precisely of the kind that demonstrably attract artists and other live-work craftsmen, initiating spontaneous and self-organizing renewal. Indeed, so much renewal is happening so rapidly that the problem converts to how to make an undesirable neighborhood into an attractive one less rapidly.

Of course the community's plan does not promote any of the vicious and destructive results mentioned. Why would it? . . .

But the proposal put before you by city staff is an ambush containing all those destructive consequences, packaged very sneakily with visually tiresome, unimaginative, and imitative luxury project towers. How weird, and how sad, that New York, which has demonstrated successes enlightening to so much of the world, seems unable to learn lessons it needs for itself. I will make two predictions with utter confidence. 1. If you follow the community's plan, you will harvest a success; 2. If you follow the proposal before you today, you will maybe enrich a few heedless and ignorant developers, but at the cost of an ugly intractable mistake. Even the presumed beneficiaries of this misuse of governmental powers, the developers and financiers of luxury towers, may not benefit; mis-used environments are not good long-term economic bets.

Come on, do the right thing. The community really does know best.

Sincerely, Jane Jacobs

This letter clearly articulated well-defined principles without any prescription for style, design, or use designations. But that was what she was about. This is pure Jacobs and the antithesis of generally accepted government policy.

SoHo regenerated organically through the private actions of many individuals, mostly artists to start. But that was in the 1970s when few cared about this district. Few noticed what was happening because it was ad hoc and in small, almost unnoticeable, steps. Few recognized the significance of these small things slowly adding up to big change. As noted, this was happening unnoticed as well in neighborhoods around the city, from the Upper West Side to the South Bronx to Park Slope. The unfolding change was different in each neighborhood because the people and neighborhoods were different, shaped by many individual doers, including some developers. But those development plans for the most part were in scale with the neighborhood, too contained to spur cataclysmic change. But by the 1990s and surely by 2000, real estate investors discovered similarly gritty Greenpoint-Williamsburg and other Brooklyn neighborhoods. Planning officials were right there to initiate rezoning plans to expedite new frontiers for excessive neighborhood-altering new development. Jane's letter to the mayor could have been sent on behalf of any of those neighborhoods targeted for rezoning.

How ironic! The historic district, SoHo, that showed the nation the potential for regeneration of industrial neighborhoods had unleashed a redevelopment frenzy now undermining the virtues and authentic character of similar neighborhoods across the city.

SoHo's earlier history exposes the intentional destruction of New York's industrial economy. This is little recognized. SoHo is only one example of this destructive path. The conventionally accepted view that industry died a natural death or spontaneously left town for suburban locations is contradicted by the SoHo story, as with other areas of the city, as we will see.

-5-

RECONSIDERING ROBERT MOSES
What's to Reconsider?

> Robert Moses' legacy is highly overrated. If he hadn't had FDR priming the pump with money, little that he did would have gotten done. And while Moses was pouring cement for highways, plenty of people elsewhere were building public buildings and other essential projects. WPA money flowed into socially useful projects of immense variety, such as schools, day care centers, hospitals, clinics, colleges, firehouses, police stations, libraries, and markets.
>
> MIKE WALLACE,
> *historian, director, Gotham Center for
> New York City History*
>
> Routine, ruthless, wasteful, oversimplified solutions for all manner of city physical needs (let alone social and economic needs) have to be devised by administrative systems which have lost the power to comprehend, to handle and to value an infinity of vital, unique, intricate and interlocked details.
>
> JANE JACOBS,
> *The Death and Life of Great American Cities*

A growing kind of revisionism is apparent today, championed by some planners, developers, architects, historians, critics, and politicians who wish for a new Robert Moses "who could get things done in New York." The crescendo of this call rises to its greatest pitch when a coalition of citizen and issue-based groups vigorously oppose or manage to delay some megascheme. Sometimes, in all seriousness, this suggestion comes with the caveat that this should be a "modified Robert Moses," a little gentler, more benign, somewhat humane, and, even, with a dose of Jane Jacobs thrown in. This is a hilarious oxymoron. The assumption that the audacity of a Moses can be tempered by a dose of Jacobs is erroneous to the core. The writings and advocacy of Jacobs make this clear. Occasionally, a wishful speaker wants to demonstrate fairness to both Moses and Jacobs or to pick and choose from each. Not possible. This is an either-or, black-or-white condition.

No matter that in his early good government career Moses was a legitimate reformer, no matter how noble one thinks Moses was because he amassed only unbridled power and not bags of money for himself, no matter how wonderful one might judge Moses's parks, he was probably the most undemocratic, arrogant, ruthless, and racist unelected government official of the twentieth century.[1] One can't separate the man, his methods, and his monuments. This is a leopard with immovable spots.

His most contemptuous quotes are the stuff of legend: "When you operate in an *overbuilt* [emphasis added] metropolis, you have to hack your way through with a meat ax." Overbuilt? Back then? If overbuilt then, what would he say now? And: "To make an omelet, you have to break an egg." And: "If the ends don't justify the means, what does?" And, "Cities are made by and for traffic."

Take him in all his autocratic glory or reject him entirely. No in between is possible. Trying to blend Moses and Jacobs is like trying to push together the old black-and-white Scottie dog magnets: the harder you push, the more resistance you feel.

THE PARK DEFENSE

Some of the exuberant praise for Moses's parks is even questionable, such as all the green grass around public housing—a legacy of the tower-in-the-park plan with the ubiquitous little black sign with white letters, "Keep Off the Grass." The same was true in city parks. I remember as a child occasionally ignoring that prohibition in Washington Square Park and getting summoned off the green by some park official. Since then, some of the unused grass areas around public housing have been converted to parking lots or play areas. Some have just been left as fenced-in grass.[2]

In the early 1960s, Central Park was under assault by Moses, notes Anthony C. Wood in *Preserving New York: Winning the Right to Protect the City's Landmarks*. Robert Moses was pushing to let Huntington Hartford build a thousand-seat, two-story café, designed by Edward Durrell Stone, in the southeast corner of the park across from the Plaza Hotel. Only fierce citizen opposition stopped this plan. And, of course, there was the Tavern-on-the-Green episode related earlier in this book.

Landscape historian Betsy Barlow Rogers, who led the monumental restoration of Central Park starting in 1975, wrote in detail how Moses ignored the purpose and design of the park as a masterpiece of scenic, passive recreation to impose his notion of a site for monuments, active play facilities, and increased automobile convenience.[3] While accepting some of his encroachments as worthy, Rogers notes that Moses created the twenty-two fenced-off playgrounds around the perimeter of the park "to preserve the surrounding scenery. To further discourage romping on the grass, he encircled lawns with pipe rail fencing, posted 'Keep Off the Grass' signs, and made infractions of this rule punishable by fine."[4] He should see the throngs sitting or playing on that grass today.

Moses must be turning over in his grave looking at Bryant Park, with all the countless people every day sitting on movable chairs or on the grass itself.[5] It was his rendition of that park as a walled-off sanctuary in the 1930s that made it so hospitable for drug users but hostile for everyone else. The current redesign, based on principles of sociologist and author Willian H. Whyte, returned the park to daily users by the thousands when it reopened in 1992.

And Jones Beach? A masterpiece started in the 1920s with state bonding funds and continued during the Depression when the federal government thought it good policy to put people to work on great public works around the country. Building a public amenity with public funds was still an accepted notion. Most surviving Works Progress Administration projects built everywhere in the country still have similar enormous appeal.

But as beautiful as it is, Jones Beach purposely excluded the poor. Moses engineered the Southern State Parkway and other roadways leading to it so that the overpasses were built too low for public buses to drive under. Moses's key staff person revealed this to Robert Caro. Some of those bridges have since been rebuilt with higher vehicular headroom. But, for the most part, buses still can't get through them with ease, according to Department of Transportation officials. Buses could fit under part of some of them but not entirely, thus rendering it improbable any bus would risk it. By his order, no mass transit could be built in the rights-of-way along the highway routes that would have made beach access available to the poor—then mostly immigrants or anyone without a car. Is that an appropriate *public* park design in a democracy, no matter how aesthetically appealing?

If he could help it, Moses built only for the white middle class *in cars*. That what he built eventually benefited the poor and working class was surely not his intent. When the middle class left the neighborhoods in which Moses inserted desirable recreation sites, the poor moved in and benefited. Moses's playgrounds are also a celebrated accomplishment—658 of them citywide, one in Harlem, none in Bedford-Stuyvesant. And La Guardia had to force Moses to landscape the ten blocks of Riverside Park he had cheaply created for Harlem from 145th to 155th Streets, after fierce resistance. As if in retaliation, he built there the only comfort station with a frieze of stone monkeys in the entire city.[6] When he built Riverside Park by covering the open train tracks and adding 132 acres of landfill, Moses had stopped the park at 110th Street, leaving the black community with the noise and grime of the trains eliminated in the park below 125th Street and above 145th Street. Even a wide wharf at 125th Street, easily converted for recreation, was ignored, and the ten-block stretch above was left with difficult pedestrian access.[7] The lush lawns and extensive planting that mark the park's beauty did not appear on that omitted stretch covered by a roadway viaduct. In fact, few amenities grace the six miles of Riverside Park and parkway in the Harlem stretch. Only one of seventeen playgrounds in the park was built in Harlem, and only one of five football fields. He had spent $16.3 million on the first 2 miles from 72nd Street and $7.9 million on the next 4.7 miles.

HIS WAY OR NO WAY

For decades, New Yorkers have cursed Walter O'Malley for moving the Brooklyn Dodgers to Los Angeles. But Michael Shapiro in *The Last Good Season* documents in gruesome detail O'Malley's effort to stay in Brooklyn, an effort tenaciously thwarted by Moses. Moses refused to condemn land in downtown Brooklyn for a new stadium (as the state and city have been anxious to do for the Nets arena included in the Atlantic Yards project on that site), insisting that O'Malley take land in Bedford-Stuyvesant that O'Malley knew was too distant and inappropriate for the purpose.

One can't ignore how ruthlessly Moses took funding from upstate parks to finance the Long Island parks he favored. Nor can one minimize how he moved the Northern State Parkway 3 miles and then curved it to preserve the property of well-connected wealthy estate owners like Otto Kahn, or the Long Island Expressway for J. P. Morgan. Yet he had no compunction about splitting the working farm of James Roth, covering his most fertile soil with asphalt and making it impossible for the struggling farmer to get his tractor across the highway.

The New York–born Moses never learned to drive, but he set about trying to create a spaghetti network of highways on a scale the country had not yet seen. Most significantly, Moses's roads went *through* cities versus *around* them. In retrospect, it is difficult to realize how far ahead of the rest of the country Moses was in highway projects. Other cities' officials watched and followed, going so far as to borrow construction contracts and loan documents he created as models. The erroneous, actually false, assumption is that Moses improved transportation in New York City and the region. What he did was improve only automotive transportation while undermining or killing some transit and preventing its future expansion.

Moses's highway construction was infinitely more destructive of the functioning city than most people recognize. It boggles the mind to consider how much of that functioning city was in the way of the 130 miles that went through New York City and then to imagine the damage that rippled out from each roadway's path like stones tossed in the water. No real calculation has ever been done of homes, businesses, social institutions, and churches lost.

The Urban Renewal Bulldozer

Moses was equally influential in shaping the country's urban renewal policies. Caro notes that Moses's Yale classmate Senator Robert A. Taft reached out to him to discuss "details of a new type of federal slum clearance program—'urban renewal'—that he was considering sponsoring."[8]

Moses was not alone in his vision for a new urban form. "The era's leading housing reformers, Henry Wright, Clarence Stein, and Lewis Mumford of the Regional Planning Association of America, wrote off tenements as relics of nineteenth-century industrialism. The metropolitan future, they argued, lay in towns planted in regional 'greenbelts' where there was room for a new communal civilization."[9] This was clearly the idea of the moment, but only Moses had the power to make his version of the vision come true.

Title I of the 1949 Housing Act was the primary vehicle for building middle-income housing on cleared land, which Moses aggressively pursued.[10] While Congress was working out the details of this program with Moses's help, Moses persuaded Mayor William O'Dwyer in 1948 to appoint a Mayor's Slum Clearance Committee of which Moses was made chairman.[11] O'Dwyer had already appointed him construction coordinator and chairman of the Emergency Commission on Housing. Understandably, New York was first in line with the most urban renewal proposals of any city in the country and, in the end, gained the largest share of funding.[12] Moses was the master all others emulated. Joel Schwartz describes what this incredible program meant:

> Title I's impact proved enormous. Projects removed 100,000 people from Manhattan and downtown Brooklyn, and, with their accompanying public housing, generated a diaspora of at least twice that number. Site clearance forced out at least 5,000 businesses of all sizes, and public housing forced out thousands more. Municipal experts declared that these losses . . . were negligible. But in Central and East Harlem, Bedford Stuyvesant, and other minority ghettoes, these enterprises nurtured a sizable portion of the black and Hispanic middle class. In other neighborhoods, redevelopments wiped out larger businesses or forced their ruinous shift to other quarters. Job loss as a direct result of redevelopment was between 30,000 and 60,000 in the postwar period. By the late 1950s, the number had risen to several hundred thousand.[13]

These were direct impacts. No way exists to measure the ripple effects of the lost businesses, residences, and institutions near the newly formed gaping hole. It is safe to say, however, that once the undermining began in one area, fraying of the larger surrounding fabric took on its own momentum.

Gay Talese described how a big project's clearance spreads deterioration beyond the specific cleared site. In a 1964 *New York Times* story about the massive dislocation impacts in Bay Ridge following the demolition of five hundred homes and the dispossessing of seven thousand people for the expressway leading to the new Verrazano Bridge, Talese wrote:

> In all, it took 18 months to move out the 7,000 people. Eventually, even the most stubborn—or out-of-touch residents of Bay Ridge abandoned their homes because of resignation or fear—fear of being alone in a spooky neighborhood; fear of the bands of young vagrants who occasionally would roam the area smashing windows or stealing doors, picket fences, light fixtures or shrubbery; fear of the derelicts who would sleep in empty apartments or hallways; fear of the rats that people said would soon be crawling up from the shattered sinks and sewers because, it was explained, "rats also are being dispossessed from Bay Ridge."[14]

The federal official in charge of the program in the early years told Caro, "Because Robert Moses was so far ahead of anyone else in the country, he had great influence on urban renewal in the United States—on how the program developed and on how it was received by the public—more than any other single person."

Urban renewal became a favorite of mayors across the country because of the lava flow of federal funds that came with it, especially if coupled with a highway project. Few cities resisted like Savannah, where, a local resident reports, "it was resisted as a communist plot." Where the demolition derby got started, it was hard to stop. Each massive project inevitably led to further decay and an accelerated cycle of clearance. The holes in the urban fabric of American cities are still visible today from Buffalo to Cleveland to St. Louis and beyond.

Title I was, indeed, producing middle-income housing, as progressive Democrats, Regional Plan advocates, the press, and all Moses's supporters wanted. Between June 29 and July 2, 1959, the *New York Times* published a series of articles, "Our Changing City," surveying the state of public housing and urban renewal. Barren looking, devoid of hope, and overwhelmed with relocation problems are how the articles found public housing. Ford Foundation staffers "became convinced that Title I had aggravated the city's housing shortage, destroyed many Old Law tenements that could have sheltered low-income residents, and created sterile, crime-ridden environments."[15]

Deborah Wallace and Rodrick Wallace wrote a very important book, *A Plague on Your Houses: How New York Was Burned Down and National*

Public Health Crumbled, that shows the enormous impact all this dislocation had on the mental and public health of the distressed population and the entire city and region. They wrote:

> Many poor neighborhoods simply collapsed from the spatial concentration and temporal peaking of these modes of housing destruction. Health areas of the South-Central Bronx, for example, lost 80 per cent of both housing units and population between 1920 and 1980. About 1.3 million white people left New York as conditions deteriorated from housing overcrowding and social disruption. About 0.6 million poor people were displaced and had to move as their homes were destroyed. A total of almost two million people were uprooted, over 10 percent of the population of the entire Standard Metropolitan Statistical Area (25 counties).

Just thinking about the magnitude of this forced migration helps focus on why, by the 1960s and '70s, New York was a collapsing mess. As Moses said, it was the "meat ax" approach to city building.

THE HUMAN TOLL

What is not recognized sufficiently in regards to any of Moses's cataclysmic urban development schemes is exactly what the Wallaces were referring to: the thousands upon thousands of lives disrupted, the downward spiral of so many lives often jump-started by such massive demolition projects, the endless tales of social dislocation. The Wallaces have provided additional insights not often discussed.

Based on years of study, they document how the fires of the 1970s continued to destroy what Urban Renewal started. What they shockingly outline is that this occurred within a framework of deliberate city policies that were based on erroneous information, pseudoscience, manipulated data, and malevolent policy goals.[16] The Wallaces effectively show that the closing of firehouses, guaranteeing inadequate responses, and the withdrawal of other municipal services in the most vulnerable neighborhoods purposefully continued the clearance that Moses started.[17] This all occurred under the post–Urban Renewal policy of "Planned Shrinkage" with the overt goal of killing off "sick" neighborhoods.[18]

What was often destroyed, the Wallaces note, were, in fact, "stable 'slums,' i.e. poor neighborhoods of old, mildly overcrowded housing that

5.1 Ricardo Levins Morales designed this poster in the aftermath of Hurricane Katrina for the people left out of the rebuilding planning process in New Orleans. He could just as well have designed it for the people of New York City left out of Robert Moses's construction process. (To view it in splendid color, visit his website www.rlmarts.com.)

are not experiencing rapid deterioration physically or socially, are true communities, often with a history decades long." They then quote a 1977 book on public health and the built environment by Loren Hinkle, published by the Centers for Disease Control. It goes to the heart of the issue: "It is the social environment and not the physical environment which is the primary determinant of the health and well-being of people who live in cities. . . . The importance of the social milieu is such that the dislocation and disruption of social relations that are produced when one moves a family from a dilapidated dwelling [within a functioning community] to a modern apartment [outside that community] may have adverse effects upon health and behavior that are not offset by the clean, comfortable, and convenient new dwelling."[19]

Such a massive scale of social disruption would not have occurred if organic change and a different scale and form of progress had been allowed to take hold—the kind that Jane Jacobs identified as building up the fertility of the land instead of eroding it. So many dismembered lives could have been uplifted instead of undermined, given a different path of development. Voices advocating that alternative path were drowned out by Moses and stilled by the deaf ear of a press and the policy-making community enthralled with his message and accomplishments. Projects on the scale that Moses built inevitably and severely and destructively disrupt the social, economic, and psychological life of thousands. Destabilization is a given. The benefits cannot match the losses.

LEARNING BY LISTENING

Jacobs's views about city development evolved. As noted in the introduction, she first learned in East Harlem how the delicate urban fabric worked to stabilize neighborhoods. By visiting the area, walking the streets, and talking to residents, she learned how the row houses, small apartment houses, tenements, stores, and local businesses created an intricate web, the whole of which gained strength from the complex, often invisible connection of the parts. Through the eyes of Union Settlement House director and Episcopal minister William Kirk and social worker Ellen Lurie, she also watched it being torn apart by one public housing project after another, wiping out an estimated tens of thousands of dwellings and 1,500 businesses.

Moses plowed through the South Bronx to build the seven-mile Cross Bronx Expressway, connecting the George Washington Bridge to I-95, as Caro vividly details.[20] In just one mile, 1,530 families (more than 60,000 people) and businesses were dislocated and 159 buildings demolished.[21] This occurred despite the existence of an alternate route a few blocks away that would have been quicker and cheaper. Only six tenements and nineteen families were in the way of the alternate route. Moses dismissed the thousands of Bronx residents and businesses pleading for the alternate route to save their homes, livelihoods, and community, saying only, "It was a political thing that stirred up the animals there." Residents and businesses were given ninety days to leave. Like so many other wiped-out neighborhoods, it had solid schools with involved parents, local businesses, seven movie houses, synagogues, churches, old walk-ups with affordable apartments that had light and air, and all manner of social institutions and networks.

And what do we have there now? A traffic nightmare with four of the eleven worst bottlenecks in the country. Nineteen of the country's fifty worst bottlenecks are either in the five boroughs or in nearby counties, as Tom Namako reported in the *New York Post* on February 26, 2009. On September 20, 2002, Alan Feuer in the *New York Times* described the truck-clogged, congested road as "arguably the most savage road in New York City."

THE HUMAN TOLL

What is seldom mentioned in regards to any of Moses's cataclysmic urban development schemes is the thousands of lives disrupted. Caro's chapter "One Mile" recounts how this devastation undermined the South Bronx and is famously cited for detailing the resulting human pain and suffering. Rare is any similar examination of the human costs of other such disruptive projects. Moses and his public relations machine, along with the political leaders, did such a good job of selling the public on the false notion that these strategies cleaned up "slums," cleared "blight," and replaced "deteriorated" neighborhoods that most people today are unaware of the true condition and quality of these communities and the lives of the people in them.

The true mark of Robert Moses has to be the way he treated the people who stood in his way. Elizabeth Yampierre, a Brooklyn lawyer and citywide leader of the city's environmental justice movement, recalls:

> My family lived on the Upper West Side, in a blue-collar community. We had a family infrastructure that made it possible for the women in my family to work, for the children to be cared for, and although we were not wealthy by any means, we were doing okay. When we were displaced, we became "roadkill" in Robert Moses' vision. Our family was scattered to the Bronx to Queens and throughout Manhattan. I went to five schools in eight years, and, in my family, some people went on to become drug addicts and some women went on public assistance. The entire fabric of my family was destroyed as a result of that displacement.

Yampierre told her story at a public celebration of Jane Jacobs's life held in Washington Park after Jacobs's death in 2006. Yampierre had not read Jacobs's books.

A similar human tragedy unfolded in South Brooklyn when Moses ignored the pleas of residents of Park Slope and Windsor Terrace to move the Brooklyn/Queens Expressway to avoid razing five hundred buildings, mostly homes. An alternate route, again only a few blocks away, would use mostly vacant lots and "save money and heartache," the *Brooklyn Eagle* newspaper reported in March 1945. Even the state legislature unanimously voted a resolution asking for relocation since the road was partially state funded. He ignored them all.

Moses became known as the country's foremost "master builder," an American Baron Haussmann, the man who shaped nineteenth-century Paris. But Moses didn't start out in that direction.

A REFORMER TO START

Moses started out as an advocate of government reform and rose to power under Governor Alfred E. Smith, who in 1919 assigned him the task of reorganizing state government, heavily centralizing it and shifting considerable power from the legislature to the governor. As Moses filled an assortment of appointments, he learned how to navigate that governmental power better than anyone. He didn't override the political system; he used it. With each agency and authority he created and then took over, he began building, first with the Long Island Park Commission, then the New York City Parks Department, the New York State Power Commission, and eventually twelve state and city positions at one time.

The concept of the public authority—an independent agency separated from normal government process of checks and balances and with the ability to issue its own revenue bonds—was Moses's. Proceedings are secret, and records are not public. Authorities were purposely designed to be impervious and impregnable to outside voices and impacts. The public authority, Caro notes, "became the force through which he shaped New York and its suburbs in the image he personally conceived." To this day, the public authority remains a favorite government device "to get things done" and to avoid a genuine public process that includes community input, real negotiation, and compromise.

Probably no one, elected or not, in any other state held such vast power over such an extended period. He served under five mayors: Fiorello La Guardia, William O'Dwyer, Vincent Impellitteri, Robert F. Wagner Jr., and John V. Lindsay. "No law, no regulation, no budget stops Robert Moses in his appointed task," La Guardia once boasted. Since Moses usually wrote the rules for the agencies he led, his task was usually his to define. And he served under six governors: Alfred E. Smith, Franklin D. Roosevelt, Herbert H. Lehmann, Thomas E. Dewey, Averell Harriman, and Nelson A. Rockefeller.

With all the leaders under whom he served, Moses was famous for threatening to resign his position if he did not get his way. Each relented—until Rockefeller. In 1962 Rockefeller wanted Moses to resign as chairman of the State Council of Parks to make way for his brother, Laurence, long a member of the Palisades Interstate Commission and a known parks and conservation advocate. Rockefeller told Moses he could retain his Long Island parks chairmanship. Moses refused and resigned from both state park positions and the State Power Commission, fully expecting Rockefeller to back down. He didn't. "For decades, governors had dreaded what would happen if they had to be the one to fire Bob Moses. Now one governor had fired Bob Moses. And nothing happened."[22]

Because he created parks all over the state, he is most favorably known as a great park builder. "As long as you're on the side of parks, you're on the side of the angels. You can't lose."[23] Caro quotes Moses here to illustrate how well Moses knew how to manipulate public opinion. And while his highways and urban renewal projects are sometimes considered inevitable, there is nothing inevitable about the routes and sites he chose that destroyed dozens of productive and vibrant residential and industrial neighborhoods and uprooted and undermined the lives of more than a million people and businesses. While the estimates of displaced residents and businesses are known for only some projects, a total seems impossible to calculate but is acknowledged to be *at least* five hundred thousand people. Some estimates exceed one million. There is no estimate for the displaced businesses. And there was nothing inevitable about his building only residential towers in the park without the traditional mixed uses of an urban neighborhood.

To assume improved roads, housing, parks, and expanded universities and other institutions would not have happened is foolish. They would indeed have happened but differently. Revisionists would have us believe that Moses was operating in the context of his time, doing what everyone else was doing. Evidence indicates otherwise. He shaped the context of his time. Others learned from him and followed his path.

THE IMPACT OF THE WORLD'S FAIR

Moses started the reshaping of the country for the car first through his facilitating the 1939 World's Fair, then through his New York projects, and then by helping other cities plan and design their projects. It was a perfect combination since Moses's vision of park creation always included—and sometimes started with—the necessary vehicular access.

In 1935 Moses took the suggestion that the city should hold a World's Fair in Flushing Meadow and, as city parks commissioner, made it happen.

He quickly recognized the immense potential of the project to enhance his own power and agenda, given the contracts and jobs involved in building the pavilions and the vast network of new Queens highways needed to reach the site and, of course, the enormous park to be created in the process. Nothing about the fair could happen without the approval and input of Moses.

The 1939 World's Fair, with its theme, "The World of Tomorrow," had a greater impact on the subsequent development of the country than most people realize. The fair is widely acknowledged as the icon of the Art Deco period of design. Less recognition, however, exists of its role in shaping urban planning and setting the nation on the car-oriented course that has existed ever since. "The story we have to tell," critic Lewis Mumford said of the fair's theme, "is the story of this planned environment, this planned industry, this planned civilization.[24] If we can inject that . . . as a basic notion of the fair, if we can point it toward the future, toward something that is progressing and growing in every department of life and throughout civilization . . . we may lay the foundation for a pattern of life which would have enormous impact in times to come."[25] Indeed! Instead of being an enormous trade show at which manufacturers could discover the newest products and technologies, as in fairs past, this fair was directed at consumers. Manufacturers would have the opportunity to exhibit their products and persuade viewers how their lives would be improved.

Two major exhibits vied for and received the most attention. The first was the fair's symbol, the Trylon and Perisphere designed by architect Wallace K. Harrison. Inside the Perisphere was the World of Tomorrow, designed by Henry Dreyfuss, in the form of a model of Democracity. Democracity broke with the tradition of looking for solutions to problems in existing cities and imagined a whole new configuration of highways linking bedroom communities for the middle class, industrial districts with workers' housing nearby, and a business and cultural district at the center marked by a single skyscraper. The message was clear: the current city was no longer viable and its problems intractable. The solution: demolish and rebuild the city and provide alternatives outside of it for those who could afford it.

The more popular exhibit, in fact the most popular of the fair, was General Motors' Futurama, created by industrial designer Norman Bel Geddes, which actually dovetailed nicely with Democracity. Here, viewed from a moving platform, was the future with cities built from scratch around highway interchanges. Tiny cars—no congestion, plenty of space between them—on multilane roadways went over mountains and bridges and ran on liquid oxygen. A fantasy, yes, but an extraordinarily seductive one. Walter Lippmann wrote: "General Motors had spent a small fortune to convince the American public that if it wishes to enjoy the full benefits of private enterprise in motor manufacturing, it will have to rebuild its cities and its highways by public enterprise."[26]

From then on, the cleverly crafted advertising campaigns of the car manufacturers equated cars with modernity and middle-class status, and the automobile industry became the foundation for our postwar economy. Caro notes in a similar vein:

> The three automotive giants would later plow tens of millions of dollars into his World's Fair at a time when other major companies were shying away from it. In the sense that he was America's, and probably the world's, most vocal, effective and prestigious apologist for the automobile, that he designed highway networks not only for New York but for a dozen cities, that by his success in building expressways in the city he did more than any other single urban official to encourage more hesitant officials to launch major highway-building programs in *their* cities, and that, by building them to new, high standards, he did more than any other single urban official to set the early standards for urban expressway design—he was the spearhead, the cutting edge, of this Panzer division of public works.[27]

The fair's message seems to have altered even Moses's vision for roads. Until then, he built "parkways"—the Taconic, Bronx River, Henry Hudson—all built to connect middle-class car drivers to parks for leisuretime enjoyment and some commuting. They were four lanes, beautifully landscaped "ribbon parks," with graceful curves offering bucolic views. Roads went around cities. Early suburbs had evolved along rail lines. The car was an additional means of transportation, not a replacement for the enviable transit system that knitted neighborhoods together into one city and wove the country's cities into a national fabric. That pattern remained until after World War II.

The car culture was *emerging*, not yet *booming*. The auto industry was to be the vehicle to put the nation back to work. An assortment of postwar national policies, including the 1956 Interstate Highway Act, purposely spurred that emerging car culture and industry. Those highways would be designed for practical use by commuters and truck traffic, even though many of Moses's roads were still routed to connect parks. Some roads actually sliced through parks, like Upper Manhattan's Van Cortlandt and Inwood. Moses's roads created more traffic, as all new roads do. Experts told him this. They strongly urged him to build transit, too. He refused to listen.

Moses set his own course. One massive clearance project followed another in what former Random House editor Jason Epstein called "periodic paroxysms of self-destruction in the name of renewal."[28]

THE COUNTRY FOLLOWS MOSES

As the first big highway builder, he created the vision and then the template for the nation. He helped craft the funding and authorizing legislation in Washington for urban renewal and highways nationwide. Then he was first in line to get funding for local projects, with the growing strength of the highway lobby behind him.

Aides to President Eisenhower consulted with Moses about national highway needs as they crafted the 1956 Highway Act. One of the early managers and the de facto head of the Interstate Highway System, Bertram D. Tallamy, had formerly served as superintendent of the New York State Department of Public Works. He revered Moses. In the 1920s, Tallamy used to come down from Niagara to attend lectures given by Moses on the art of "Getting Things Done." Tallamy told Caro that "the Interstate Highway System was built by principles he had learned at those lectures."[29]

After the '56 act was proposed, University of Michigan professor Robert Fishman notes, "Moses became the principle spokesman of the U.S. Conference of Mayors in urging that interstates 'must go right through cities and not around them,' contrary to what President Eisenhower advocated. The president envisioned a road network between cities, like Germany's autobahn, with short connections to city centers."

Moses did not confine his strategy to New York. Other cities hired him to design freeway networks in the 1940s and '50s. Few were built. Funding was usually difficult, so many were postponed. Some were scaled back or simply canceled. Portland, San Francisco, San Diego, D.C., Baltimore, Los Angeles, Detroit, and others had Moses's help or influence. The first was New Orleans.

NEW ORLEANS

The French Quarter of New Orleans survived Hurricane Katrina in 2005 better than most of the city. But in the 1940s it narrowly missed being hit by a planning disaster engineered by none other than Moses. "A progressive spirit flourished in New Orleans after World War II. The desire for progress was reflected in the decision . . . to hire Robert Moses, the great freeway builder . . . to introduce 20th century thinking to New Orleans . . . Moses had done more to change the face of New York . . . than any other person in the 20th century. In 1946, expressways were considered avant-garde in America and Moses, with his faith in the automobile to move people in cities, was the acknowledged leader of this approach to urban-transportation planning."[30]

So the battle to preserve New Orleans's French Quarter involved defeating a proposed Moses-designed elevated highway for the waterfront, which would have demolished as much of the Quarter as his New York highways did back home. But while the waterfront route was changed, the idea of a highway through the city remained. A decimating highway did get built instead in New Orleans that cut through Treme, one of the oldest black neighborhoods in the country. Claiborne Avenue, a glorious boulevard of live oak trees and thriving local retail, restaurants, and the Capitol Theater, was the heart of this historic community. "Black people's Canal Street," one remembers it, "the large neutral ground for family barbecues, the central artery for Mardi Gras Indian parades." It was replaced by I-10. As one elderly citizen recalled for *Times-Picayune* columnist Lolis Elie, "Claiborne Avenue had gorgeous oak trees from one end to the next, not like now with a piece of concrete over people's heads. Treme was a neighborhood of white and black. They didn't go to the same school or church but the kids played together on the street and everyone sat outside together having fun. Claiborne was the heart of the business community and in 1963, I-10 ripped out the heart of hundreds of families' homes. Then they built black and white housing projects and separated the people."[31] Nearly five hundred homes were removed.

PORTLAND, OREGON

Portland is today considered the nation's best model of a popular livable city whose balanced transportation system has helped rejuvenate the city way beyond expectations. It was the first city to aggressively reinvest in public transit after World War II. In a 2005 article in *Willamette Week*, Bob Young wrote:

> If there was one event that defined Portland in the past 25 years, it was killing the Mount Hood Expressway, a six-mile, eight-lane asphalt behemoth that would have vaulted across the river from Johns Landing to Interstate 205. . . .
>
> Indeed, the godfather of the freeway was none other than Robert Moses, the fearsome architect of modern New York City. . . . In 1943, the power brokers of Portland—the five white men of the City Council and the city's utility, banking and insurance executives—brought Moses west to modernize their little town.
>
> Moses' vision called for new freeways slicing up Portland like a pizza. His plan would triple the mileage of blacktop. . . . "It was a grid of freeways with a school and church within each grid cell," says Ethan Seltzer, director of the Institute of Portland Metropolitan Studies at Portland State University. . . .
>
> The idea was to curb urban decay. . . . But what planners failed to realize was that freeways actually accelerated urban decay by destroying neighborhoods and sucking residents out to the suburbs.[32]

Resistance started with local residents of Southeast Portland in 1969 when the city started buying properties but was picked up and led by then Legal Aid lawyer Neil Goldschmidt, who was running for city council. Goldschmidt offered a totally different vision, inspired by Jane Jacobs. He won the election, went on to become mayor in 1972, led the effort to make federal highway funds convertible to transit, and launched a transit-building program that continues today and is the envy of cities across the country. Goldschmidt furthered the transit investment bandwagon as head of the U.S. Department of Transportation in 1979 under President Jimmy Carter.

HARTFORD, BALTIMORE, DETROIT

Hartford and Baltimore rejected plans designed by Moses. This was early. Hartford hired him in 1949 when, with a population of 177,000, "downtown streets were jammed with traffic all day long, much of it carrying shoppers to five big department stores," reminisced Joel Lang in the *Hartford Courant* in 1983. Hartford may have rejected Moses's specific proposals, but the highways that got built still plowed through and decimated the downtown.

In Baltimore in 1944 Moses was hired "to recommend a route for what was then known as the East-West Expressway (which still hasn't been built)," wrote Gwinn Owens in the *Baltimore Sun* in August 1981, upon Moses's death. Opposition was immediate in both West and East Baltimore and, like a dozen proposals that were to follow, Baltimoreans made it clear they weren't going to have their communities plowed under for a Moses-type expressway. The routes selected as alternatives to Moses's ideas still heavily damaged the central city. The idea of cutting *through* a city was now a widespread and accepted policy. If it wasn't the Moses-designed route, it just as well could have been. The elements were all the same.

In 1942, at the request of Michigan's commissioner of highways, Moses reviewed plans for Detroit's crosstown expressway between Detroit and Willow Run that ran through established neighborhoods of the city. In a fifteen-page letter, Moses wrote that generally speaking, the plan for the expressway "seems to us to have been admirably conceived and laid out."

PITTSBURGH

He also had a hand in the Pittsburgh urban renewal plan, one of the first in the country that erased a substantial part of the heart of the city's industrial and downtown heart. In its place was a vast expanse of grass with a few stand-alone buildings placed at a distance from one another with the two sides of the triangle graced by the Allegheny and Monongahela Rivers. As Lewis Mumford noted in his book *The Highway and the City*, "One look at the cluster of skyscraper offices that now rise in the 'rehabilitated' area of Pittsburgh known as The Point should convince them of their error; a handful of skyscrapers standing in a glittering freight yard of parked cars is a contribution to neither business nor urban beauty."

In 1957, one hundred acres of the Hill, the heart of the city's black community and center for jazz-filled nightspots, was cleared for a Lincoln Center–style cultural island with an opera house, symphony hall, and theaters. It was never built, but eight thousand residents were displaced.

Clearly, highways halted in midconstruction or before construction—not necessarily designed by Moses—in communities across the country were stopped by citizen protests that usually included long, delaying lawsuits. Where highway projects were derailed completely or in midstream, downtowns and neighborhoods have held on or regenerated—if enough urban fabric was left to do so. In many cases, however, the highway fever did not cool with Moses's departure. Alternative routes were selected, some implemented. Whether they were better or worse is hard to know, but too many cities have been crippled by highways through the city. Even more were started but never finished, leaving unnecessary cleared land in their wake.

San Francisco

An earthquake in 1989, not common sense, took down San Francisco's vigorously opposed and never-completed Embarcadero Freeway on the waterfront and redirected federal transportation funding into investment in the city's subway system. The rejuvenation of that moribund waterfront is now a model of success with its seven-mile promenade of sidewalks, palm trees, and historic trolleys connecting to Fisherman's Wharf, a restored ferry terminal, farmers' market, and new hotel. Nearby property values have skyrocketed 300 percent.[33] But citizens, led by a straight-talking Mayor Joseph Alioto, had stopped the freeway's completion years before. He said during a 1974 Senate hearing on the cause of our transportation crisis that placing an interstate highway link along the San Francisco waterfront just to give cars access to the Golden Gate Bridge was unacceptable. "I wouldn't let them complete it," Alioto recalled. "I said tell everyone to slow up and enjoy themselves in this beautiful town. . . . There isn't a view like this in the world. You don't have to zip through it." Alioto had wrestled long and hard with strong-arming highway builders. "That crowd would put a freeway through the Vatican if they had a chance and could save space or money," he said.

Pittsburgh, Detroit, Portland, New Orleans, Hartford, Baltimore. These were significant cities in the 1940s. The country watched them, along with New York, and followed the path being forged by Moses. "In 1964, when Robert Moses completed his major highway building . . . no other metropolitan region in America possessed 700 miles of such highways. . . . Even Los Angeles, which presented itself to history as the most highway-oriented of cities—which was, in fact, not a city in the older sense in which New York was a city but a collection of suburbs . . . —possessed in 1964 only 459 miles of such highways. No city in America had more than half as many miles. . . . But nothing about his roads was as awesome as the congestion on them."[34]

MOSES LISTENED TO NO ONE

In June 1955 urban critic Lewis Mumford wrote in the *New Yorker*, "Before we cut any more chunks out of our parks to make room for more automobiles or let another highway cloverleaf unfold, we should look at the transformation that has taken place during the last 30 years in Manhattan." This, of course, did not happen.

But equally significant, Moses and the highway lobby starved the subways, bus, and railroad systems of funding. Even before the war, Caro points out, the realization emerged that more roads breed more traffic, that building more roads would not solve traffic congestion, and that the only answer was coordinating mass-transit improvements with highways. Moses adamantly opposed this idea in every way possible and controlled all possible funding to thwart it. Worse, he designed every road in such a way that transit cannot be added either on the highway median or parallel to the road, as many planners advocated, even passing up the opportunity to cheaply buy the land adjacent to highways for future transit.

City planner F. Dodd McHugh, working on a master plan for New York airports in the 1940s, urged Moses to provide space along the Van Wyck Expressway to JFK. In the 1950s, Moses ignored studies demonstrating economic value by providing mass transit along the Long Island Expressway. When the Triborough Bridge and Tunnel Authority, under Moses's firm control, piled up surplus after surplus, Governor Rockefeller and Mayor Lindsay tried to spend some of that surplus on mass transit. Instead, Moses refused to let that happen and instead just planned another road.

The Moses image of being above politics was a myth; he fed the political machine with lucrative contracts, fees, and all kinds of favors to ensure support for his projects, especially, as Mumford wrote, from the well-placed "real beneficiaries of the system to whom it means jobs and prestige, contracts and profits." As Joel Schwartz points out, "Behind closed doors, he handed choice locations to redevelopers, allowed them to occupy sites at their leisure, and encouraged them to build luxury high-rises without regard for city plans. At Manhattantown, Moses allowed redevelopers with Tammany ties to squeeze rent from the black occupants of condemned tenements. Manhattantown showed Moses's consort with the powerful, his contempt for the helpless, and his racism."[35]

If anyone deigned to oppose or seriously question one of his projects, those contracts instantly dried up. He so mesmerized the New York press for decades that it turned a blind eye to his ruthless manipulations and the scandals and inequities his policies fostered. He conducted government in secret and by fiat and showed nothing but contempt for critics. He often did more than that. As Caro discovered:

> And if Moses possessed no derogatory information at all about an opponent or his forebears, this was still no guarantee against attack. For Moses was an innovator in fields other than public works. He practiced McCarthyism long before there was a McCarthy. He drove Rexford G. Tugwell out of his City Planning Commission chairmanship—out of New York, in fact—helped drive Stanley F. Isaacs out of his borough presidency and destroyed public careers of a dozen other officials by publicly, and falsely, identifying them as 'Pinkos' or 'Planning Reds' or 'followers of the Ogpu,' the Soviet secret police.[36] There were two widespread Communist witchhunts in New York City, one in 1938 and one in 1958. Both relied heavily on 'information'—much of it innuendo and outright falsehood—leaked to newspapers by Moses.[37]

He went after Joe Papp, trying to cancel his already extraordinarily popular Shakespeare in the Park. In 1958 Papp had been called before the House Committee on Un-American Activities. He refused to say whether he had been a communist but denied he presently was one and refused to identify friends who were or had been. Moses only learned about this a year later through one of his key assistants. He sought to cancel Papp, spreading lies that Papp was a "communist of long-standing" who "took the Fifth Amendment again and again." But, as Caro points out, the Senate hearings that brought McCarthy's downfall were in 1954, and this was 1959. Papp was a street fighter and knew how to play to the press as well as Moses and, in this case, better.

MOSES IS BUILT INTO THE SYSTEM TODAY

But as much damage to urban America that I believe Robert Moses wrought, I, too, long for a new Robert Moses. Why? Because then we would have an easy target to fight as new oversized, heavily public-financed, isolating "demolish and rebuild" projects are proposed and continue to erode our cities.

In New York, if Moses or a look-alike were in charge, it would be a lot easier to fight such plans as the oversized Atlantic Yards development with thirty-three hundred parking spaces at one of the best transit hubs in the city,[38] new Yankee Stadium parking garages replacing local parks, the Ground Zero separateness, the shopping mall and office-park mentality, and the Willets Point and Columbia University clearance plans. What we actually have is the ghost of Moses haunting the "system." Most big schemes—including new waterfront parks and big developments—bypass the local review process. Instead, they proceed under the auspices of the Empire State Development Corporation, a state authority that makes all decisions and holds public hearings but is not subject to the same local approval standards, just as Moses invented.

Private developers now get public dollars and tax incentives with impunity. Eminent domain—or just the threat of it—is used more for private profit than legitimate public purposes; Moses used it for what he, at least, defined as a public purpose even if his definition of "slum" was self-serving. Planning departments today are powerless in the face of well-placed developers, assuming those planners even object to the oversized and inappropriate development overwhelming all corners of the city today. Often those planners seem to see their mission as expediting new development, confusing development and planning. Some projects exhibit design appeal, but a well-designed, wrongheaded project is just that—a wrongheaded project well designed. Good design is never enough to overcome inherent urban weaknesses.

Except where public opposition succeeds, citizen participation is a mirage. Scores of public hearings occur, and negotiations are well publicized. In the end, final agreements reflect what the developer and politicians wanted in the first place, with givebacks built in as sops, creating the illusion of compromise. The final plan has no relation to what a complex, organic addition to a particular place might have been. And the public participation never comes until the plans and designs are set, not in the beginning when the agenda is formed. At that point, public input can only tinker, not really shape, any plan. In fact, the process today might just as well be designed by Moses. "We have a development czar in New York State now who can override any local control issue," says Kent Barwick, former president of the Municipal Art Society, referring to the Empire State Development Corporation. "Robert Moses would be deeply jealous of that authority. It has the power to go in and do what it wants with the vague requirement that it consult with local officials with no public input required." Now, if Robert Moses were here leading all these movements, what a field day we critics would have.

Despite what Moses believed, the end does not justify the means. "Getting Things Done" in a democracy is not as important as *what* gets done and *how*. And on both counts, alternative methods and programs to Moses's would have done New York better, along with the cities that followed its course. Revisionists view him as more constructive than destructive, more builder than demolisher, more a creature of his time than the shaper of his time, and the man we have to thank for the modern city. I disagree.

The physical achievements, whether judged good or bad, are undeniably mighty in breadth, scale, and obstacles overcome. But the danger in a revisionist view of history is that it takes on a life of its own. That life often becomes myth, like the incorrect belief that Mussolini "at least got the trains to run on time." Two questions are critical: Did the damage he wrought outweigh the good? My answer is yes. Were alternatives available to meet the city's need for infrastructure, transportation, and neighborhood repair? My answer again is yes. Without Moses, those alternatives had a chance; with Moses, they did not.

If you want to put Moses in a positive light, then favoring the car-centric, lower-density suburban vision of the city goes with it. Fortunately, many understand that under that scenario, cities are doomed. The reviving cities today, in fact, are redensifying; rebuilding local transit; revaluing existing assets like traditional neighborhoods, historic and plain architecture, and shopping streets; and taking down elevated highways and skyways. A good observer can't miss seeing this.

WHOSE URBAN VISION?

Moses's own view of his era and rationale for his actions was that the city needed saving, but the question should be, "From what?" After the war, cities had problems that needed to be addressed. The infrastructure of existing roads and transit needed repair and expansion. Deteriorated buildings needed upgrading and some replacement. Public facilities needed renovating and additions. Slums were a problem, but how to define the problem and the solution was open to question and debate that Moses would not permit. No consensus existed that wiping out whole working-class neighborhoods was a solution to real problems nor that the towers-in-the-park were the answer to anything. Social and economic challenges cannot be met solely by physical creations.

Urban vibrancy had dimmed when resources were directed to the war effort, but the solution was definitely not to demolish whole swaths of the urban fabric and hope that what remained would not fall apart. The value of social and economic networks was greater than the new structures to be built by dispossessing them. Mending the urban fabric, repairing and replacing different pieces around the whole city, could have included many new projects, large and small, but never on the ripping scale of what Moses proposed and never at the same staggering social or financial cost. For example, investing more in the neglected public transit instead of just the convenience of the private car would not have precluded vehicular access, just not made it the priority. Today we struggle to re-create a transportation balance.

Was the city better off after Moses? We had thirteen expressways to help people get in and out of the city, but we had less mass transit to get people around the city. We had some celebrated new projects like Lincoln Center, the United Nations, the Coliseum (now gone, replaced by Time-Warner Center), and a money-losing 1964 World's Fair that gave the city Flushing Meadow Park. But we still had a crumbling infrastructure and a maintenance burden for the new projects that continue to cost dearly. And as investigative reporter Fred J. Cook wrote about Moses's slum-clearance program in a 1956 exposé in the *World-Telegram and Sun*: "It is a system under which neighborhoods actually have deteriorated; it is a system under which the number of apartments, already inadequate, has been reduced for years to come. It is a system . . . beginning again the cycle of overcrowding and bad housing that creates slums." And as architect and planner Robert Goodman observed, "The inhabitants of our dormitories for the poor have all the 'symptoms' of poverty as those living in adjacent tenement areas, without even the consolation of the corner stores, storefront churches, street life and lack of bureaucratic administration of their old 'slum.'"[39]

DENSITY IS NOT THE PROBLEM

Moses and many planners since made the fundamental mistake of thinking density was the problem, failing to distinguish between density and overcrowding. Diminishing density, which almost all urban renewal and slum-clearance projects did and still do, does not diminish or solve problems. Problems are just shifted elsewhere and, in fact, exacerbated as new units built are rarely in the same quantity as those destroyed. Fewer units mean more chances of overcrowding.

Density is critical to vibrant urbanism. Mass transit, local retail and the jobs that go with it, well-used public spaces, and other elements of genuine urbanism can't survive without density. Car-based neighborhoods in a city function like suburbs out of the city. They are holes in the urban fabric, undermining the whole by weakening specific parts. There are, as the late *New York Times* architecture critic Herbert Muschamp described, "projects physically located in a community but contributing little value to it." And as Jacobs explained, "Densities are too low or too high when they frustrate city diversity instead of abetting it."[40] They can't be determined by the formulas and ratios planners favor.

Moses diminished both density and the number of affordable dwellings, thus guaranteeing continued overcrowding. He also guaranteed inflexible projects that stood like islands apart from areas of the city that would eventually dynamically and organically rebuild themselves around those islands. The real causes of slums were unaffected and in many cases made worse.

Ironically, today people assume that high-rise means high density when, in fact, the modest low-rise mixture of individual buildings bulldozed for urban renewal was higher in density than the tower replacements that were purposely less dense than what was demolished.[41] Three- or four-family modest-scale houses built close together with tenements and slightly higher but still small apartment houses in between provided the density of once vibrant neighborhoods. That is what was lost. Today, this same density is so admired and expensive in Brooklyn.

The myth of density was so promoted that today the idea remains pervasive that density causes crime, poverty, and other urban ills. Ironically, in communities where density has either been thinned or resisted, overcrowding is often the result.

The Social and Psychic Dimension

Moses dismissed all suggestions of alternatives to total clearance and to the misery caused by displacement. "No one has yet suggested a way to clear slums without dislocating people," he said. He was correct. Clear slums without dislocation, no; regenerate slums with minimum dislocation, yes. One is strictly physical and simple, the other organic and complex.

But what were the causes of slums? Redlining, racism, blockbusting, land speculation, disinvestment, rent gouging by slumlords, migration of rural Southerners into the city, and the gradual departure of the middle class all undermined healthy urban neighborhoods across the country. Slum clearance solved none of these problems and, in fact, exacerbated many of them, especially land speculation, racism, and poverty.

Urban renewal and highway building reduced the number of low-income housing units, dislocated between five hundred thousand and one million people in a city of approximately eight million, and increased rents for many, all while providing a financial bonanza for private interests. Those interests profited from slum-clearance land sales, construction loans, and subsidies. The kind of societal damage described earlier by Elizabeth Yampierre was the result. Much of the social dysfunction created by such dislocation led to so many of the social problems that peaked in the 1970s. "Indeed, when the construction was done, the real ruin of the Bronx had just begun," wrote author and CUNY political science professor Marshall Berman, who as a child was displaced by the Cross Bronx Expressway.[42]

The impact of serial displacement was already a citywide issue in 1958. Only Caro has focused on the human side to a notable extent and only in the one case of the Cross Bronx Expressway. The dimension of the problem and its lasting impact were and are citywide. Dr. Mindy Thompson Fullilove, professor of clinical psychiatry and public health at Columbia, wrote a revealing book, *Root Shock: How Tearing Up City Neighborhoods Hurts America and What We Can Do About It*, analyzing in excruciating detail the social and psychological effects of the displacement caused by urban renewal and highway construction in cities. Her study covered several cities, with similar patterns appearing in each. Referring to the effects of all the cataclysmic disruption, serial dislocation, and the shattering of the critical web of social connections and familial relationships, she wrote:

> It was in a state of overwhelming injury that black people faced a series of crises: the loss of unskilled jobs, the influx of heroin and other addictive drugs, the slow collapse of the family, and the incursion of AIDS, violence, asthma, and obesity. Each disaster increased the impact of the next, and the spiral of community disintegration began to spin faster and faster, just as the last domino seems to fall much more quickly than the first. The present state of Black America is in no small measure the result of "Negro removal."

That is a powerful conclusion, one that most officials ignore or reject rather than take seriously. "We have had a series of policies that continue to displace people," Fullilove noted, "and no real policies to stabilize places."[43] The poor are just placeholders for the next development plan, she observed. The value of the places they are relocated to is destroyed and then can be bought cheap when the time is right. Any genuine stabilization plan or policy, Fullilove argued, echoing Jacobs's articulation of "unslumming," would include investment in an area while keeping the people in place. This preserves the social networks and all the other components of a stable urban neighborhood.

The bottom line is that social dislocation, whether in small numbers or large, is a primary cause of urban instability, costly to the people affected, and costly to the larger city. This is not just logical, an assumption easily understood by anyone who recognizes the authentic urban process. But it is also shown to be true in clinical studies that Fullilove and others have conducted. Between 1991 and 1995, for example, Fullilove interviewed people living in randomly selected households in Harlem. Of those interviewed, twenty-five reported that they had been homeless at some point in their lives. An astounding 25 percent had come from dislocated homes and had been separated from their parents for at least a year prior to the age of eighteen. Some experienced both. "This geographic area," Fullilove points out in conversation, "experienced dramatic disinvestment where familial and social bonds had come apart." What keeps people healthy, she adds, are the "social connections and social solidarity that come with dense social networks."

THE RESURGENT CITY

The city hit bottom in the 1970s. The spiral of urban decay had descended pretty low, following the massive disruption caused by the Moses era. The worst damage was done. The rest was left to burn through most of the 1970s.

Between 1950 and 1975, the city lost one million people. The federal money for big clearance projects eventually either diminished drastically or went dry. Forced to change course, government leaders found new, creative solutions, often following citizen-led efforts. The natural organic process that was taking root around the city finally had a chance to take hold and grow. Where successful, that process enhanced rather than displaced the rich assortment of people, culture, and economy we now celebrate. The unarticulated strategy was to improve conditions and lives where they lived, not try to move people around, what Jacobs described as "unslumming." Unslumming comes not when new people are moving in but when people choose to stay, make their own neighborhoods. This is distinguished from gentrification.

What has evolved organically since the 1970s is exactly what was advocated by Moses's critics, first led by attorney and housing activist Charles Abrams and later Jacobs, Whyte, and others. Demolish judiciously. Replace the unrepairable strategically. Leave standing viable buildings ranging from modest apartment houses to structurally sound tenements to run-down brownstones in need of remodeling. Discourage erosion of industrial space. Invest in transit. Respect and enhance existing schools, community services, and social institutions, all of which contribute to the critical social fabric necessary for stable neighborhoods and cannot be created from scratch. This strategy—Urban Husbandry was how I described it in *The Living City*—left plenty of room for needed demolition of the hopeless tenement or commercial building. But the basic stability of socially cohesive neighborhoods was not further destroyed. And a good deal of the city's wide variety of economic activity was not massively dislodged. (Studies have shown that one-third of dispossessed firms went out of business—a rate significantly above normal business failures.)

Revisionists argue that Moses did what he did because of his love for the city. Even that is questionable. He didn't love New York City as much as he loved his view of what it *should* be, how it *should* function, what *should* replace it. He reshaped New York in his image and with it cities near and far. As Lewis Mumford points out, "In the 20th century, the influence of Robert Moses on the cities of America was greater than that of any other person."

Of all the harmful urban strategies Moses perpetrated, none is as long-lasting and economically destructive as the idea that industry was either dying or dispensable or that its location is easily manipulated. As we will see next, Moses's thinking on this subject remains fully ingrained in the thinking of New York's city planners with the power to continue what Moses unleashed.

-6-

THE FACTORY
The Secret Life of New York Industry

> Urban manufacturing is mostly unrecognized
> by economic development experts, or seen as
> an anachronism. This is a mistake.
>
> SASKIA SASSEN,
> *economist*
>
> A city is a settlement that consistently generates its
> economic growth from its own local economy.
>
> JANE JACOBS,
> *The Economy of Cities*

Donald and I were married in May 1965, five months after I became a full reporter. We returned from our honeymoon, and without telling him, I changed my byline from Roberta Brandes to Roberta Gratz. It did not seriously occur to me to keep my maiden name, something so many professional women do today, including our two daughters, Laura and Rebecca. But three months later my father died. I learned from my mother that my father had been saddened—though he did not tell me—that I had dropped the family name. In his memory—not for feminist reasons—I retrieved the maiden name and changed the byline to Roberta Brandes Gratz. To some of the editors this was a nuisance at best, an annoyance at worst.[1]

6.1 Ramsammy Pullay, nicknamed Dez, has been with the company since 1996. Here he is "benching" or bending a steel furniture component. *Joshua Velez.*

Donald, like me, had been living in the city with no interest in leaving. He had moved in happily after college, having grown up in Pelham, a near-in Westchester suburb. He took a one-room ground-floor apartment facing a small courtyard on East Twenty-sixth Street. He walked to work.

In 1955 Donald had joined the family metal fabrication business, started in 1929 by his father and a partner.[2] Metal fabrication simply means a process by which objects are made out of metal. Steel, aluminum, and copper, primarily, are bent, drilled, welded, polished, and assembled into chairs, tables, architectural elements, exercise equipment, and custom-designed objects. None of this is mass produced. Instead, skilled and semiskilled workmen individually operate the assorted machines that make up the process. Treitel-Gratz (now Gratz Industries) was located on the sixth floor of a six-story loft building on East Thirty-second Street between Lexington and Third Avenues.

Watching the fate of this building and business unfold was for me another source of learning about both the changing city and the working of the urban economy. The evolution of the Gratz family business continues to be instructive, just as my own father's dry-cleaning business provided urban lessons. Gratz Industries, like most city manufacturers, faces an ever-changing array of challenges from both the national economy and city policies. More than eighty years old, it is as contemporary as it ever was.[3]

A 1997 report, *Designed in New York/Made in New York*, noted about the city's "large, complex manufacturing sector": "Although manufacturing in New York struggles with high costs and a continual need to reinvent itself, the frequent public pronouncements of its demise are, as the pundit said, premature. Twelve thousand firms employing a quarter of a million production workers endow New York with what is still one of the densest concentrations of manufacturing in the United States."[4]

Manufacturing: Ever Changing

Treitel-Gratz had moved to Thirty-second Street in the 1930s from a small brownstone on lower Lexington where it started in the 1920s. The East Thirties were filled with furniture manufacturers. By the 1960s, an assortment of small manufacturers and esoteric businesses occupied this loft building: a menu printer, a bra manufacturer, a cabinetmaker, three decorative wood finishers, a manufacturer of machines for glove makers, a typesetter, an umbrella manufacturer, a drapery and slipcover maker, a dinette furniture seller, a gold stamper, a store display maker, and a woman who raised rats. Quite a combination! Some of the businesses worked together on special jobs and were spontaneously and conveniently clustered for the decorating trade. We did metalwork for the cabinetmaker and store display maker and used the upholsterer when we needed that work. Everyone did odd jobs for one another. It is difficult to place a monetary or operational value on this kind of synergy. "By the early 1930s, the company had established itself as the metal shop of choice for, among others, the celebrated industrial designer Donald Deskey," wrote Charles Gandee in an article about the company titled "Heavy Metal" in the *New York Times Home Design Magazine* in spring 2003. Deskey was then doing the celebrated interior furniture for Radio City Music Hall, including the Art Moderne furniture for the office of the great impresario S. L. Rothafel, known as Roxy. Other great industrial designers, like Raymond Loewy with his iconic Coca-Cola machine, George Nelson with his furniture prototypes, and John Ebstein with his toy models for Gabriel Industries, were also customers. The company's history parallels the history of twentieth-century design.

In 1948, Hans Knoll, a German émigré, wanted to bring the furniture of legendary Bauhaus architect Mies van der Rohe to the United States and enlisted the company to engineer and manufacture the Mies line of chairs and tables now considered classics—Barcelona, Bruno, Tugend-hat—all first exhibited at the 1929 International Industrial Exposition in Barcelona. In 1958 architect Philip Johnson turned to Deskey for the interior of the Four Seasons Restaurant when it opened in the base of the Mies-designed Seagram Building on Park Avenue that was also filled with Mies furniture. Johnson was a protégé of Mies and coarchitect on the building, and he designed the restaurant interior with Garth Huxtable. That restaurant, a city-designated interior landmark, was—and still is—furnished with the classic Mies furniture.

In the 1940s, '50s, and '60s, American furniture design was in its heyday. Treitel-Gratz furniture and metalwork were going into scores of new office buildings in New York, Chicago, and other cities and suburbs, especially those designed by Gordon Bunshaft of Skidmore, Owings, and Merrill.

But aside from the building interiors, Knoll furniture, a line of furniture designed by Nicos Zographos, and the industrial-design model work, most of Treitel-Gratz business in the 1950s and early 1960s was actually precision sheet metal for electronic equipment, before that field of work moved to California with the aircraft industry. But as can—and often must—happen in any kind of business, especially manufacturing, as one product line diminishes or moves away, another fills the spot. It happened for Treitel-Gratz as the art world was transformed in the 1960s. Isamu Noguchi had long been a customer for many of his metal sculptures since the 1940s, but Alexander Liberman was the first of a new group of sculptors who came to Treitel-Gratz not just for its reputation for skillful implementation and metal craftsmanship but because of its proximity to Manhattan. Liberman often visited the shop and worked alongside one of our machinists.

People fail to understand the importance of New York City–based manufacturing if they don't recognize the value that industry has to the fields, like art and architecture, for which the city is famous. For designers, being able to implement ideas locally is critical to their craft. Surely, it was true for the long line of leading artists, architects, and furniture designers who passed through our factory. We've always been convenient to a subway. "Urban manufacturing needs to be done where it is used," observes Columbia University professor Saskia Sassen, who has written several books on global capital and the mobility of labor. "This is not an old, outdated condition but a very contemporary one. This is not about the past; this is cutting edge. The specialized service economy demands it; the new economy needs this kind of manufacturing." Designers benefit from proximity in many ways but none so important as what architect David Childs calls "the knowledge of the skilled workers who operate the machines, work with the materials and understand what those can do. They know things you can't put in books. Designers need that knowledge more than ever."

THE CHANGING ART WORLD CHANGED US

In the 1960s Alexander Liberman brought sculptor Barnett Newman to the shop. Newman subsequently brought in a whole group of young Minimalists who were either his friends or protégés, all little known. The Minimalists were changing the nature of contemporary art. Many of them made a big splash with the 1966 Minimalist show Primary Structures at the Jewish Museum. That landmark exhibit defined the Minimalist movement. Donald Judd, Walter De Maria, Sol Lewitt, Robert Rauschenberg, Forrest Myers, Michael Heizer, Robert Indiana, and more—it was a cast of soon-to-be stars.

Just as the company history parallels the evolution of interior and industrial design of the twentieth century, so does it parallel the evolution of the Minimalist and post–Abstract Expressionist art that emerged in the 1960s when the center of the art world shifted from Paris to New York. In New York, the art scene shifted from the Upper East Side to SoHo with the new trend in larger and larger artworks and the opening of the Paula Cooper Gallery in 1967. Key artists exhibiting there came to us.

From the 1960s on, office furniture, custom metalwork, and sculpture dominated. As the field of architecture evolved, so did the content of our production. I. M. Pei, Charles Gwathmey, Deborah Burke, Masimo and Lila Vignelli, Robert A. M. Stern, James Polshek, and Skidmore, Owings, and Merrill, and others, looked to the company to solve fabrication challenges.

Change is inevitable in manufacturing. One big change with a company like ours can shift the whole picture. In the mid-1960s, Knoll took its business away to its own manufacturing operation in Pennsylvania. At the

6.2 Barnett Newman with his first steel sculpture, *Here II* (1965), at Gratz Industries. *Ugo Mulas, courtesy of the Barnett Newman Foundation.*

same time, a new item for production was added. Romana Kryzanowska, the chosen successor to innovative exercise master Joseph Pilates, came to Donald to produce metal exercise equipment, long before his Pilates Method became the rage. In time, Pilates exercise equipment surpassed custom metalwork and furniture as the company's primary product.

Like many New York manufacturers, our work goes all over the country and abroad, more heavily abroad with the weak dollar. But also, like many local companies, our work is part of the fabric of the city, in homes, museums, offices, building lobbies, and the public realm—Maya Lin's *Time Piece* in Penn Station, the button and needle in the Garment District, the Martinelli sculpture on the facade of the United Nations, the Robert Indiana *LOVE* sculpture at Sixth Avenue and Fifty-fourth Street, and the stainless steel and glass Bank of America sculptural logo hanging in the lobby of its new building at Forty-second Street and Sixth Avenue. As the city loses businesses like ours, often unnecessarily, the ability diminishes to design or invent and fabricate locally. As the report *Designed in New York/Made in New York* noted, "New York is home to a highly evolved manufacturing sector, which . . . retains a strong core of production facilities capable of producing goods for world markets. Many of these manufacturers produce for the design-driven market. Fashion, jewelry, publishing, advertising, and marketing—these are New York City's best-known industries in which design plays a key role. But designers are also essential in other lower profile but important New York industries such as custom furniture, architectural woodwork and metal, accessories, lighting fixtures and toys."

In fact, the whole country still manufactures much more than is popularly understood. America remains by far the biggest manufacturing economy in the world, producing more by half than China and two-thirds more than Japan. This is difficult to comprehend because all sorts of primarily technological innovations have increased productivity and diminished dependency on a large labor force. That labor is now increasingly higher skilled than before.[5]

THE INDUSTRIAL NETWORK IS COMPLEX

Manufacturers form a complex web of similar and disparate operators that function both individually and interdependently. The modest and small scale of most of these manufacturers allows for considerable flexibility, quick production, and innovation. As Scott E. Page, professor of complex systems, political science, and economics and author of *The Difference: How the Power of Diversity Creates Better Groups, Firms, Schools, and Societies*, told the *New York Times*: "New York City is the perfect example of diversity functioning well. It's an exciting place that produces lots of innovation and creativity. It's not a coincidence that New York has so much energy and also so much diversity."[6]

The ability of the designer to participate in the fabrication process can be critical, especially since so much of local manufacturing is customized work. In 2007, for example, we fabricated at the behest of Gensler, the national design firm, a rather complicated floor-to-ceiling bronze screen for the lobby of the Park Avenue UBS office building. Ed Wood, the principal at Gensler who designed and engineered the screen, made frequent trips to both the factory and our affiliated space in Harlem where the massive screen was assembled. Most of the fabrication occurred at the factory, but specialized parts requiring machinery we didn't have were produced by a Bronx fabricator. A patinator in Beacon, New York, another fabricator in New Jersey, an engineer in Massachusetts, a rigger in Philadelphia, and a score of local shops all had a hand in this complex structure. At one time, all of these operations could be found in the scattered industrial neighborhoods of New York. No more. And while most of the work stays local, or not far away, the proximity issue makes a difference at every step of the process and in the final cost. Our complex, mostly local network of suppliers numbers close to 150 businesses.

While "experts" have long been quick to declare manufacturing dead in New York and other places around the country, many manufacturing companies like Gratz Industries stay very much alive if flexible enough to adjust to changing times *and* if not undermined by government policies. Too often, industrial districts are declared "blighted" when many diversified businesses exist in the seemingly run-down assortment of industrial spaces.

In an article titled "The Changing Face of Manufacturing in New York City," Sara P. Garretson, executive director of ITAC, the Industrial Technology Assistance Corporation, wrote: "No question, manufacturing has experienced a drastic decline. The cost of doing business here (particularly labor, energy and taxes) has driven away many manufacturers who depend on high value volume and narrow profit margins. Land costs discourage companies that need to expand, particularly those that want large, single-floor production facilities, and environmental regulations have hampered others. The manufacturers who thrive here offer a wealth of lessons the city can use to stabilize, or even expand, its manufacturing base."[7]

Few factory buildings or their districts ever look spiffy. Architecturally, they range from the design worthy to the plain. But together they form a comprehensible pattern built over time as industry evolved. Significantly, industrial neighborhoods contain a mix of scale that accommodates the large factory or the small job shop with residential buildings scattered throughout. The mix of buildings and uses is exactly what sustains the district if not knocked off balance by inappropriate rezoning.

The uneducated or uncurious observer would be unaware of what productive businesses exist in such areas that play an important role in the city's overall economy and social fabric. Few city officials or planners comprehend or appreciate the hodgepodge, gritty nature of an industrial district, nor do they want to. As architecture professor John A. Loomis wrote in the *Livable City* article "Manufacturing Communities—Learning from Mixed Use": "Mixed-use neighborhoods defy neat zoning categories. They are mature communities with integrated networks of activities and building types, woven together over many years from countless incremental, often spontaneous acts of building. They are often inhabited by one or more distinct ethnic groups, which contribute to a rich cultural life."[8]

The city's Planning Department is quick to measure an area when it can show a statistical decline in the number of businesses as justification for an already planned upzoning. Rarely are surveys designed to show an area's hidden strength. One former Planning Department staffer conducted a very revealing survey in the 1990s of Brooklyn's Greenpoint and Williamsburg waterfronts about to be rezoned. "Don't show me those maps of job density," a hostile department boss said. The genuine survey with door-to-door canvassing to really understand what was going on undermined the pronounced assumption that a residential rezoning was in order and would have no negative effect. Honest surveys actually reveal what is needed to improve business rather than replace it. New innovations and new businesses in the incubating stage become known. In fact, one former staff planner says, "They made it clear they did not want to know."

"City government needs to protect the opportunity for new things to get a foothold and live," Jacobs said. "Just keeping things open for opportunity is important. Opportunity, not necessity, is the mother of invention."

Urban Renewal Interferes

Manufacturers, like any business, experience many ups and downs but survive if they can change with market demand. But undisturbed was not to be for Gratz Industries. The story of Gratz Industries should not be viewed as unique. Similar tales are found in all cities.

In the early 1960s, the entire Thirty-second Street block—a mixture of small apartment houses, industrial lofts, and six-story tenements—was condemned for urban renewal to make way for a post office. Because emptying some of the buildings on the site, especially one apartment house around the corner, was a politically hot topic, Senator James Buckley opposed the project. That killed it but not before most of the properties had been condemned as blighted, businesses and residents displaced, and then properties demolished.

The block had exhibited traditional urban vitality, regardless of its worn look. No vacancies existed. In each building, a new tenant appeared when one moved out. Pedestrians filled the street. Shopping and other uses drew them nearby. But, by law, to be an official "Urban Renewal" site, the block had to be declared "blighted." Blighted, in this case, as with so many others, simply means the property is wanted for a different purpose from the one for which it is currently used:

- That the Thirty-second Street buildings were filled with economically viable uses was irrelevant.
- That the buildings were merely neglected by owners waiting for a lucrative government buyout was irrelevant.
- That the buildings could have been economically renovated and upgraded, like thousands of similar surviving properties around the city have since, was irrelevant.

The only relevant fact was, as usual, simple: a new development agenda was set, and manufacturing was not on it. This was just like what was illustrated in the chapters about Greenwich Village and SoHo. Manufacturers and manufacturing districts have experienced this over and over and not just in New York. This is *not* a natural process; it is about real estate.

The federal government continued to own the cleared Thirty-second Street site after the post office project died. Empty land is a monumental lost opportunity in cities everywhere. In this case, it was even more: an unnecessary loss of economic diversity. Years later the land was sold to a private developer. The federal Urban Renewal program was notorious for condemning *privately* owned property for a *public* purpose with the help of eminent domain, then eventually selling it to another *private* property owner. This still happens today and is a source of great injustice. The abuse of eminent domain is a scandal of national proportions.

Until a U.S. Supreme Court decision (*Kelo v. New London*) in 2005, the purpose of eminent domain was understood to have been primarily for taking private property for a public purpose such as school construction, roads, public utilities, or other clearly public uses. Over time, however, this fundamental idea had been corrupted to permit the taking of private property from one owner to give to another private owner, this time a real estate developer or commercial user.

All over the country, small businesses have been erased by eminent domain to make way for shopping centers, big box stores, or corporate office parks. Modest, middle-class residential communities have been partially or completely erased for a commercial, so-called mixed-use project of a grand scale or for a stadium or casino.

One woman, Susette Kelo, a divorced nurse, renovated a falling-down Victorian house. She and her neighbors in New London, Connecticut, had watched neighboring land confiscated for development that hadn't even materialized, again empty land representing an erasure of economic and social value. This area was once the heart of a downtown community that many cities once had but lost to "renewal" projects over time. These were traditional areas where people walked to work, to shop, to school, or to the movies, the very kind of neighborhoods experiencing great popularity today where they still exist. Susette Kelo and her neighbors sued to stay. The city wanted their land as part of a Comprehensive Plan that included condos, a hotel, and labs for Pfizer, Inc. The case went to the U.S. Supreme Court, ending with a decision broadening government's power of eminent domain.[9] Jane Jacobs, who didn't oppose eminent domain in principle, contributed to the brief and noted: "Eminent domain is being terribly abused, almost as a war-making instrument, an instrument of force, not being used decently." Enormous repercussions have ensued across the country since the decision.

And, as on Thirty-second Street, this urban renewal project has been another debacle. Eight years later, no construction has occurred. The land is empty. The promised 3,169 new jobs and $1.2 million a year in tax revenue never materialized. Developers, desperate to obtain financing, even applied to HUD for taxpayer-backed loans to build luxury rental housing. So far $78 million in public funds have been spent on the project with nothing to show for it but ninety acres of emptiness and lost businesses, jobs, and retail uses, disrupting lives and erasing a community. Quite a definition of economic development. (In November 2009 Pfizer Inc., for whose expansion the land was cleared, announced the closing of its already huge New London R&D headquarters and made plans to sell or base those offices and leave New London entirely.)

To Long Island City

In 1967, with the impending demolition of the Thirty-second Street building, Gratz Industries moved across the Queensborough (Fifty-ninth Street) Bridge to Long Island City, Queens, where it remains today. The first move was to a rental building. Then we purchased the current eleven-thousand-square-foot cinderblock building in the shadow of the Queensboro Bridge. At the time, Long Island City, on the east side of the East River across from Sutton Place, was primarily a manufacturing district, the city's most concentrated in-

6.3 **Gratz Industries today in Long Island City. Mural was painted by a local youth organization.** *David Rosencrans.*

dustrial district outside Manhattan. Three subway lines, the Long Island Railroad, and the Long Island Expressway are all accessible here. Tenements, small apartment houses, apartments over retail shops, and even a one-block designated historic district of brownstones mark the area. Enclaves of classic working-class areas in Long Island City have shops, churches, small workshops, and single-family homes. The majority of firms are like ours with twenty-five employees or less. Within its 330 blocks are twelve hundred industrial firms employing forty-five thousand people.

The proximity to Manhattan was critical to the location choice, since our customers are mostly Manhattan based. And Long Island City was filled with the kind of suppliers we used, minutes away as unanticipated needs arose during the manufacturing process. This complex and delicate assortment of seemingly unrelated businesses enables all to network easily among themselves. Even the gas station next door to our present location has found need for our services and we for theirs. Time is money in any business, and these critical connections make this delicate economic network work.

Taking the business out of New York never tempted Donald. Fully one-third of the district's businesses moved from Manhattan.[10] The upholsterer moved to Long Island City, too. Several of the businesses from Thirty-second Street closed for good, years earlier than they otherwise would have. Others scattered. Several left the state. Some would have evolved into different businesses, if not fatally disturbed. Undoubtedly, some of them would have disappeared naturally as their markets dried up or they sold out to larger companies, but, as can be observed today in similar types of buildings, new businesses would have moved in. Furthermore, just because a business might eventually close doesn't justify closing it down before its time and denying the business owner the opportunity to sell profitably to a subsequent owner or to reinvent the business.

Many companies manage to reinvent themselves, as *New York Times* economics editor Catherine Rampell has demonstrated. With a combination of "perseverance, creativity, versatility and luck," she notes, many companies have survived, and some, like IBM, have transformed themselves many times. Few remember, as she points out, for example, that radio was pronounced dead in 1953 with the advent of television. "But the industry revitalized itself by tapping into new markets," such as "the youth music market, congregating around the car radio . . . longer-form news and talk radio."[11]

Gratz Industries reflects this pattern, and our production assortment continues to evolve. Some of it stays the same, like the classic modern furniture and Pilates equipment. Some of it continues in a different form; the cast of architects, industrial designers, and sculptors changes. New markets open up, like interior work for hotels, high-end retail stores, and restaurants in New York and abroad. And who could have predicted a renewed interest in Modernist furniture, giving us an opportunity to again manufacture Modernist pieces long out of production, or the global spread of Pilates, with our equipment in demand from Sweden to South America to Russia?

Some materials, like bronze, or processes, like chrome plating, are too costly to offer easily. And some items are more cost-effective to outsource. But all of these are normal adjustments in any business. Yet the skills of our twenty-five or thirty workers—machinists, welders, benders, polishers—remain applicable, as adjustments come along. And our pay scale and health insurance—as in all manufacturing—are probably double the pay of chain-store retail or tourist industry services, the kind of businesses

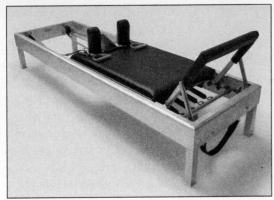

6.4 Pilates Classic
Reformer is the
primary piece of Pilates
equipment. The whole
Pilates line is now
a major portion of
our business.

whose job-creation ability is overpromised by city officials. And unlike chain stores and hotels, our profits stay in the local economy.

Our employees mirror blue-collar New York. The city's production workforce is 63 percent immigrant and 78 percent people of color, similar to ours. In classic manufacturing form, some employees come with one or no skills and learn new ones as they move along. A few have been with the company for ten, fifteen, even thirty years.

As the number of New York businesses employing these kind of workers diminishes, the opportunities disappear for blue-collar workers and the immigrants who keep coming. Yet these employees live in neighborhoods around the city, support local stores, send their kids to local schools, fill church pews, and volunteer in civic activities. They are not suburban commuters. They pay local taxes. None would find a place on Wall Street or in the tourist industry to which the city so heavily caters.

INDUSTRIAL SPACE IS BEING NIBBLED AWAY

In recent years, Long Island City has gone through a number of zoning changes that have eroded its status as the heart of industrial New York. City Hall and the Planning Department, through several administrations, have devalued and dismissed the importance of this district. Such a view can only be based on ignorance. Notes Professor Sassen, "City agencies don't understand this aspect of the economy. Misunderstanding continues since the 1980s that we need only luxury office buildings. New York has steadily been getting rid of or shrinking industrial zones. They fail to distinguish be-

tween what can leave the city and what benefits from being in the city."
Sassen is a world-renowned economist known for her specialized knowledge and understanding of urban economies, with several books to her
credit. She is called upon and listened to in cities around the globe, but the
message she has been delivering to New York for several decades has fallen
on deaf ears. She has repeated these messages many times over the years,
noting years ago, for example, that the "ripple (or 'multiplier') effects of
manufacturing in the regional economy are as much as one third larger than
those of comparable service sector activities." Her voice is not alone.

A 2003 report, *Engine Failure*, by the Center for an Urban Future and
funded by the Rockefeller Foundation, suggested a dramatic shift by the
city away from traditional FIRE (finance, insurance, and real estate) businesses, large-scale commercial properties, and policies that increase real
estate costs and overwhelm small businesses with multiple permits and
diminished services. A "doomed strategy," the report labeled existing policies. And this was before the biggest wave of upzonings that priced out so
many. While large firms shed jobs and small ones add them, New York
"has become one of the worst environments for entrepreneurs and growing firms," the report said.

What city shapers value in Long Island City and other industrial neighborhoods is the proximity to the East River waterfront with its views of the
New York Harbor and Manhattan's East Side. Real estate is king in New
York. That manufacturing is "dying," "dead," or "going overseas" is the
usual false justification for rezoning. Reality is more nuanced and not as
simplistic. If you repeat an untruth often enough, however, and it gets repeatedly quoted in the press, the unknowing public believes it. The erroneous notion is promoted that space for industry is protected under the
upzonings and through other nonzoning policies. Those other protections
don't work, however, and enforcement of the so-called protections is lax.

In fact, these planners cling to the pre–World War II idea of questionable validity that there is no manufacturing in the future of New York
and only the FIRE and service (some say "servant") economy is appropriate for the city. No matter how many times the city loses *all* the financial
job gains of recent years each time it experiences a recession, officials continue to pursue an all-out effort to revive the same financial sectors and ignore the industrial. Often they cite amazing statistics for vacant industrial
space, but it is always a lie. The lie is this: counted in those statistics are
underwater and marshlands, airports and low-density space near airports,

public transportation yards, water and sewer services, and solid waste disposal and other unusable sites. This becomes the rationale for a policy of continuous upzoning of industrial neighborhoods.

Upzoning, the method by which the local government increases what a developer can build, inevitably drives up the cost of industrial space. This is not rocket science; this process never fails. If you zone for high-rise development and offer incentives as well, it will happen. No comparable incentives exist for property owners to retain a manufacturing use. Predictably, slowly but surely, industrial space is being lost. As it diminishes, nibble by nibble, the cost of creative production in New York becomes increasingly prohibitive. The death of industry becomes a self-fulfilling prophecy. Long Island City is only one example.

A 1991 study of Long Island City commissioned by the Public Development Corporation under Carl Weisbrod and produced by planner John Shapiro describes in great detail its strength as an industrial area, identifies the threat posed by greater commercial development, and encourages retaining industry. Three major recommendations were made to spur new office development but reduce the risk to manufacturing:

- Upzone close to the subways and provide incentives to stimulate new office development in a concentrated and limited core.
- Invest in the subways, sidewalks, roadways, and open space to attract office tenants.
- Create more restrictive zoning in the industrial ring—"manufacturing sanctuaries"—to reduce real estate speculation, preserve space for manufacturing, and prevent the conversion pressures from spreading.

Adam Friedman, former head of the New York Industrial Retention Network whose mission is to assist the survival of the threatened industrial sector, endorsed these recommendations and added a few innovative ones as well. In an op-ed article in *Newsday* in 2001, Friedman suggested, "If a developer prefers to create a building without manufacturing uses, he could pay an assessment fee that goes into a fund to help manufacturers purchase their buildings, to subsidize their relocation or to encourage the development of new rental properties for manufacturers. Developers could also purchase the unused development rights on industrial properties in the surrounding areas, allowing them to build more in the core."[12]

Not unexpectedly, the city did (1) and (2) but not (3) and ignored NYIRN's suggestions. Speculation that his article predicted is exactly what happened, clearly what the planners wanted. Manufacturers were priced out and continue to be. In addition, it actually hurt the commercial development by dispersing it beyond the core. Without density in the core, it was harder to attract restaurants, shops, and other desired amenities.

Friedman also wisely suggested creating a new "balanced mixed-use" district that would deny conversions to residential use if 50 percent of a block was already converted. Lots of less than six thousand square feet, he added, could be converted to residential. Those ideas as well were ignored. It seems that it's okay for government to intervene to encourage office and residential development and give tax breaks to big box retailers, but it is beyond the role of government to preserve the conditions that foster manufacturing.

I, too, testified at that Planning Commission hearing on behalf of Gratz Industries. Picking up on some of Friedman's ideas and adding some of my own, I said:

> Create manufacturing sanctuaries. Assess new office or residential developments with a manufacturing retention fee. Assess, as well, current property owners whose property values will jump considerably. Use the money to help manufacturers either buy their building or underwrite the predictable rent increase that will follow your up-zoning. Where possible encourage development of new manufacturing space but require its rent to be affordable in a manner similar to requirements of a percentage of new residential apartments be kept affordable.
>
> Give incentives to manufacturers, like my husband, to retain their manufacturing business. This city knows how to offer gargantuan financial incentives to big new developments. Only modest ones are required here. And you know inevitably incentives will be offered to new development in this area. Why not offer it to those who don't sell their industrial property for another use?
>
> And why not think along the lines of farm trusts and land conservancies who buy the development rights from land to retain agriculture and open space? Gratz Industries would be the first in line to entertain such a proposal, one that would guarantee beyond our ownership that our space would remain industrial.

Industry Nurtured and Sustained New York

For its eighty years of existence, Gratz Industries has represented the kind of small, individualized manufacturing resource that once sustained New York. The city's once-booming economy was almost entirely based on just this kind of small and medium-size manufacturer. Collectively, the city's manufacturers produced a dizzying and endless array of goods shipped around the globe. Until the 1980s, even while the city was losing jobs, tax collections from industrial New York underwrote the bulk of the city's budget for public services.

New York was never the classic smokestack city dominated by a single large industry like steel in Pittsburgh and Youngstown, automobiles in Detroit, Boeing in Seattle, rubber in Akron, or Kodak in Rochester. What heavy industry New York had was gone by the 1940s, notes sociologist and professor Robert Fitch, such as "chemical plants, slaughterhouses, animal-fat rendering plants." Instead, small production and processing industries formed the bulwark of New York's economy. As Fitch observes further: "The whole form of industrial life was practically invented in New York City. As early as the 1940s the city's chief manufacturers were not producing standard, assembly-line products. . . . They were a bunch of little guys practicing 'agglomeration' economies—the cost savings that result from businesses locating next to each other . . . small inventories, design driven, relying on 'external' rather than 'internal' economies of scale. Instead of savings from long production runs, capital savings arise from not having to sink capital in expensive equipment available nearby."[13]

The breadth and diversity of its economy and greatest concentration in the world of manufacturing jobs insulated New York well from the ups and downs suffered by the singular-industry cities. In large measure, it is the reason New York fared better during the Depression than many other cities. New York's bewildering array of businesses provided entry-level jobs for the steady flow of immigrants, many who eventually opened their own businesses elsewhere in or out of the city, adding to the national economy. The same immigrant absorption and new business creation process is visible today. New immigrant-generated, innovative businesses exist all over the city and since the 1980s have been probably the most unacknowledged source of the city's regeneration.

The staggering variety of products once made in New York City is long forgotten, and what is made here today is hardly known. Whereas

Manhattan was a manufacturing center dominated by the garment, jewelry, and printing industries, Brooklyn probably had the greatest variety of products. Brooklyn was the fourth-largest manufacturing center in the country by the early twentieth century, home to makers of Brillo soap pads, Heinz ketchup, Spalding sporting goods, Eberhardt-Faber pencils, Domino sugar, Pfizer Pharmaceuticals, Pechter Fields Rye Bread, Topp's chewing gum with its popular baseball cards, Rockwell chocolate bars, Gretsch musical instruments, Corning Glass Works, Esquire Shoe Polish, and Meri-lei's that were exported to Hawaii to be sold to tourists, many from New York. Coffee, tea, machinery, paint, paper boxes, shoes, soap, and beer added to the variety of goods manufactured there. Queens had Swingline staplers and still has Steinway pianos and knitwear. The Bronx had American Bank Note and Farberware. Harlem had Madame Alexander Dolls, furniture repair, high-end woodworking, and window manufacturing. And the Brooklyn Navy Yard produced an assortment of vessels.

The diversity and number of manufacturers are comparable today. The variety is huge, the individual scale of each often modest. Many big companies that started small and grew large and then left the city did so because at a certain scale, experts note, large companies don't need the advantages cities offer smaller companies. As Jacobs emphasized, the important point is not how many mature companies leave the city; the important measure is how many new ones grow in their place. That is the measure of a dynamic economy.

From the 1890s to 1950s, the New York City region was the dominant manufacturing center of the country, and the city's economy was its most robust.[14] Industrial production dominated. Then the agenda changed to office and residential priorities, public investment in supportive infrastructure plummeted, and decline set in. All the areas designated for demolition and rebuilding were doomed, no matter how many successful businesses remained and wished to stay. For its two decades of subsequent steady decline, New York still had the nation's largest concentration of manufacturing jobs. They were not disappearing for natural causes. It is not a coincidence that the decline of industry here, although started before World War II, paralleled the increasing momentum of Urban Renewal clearance projects planned and implemented by Robert Moses. For the century of its economic preeminence, New York's economy had grown organically with a spontaneity that produced its unpredictable hodgepodge of businesses. This unique economic system remained a national stronghold longer than conventionally believed.

By the 1950s the combination of a technological revolution and low-wage competition from the South or abroad threatened New York's and the national industrial economy. Many factors were cited, including containerization and cheap suburban land available for the preferred one-story plants instead of the multistory lofts. This was the favored rationale for assuming the inevitability of deindustrialization and planning to make it so. Yet if global competition made it all so inevitable, how is it that in the 1980s, Los Angeles gained precisely the manufacturing jobs New York was losing, especially in the garment industry that doubled there? Some manufacturers moved elsewhere, but there were plenty left behind.

Clearly, attention and investment went elsewhere during the war. A neglected infrastructure made doing business in New York more challenging, while new, cheap suburban alternatives multiplied. Rail freight diminished, while highways multiplied and cheaper truck freight increased. But as has been pointed out in many ways in this book, the answer to neglect and deterioration is not replacement. The assumption that manufacturing was dead, of the past, or anachronistic was as ill-considered as the idea that a financial- and information-based monoculture could fully sustain a "new" economy or that it did not have production needs.

POSTWAR OPPORTUNITIES MISSED

Three directions were possible after the war. One focused on nurturing the strengths of an innovative entrepreneurial class and the workforce behind it. The second focused on replacing it with a real estate– and service-based economy. The first valued the tradition of individual innovation and entrepreneurial instincts; the second valued the city's real estate almost like a natural resource to be mined into a shining replacement. A third possible direction would have been to balance the first two, providing for the survival and strengthening of the old economy and recognizing its contemporary value and emergence and growth of the new economy. Under this direction, neighborhoods would not have been replaced wholesale. New housing would have been fitted in where opportunities allowed. Small numbers of businesses would have been forced to relocate, but appropriate neighborhoods would still be available to locate in. But that third option is not what happened.

"Information-" or "knowledge-based" jobs, in the FIRE sectors, so the conventional rationale went, were the wave of the future. Thus, a carefully planned, neat, newly created city to house a financial-based, information-age, and service-based economy would purposefully replace a messy, organically grown, unpredictable, and fundamentally flexible economy that had evolved according to no imposed plan. For this scenario, growth of the city economy was overly dependent on leveraging the value of real estate instead of the entrepreneurial spirit and energy of people whose innovative ideas create the new businesses, jobs, and meaningful expansion and growth. This scenario is also heavily dependent on public funds or incentives of all kinds, what many call "corporate welfare." This distorted economic policy at best leaves the city vulnerable to economic shifts that would be mitigated with a more balanced and diverse economy in place. Instead, the current overdependence on Wall Street evolved.

In the 1980s, for example, white-collar jobs on Wall Street and in other FIRE sectors proliferated with head-spinning growth. Proponents of this "new economy" strategy patted themselves on the back. Then in the late 1980s, the stock market took a nosedive. Jobs were lost with the same head-spinning velocity they had grown. According to the Federal Bureau of Labor Statistics, Manhattan, where most FIRE-economy jobs take place, lost 149,000 jobs between March 1989 and April 1992. This equaled the entire gain since 1980. In other words, by the early 1990s, all the job gains of the 1980s were lost. Considerable revenue was lost, too, due to all the corporate tax breaks given to businesses to remain in the city and create jobs.[15] Even more jobs were lost during a period of heavy mergers and consolidations. Of course, jobs in this sector multiplied again in the boom of the late 1990s. A bigger loss occurred in 2008. If, however, New York had nurtured its multiple economic assets, tumultuous ups and downs in one dominant sector might have been balanced by sectors experiencing less dramatic shifts.

Also during the 1980s, as city policy and investments were focused on nurturing this white-collar economy, industry experienced insult upon injury. Developers were getting tax breaks, subsidies, and cheerleading from all city agencies. But industrial districts were suffering service cutbacks and infrastructure neglect. Gratz Industries experienced periodic break-ins in the 1980s. When Donald sought some police assistance, he was told there was one patrol car for the entire district. When it rained, the street in front of the shop flooded due to a clogged drain that caused long-lasting backup.

All pickups and deliveries occurred at this frequently flooded entrance and were made exceedingly difficult. I remember Donald's innumerable frustrating attempts to call one city agency after another, over and over again, pleading for relief. It took years.

FALSE GOD OF EFFICIENCY

The 1929 plan of the Regional Plan Association (RPA) first reflected in a formal way the emerging disdain for the messy, difficult to define, individualized assortment of industries and the similarly varied residential neighborhoods. While this view of urban life already had been growing, it was codified in the 1929 Regional Plan and embraced and implemented enthusiastically by Robert Moses.

Here was the first potent articulation of the view still in force today that the city's major asset was not its pulsating, complex industrial economy, its diverse entrepreneurs, its patterns of innovation and new start-ups, its energetic immigrants, and its skilled and semiskilled workers but its residential and corporate real estate. Rearranging the city's built form to be more orderly, less congested, and cleaner was the goal. Real estate became the resource of choice to effect the change.

This transfer of economic priority was not a natural market shift but one of official policy. The RPA, the establishment's favorite nongovernmental voice, led the chorus for this refrain, supported by "The Plan." City officials, financial leaders, corporate heads, newspaper editorial boards, unions, architects, and the emerging profession of city planners embraced it wholeheartedly from 1929 forward. The appeal of this strategy was strengthened by the federal funding that would fuel it.

The broad acceptance of this urban strategy in effect gave Robert Moses carte blanche to pursue his vision of the efficient city of demolished, replaced neighborhoods connected by an efficient spaghetti network of highways. Under the skillful direction of Moses, the master builder who could get things done, all things would be put where they belonged. Productive efficiency would be the result, so the thinking went.

Cities, however, cannot be reduced to an efficient order like a machine, as Jacobs has taught. Efficiency stifles innovation and a diverse economy, as one learns well from her book *The Economy of Cities* (1969). In this, Jacobs's second and probably most important book, she shows in several ways how "efficiency fails to make a city prosper." In her chapter "The Valuable Inefficiencies and Impracticalities of Cities," Jacobs describes how Manchester, England, stagnated due to its "efficient specialization," becoming an "obsolescent city" and "the very symbol of a city in long and unremitting decline." The economy of Birmingham, on the other hand, "did not become obsolete, like Manchester's. Its fragmented and inefficient little industries kept adding new work, and splitting off new organizations, some of which became very large but were still out-weighed in total employment and production by the many small ones." The key measurement of the economic rate of a city, Jacobs points out, is "the addition of new work to . . . older work" in which Birmingham excelled.[16] Her analysis of efficient and stagnant Manchester contrasted to fragmented and diverse Birmingham remains instructive.

The efficiency that has great value, Jacobs also shows, is the efficiency of density, what she calls the "concentrated market." That concentrated market "is, in itself, an efficient thing. And its chief characteristic, that it is concentrated, makes it possible for small, fragmentary, exceedingly special, weak or much-duplicated enterprises to operate with considerable inefficiency and yet often get away with it. But apart from this, as far as I can see, the conditions in a city that promote efficiency of operation are in conflict with the conditions that promote development work."[17]

Economist Sandy Ikeda provides a similar take on this idea:

The modern demand to rationalize the city and to make it 'more efficient' is misplaced. A living city cannot be efficient. Efficiency, in the economic sense, presupposes an overarching plan against which measured outcomes can be evaluated. A living city, however, follows no such plan. It is itself the unplanned, collective result of the countless individual plans executed continuously in it day after day.

Neither can it be inefficient, because that too presupposes a system-wide plan. Both efficiency and inefficiency presume that we know how things ought to be, what success and failure look like, and that's impossible in the urban dynamic. Instead, . . . a living city is a 'dynamically stable' process . . . [that] generate[s] order through time. It embodies trial and error, surpluses and shortages, apparently useless duplication, conflict and disappointment, trust and opportunism, and discovery and radical change. These are in the nature of the living city.[18]

The valuable economic density that Jacobs refers to, fostering new business formations and breakaways from existing businesses, is what is being eroded as the city's industrial neighborhoods are purposefully transformed into high-end residential communities, erroneously labeled "mixed use" because some retail and commercial space is included. This continues the never-ending search for order. Overdesigned order represented by large-scale redevelopment projects inhibits new patterns of activity. It stifles the fundamental DNA of the New York economy, which is more complex, unpredictable, fluid, and diversified. The result is a monoculture revolving around financial and related services—in other words, Moses's sterile vision of efficiency.

Thus, in the name of rational planning for the efficient service and financial economy, many of New York's industrial jobs were deliberately and needlessly lost, an occurrence still happening in twenty-first-century New York. City officials boast of a much diminished rate of displacement from renewal-type projects since the days of Robert Moses. Maybe the loss is less, but, of course, what's left is already diminished considerably. And maybe it is more scattered around the city. But it is like being a little bit pregnant: first month or ninth, you are still pregnant. Displacement is displacement at any rate. The loss continues to be unnecessary and avoidable, given available alternatives. The pursuit of oversized replacement projects continues to cause needless disruption and economic and social loss.

City officials, for example, are enthralled with new mall development where possible, missing the opportunity to preserve small, growing businesses or create new, much-in-demand industrial space to incubate new ones. In 2007, a large city-owned vacant industrial building provided a redevelopment opportunity for which the city sought a developer. The location was in Sunset Park, a traditionally mixed industrial and residential area in Brooklyn. One development team proposed to recycle the existing building, making it totally energy independent and giving it a modern new design. Most of the space would be retained for industry, but retail and residential would be added modestly. The developer's primary goal was to preserve industrial space and advance a sustainable development opportunity. The proposal offered an interesting mix of uses asked for by the city. But, instead, the city chose a politically well-placed developer planning a conventional shopping mall and upscale housing mix. The idea of preserving some space for industry was dropped entirely. Fortunately, the economic collapse caused the winning developer to withdraw, and a chance exists that the first developer interested in industrial space may be the winner after all.

Moses's power diminished and then disappeared in the late 1960s and '70s, but the industrial erosion continues under new policy formations.

Long Island City Escapes for a While

For reasons not apparent, most of Long Island City escaped the worst of this urban strategy for a long time, probably because the focus and interest of planners and real estate speculators were elsewhere in the city. Our factory is just south, in the shadow of the Fifty-ninth Street Bridge. North of the bridge had been totally bulldozed and replaced in the 1930s with a thirty-six-hundred-unit tower-in-the park public housing complex—twenty-six six-story buildings on six superblocks and a lot of fenced-in green grass. But south of the bridge—down to the entrance of the Queens-Manhattan Tunnel and the beginning of the Long Island Expressway—escaped major surgery. It was the strongest and densest area of the whole city's industrial economy until recent years.

Long Island City's escape from the worst was not through any positive action on the city's part. In fact, commercial and residential development was heavily encouraged by the city but went nowhere fast because the market wasn't there yet. But even at slow speed, redevelopment began a nibbling trend that has accelerated over time. In 1989 CitiCorp built a huge tower with a facade of green glass and ninety-seven million dollars in tax abatements. Several suppliers of materials like aluminum and small job shops disappeared. All sorts of ancillary service businesses—pattern makers, cabinet shops, upholsters, machine shops—were priced out and moved away. The farther they moved, the higher became our cost of doing business. The serious erosion of this industrial heartland was perhaps later than other areas but gaining momentum.

Queens West, at a onetime waterfront port and terminal site with varied industrial buildings, was begun—a massive, highly subsidized complex of high-end residential and commercial towers meant to be a whole new neighborhood, not unlike Battery Park City but surely out of place in a functioning industrial district. Five apartment buildings went up in ten years. The plan for sixteen apartment buildings with forty-four thousand apartment units and four office towers on this seventy-four-acre site gained momentum in recent years as new development raced forward all over the city.

Long Island City's Hunters Point community was hardly a blighted outpost. A longtime industrial and manufacturing district was mixed in with a historic Italian working-class community that included small locally owned businesses. Thirty-two companies were located there, employing two thousand people doing everything from baking to servicing elevators. Some land had been vacant for years, left from the 1940s when land-banked property was held for large-scale schemes, such as a possible UN residential village, directly across the East River. The Planning Department staff member who surveyed the area in 1980 found that this was a robust mixed neighborhood with a fair amount of thriving industrial businesses. Her bosses did not want to hear it. They demanded instead that she sign a document reporting it was blighted. She resigned instead.

THE PAST IS PAST

Absolutely no one is suggesting that New York City will or could once again become an "industrial" city, but this is a simplistic way of dismissing economic realities that question current thinking. The challenge the city fails to face is allowing existing industry to survive instead of being excessively sacrificed on the altar of real estate development. The loss of industry is no more now a natural process than it was over the past fifty years.

The twenty-first century needs a new set of definitions for such things as "manufacturing," "industry," and "crafts." New York has become a so-called service, not production, economy. But what is service and what is production? Is Kinko's a service provider with its copying services or a manufacturer with its production of bound books or both? Is the stained-glass craftsman who restores deteriorating old church windows but also designs and produces new lighting fixtures a craftsman, service provider, or object producer, or all three? And what is the designer who designs for others and also produces a small inventory to sell retail on-site? Then there is Sarabeth's Kitchen, which started twenty-nine years ago as a jam-and-jelly shop and became one of the city's top gourmet-food brands. Two Sarabeth's Kitchen restaurants are quite popular. The brands are sold in grocery stores, with baked goods and soups added to the mix. So is it a restaurant, wholesaler, or retailer, or all three? And what about the hairdresser who provides the usual services but also produces his own line of products, manufacturing and selling them? In what categories are these businesses classified and measured in the economy?

Likewise, one need not advocate bringing back lost industry to promote the idea that manufacturing is not only alive but actually an undervalued economic sector with new things bubbling up that could be nurtured instead of strangled. Industry can't be brought back to what it was, but neighborhoods where new innovations might emerge could be protected and nurtured. New elements of a green economy—products to serve the new interest in green construction—are starting here in hidden ways, but may not be able to find the space in which to grow, expand, and add new work to old.

The important thing is to recognize the multiple values that existing industry has for the city and its workforce and not lose what exists because a real estate speculator has designs on a site or a district. A manufacturer today may lose a market or find a more economical way to produce overseas, but that does not mean another form of production won't fill the unused space or employ the same skilled labor, just as Gratz Industries has over the decades. And who could anticipate production work returning to our shores because of the weak dollar, increased production costs abroad, and high shipping costs?

CREATIVE CONVERSIONS

As larger businesses leave today, the spaces once occupied by single-use tenants are sometimes being divided up for multiple smaller businesses. One of several buildings once occupied by the Eberhardt-Faber Pencil factory in Greenpoint was divided into dozens of smaller spaces for woodworkers, designers, jewelry manufacturers, printers, and artists. The forty-thousand-square-foot former Nassau Brewery in Crown Heights has been carved up into two dozen smaller spaces ranging from four hundred to four thousand square feet, and includes a mix of metalworkers, designers, video producers, and others. The former Monti Moving & Storage building, also in Crown Heights, is now home to twenty-five workspaces that include artists, woodworkers, film editors, set designers, and architects.

Also significant is the proliferation of food-preparation businesses occupying old factories. This is especially true of ethnic specialty foods, the fastest-expanding segment of the growing New York food industry that includes everything from a variety of breads to chocolate and beer (again). The problem comes as these small companies succeed and grow and need larger spaces, the kind the city is losing rapidly. Many will be forced out of the city. At the same time, Friedman notes, not enough big spaces are being divided into small spaces, as O'Connell and Sweeney have done, as we will see. Start-ups need rental spaces under ten thousand square feet. A space mismatch exists. The supply is the bigger older buildings for single-use tenants, and the demand is for small and medium-sized properties. This seeming contradiction becomes understandable when one observes that the big ones frequently are converted to high-end condos, not new industrial space.

TRUE ECONOMIC DEVELOPMENT IS A RENEWABLE PROCESS

Many familiar corporate giants—Kodak, General Motors, Apple Computers, Macy's—were started by a single innovative entrepreneur. Starting in a small, limited way, each one expanded, shifted its product mix, and evolved into a corporate giant. That process is not anachronistic. It repeats itself regularly when not stifled by city policies. This is the DNA of economics. Some famous companies didn't start out making what they became known for, as Catherine Rampell pointed out in her article mentioned earlier about companies reinventing themselves. Nokia made paper before cell phones. Toyota made looms before cars. Some auto-parts manufacturers today have reinvented themselves into windmill turbine producers. For city planners to continue to plan and rezone as if industry can't survive, grow, and be a significant contributor to the city economy is dramatically shortsighted. The rezoning of almost every industrial district in the city reflects that shortsightedness.

Ironically, one city agency is actually proving the wrongheadedness of the official no-confidence vote in industry. The Brooklyn Navy Yard with more than forty buildings, four million square feet of industrial space, 230 tenants, and five thousand employees has a never-ending waiting list for production businesses wishing to get in. It can't build new buildings fast enough to fill demand. Only one business, so far, has folded during the economic collapse, and another was right there to fill the space. Current tenants keep growing and want more space. Demand grows while available space citywide keeps shrinking.

The entrepreneurial processes from which new businesses emerge and grow have a timeless legitimacy and repeat themselves if conditions exist to allow the process to continue. The repetition of the process often looks somewhat different over time, but the repetition of a natural process remains nonetheless. *Real estate development doesn't create economic growth; it follows it.*

Again we return to Jacobs's point that economic growth comes when new work is added to old and imports are replaced with local production. One of the most important and oft-cited examples she presented to demonstrate new work created by import replacement was the Japanese bicycle industry, which, when her book was published, was a world leader. She wrote: "Innovations are the most important kind of goods and services added to older work. But for every true innovator, there are many, many imitators. Innovations make up only a fraction of the many individual instances in which new goods and services are added logically to older work. Imitation is a shortcut. It seldom requires as much trial and error as innovations do. The repairing of things is often the older work to which the newer work of making the same things is added."[19]

In late-nineteenth-century Japan, Jacobs observed, the Japanese economy was in the doldrums. The import of Western goods was preeminent, including bicycles, a popular means of transportation. A conventional response by government to this evolving business would be to invite a Western manufacturer to set up shop, as has been done in many places with car companies. Alternatively, the government arranges for the establishment of a manufacturing business, copying Western models and importing Western machinery and professionals to operate the new facility.

Instead, Jacobs observed, the Japanese production of new bicycles grew out of the extensive network of one- and two-man repair shops that sprang up to service the growing demand. Instead of importing expensive parts or cannibalizing valuable existing bikes, the "repairmen" learned to manufacture replacement parts, thus becoming light manufacturers. New entrepreneurs became the "assemblers," in effect producing their own line of bicycles. "The Japanese had acquired a pattern for many of their other achievements in industrialization: a system of breaking complex manufacturing work into relatively simple fragments, in autonomous shops," Jacobs wrote. "Parts making has become a standard foothold for adding new work." In fact, Sony too, she noted, began at the end of World War II "as a small-parts shop in Tokyo, making

tubes on contract for radio assemblers, and was built up by adding to
this the manufacturing of whole radios . . . and other types of communication and electronic goods."

Ford Motor Company had a similar beginning, Jacobs pointed out.
Henry Ford failed twice to set up complete car-manufacturing operations
but succeeded the third time by buying "from various suppliers in Detroit
every single item he needed for his cars—wheels, bodies, cushions, everything." Ford evolved into a manufacturer from there. Philco, Motorola,
Lockheed, Grumman, and others followed similar patterns. Today, parallel success stories are all over the place, including Apple, Google, and Mi-
crosoft, all garage start-ups.

Ironically, a variation of this very process can be observed today in, of
all industries, bicycle manufacturing. Portland, Oregon, often hailed for
its early farsighted public transit policies, built an ever-expanding light
rail network, increased densities, and rolled back its greenhouse emissions.
It was also early in planning and developing bike lanes. This was in the
1970s when the focus of that city's transportation planning shifted from
accommodating the automobile to promoting the revival of mass transit.
Today 3–5 percent of Portlanders commute by bike, the highest percentage in the country, according to the Census Bureau.[20] The increasing popularity of biking caused an increase in sales of national brand bicycles
produced elsewhere by large corporations.

Now, Portland has an expanding twenty-mile network of bike boulevards, and a growing number of custom-made bike builders. These are
the import replacements Jacobs cited as crucial to expanding a local economy. An estimated 10 small shops produce high-end handmade bikes, and
approximately 125 bike-related businesses produce racks, components for
manufacturers, and clothes. Bike sales and bike tourism keep growing as the
city increases bike lanes and bike-friendly amenities. A cycling industry
and its offshoots now account for an annual one hundred million dollars
and a thousand jobs in the local economy. Ten years ago, a small number of those employees were working for retailers selling mass-produced
bikes—the imports in the process Jacobs described.

The public health– and environment-minded city government recognized an emerging new industrial sector. Now it is working with the small
number of bike builders to improve business and accounting skills as well
as hosting handmade bicycle trade shows. This is government at its best,

nurturing spontaneous and genuine economic development. Often, assisting small businesses in marketing, accounting, and joint advertising is more beneficial than tax breaks or incentives. For genuine economic growth, nurturing the homegrown business beats luring the mature one from elsewhere with tax breaks and other expensive incentives.

Unplanned economic growth has occurred in New York City over the years, but in most cases that growth has been nurtured by not-for-profit developers or under-the-radar small entrepreneurs, especially in the furniture-making industry.[21] The Greenpoint Manufacturing and Design Center started by David Sweeney, for example, rehabilitated five vacant North Brooklyn buildings containing five hundred thousand square feet, creating space for more than a hundred firms. Officially, this spontaneous new growth has been handicapped at best and stifled at worst.

OFFICIAL LOGIC IS ELUSIVE

The current official approach to industrial districts in New York is schizophrenic. Officials go through the motions of protecting them, and then undermine them with erroneous planning and zoning policies. On the one hand, for example, the mayor created the Office of Industrial and Manufacturing Businesses and charged it with creating sixteen special Industrial Business Zones offering industries additional services but no legal zoning protection. Zoning in manufacturing districts still allows hotels and big boxes that erode needed space. Land values escalate because of proximity to new residential and commercial development that the upzoning encourages. Industry continues to be priced out. Incentives are available to relocate into an industrial zone but not to survive if you are already there.

A 2008 study revealed that big boxes are like big vacuums, sucking up local retail dollars and sending them to home offices out of the city.[22] In addition, they are huge automobile and truck traffic generators, low-wage job creators, and magnets for more vehicular-dependent businesses. In manufacturing districts, they squeeze out industry. Take, for example, the city-approved—actually encouraged and subsidized—Ikea superstore, the largest in the country, on Brooklyn's waterfront in Red Hook.[23] Why, one might ask, would the city want to encourage a mile-long site with spectacular harbor views of the Statue of Liberty and Lower Manhattan to be given over to a windowless superstore surrounded by parking?[24] But that is the least of questionable notions apparent in this project.

Peninsula-shaped Red Hook once formed the heart of Brooklyn's rough-and-tumble working waterfront with multiple cargo piers, location for the immortal film, *On the Waterfront* (actually filmed in Hoboken). Here is the Erie Basin, the southern terminus of the Erie Canal, and the reason for its vibrant shipping history. In the 1930s, bustling streets and solid housing were cleared to build the Red Hook Houses, a twenty-eight-building public housing complex with 8,000 residents, the city's biggest and most insular. A combination of two- and six-story redbrick buildings, this was the country's first high-density public housing and Brooklyn's largest. Another eighty acres were cleared for an enormous containerport. But after many buildings were demolished and businesses displaced, the project was considerably downsized and land left vacant. To accelerate the area's demise, also under the direction of Robert Moses, the Gowanus Parkway was built on the pillars of the former elevated BMT subway line, bisecting South Brooklyn along Third Avenue. The once job-rich waterfront was cut off from the upland neighborhoods and the rest of the borough. More than 1,300 families and 100 businesses were erased and the area sent into a permanent downward spiral.

After the war, federally subsidized mortgages and the new suburbs did the rest to undermine Red Hook. The 1990 census showed 11,000 people living where 22,000 lived in 1950. Most of them were then and still are on public assistance. Containerization and the Port Authority's shifting of waterfront work to New Jersey accelerated the decline. The most imaginative idea city planners could come up with for this view-rich acreage of waterfront was luxury high-rises with ferry access to Manhattan so residents didn't have to pass through the rough neighborhood.

While city planners plotted rezoning scenarios, one man had a different vision. Greg O'Connell, a former cop, started buying Civil War–era warehouses on abandoned piers in the late 1980s. He renovated and slowly converted them for small businesses hungry for the space. Rejected for financing by banks and with no public money and, in fact, in the face of official government skepticism, O'Connell single-handedly proved experts wrong. More than 120 businesses and 1,250 jobs occupy O'Connell's seven buildings, everything from a glassworks to a music set–making studio.

I first encountered O'Connell in the 1990s while researching *Cities Back from the Edge*, and I included the beginning of his story in that 1998 book. But O'Connell, probably the star example of the civic-minded developer, was really just beginning then. He had transformed only the first warehouse, a nineteenth-century massive brick structure with heavy timber frames, some with terra-cotta arches. Subsequently, he renovated more waterfront warehouses and other spaces, gave free space to community groups and community activities, built a public park and walkways along the water using all recycled materials and solar night-lights, and renovated neglected inland residential properties for affordable housing.

Slowly, officials and the public took notice. Artists were moving into Red Hook, priced out of the string of earlier successful artist neighborhoods. Then O'Connell redeveloped a former warehouse for the city's premier fresh food market, Fairway, founded on the Upper West Side in the 1940s. The plan was both brilliant and community sensitive: supermarket on the first floor, prepared-food operations with jobs for local residents on the second floor, and live-work spaces on two floors above. And since Red Hook is nowhere near a subway stop and is served poorly by bus service, Fairway—at O'Connell's insistence—developed a shuttle bus going to the public housing where few residents had cars. The city has since improved regular bus service, and a water taxi stops at its waterfront entrance.

By then, it was all over for Red Hook as a fairly priced, remote outpost of the city. Red Hook was on the map. Ikea landed the next choice site. But a very significant and historic business remained on this twenty-two-acre site—a Civil War–era graving dock, one of the few working graving docks left in New York Harbor. Graving docks are used for ship repair and are based on relatively simple technology—a ship floats in, a door closes behind it, and the water is pumped out, leaving the hull exposed for repair. Red Hook's dock was in continuous use from 1866 until evicted by Ikea. In fact, it was where the city's own sanitation and sludge-removing vessels were repaired and one uniquely large enough to handle a 750-foot vessel where others can't.

Ikea went through the motion—pro forma, of course, for every new development—of promising jobs, "500 or 600" of them, none of which would be promised for local residents. Understandably, even the remote prospect of jobs was enough of an enticement to excite the local job-seeking population.

Now this was curious. This 346,000-square foot facility would be Ikea's largest in the country. But the 311,000-square-foot Ikea in New Haven, Connecticut, has only 350 employees. Why the Brooklyn store would need 50 percent more than that number of employees is inexplicable indeed. (Ikea refuses to disclose the actual number of jobs created and how many are local.) Nearby neighborhood businesses see the Ikea traffic go by, but none of it also comes to them.

Speaking of jobs. The graving dock had 100 well-paying skilled jobs with additional ones added when a supersize ship repair came in. Apart from their own inherent value and higher pay scale, these kind of jobs are better than retail jobs as an economic multiplier for goods and services in the community. Certainly, no economic growth will emerge from Ikea, no innovations or new work. That all happened years ago in Sweden, Ikea's home country. Instead, what is emerging is more big box development nearby where a fabulous old manufacturing building sits. It will probably be demolished instead of creatively reused.

So first we have a spectacular waterfront site given over to a big box. Then we have a singular and significant operating business displaced. Then we lose 100 solid skilled jobs. But there is more, much more.

The graving dock is paved over for a 1,400 car parking lot *even though* two alternative designs showed how Ikea could have the same parking lot just as conveniently on the store's other side, sparing the graving dock. This parking supplements generous parking under the building. Here is yet another classic example of where the city could have had both, *not* either-or, but both big box *and* big boats. Officials chose not to force Ikea to move the parking lot to achieve both. As of April 2009, the parking lot has been full twice![25] Most weekdays it is completely empty.

Also on the site were two significant rows of historic redbrick warehouse buildings, of the same Civil War vintage as the O'Connell buildings and several designated city landmarks elsewhere on the Brooklyn waterfront. In these buildings could have been the kind of innovative new businesses incubated in O'Connell's buildings and more economically beneficial.

That the graving dock was of great local and national historical significance apparently made no difference to city officials who treat preservation lightly. The National Trust for Historic Preservation, the Preservation

League of New York State, the city's Municipal Art Society, and other similarly prestigious organizations appealed to city officials to intervene but were ignored. In fact, it was pointed out that the whole Ikea project was contrary to the Planning Department's own 1992 Waterfront Plan for the site, which strongly called for this piece of the waterfront to remain zoned and dedicated to continued maritime activity. Public access and commercial activity were to happen in other areas of the peninsula, including where Fairway opened. So much for official "plans" and officially protected economic uses.

All this comes while the city is expanding its use of the waterways for commuting, commerce, garbage transport, ocean liners, and park development. Where will the ferries, tugs, passenger ships, and other vessels be maintained and repaired? The city is reportedly investing a half-billion dollars for new passenger ship terminals, ferry landings, and transfer stations, yet eliminated a functioning graving dock. In fact, now the city is reportedly looking to create three new graving docks.[26] Where is the logic in that? A Maritime Support Services Location Study, begun in the summer of 2006 by the city's Economic Development Corporation, noted that the "port has experienced a resurgence in waterborne transportation" and a considerable increase in the barge and tugboat fleets in recent years.

So many of these development conflicts are presented erroneously as either-or, take-it-or-leave-it proposals. Invariably, alternatives offered by the public make possible a better combination. But without pressure from city officials or the city council that rubber-stamps these Planning Commission approvals, Ikea and all developers hold fast. The fallacy of designating protection zones while destroying viable places has never been satisfactorily explained. "Conformity and monotony, even when they are embellished with a froth of novelty, are not attributes of developing and economically vigorous cities," Jacobs wrote. "They are attributes of stagnant settlements."

In the press, the favorite themes are jobs versus home owners, gentrifiers versus the poor, affordable housing versus historic preservation, all individually legitimate issues made out to look like they are in intractable conflict, a competition among worthy values. These are easy, formulaic interpretations that include some truths but miss the bigger picture, the picture that illustrates the potential for balance that achieves multiple goals, not just blind development goals. Ironically, this comes at a time when new fields for innovation are clear and in need of the space to incubate.

Products and processes are in demand to address the market for green products, environmental cleanup, new sources of energy, building restoration. Space for these economic opportunities continues to diminish. Jane Jacobs foresaw this potential in 1969 at the end of *The Economy of Cities*: "In highly developed future economies, there will be more kinds of work to do than today, not fewer. And many people in great, growing cities of the future will be engaged in the unroutine business of economic trial and error. They will be faced with acute practical problems which we cannot now imagine. They will add new work to older work."

Less and less of this is possible in New York City.

-7-

THE UPPER WEST SIDE
What Moses Couldn't Kill

> A living city is always becoming.
>
> ———————
>
> SANDY IKEDA,
> *economist*

Then as now, it is spoken of as THE West Side—sometimes Upper, more often just *the*—but in reality it is dozens of communities lumped together under one geographical umbrella, running roughly from 59th Street to 110th. More than a community, the West Side was and still is a state of mind.

The earliest hints of the city's turnaround were first recognized in the 1970s on the Upper West Side, even though signs could also be seen in other parts of the city, notably Brooklyn. But the Upper West Side was in the spotlight with all the massive urban renewal clearance projects going on and the presence of Lincoln Center. And the press was, at the time, very Manhattan-centric. Lincoln Center kept the media's attention.

Flanked by two great Olmsted parks, divided by three distinct shopping streets, and served by two subway lines and several crosstown buses, the West Side had solid urban assets that helped it sustain considerable urban renewal erosion without killing it entirely. What the West Side also had that served as a crucial ingredient of rebirth was a wealth of solid, if badly abused, brownstones—blocks after blocks of them. Renovators started slowly buying them in the 1960s. In 1969, Donald and I bought

7.1 Our brownstone on Eighty-seventh Street. We occupied the basement and parlor floor and rented the top two floors.

and fully renovated a four-story brownstone, creating a duplex for ourselves and two floors of rental apartments above.[1]

Most West Side brownstones had been built in the late 1890s for middle-class families but had not fared well over time. They had been broken up into tiny apartments and neglected by absentee landlords. But they were easily converted back to single-family, double-duplex dwellings or other combinations. House tours became a popular vehicle for early "brownstoners" to publicize the alternative lifestyle they were pioneering. Donald and I happened to go on one, were impressed, and thought a brownstone was the answer to our desire to stay in the city. We were already comfortably settled in a two-bedroom apartment on West Eighty-first Street across from the Planetarium and a half block from the Central Park playground. But the brownstones we saw were extremely attractive and still cheap. A house, backyard, barbecue, sandbox, and still be in the city? What an appealing concept, a compromise for the suburban resister.

I never thought of Donald and myself as urban pioneers, but when we bought the brownstone on the Upper West Side, many of our friends and relatives thought of us as such. How could we not want a house in the suburbs? When the kids started to come, most young couples at that time in the late 1960s headed out. This was the pattern expected of our generation. Neither Donald nor I would hear of it. Donald had been raised in a near-in suburb but wanted to stay in the city, as I did. Other city couples were resisting the outward trend, finding ways to stay in the city.

A NEW URBAN RENEWAL PARADIGM

Three years later, we were gone, back to apartment house living. It was too much "pioneerism." The neighborhood was in a state of flux. Our area of the Upper West Side was under intense pressure from the thousands of legitimately angry West Side residents displaced for Lincoln Center and Lincoln Towers to the south. We were on the southernmost block of the West Side Urban Renewal area that uniquely called for a combination of brownstone conservation on the midblocks and new apartment-house construction on the avenues. This plan was promoted by the City Planning Commission, under chairman James Felt, in contrast to the Moses total-clearance pattern. Here, primarily the avenues were cleared and replaced with both public housing and high-rise, economically mixed apartment houses; the midblock brownstones were, for the most part, spared. These were the same quality brownstones Moses declared irredeemable elsewhere. This was a new urban renewal model, new for New York City and, in fact, for the country.

The *AIA Guide* notes:

> The concepts that emerged were radically different from those of earlier renewal efforts. Exploitation of the highest possible rental scales was abandoned. Clearance and rebuilding from scratch, once the only redevelopment tools, were combined with rehabilitation and renovation, particularly of the basically sound side-street brownstone row houses. Steps were taken to ensure an economic and social mix within the district by providing not only separate low-rent projects but also low-rent families within middle-income developments. Finally, the plan provided for phased development from West 97th Street south to encourage the relocation of on-site tenants.[2]

The idea of a neighborhood of mixed-income housing really appealed to us. But understandable unrest on the part of displaced low-income families to the south had resulted in frequent protests, community conflict, and personal unease. Hundreds of displacees were now demanding replacement housing.

Urban renewal never produced new quantity as much as it destroyed old. The bulk of what was built, in this case Lincoln Towers just north of Lincoln Center and most of the West Side Urban Renewal area, was intentionally for the middle class, beyond the financial reach of the displaced poor. Keeping the middle class in the city was the avowed purpose. Thus, the legitimate pressure for more low-income housing made life difficult and unpleasant for many pioneering young families. The tensions, heated community meetings, and angry protests were unsettling, to say the least. Neighborhood stabilization was difficult to achieve. An overall tension in the community impeded the potential for community spirit and comfortable integration. Crime was already a problem. All this discouraged us.

It was a particularly painful situation for me, already juggling full-time work at the newspaper with motherhood at a time when this combination was not common and very difficult. The idea, so accepted today, of taking a few years out of a career to stay home with young children was for me not an option. I would never have gotten my job back. Some of my editors were already leery of having a working mother as a reporter. I was the first at the *New York Post* since World War II. Other women reporters were married, but the only other one with children was the fashion editor and she was a grandmother. I did, however, find ways to restrain my career in order to give me more time with my kids. Feature assignments allowed me to leave home late in the morning or come home early in the afternoon. Occasionally, I persuaded an editor to let me write the story at home. I also had wonderful child care, but our babysitter even felt unsafe taking the children to the playground during the day.

My mother lived around the corner, frequently visited my kids, but she, too, was uncomfortable walking with them in the neighborhood. The accumulated tensions were too much. I was confident that in another decade, the neighborhood would be fabulous, but in the meantime, we had two daughters to raise and a life to lead. We couldn't wait. I was correct about the neighborhood eventually being fabulous. I was off by only a couple of years. It took a little longer than a decade, but, for sure, today the area's an established winner.

THE ERA OF FEAR

It is easy to forget the well-founded fears we lived with in the New York of the 1970s. Crime seemed rampant. Fear was the emotion of the day. It motivated many residents to move away. The 1970s saw the explosion of drugs, especially crack.

Gold necklaces were torn off pedestrians. Handbags were snatched, giving rise to the popularity of the shoulder bag. Young kids had the sneakers they were carrying taken away from them as they traveled to and from school. In parks, kids were known to have their bikes taken out from under them by menacing kids. Flower boxes were emptied or taken in total. Cars were constantly broken into or stolen. And bikes were an immediate invitation to disappearance even if locked with a heavy chain. These were facts of life all New Yorkers lived with, not just pioneering brownstoners. But despite the hurdles, slowly but surely, more families were buying brownstones and were taking the risk.

Not us. We tried but wanted out. We jumped at an opportunity in a wonderful Central Park West apartment house, one of the Art Deco twin towers that makes the Central Park West skyline famous. Back to traditional door-man apartment-house living. We sold the brownstone at a loss and have not moved since. That was 1972.

We had experienced petty crime firsthand. Most was nonthreatening. Prowlers on the roof. Unsuccessful break-in attempts. Stolen bikes and plants. But the worst occurrence I recorded in the following story. Ironically, this style of the firsthand story became a New York City journalistic art form in the 1970s—writers detailing their personal encounter with crime. In the New York of today, this experience isn't remotely anticipated.

It might seem strange, but the following incident was not what caused our departure. It was more of an accumulation of things—disappointment in the neighborhood, the hostilities and tensions in the community, the difficulties raising young children under tense conditions, and, of course, daily fear. But many families remained undaunted, and some neighbors and friends from those days are still in place and happily so. And although the following occurrence did not drive us out, it was indeed traumatic.

"Mugged: A Victim's Story"
New York Post Daily Magazine, February 6, 1971

"You've now had the prototypical New York City experience. You've totally committed yourselves to remaining here and raising your children here. You've renovated a brownstone and now you've been mugged."——A Friend.

It is the ultimate fear we all live with in this city, the fear of being mugged. It is the nightmare that all New Yorkers shared but until it happens to you, it remains just an abstraction, something you've heard about or read about, something that happened to someone else.

Then it happens to you and you discover that the reality is more brutal, more psychologically devastating than you imagined possible. You know it could have been worse physically, you know you could have been killed. But you can't imagine how anything could jar your psyche more.

It happened to me. I know.

It was a weekday evening. My husband and I had just come out of an apartment house on 86th St. between Amsterdam and Columbus Avenues. The hour was 11:30. We had only a three-minute walk to our house around the corner on 87th. It was snowing slightly. The ground was slippery. We walked carefully, focusing on the ground.

Eighty-sixth is a major crosstown street, rarely deserted, always plenty of cars and buses passing by. Upper West Side residents hardly concern themselves with the major thoroughfares; it is the side streets, like the one we live on, that we worry about. They are frequently deserted. Anyone with normal city fears would anticipate a mugger lurking in the shadows.

But we were on 86th and there were several pedestrians not far away. We saw two youths walking toward us, one about 5-5, the other about 5-9, both black. The tall one wore sunglasses. I thought of nothing at the sight of them except that I had to turn slightly to pass them and that I should be careful not to slip.

Suddenly they were right in front of us. I don't even remember falling, just landing. I was apparently pushed with such force that there wasn't even time to try to break the fall by instinctively turning to the side.

I landed squarely on my back, with the back of my head and spine hitting hardest. I didn't lose consciousness and as I started to get up I saw my husband fighting with our assailants. I screamed like I never thought I knew how, so loud it was heard on the 19th floor of a nearby apartment house.

They hadn't laid a hand on my husband when they pushed me down. In fact, he hardly realized what had happened until he saw the short one pick up the bag I dropped and start running. Instinctively he went for him, yelling the profanities of an outraged husband. They fought. My husband doesn't recall the mugger putting up much of a fight.

Then the second youth jumped on my husband and it was at that point I screamed. I spotted a police car passing in front of us on 86th. The policemen heard the scream, came running. The muggers fled in opposite directions, the pocketbook left behind.

The police gave up the chase after only a block or so and I wonder if they really tried hard enough to catch the pair. The muggers had a very slight lead. They could have been caught. But I also wonder if I can blame them for not trying harder.

So many times police have risked their necks to catch such people, only to discover that the victims, fearful of reprisal, refuse to press charges. How did they know I would have gone to court? Is the policeman wrong for feeling, "I don't want to get killed either." Or, to complain that he arrests criminals only to see them back on the street in a short time doing their thing?

. . . I have written about victims of all kinds of crime, heard their agonies, listened to their demands for action. I have wrestled with the issues of crime and justice. Still I have no answers, just questions.

The whole incident was over in less than five minutes. The police offered to drive us to the hospital. I declined, thinking my injuries were not serious. All I wanted was to go home and get into bed. They drove us around the corner. I called a doctor friend and inquired what I should do for myself. He advised a hospital for X-rays, just to be sure.

The aches and pains were beginning to surface but their severity still hadn't occurred to me. In the next few hours I was to discover a fractured skull, badly bruised spine, jaw knocked out of line, bleeding tongue and elbow, stiff neck and a score of minor injuries. My husband suffered a few bruises from the fight.

Twice before I have had to go to hospital emergency rooms but never at night. It was already 12:30. We went to Mt. Sinai. It seemed to me to be a slow night. Not many people waiting, no accident or other mugging victims. I watched the others. A child with a painful earache, sobbing in his mother's arms, waited the same hour-and-a half that I did.

Another child and a woman had fevers. A mother having a bad asthma attack was accompanied by her young children. All were black or Puerto Rican. I was struck by the thought that the poor rely on the emergency rooms of our hospitals the way the middle class relies on family doctors.

My turn finally came, X-rays were taken, a fracture noted, a neurologist called, a decision made to admit me for observation and tests. There was one bed available in the whole hospital. By 4 a.m. I was in it and my husband finally went home.

The head nurse came in, a warm, sympathetic girl who just wanted to assure me they would do their best to make me comfortable. Suddenly, everything finally began to sink in and I broke down, sobbing uncontrollably. She let me talk it out. I felt better but the full reality of what had happened less than five hours earlier was just beginning to register. I had become a statistic, a victim of crime.

I spent the next five days in the hospital and fortunately no blood clotting or other possible effects of a fracture occurred. All the tests indicated there would be no after-effects.

Not for one minute in those five days and for several after I got home did my mind wander from what had happened. I kept seeing that face, that blank, cold expression of the man who pushed me. It is now just an impersonal face, just an expression. I doubt I could identify either assailant. It's like every B crime movie you've ever seen where there's a police line-up and a witness tried desperately to identify the criminal.

Everything about the incident ran counter to what we anticipate will happen. I had never worried about walking at night with my husband. It is only women alone who think they must be extra careful. You think if it happens, someone will come up and grab your bag or demand you turn it over. You promise yourself you won't resist, to save your neck. I never had the chance.

As I tried desperately to drive the details from my mind, I realized we never really expect this kind of thing to happen to us. The fear of it has become woven into the fabric of this city's life. We continue to think it will always be the other guy. We refuse to accept the fact that this city can be dangerous. It can't happen here. But it can and it does.

The reactions, concern and questions of friends were interesting. Immediately they asked, "Are you sorry you're still living in the city?"

They know what my husband and I went through to renovate our brownstone. They know the agonizing process of deciding to totally commit yourself, your family, your resources to a community still fraught with risk and aggravated urban problems.

They know how desperately we wanted to be able to live in this city. Yet I know my children, now only 1 and 3 years of age, will never have the freedom to enjoy this city as I did as a child. And I am sad for them.

I have friends who have made the move out. They called, too. Interestingly enough, only one said, "So when are you moving out?" Others were more honest. One told me of a child in her neighborhood who was mysteriously kidnapped while playing on the lawn but fortunately released a few blocks away. "There are problems everywhere," she said . . .

The genuine concern of my city friends was overwhelming. It was almost as if it had happened to them. In a sense it has. They have been brought one step close to the reality. Many people reacted by saying we should all walk around with guns in our pockets. Yes, the same people who wanted all firearms banished in the wake of the Kennedy and King assassinations were now telling me I should carry a gun.

To the first such comment, my husband observed: "I would have shot my foot off going for it." Even if it were not a frightening solution, it would remain an impractical one. We never would have had the chance to reach for a gun. And would we have wanted to risk shooting a bystander, ourselves or even our assailants? . . .

I don't know where it will all lead. Were our assailants drug addicts? It seems likely. Even if they weren't we know that the habit's cost is the genesis of much of our city's crime. God knows, we are not doing enough about that problem.

I haven't yet tried to resume my normal routine, which kept me traveling around the city a good part of each day. Soon I will be physically up to it, but God I'm scared. I have ventured out of my house a few times, mostly to walk my dog. I know I will only feel safe when I have that dog at my side. The fear has not left me. I wonder if it ever will.

Now, like so many people, young and old, I move around the city at all hours of the night without fear, ride the subways, always finding many people around. Safety, or the feeling of safety, comes with the numbers of people around us. If you hadn't lived through the 1970s in New York, it is easy to wonder what all the safety talk is about.

URBAN RESETTLEMENT

Until the 1973 oil crisis, the trickling trend of returning young urban settlers went almost unnoticed. Experts declared the numbers of returnees insignificant. Statistically, they were correct. But meaningful urban change evolves *only* slowly and doesn't even show up statistically until the trend has dramatically progressed. Thus, experts were oblivious to the on-the-ground shift that was definitely occurring—until, that is, the oil shock of 1973 when the questioning of the auto-dependent lifestyle began in earnest. This was a good example of a totally spontaneous trend, the kind that undermines highly developed, inflexible official plans. No plan can anticipate cataclysmic events that are bound to occur. Questioning the car-centric lifestyle until then was almost sacrilegious. The automobile industry had by then reshaped the country's lifestyle values.

By the 1970s, as noted, the trend of returning urban residents was gaining visibility but did not accelerate and gain much media notice until the late 1970s or early 1980s. The Brownstone Revival Movement had already begun in Brooklyn's Park Slope and Cobble Hill where Everett and Evelyn Ortner had organized the Brownstone Revival Committee in 1965. Their newsletter, the *Brownstoner*, inspired like-minded urban pioneers around the city. Dedicated brownstoners banded together to beat back urban renewal programs that targeted brownstones for demolition. They cajoled the banks into giving mortgages, the same banks, in fact, that had earlier redlined their neighborhoods. They also harassed speculators to prevent stripping of precious ornamentation and proselytized among friends about the brownstone life. In a May 1973 article about books that had just been published aimed at the brownstone renovator, I wrote, "In the early '60s the 'brownstoners' were called New York's modern pioneers, long on guts but short on sanity. Later they were seen as the most hopeful sign that the city would not lose all of its middle class to the sprawling suburbs and as—maybe, just maybe—the ones with the best idea of how to live in a city of vacancy decontrol and spiraling rents."[3]

The state of the Upper West Side in the 1970s had its parallels in other cities where slum clearance had not totally erased the nineteenth-century

7.2 Park Slope brownstones, probably the signature housing style of the borough of Brooklyn. *Ron Shiffman.*

building form—whether brick or limestone row houses, clapboard or brick triple-deckers, or freestanding Victorians with back and front yards separated from neighbors only by driveways to rear-yard garages. In 1970 the first Back to City Conference was held in New York. Activists attended from eighty-two cities across the country, representing reviving historic neighborhoods. They compared stories, shared problems, and learned lessons from each other's successes and failures. Most important, they discovered they were not alone. Clearly, something bigger than their individual efforts was going on. Small efforts, almost unnoticeable, were evolving around the country, the beginning of a big, in fact monumental, national shift. The event led to formation of the national group Back to the City, Inc., an informal network of reviving communities. In January 1974, I wrote in part:

> For years, urban loyalists have been predicting that those fresh air and free school seekers would return. Well, it's happening, although slowly for now. But if there's one new factor ready to turn the current trickle into a full-fledged trend it's fuel.
>
> In short, the energy crisis is stemming the exodus and bringing suburban residents back. The two-car family with the roomy oil-heat

dream house, the shopping center miles away and children with distant friends and schools is "going bananas," reports one former Bronx resident seeking to return from Long Island.

THE WEST SIDE: THE HAPPENING PLACE

The Upper West Side reflected the best and the worst of what was happening in New York in the 1970s. It was one of the most concentrated Robert Moses battlegrounds but also in the vanguard of incremental renewal. This area was a trendsetter nationally for row-house living in a similar way that SoHo was for loft living. The New York City lifestyle, personified here, made good media copy. Brownstone living, especially the "urban duplex," was making it into national magazines. My editors recognized what was happening and knew I was living in the midst of it. They assigned me to write at length about the West Side.

Today, the West Side is actually chic, a shocking development for long-time residents like myself. But in 1974, it was far from it. In fact, you had to be a keen observer to recognize the precursors of good things to come. In December 1974 I wrote:

The area seems to spawn more urban chauvinists per square foot, more promoters of community spirit and defenders of have-not groups than any other neighborhood. It seems, as well, to contain more activists in far-flung causes, more aspiring politicians, more improvement groups and, certainly, more beards and blue jeans than any area outside Greenwich Village.

Most West Siders will recite as if by rote the same litany of advantages that makes their neighborhood so appealing—sound housing of every kind, sometimes even at rational prices; excellent transportation including two subway lines and a variety of buses; ethnic diversity that is not only reflected in the faces and accents of residents but in the local stores, restaurants and cultural groups; small playgrounds and large parks; museums, uncrowded movie theaters and of course, Lincoln Center.

Back then, West Siders lamented the loss of local businesses, the pushing out of more low-income residents, and the unending influx of the rich and famous who do not share the civic activism that was once the West Side trademark. Movies were getting crowded. Tourists seemed to be everywhere, and the idea that, as one observer noted at the time, "the city seems smaller here" was a fading memory.

Historically, the West Side has always been "the other side of town." It was always twenty years or so behind the East Side in development trends, and it wasn't until mansions and townhouses spread over the East Side that the developers gave serious attentions to the West Side north of Fifty-ninth Street.

When in 1880 Singer Sewing machine heir Edward S. Clark began construction of the city's first luxury apartment house—a chateau of gables, bay windows, and incomparable detail at Seventy-second Street and Central Park West—observers teased that he was building so far into the country that he might as well be in Dakota Territory. The name Dakota stuck, and today it is still considered one of the city's most exclusive addresses.

Soon after, the Ninth Avenue El (elevated train) was completed, opening the West Side to the first of many waves of upwardly mobile middle-class families and the beginning of serious development. Row houses were built in great numbers for single-family elegance through the last fifteen years of the nineteenth century. Gracious high-rise apartment houses—not as opulent as the Dakota—started going up slowly on Broadway after the turn of the century with the Beaux Arts Ansonia at Seventh-third Street and the more sparsely ornamented Apthorp at Seventh-ninth Street and Belnord at Eighty-sixth Street. By the 1920s and '30s, Central Park West, West End Avenue, and Riverside Drive were lined with fashionable high-rises that remain the housing anchors of the entire area.

After World War II, as the middle-class Irish and Jewish occupants moved farther north to the Bronx, to the East Side, or to suburbia, brownstones were subdivided to house waves of new immigrants—blacks from the South and the West Indies, Hispanics from Puerto Rico, Cuba, and South America. Because the units were small, overcrowded, high in price, but low in maintenance, many rapidly deteriorated.

CATACLYSMIC CHANGE KICKS IN

Then, in the late 1950s and early '60s, came the beginnings of the city's two largest urban renewal programs—the twelve-block (fifty-three-acre) Lincoln Center and the twenty-block West Side Urban Renewal Area between Eighty-seventh and Ninety-seventh Streets—and construction of two large-scale middle-income developments, Lincoln Towers at West End Avenue in the Sixties and Park West Village at Central Park to Amsterdam, Ninety-seventh to One Hundredth Streets.

When I referenced this urban renewal area in my 1974 articles, I didn't mention Robert Moses's connection to Urban Renewal policies up to that time. But I did note in my article a major population shift taking place: "Co-operative conversions of pre-war high-rises started in the 1960s, anchoring the professional middle-class that had moved there for the large rent-controlled apartments. The brownstone movement spread north and south from and west of the Urban Renewal Area, reclaiming some of the most solidly built housing in the city for young middle-class families seeking space, elegance, value and backyards."

The article noted that the scores of low-income residents displaced by assorted Urban Renewal projects were now concentrating along Amsterdam Avenue and north to the Manhattan Valley area, 107th to 110th Streets, Central Park to Broadway. Many also relocated into the ten public housing projects containing 4,628 apartments scattered around the area or in buildings leased by the Housing Authority and rented to low-income families. The West Side's low-rent apartment supply filled up, and many displaced families moved to other boroughs.

More than just the housing supply was rapidly changing when I observed this scene in the mid-1970s. Seven new public schools had been built since 1960. Private schools, too, had built new facilities or expanded old ones. And there were now seventeen day-care centers, including four Head Start programs. Block associations had planted trees; Broadway malls had been relandscaped. Playgrounds had been rebuilt.

Signs of renewal were showing more and more in the commercial fabric of the West Side as well. The impact of the women's movement was evident in the growing number of entrepreneurial women opening the small, local businesses appearing on the scene. This trend—women-owned businesses—was new, and it was emerging early, as many trends did, on the Upper West Side. Restaurants and bars, in the blocks from the Eighties through the Nineties along the avenues, offered live jazz and had become favorite spots for the steadily growing black middle class moving into the area.

Slowly but surely, theater groups were taking hold, with *Godspell* in its fourth year at the Promenade Theater and *Sgt. Pepper* at the newly renovated Beacon. New restaurants gained a loyal local following. "We won't eat anywhere but on the West Side, where prices are still reasonable," I quoted one resident saying.

In the second of the two articles I wrote on the Upper West Side, I focused on the problems. I wrote in part:

> Behind the facade of renewal and renaissance that covers great chunks of the West Side from 59th to 110th St., there are areas of great discontent and frustration.
>
> The "great sore" of the West Side—the Single Room Occupancy-Welfare Hotel problem—floods the area with unsupervised former mental patients, alcoholics, junkies, multi-problem families, and leaves the elderly vulnerable and the younger families scared.
>
> A 1969 city-wide study of SRO buildings indicated that almost 50 per cent of the entire city's SRO tenants live on the West Side, occupying some 25,000 apartment units between 74th and 110th Streets. Although the hotels Hamilton and Hargrave have been converted to housing for the elderly and the Kimberly at 73rd and Broadway is vacant, not much has changed in five years.

The West Side Urban Renewal Program was initiated in the 1950s as the nation's model for economic integration within buildings. Promoted by Planning Commission chair James Felt as an alternative to Moses's clearance strategy, the plan had been stumbling past the half-completion mark with a few years of stormy community debate. Some groups called for increasing the proportion of low-income housing. Others claimed any increase would cause the community to tip into a slum or ghetto. The argument was whether 20 or 30 percent was the right amount of low-income housing. And while the conflict was enough to cause some of the bitterest community battles the neighborhood had seen in years, federal housing funds stopped and made things worse.

The spreading phenomenon of the fast-food chains was another issue of debate. At one point a rumor circulated in the area around Seventy-ninth Street and Columbus Avenue that a McDonald's would open. "The community was up in arms," said the late councilman and then congressman Ted Weiss. "Five years ago a McDonald's would have been considered a neighborhood improvement. Today it's an anathema."

Fast-food chains have become an accepted way of life today in almost all urban neighborhoods. Now they are not as threatening as in the time

I was writing these articles. A generous selection of local food outlets of every scale and price exists and flourishes.

Crime, of course, was a constant worry, but statistics don't seem to affect the way people live with the reality of crime as much as people's "feel" for it does. As more stores stayed open late, as new restaurants proliferated and nightlife in general picked up, many residents felt the community had gotten safer. One guide was the newsstands. Only a few years earlier, none stayed open late except at Seventy-second Street. Now they were open late up and down Broadway.

The article also noted the small-town feel of residents:

> Consistently, when you speak to residents about what's good and bad on the West Side, they will tell you everything that's happening within a small radius of their home. They know who lives above and below them, those their children meet in the playground. They organize food co-ops or babysitting services and they know the local shopkeepers as well as their neighbors.
>
> Actor Jordan Charney, who lives in a 10-story apartment house on 74th between Columbus and Amsterdam Avenues, talks of "the marvelous shops offering home-made things" and "the assortment of people going into their own business."
>
> "Lincoln Center has pushed problems uptown," Charney says, "hiding them a little better because they're out of my neighborhood. Up there it's as scary as it used to be when we moved here seven years ago."

Boundaries differed. Problems varied. But a do-it-yourself state of mind pervaded each subcommunity. Whether it was tree planting, day care, playgrounds, block-by-block security guards, or housing problems, West Siders didn't wait for City Hall to solve them. Residents lived with the realities of the problems; alternatives were less desirable. Sometime in the 1970s and '80s, however, a real upward shift began. Government money for big projects had stopped flowing, as it had in the heyday of Urban Renewal in the 1950s. The city was flirting with bankruptcy. The state was suffering serious financial setbacks, and the federal government was no friendlier to New York than in the "Ford to City: Drop Dead" 1970s days. The cessation of the big projects gave license to the smaller ones to advance. No one thing is identifiable. Instead, an accumulation of successive steps occurred. It was a clear case of incremental change, if ever there was one.

A variety of new stores opened, more upscale now, a sign that someone thought the area was an underserved market to which nonneighborhood shoppers would also come. New children's clothing stores appeared, a clear reflection of the increasing number of new families. Until then, one small children's department store, Morris Brothers, had been the sole outpost for shopping parents.[4] East Siders began to consider the West Side's private schools for their children. An assortment of new banal apartment houses went up across from Lincoln Center, a sign that big developers decided the district had value. And young singles and families kept buying and fixing up the brownstones not destroyed by Urban Renewal.

The Lincoln Center Myth

Credentialed experts often attribute urban regeneration of any kind to the official plans and developments of the day. Most planners and government officials and observers don't give credence to the gradual block-by-block and business-by-business improvements that mark organic incrementalism. They can't recognize it until it is full-blown. They insist that ad hoc change is insignificant. They are wrong on all counts. One needs to recognize the often small precursors of positive change to understand its emerging appearance. The precursors were in abundance on the West Side, as all the gradual changes already mentioned indicate.

According to conventional wisdom, Lincoln Center was the catalyst for regeneration of the West Side. This is a myth. Simple observation illustrates how this was not the case. *If* this were true, renewal would *only* have occurred in the late 1960s and '70s on the West Side around Lincoln Center, or in proximity to other big new construction projects. This was definitely not the case. SoHo, the Lower East Side, areas of the South Bronx, and the many areas of brownstone Brooklyn showed early signs of nascent rebirth at the same time as the Upper West Side. Positive change was bubbling up in small doses all over the city. It was observable, anecdotal, and nowhere yet ready to be measurable. And, indeed, it was happening in many traditional and historic neighborhoods all over the country. Thus, experts and the press did not recognize its significance as the beginning of a shift. They couldn't imagine this happening without a big catalyst like Lincoln Center.

Ignoring where else regeneration was slowly taking hold, the myth prevails that Lincoln Center rejuvenated the West Side. In reality, it did not. The rebound of the Upper West Side and scattered neighborhoods throughout the city was people driven by the vanguard of urban pioneers. Value-hunting brownstoners and apartment dwellers were attracted to the solidly built historic building stock and middle-income apartment towers. They were resisting the expected move to the suburbs. In neighborhoods farther out, way off the radar screen of city experts, immigrants were filling largely vacant housing where people had moved out. With them came new businesses as well. The Russians went to Brighton Beach and the Syrians to Atlantic Avenue, both in Brooklyn. The Chinese filled the Lower East Side. The Koreans went to Astoria, Queens. In each neighborhood, the new residents sparked a gradual rebirth that is explosive today.

Trends always start small, almost invisibly. Values and lifestyle choices brought new settlers to the West Side. Lincoln Center was clearly a sign that government and financial institutions thought the West Side was worthy of reinvestment in big government-supported projects. But what Lincoln Center really did was bring East Siders and suburbanites to the West Side in the evening—all visitors who had been afraid to venture into the area because of its reputation for crime and poverty.

Visitors, whether from other neighborhoods or out of town, are never enough to spark rebirth. Local residents and businesses do the spade work, reenergize a place or district, give a place character, and make visitors comfortable. Visitors follow locals in the process; they are never catalysts for the rebirth process. Years later, after the Upper West Side had turned dramatically upscale, many of those visitors came there to live, too.

If anything, Lincoln Center and, later, Lincoln Towers made rejuvenation more difficult, if one understands rejuvenation as the gradual return of young, middle-income families and new businesses to a stabilized, existing population mix with new buildings fitting in with existing ones. Enlivened street life, diversity of population and activity, and social interaction follow that new population. That was not what followed the development of Lincoln Center. What did follow were several large new developments, including a series of dull residential towers across Broadway. Together with Lincoln Center, they do not add up to a definition of natural, positive change. In fact, unrest caused by the displacement of seven thousand families and eight hundred businesses[5] in twelve blocks demolished for Lincoln Center complicated life and made it unsettling and stressful for longtime residents and new.

It is worth pausing for a moment to look further at why Lincoln Center is a signature Moses creation. This is difficult to do now without offending many good people who have worked hard to make this world-renowned seat of culture a great success. But that success is due to the content and programs, not the vessel they come in. As soon as a critical word is said about the physical design of the complex, such people take offense, even though they had nothing to do with designing it, only in making it succeed as an artistic center despite itself.

First, it must be said loud and clear that the institutions of Lincoln Center have become star performers on the city's cultural stage. But that is about cultural programming, not bricks and mortar and urban design values. Paul Goldberger wrote a very perceptive Sky Line column in the *New Yorker*, "West Side Fixer-Upper: New Ideas for Lincoln Center That Don't Involve Dynamite," giving high marks to the first steps in a planned redesign. He credited architects Diller, Scofidio + Renfro with "figuring out ways to weave the atoll back into the fabric of the city." He noted, "There were complaints about the facilities at Lincoln Center from the beginning." But more significantly, he hit at the heart of the matter:

> But the raison d'etre for Lincoln Center was dubious from the beginning. . . . Moses didn't care much for opera, or theater, or symphony orchestras. He just figured that they could serve as a magnet for development. Using culture in this way was a new idea in the fifties, although almost everything else about Lincoln Center was stuck in the past. As a piece of design, it was as retrograde as the halls that it replaced—and much less successful. . . .
>
> The idea of a cultural campus set apart from the city never made much sense, even though Lincoln Center did, to be fair, promote the urban renewal effect that Robert Moses intended. The neighborhood would probably have been gentrified without Lincoln Center, of course, but hardly in the same way, or on the same timetable. . . .
>
> Lincoln Center has sometimes seemed less the vibrant source of the neighborhood's energy than the empty hole in the middle of the doughnut. . . . Lincoln Center reflected [Moses's] social philosophy, which was on the side of public subsidies for middle-class amenities and against the visible presence of the poor.[6]

Centers, like other big stand-alone separatist projects, breed more new development mislabeled revitalization. But more than anything, they continue nibbling away at traditional streets and diverse uses, the ingredients of real places. Here, too, Moses (in partnership with John Rockefeller) led the way, as Martin Filler notes: "This cultural one-stop shopping center launched a nationwide boom in performing- and visual-arts complexes."[7]

Moses was a separator, segregator, and isolator, designing the world for the car. He was a "centerist"—meaning cultural (starting with Lincoln Center), retail, industrial, sports, entertainment centers—isolating uses within the city, suburb, or town in a way that disconnects them from the rest of daily life, creating islands of singular activity in the urban fabric. Again, he created the model, and the nation followed.

The Moses pattern undermines the potential of vibrant, vital, economically and socially robust, integrated, and connected "places" in a city, suburb, or town. And it is a form of growth that annihilates and replaces versus replenishes and adds. Communities throughout the country today are trying to reconnect what that separating era of planning destroyed. Now, Lincoln Center, cited as one of Moses's great achievements, has embarked on a billion-dollar effort to remodel itself in a more urbanistically connected way, undoing Moses's isolationist vision.

Lincoln Center is a good place to understand the Moses philosophy, even though its widespread popularity as a cultural destination blinds people to the underlying fallacies of its creation. Understanding what was wrong with the barracks-style high-rise housing projects is easy today, especially since so many of them have been and continue to be blown up and rebuilt around the country. And widespread understanding exists more than ever that massive highway building and disinvestment in mass transit were the fatal domestic flaws of the second half of the twentieth century. But there are few signs of public or official understanding of the antiurban nature of cultural centers or, for that matter, entertainment centers, sports complexes, or similar concentrations of singular uses. Superblocks, whether for residential towers or entertainment, are disruptive and destructive in a city. Robert Moses launched his approach to city building in a big way on the West Side.

WEST SIDE STORY

Elizabeth Yampierre's family displacement saga was recounted earlier. Yampierre actually lived on the site, known as San Juan Hill, where the musical *West Side Story* purportedly takes place. A number of scenes in the movie were actually filmed on those streets. The movie's producers had persuaded Moses to hold off demolition a short time while they used it as a stage set.

Looking at the stills of those scene shots now is startling to anyone who thinks what Moses was clearing was really a slum by any honest standard. Not that deterioration wasn't clear, and not that living conditions weren't seriously deficient. But if one studies the photos of empty tenements and small apartment houses with windows already missing and evidence of the accelerated decay that sets in once urban renewal is declared, it is hard not to question how so much reusable, renovatable fabric could be consigned to the garbage dump. Many comparable buildings today have been converted to upscale apartment houses and condominiums. As Filler also wrote, "Today, that 19th-century housing would be gentrified before you could say Jane Jacobs, but in the 1950s, tabula-rasa development was standard operating procedure."[8]

THE REAL DRAW OF THE WEST SIDE

The traditional mix of dense and architecturally masterful West Side buildings experienced a real image problem during the era of massive slum clearance and new project building. The incomparable prewar apartment houses of Central Park West, West End Avenue, and Riverside Drive north of Lincoln Center had never lost their appeal, although they had lost their status as chic. For a long time the "chic" label applied only to the Upper East Side. But the architectural appeal, solid construction, and size of apartment rooms could not be matched by anything built after World War II.

In time, the West Side became overchic, and for many longtime West Siders, it lost its charm. Real estate values are off the charts. The area is so overrun by tourists at the southern end around Lincoln Center, where I live, that little local flavor remains. Mall stores dominate. This is one of the city's worst traffic-congestion hot spots. More and more superwealthy people have moved in and brought their sense of entitlement. Three lanes of traffic on Central Park West, for example, are sacrificed for angled parking for private cars of the policemen and double-parking (sometimes triple-parking) for private cars and limousines at the Trump International Hotel and the new superluxury condominium 15 Central Park West. This new addition to the West Side opened in 2007 at such through-the-roof sales prices that the area was dubbed "the new Gold Coast."

Essential qualities hold strong. Some things are almost immutable because a large swath of the area was declared a historic district in 1990. Actually, several historic districts cover a lot of the Upper West Side. The largest is the Central Park West district from Sixty-second to Ninety-sixth Streets, with parts of Columbus Avenue included. A scattering of smaller districts is found along Riverside Drive and West End Avenue. Effectively, nothing within those designated areas can get torn down or altered without approval of the Landmarks Preservation Commission. That is not to say things don't get torn down that shouldn't and that new large-scale buildings of mediocre design don't get built. But the basic effectiveness of the area's landmark protection is clear. Enormous change has transpired on the Upper West Side, but its essential physical character has been sustained. The glaring compromises remain isolated and contained. That is the fundamental virtue of designated historic districts in the first place. Change evolves within the context of authenticity, a good definition of regeneration.

Positive Change, Negative Change

The West Side exhibits the result of two kinds of change—change that is regeneration and change that is replacement. This kind of duality can be found in cities around the country. Here it is dramatically pronounced because of the large scale of both kinds of change.

The substantial areas of the West Side most dynamically regenerated are those with the large stock of renewed brownstone and limestone row houses, small-scale and large-scale prewar apartment buildings, and the varied assortment of combined residential and commercial structures that line the three primary commercial corridors. Then there are the replacement areas: Lincoln Center; the eight-building, 3,837-unit apartment complex of Lincoln Towers (Sixty-sixth to Seventieth along West End Avenue); the six-building Park West Village (Ninety-seventh to One Hundredth from Central Park to Columbus); and a number of public housing projects north of Ninety-sixth Street that totally replaced a diversified fabric. Robert Moses had declared each of these areas a "slum." One has to question how much of a slum these areas could have been when comparable assortments of diversified buildings that stood on the cleared and rebuilt sites are today significantly upgraded and regenerated.

The replacement projects have remained static—physically no different from when constructed under Urban Renewal. Granted that Lincoln Center's Philharmonic Hall has had to be rebuilt inside twice because of poor acoustics. The central plaza, too, was rebuilt, and recent years of creative outdoor programming have dramatically enlivened that space. The open-air band shell of Damrosch Park at the southwest corner was added after completion. But Lincoln Center remains the isolated and isolating island of culture it was meant to be. And while sections of Lincoln Center are being redesigned to connect to the vibrant area across Broadway, no attempt appears to be in the planning to open up the west side of Lincoln Center that is walled off in the most hostile way possible from the public housing projects on the other side of West End Avenue. North and south along West End Avenue across from the public housing, street-level retail can be found. A solid brick wall in the rear serves as both an impenetrable boundary and a break in that retail strip. Clearly, it was designed to be fortresslike.

DEFINING PROGRESS

The impact of Urban Renewal is probably more benign on the Upper West Side than in most other New York City neighborhoods. Several things explain this. To start, the area was a dense, rich fabric with a variegated texture that could sustain considerable loss without losing its essence. And considerable losses it did indeed sustain. Ironically, the large swaths of alleged slums that were demolished and rebuilt would be gentrified middle-class neighborhoods today. Additionally, the replacements, besides Lincoln Center, are an assortment of well-maintained and well-managed middle- and low-income developments. Over time, they have woven themselves into the surrounding community. Nevertheless, they represent big tears in what was and could be today an untorn urban fabric that could have had a diversified assortment of economically and socially mixed housing of every scale, national and local businesses, and varied institutions, simply more of what it already is in the regenerated areas.

Many neighborhoods and downtowns in New York and around the country are not so lucky. They have sustained too enormous a scale of clearance. From Bushwick in Brooklyn and the South Bronx to St. Louis, Indianapolis, Louisville, Detroit, Buffalo, Charlotte, and others, only remnants are left. To regenerate by building on a modest remnant is possible but much more difficult. The cities regenerating the best today have the most traditional fabric left; the ones having the most clearance damage are experiencing the more difficult time. It is staggering to think of the damage done across the board to American cities after World War II in the name of progress.

With Lincoln Center, as had been true with the highways and housing towers, Moses created a template that would deceive the world into accepting the notion that this was a good way to redevelop cities—Moses style.

-8-

WESTWAY
A Conversation with Jane Jacobs

> You take some things as given: you don't want a city that's built for automobiles and not people first.
>
> ——————
>
> JANE JACOBS

> In the end, will Westway be remembered as but a symbol of abstract and competing concepts of urban renewal—the automobile against mass transit; the slow-growth philosophy of targeted renaissance against the glamour of grand-scale construction? Indeed, will it be remembered at all?
>
> ——————
>
> SAM ROBERTS,
> "Battle of the Westway: Bitter 10-Year Saga of a Vision on Hold," *New York Times*

Jane Jacobs sits at the dining room table of her three-story Victorian house in the leafy Toronto neighborhood known as the Annex. It is 1978. She is pondering the news I am bringing her from New York City, primarily the latest chapters in the ongoing fight over the Westway—the massive replacement of the West Side Highway along the Hudson River—then raging in New York. Her white hair and large eyeglasses give her an owlish look that can turn from severity to impishness at the switch of urban topic. "Why aren't you writing about this, Roberta?"

8.1 Jane loved to sit and chat on her front porch, which we did many times. *Herschel Stroyman.*

she asks in her most challenging voice. Her unrelenting gaze remains fixed on me.

This is my third or fourth visit since being introduced to her earlier that year by the first editor of my first book, Jason Epstein, Jacobs's editor.[1] We had just begun a long friendship from which I benefited enormously. Over twenty-eight years, she nurtured, nudged, challenged, and enriched my own thinking, writing, and activism. She reinforced my skepticism of official city planning precepts, occasionally rescued me from acceptance of a misguided notion, and showed me the universal lessons of Toronto's enduring urbanism. Her willingness to take controversial stands and to contradict conventional wisdom was an inspiration for my own activism. We had our differences that only made our conversations more lively. Jacobs and her family had moved to Toronto in 1968. She, more than anyone, opened my eyes early to the defining impact of transportation and manufacturing issues on cities.

On this occasion, our mutual friend Mary Nichols was also visiting. Nichols, a resident of Greenwich Village and former columnist for the *Village Voice* and then an assistant to Mayor Kevin White in Boston, had kept the expressway in the news through her *Village Voice* coverage when the mainstream press was less interested and editorially supportive.

Both Jacobs and Nichols were intensely concerned about the Westway progress. They both saw a direct link to the Moses Lower Manhattan Expressway. Jacobs and her family had moved to Toronto in 1968 during the Vietnam War when her two sons were draft age. The final defeat of the Lower Manhattan Expressway occurred after her 1968 departure. Nichols was working and living in Boston and would return to New York soon to work for her old friend and mayor-elect Ed Koch. Yet both urban activists still cared deeply about New York.

On this particular visit, Jacobs and Nichols both grilled me about the Westway fight and persuaded me to write about Westway—the twelve-lane highway proposed to be built on landfill along the West Side of Manhattan—when criticism of it in the press was rare.[2] Did I know how critical it was to the future of New York? Did I realize how important to a city its public transit is? Did I realize that so many American cities were dysfunctional because they had spent decades investing in automobile access while destroying the neighborhoods, downtowns, and transit systems they all once had? Did I realize that New York could go in the same direction? No. I had not realized any of these things to the extent they were presenting them. My focus was on neighborhood and downtown regeneration around the country: the South Bronx, Savannah, Pittsburgh, Cincinnati, San Francisco, Seattle, and elsewhere. I had just started research for my first book, *The Living City: Thinking Small in a Big Way* (1989).

I had been coming to Toronto to explore causes of recent urban decay with Jane, as well as to share with her the signs of rebirth that I was observing in my research but that conventional observers and professionals were dismissing as ad hoc and too inconsequential. She was so enthusiastic about what I was describing as the early rebirth of the South Bronx generated by community-based improvisations that she insisted I take her there when she was next in New York. We subsequently visited the People's Development Corporation and Banana Kelly in the South Bronx in 1978, led by Ron Shiffman, then head of the Pratt Center for Community and Economic Development, who first took me there in 1977.

She was, however, relentless in pushing me to stop and write about Westway. In many ways, the most important aspect of our expanding relationship was her willingness to be critical of what I was saying or thinking. My slowness to recognize the significance of Westway was one of those occasions. Sure, transit was an important issue in the urban regeneration story, but I did not yet view it as an overarching one. Jane and Mary turned my head on this topic. Transportation, they convinced me, was central to the economic, physical, and social life of all of urban America.

Persuaded, I decided to switch gears. Michael Kramer, then an editor at *New York Magazine*, liked the subject, if I could get Jane to consent to an interview on it. A few months later, she agreed. These kinds of interruptions were intolerable when she was writing. Consenting to this interview, however, was not just rare but sudden, and I asked why. "Westway is different," she said. "I just think it's the single most important decision that New York is facing about its future and whether it can possibly reverse itself, or whether it's hopeless," she explained. "This is in part because of the practical damage that Westway will do to the city. And it's also very important as a symptom of whether New York can profit by the clear mistakes and misplaced priorities that it's had in the past or whether it just has to keep repeating them."

Her son Jimmy, who lives down the block, told her she was crazy to agree to this interview. "But I told him, 'Jimmy, this is important for the fight, and what if that Westway is built and I think, 'Maybe I could have made some difference; I can't live with that.' And he said, 'Ah yeah, sure,'" she laughed.

We spent many hours over several visits discussing this subject, all of which was taped (the tapes were transcribed).[3] The substance went way beyond Westway. She talked a lot about recent New York development history, providing tales and tidbits she had never written or spoken about.

Jacobs's art is to accessibly outline a specific issue while making clear the broader implications of the substance. So much of what she covered when referring to either the Lower Manhattan Expressway or Westway—like every other issue she wrote or talked about—can be applied to highway and urban renewal fights anywhere.

At its simplest, Westway was just another piece of the Interstate Highway System, stretching from Forty-second Street down to the island's tip. The complexities are not visible at first. No neighborhoods would have been bisected or erased, although plenty would suffer through the increased traffic of the expanded highway. No land would have been taken away. In fact, land would be added with landfill under which the highway would partially go through a tunnel. Together with the six-lane inland service road, Westway would equal twelve lanes. On top of the landfill, two hundred acres of new city would be created for housing, parks, and commercial development. New highway proposals across the country often

8.2 Jane took special pleasure in the view from her porch down through the whole row of porches. *Herschel Stroyman.*

looked that simple. Sometimes they still do. Deceptively, the Westway route was drawn as a straight line on all maps. The highly land-consumptive on- and off-ramps were rarely shown. Only two ramps were apparently planned, but it wasn't clear if more would have been added.

As she proceeded through this conversation, Jacobs primarily explained the damage Westway would inflict on New York City and how it would transform the city. But she went way beyond this as well. Most significantly, Jacobs illustrated the importance of any highway debate to the future shape of all cities of any size. This was long before this fundamental debate went mainstream. Essentially, how one views a highway proposal directly relates to one's fundamental understanding of how a city functions best.

THE HEART OF THE ARGUMENT

Two fundamental points formed the heart of her argument against Westway. The first is that Westway was part of the same original overall highway network plan of 1929, as was the Lower Manhattan Expressway, thus their intrinsic connection. That plan for all of Manhattan, she argued, improperly favored development geared toward the car, not mass transit or the pedestrian. The second point was the internal contradiction between economics and the environment evident in the argument for both highways. "These are really very obvious things, but I don't think they're obvious to most of the public," she said. "The first point is that Westway is only part of the 1929 plan. Just think of that. It's almost fifty years old, almost half a century old. New York prides itself on being up to date, but it's being run by a half-century-old plan. Only pieces of it keep surfacing. Nobody would ever consent to the insanity of doing the entire thing. And yet, if, piece by piece, it gets done, the whole thing is inevitable, because each part depends on another."

In this case, if Westway were built, the same expanded highway would inevitably be necessary from Forty-second Street north and from the Battery south around and up the East Side. Robert Caro, she pointed out, illustrates well in *The Power Broker* the Moses technique of building a bridge without saying there's got to be a new or wider highway on either side. "And the bridge gets built," she said, "and aha, now the wider highway becomes necessary. Or he builds a road and says nothing about a great big bridge that's going to have to come, and aha, all of a sudden, the bridge is necessary. It's piecemeal. People would have a fit if they saw the whole thing." But, she said, that's the way these highways have been pushed and not just in New York but everywhere. "In essence, the plan is a ring, an oval really, all around the outside of the island, and then it has lacings across the middle. It's a net, catching Manhattan. The Lower Manhattan Expressway was one of these crosstown lacings for the whole system."

During the fight over the Lower Manhattan Expressway, opponents had seen the 1929 Regional Plan, both the maps and the written volumes. This put their effort in perspective. The existing West Side Highway (six lanes) was the first piece of the plan, originally called the Miller Highway. The East River Drive (six lanes), built in the 1930s, was also part of it. "The plan ran into trouble when it began to involve the lacings across the city and the ramps off of them," noted Jacobs. A crossing at Thirtieth Street was the first defeat, she said, because it would have destroyed the Little Church Around the Corner where many theatrical weddings took place. It had a loyal constituency.

"The story is told," Jacobs recalled, that "an actor and an actress wanted to get married at, I think, Marble Collegiate, and they got short-changed there, and somebody said, 'Go to the little church around the corner.' It had a different name [Church of the Transfiguration]. They were treated there with dignity. It became the church of theater people and became known as 'The Little Church Around the Corner.' This was either before the war in the '30s, or right after, not long after the Regional Plan was proposed. That would have been the first lacing across Manhattan, but because of the church, they hit resistance. So that piece was dropped. Then there was the hiatus on construction during the war."

Early tunnels, bridges, and ramps, Jacobs pointed out, were on the periphery of Manhattan. Few viewed them as affecting the city center. "There's a certain logic, you see, to drawing this through traffic over to the edges," she said. "But the plan always presupposed these lacings, this whole net, to get cars into the city expeditiously and across town. A Los Angelizing of the whole city." The "Los Angelizing," Jacobs said, is what traffic engineers want to do to all cities, a one-size-fits-all approach to any city.

> This is probably what they all are taught, that no place within a city should be more than a quarter of a mile from a ramp onto an expressway. Los Angeles comes closest to that. Everywhere in Los Angeles is fed by expressways. This is the basic idea.
>
> And this was always the plan for New York. But you see, it wasn't evident when it was just on the outside. The 1929 plan did not show entrance ramps, nor do Westway maps. Ramps require enormous demolition to create. The minute the real plan for Los Angelizing Manhattan ever goes into operation, it alarms the hell out of people because the destructive implications become very vivid. The Thirtieth Street crossing got that kind of opposition. The Cross Bronx Expressway did too, but that opposition didn't succeed.

The road through Washington Square would have been one of those ramps. Yet it wasn't clear to people for a long time, she said, that it would connect to the expressway.

FIGHTING CITY HALL

"Some people," she said, "would like New York to turn into a Los Angeles, or don't have any sense of the highway's impact on the fabric of the city, or are like Robert Moses, and there are plenty of people like this. There is no use—we found out in these fights—trying to convince these

The Begelman Spectacular: Enter Judy Garland

Frank Mankiewicz on Smuggling Cuban Cigars

NEW YORK

**How Westway Will Destroy New York
An Interview With Jane Jacobs**
by Roberta Brandes Gratz

8.3 This cover story of my interview with Jane about Westway gained a lot of attention in 1978. Jane's voice had not been heard in New York for a number of years. *New York Magazine.*

people. You fight them. If you spend all your time trying to persuade the people who really want this, instead of fighting them, you lose. This is the way to get defeated." This is a key Jacobs principle: cultivate your constituency rather than trying to persuade your opponents. "You could spend all that energy on trying to bring reason to Robert Moses, or people like him, showing him how he was harming the city, and you would waste it all because his idea of improving the city is really to wipe it out and start over with big projects."

People meet with officials at City Hall, hear expressions of empathy, even maybe agreement, think they have made their case, she said. When it doesn't go their way, they get discouraged. "That's where the expression 'You can't fight City Hall' comes from. But you can fight City Hall if you understand that trying to fight it is different from trying to persuade. You can't persuade them, but you can fight them."

The viability or regenerative potential of some areas is often not easily evident to the casual observer. Thus, officials declare blighted a neighborhood that is anything but. Deterioration along the Westway route was obvious. Buildings had been neglected for a long time in anticipation of the highway. Few people recognized it as a classic condition, like SoHo had been, where the plan for the highway decades earlier made possible the assumption that nothing else could occur there, an illustration of "planners' blight," as described in the SoHo chapter.

The question arose about what would happen to traffic without Westway. It would either continue south around the tip of the island or find its way across the streets, Jacobs predicted. But "the faster you make it for the traffic, the more of it will use these facilities, and also, the less money you have for other kinds of transportation. It's no accident that transit has gone down, while enormous amounts of money have been spent on highways in New York."

HIGHWAY AS CURE FOR DECAY

Driving down the West Side revealed the many things that were happening to make the area look bad. Aside from derelict and neglected buildings, landlords had readily rented to raunchy nightclubs, like the Anvil. Nevertheless, Jacobs insisted, "no defense is needed of how good the area is, or why it seems so bad. This highway can't be justified on the grounds that it's so bad there that things need to be taken out. What a ridiculous idea that you put in a billion-dollar highway to manicure a place!"

I raised a larger issue, arguing that the pattern of designating one area after another for renewal or a highway, as Moses did, caused the constant uprooting of people. Jacobs grew a little impatient:

I know, but that's still a very peripheral argument against the expressway, because plenty of expressways have been put into areas—or proposed for areas—chosen precisely so that that will not happen. They've been put through parkland, through ravines, along old railroad tracks. They've been put through all kinds of places where they will not uproot people, or where displacement is minimal. And it still does enormous damage to a city. And it's still the wrong priority for the money.

This is a wrong way to treat transportation in the city. And it's an uneconomic way and it's a polluting way, and it's got internal contradictions that cannot be justified. And it is a national problem. It doesn't mean that, aha, if you can, in another city, find an expressway that actually doesn't uproot anybody and doesn't cut off the waterfront, and doesn't do one of these specific things, yet cuts through the city, that it's okay. It's not.

For Jacobs, it all boiled down to certain irrevocable givens. One of those givens is that if the plan brings more cars into the city, it is wrong. And, she added, it was "cutting down the amount of money, inevitably, to deal with city transportation in other ways."

TIDE TURNING AGAINST CARS?

Neighborhood traffic has long been a sore point in many places, but most people assume that providing more parking opportunities takes moving cars off the streets. Yet, just as critics argued and showed in the Washington Square Park fight, the more you provide for cars, the more cars will come. The easier to park, the more people will drive. But how traffic cripples, if not kills, a neighborhood is not always understood.

In *Death and Life*, Jacobs summed up the problem as she had done in our interview—the erosion of the city in favor of the automobile. Roads become wider. Sidewalks are narrowed. Noise, pollution, danger increase. It's a process of erosion of everything else. When too many automobiles start coming into a neighborhood, deterioration inevitably occurs. When every other amenity of the neighborhood, or of the city, is sacrificed, and inordinate proportions of transportation money are devoted to cars, then you're eroding the city.

Jacobs was not anticar, just against transforming the city primarily for cars. "There are people who must have this metal cocoon," Jacobs added.[4] "If they will accept some of the disadvantages of it—that it's a very slow way to get about, very aggravating to be caught in traffic, and so on— okay, they make their choice. But when they want the whole city remodeled to accommodate their phobia, that's the problem. And furthermore it's an impossible thing. You cannot do it. You just can't, especially in dense and large cities, accommodate all the potential cars. Inevitably, you're eroding things."

And, of course, it came back again to priorities. "Westway is a prime example of not only, my God, the cost," Jacobs said, "but also the vision of what the waterfront will be, and what it will do to the rest of New York streets."

This becomes the first step in a new erosion process. "And a very big one," she added. "A very big step. The amount of money involved is sort of a measure of that."

THE INTERNAL CONTRADICTION

This was where her second fundamental point came in. The first was that Westway was part of the same network as the Lower Manhattan Expressway, all first provided for in the 1929 Regional Plan. The second point, similar in both fights, was the internal contradiction of the proponents' argument.

> Here it is, their big vulnerable point: two contradictory things. One is, if they say that what this expressway is going to accomplish is to accommodate a whole lot of additional traffic, then they run into the problem about air pollution. Even if they say the traffic is going to move faster. If it's going to accommodate over the next twenty years 2 or 3 percent more traffic a year, or whatever, and you begin to convert that into air pollution, it's horrifying, and it will never meet the air pollution standards. So they have to minimize the increase in traffic and downplay that it is encouraging more and more automobile traffic at the expense of transit.
>
> But these things cost so damn much, how are you going to justify spending billions of dollars on this highway if it's not going to handle any more traffic than is being handled now? The enormous costs require arguing that there is some commensurate enormous service it will do. And yet that service, carrying and generating increased traffic, implies horrendous damage to the environment. So, in one case they argue the one thing. Then they have to be inconsistent and argue the other one.

Thus, if it's going to do what it's supposed to do and justify its cost, more traffic will be created, and pollution will be generated. If you minimize the traffic projection, you're minimizing the job the project will do, and therefore you forfeit its justification. The cost can't be justified. "We may think we have problems," she laughed, "but we don't have any built-in inherent intellectual inconsistency, terrible inconsistency, ruinous inconsistency, which they do."

Now, this is the chief thing that I think is alike on both these fights. As far as I know, the Lower Manhattan Expressway fight was the first one, at least in New York, where the citizens fighting it began to focus on this inconsistency. That's partly because of the much greater awareness of what was happening to air quality than in the past.[5] And when you took the figures that were promoted for the expressway and turned them into what it would mean to the air, in Chinatown, for example, it was outrageous.

PROPONENTS CHANGE THE ARGUMENT

That's when suddenly expressway proponents switched the whole argument to the marvelous new housing and parks and all that was going to be put in on either side of the expressway; it was going to be a whole new piece of city.

And the hearing that was held, the one where I got arrested, that's what that was all about in '68? [That hearing] was put together very hastily to change the subject. They *had* to change the subject because they were hung up on this dilemma.

Now, with Westway, here's how it's similar: it *started* with a change of subject. So much about Westway has been about the landfill and what will be built on it, and the proponents of Westway keep trying to talk about that instead of about the highway. And the more they can talk about that, the less they have to face this absolutely impossible thing of trying to justify it. That's the function of the landfill.

They learned a lesson. They can't argue Westway on the grounds of how much traffic it will service because the argument then becomes the pollution. They can't argue how little pollution it will provide because the argument becomes why spend all this money if it's going to do that little for traffic. But the opponents of Westway won't let them change the subject entirely.

Now they're saying, look, even if it was 3 percent—that's nothing. But you see *these are different hearings*. They never have a hearing at which the economic justification and the pollution both have to be argued. They argue one thing at one kind of hearing, and then years later when the pollution one comes up they'll argue something else. And there's no honesty to any of these figures. And here is the basic inconsistency, the basic impossibility. Actually, it *is* impossible to deal with the traffic needs of New York in highways instead of transit; it's an utter impossibility. It's a contradiction in terms. And it's not a verbal contradiction; it's a real one. You can't do it and keep New York, keep it as a viable city.

I mentioned that the expressway fight seemed to be the first victory of its kind based on environmental reasoning, using the new federal laws passed in 1968. Jane retorted:

Yes, because before there were environmental impact laws—and in this case air quality—they could justify how this enormous amount of money to be spent had a tremendous cost-benefit ratio, because traffic was going to increase 8 percent a year, etc. They had big figures on the record early, because that's the only part of the argument that they were concerned with at first. There weren't any laws about air quality. That's why on Westway, twelve lanes for a 1 percent increase in traffic, a billion dollars for that! That's the figure that they used at the hearing, and the hearing officer said, in effect, "I can't see what you're basing this on." So, now comes leaking out in the press, if 3 percent more cars were going to use this, it still would come within the air-quality limits? In short, they have figured they could go up as high as 3 percent and not get into trouble. But that's all. And it's not enough to justify all that money. Hence the landfill, et cetera. They hope nobody asks the question: "All right, if this landfill and these parks and all these apartments and everything are so great and the city really will have money to run these parks and fill up this many more apartments and so on, why not do it on its own? Would you do it without the highway? Why is it so great with the highway?"[6] Well, it's so great with the highway because it's meant to *sell* the highway.

NEW LAND PLUS PLANNED SHRINKAGE

During the Westway debate, observers occasionally questioned whether the land-development portion of the plan made sense. And not just because the city had no money to create or run the parks, but also because the plan only included putting in a lot of dirt and maybe a token park and then zoning it for housing and parks. None of the land development

8.4 Many people
wore this button.

would occur at the same time as the highway was being built. If one liked the idea of all the parks and housing, then the question was: why are we letting the parks, already suffering from great budget cuts, that we have go to hell while talking about new parks, and why are we concerned with new space for housing when Roger Starr is talking about shrinking the city?[7]

Roger Starr was head of New York City's Housing and Development Administration from January 1974 to July 1976 and a *New York Times* editorial writer from 1977 to 1992. Starr's philosophy of Planned Shrinkage called for the concentration of shrinking urban populations in areas of high density and providing municipal services to those areas, while cutting off services and abandoning or demolishing buildings in the areas with diminishing populations. Create new land and build new housing and office towers while at the same time abandoning areas, where

> sewers, streets, parks, schools, electric lines, and more already exist? There is no sense to this, no reality in it at all. This is the reason to change the subject and get behind the pollution issues.
>
> The expressway was a running fight for quite a while. It wasn't until 1969, after the new pollution regulations had gone in, that the first hearing was held on the plan for all the grand things that were going to be built on either side of this expressway and the marvelous new piece of New York that this money was going to buy. Killing it *did* buy a marvelous new piece of New York. It bought SoHo. SoHo was already reviving, at least starting to. This new exciting neighborhood *was* being created. Chinatown and Little Italy would have been devastated too. But nobody in the media confronted this built-in dilemma. I don't think this has ever been published, or ever said, and I think this is big news. Don't you?

More Differences

Public debate over whether to build Westway was really a mirage. No debate occurred about *whether* to build a highway, just which of five highway plans to adopt: highway alternatives, not transportation alternatives. It was all about cars.

> The public has been going through a great learning process in the last couple of decades of how to defeat the highway men. In response the highway people, naturally, have worked up other defenses. The environmental impact and air pollution thing was a new weapon for the public. The changing of the subject was a defense move for proponents.
>
> Now there is a requirement for public participation. The public demanded it and got it. In earlier highway schemes, there was no such requirement. So, the defensive weapon is new ways of manipulating the public and of using public relations to give the impression of public participation. With Westway, they've anticipated a lot of the troubles that they had with the Lower Manhattan fight. And this time it's a harder fight because they know that they can't give up on Westway and start with another piece of the net.

It was becoming clear that if Westway was lost, the battle *and* the war were lost for more highways like it. "It's a much harder fight in that they are much more determined to win this battle," Jacobs said, "so they won't lose the whole net. But rather than the various differences mentioned, *this* is what makes this a much harder battle. The chips are down on this one. And herein lies the future of New York. The stakes for the people of New York are tremendously higher in this one."

Westway's defeat would be an incredible reversal. If it was defeated, then maybe, finally, there might be some notion about getting to the real business at hand, Jacobs said. In the transit field this would mean looking at upgrading and expanding transit. In the housing field it would mean rehabbing what already existed instead of first or only building more new projects. Jacobs's vision was about strategies for rebuilding the city.

> The stakes for everybody in the country are high. If Westway were built, it would be a very clear signal that there was no hope for the future of New York, that it could do nothing but repeat expensive, disastrous

mistakes, and that it can't turn itself around, and that it was okay to keep building new or expanding existing highways. Other cities will follow.

New York used to be its people, its citizens and the brilliance of many of its citizens. This was what put it ahead of other places. What's happened to a city that can have handed to it such a brilliant analysis of what its highway programs did to it, as Bob Caro did in *The Power Broker*, and it just rolls off? And they just keep obsessively repeating the same mistakes. This is what's absolutely frightening about Westway, that there's no way New York can turn itself around. That's what it would mean to me.

I asked, was this is a classic turning point, then, a crossroads? Jane stated, "Yes, it is. I do think it is that important."

-9-

BIG THINGS GET DONE

> The decline of New York's essentially efficient, energy-saving, decrepit transport system has reflected the decline of the city. But the massive rehabilitation of this arterial lifeline through a trade-in of Westway funds would be the most significant present step this city would take to assert its inner vitality and to underpin its future growth and development for the benefit of the masses of people who live and work here.
>
> JOHN OAKES,
> *New York Times* (op-ed, 1978)

And that is what happened with the defeat of Westway.

No mayor could have as much of an impact on the city as did the official defeat of Westway in 1985. In fact, Westway would have cost endless billions of dollars and stunted the rebirth of the city that is so universally admired today.[1]

Citywide, the benefits are many but not easy to recognize and hard to measure. Transportation investments were fundamentally altered. Transit, on which 85 percent of New Yorkers depend, became a priority for the first time since the 1930s. Car-oriented policies were significantly challenged and seriously rethought. The years of debate resulted in a sea of change in urban development thinking. As a result, many destructive urban policies that evolved after World War II were reversed or, at least, moderated; transportation, after all, shapes development anywhere.

9.1 The Westway landfill would surely have seen towers rise on it at least as tall as ones like this rising on the Williamsburg waterfront. *Ron Shiffman.*

The defeat of that massive highway project changed the transportation debate in New York City. It also helped change the debate nationwide. And it helped change the debate about how we understand and view cities. As Jacobs noted in conversation, one's view of the city shapes the feeling about this highway. Above all, the defeat helped renew New York City in many unrecognized ways.

If it had been built, the disruption and construction in Manhattan would rival the Big Dig in Boston. Expected federal funding would have been exhausted long before completion. Where the money would have come from to rebuild the subway and regional transit system is anybody's guess. The state legislature is unlikely to have filled the gap. The distinctively revived neighborhoods along the far West Side—Tribeca, the West Village, Gansvoort Market, Chelsea, and the West Thirties and Forties—would instead be coping with the impact of that disruption. The full range of consequence is hard to imagine.

Westway was more than a debate about a highway or even the larger transportation issues. It focused attention and drew out differences over how cities function and how they are reinvigorated. In the broadest sense, the battle over Westway should have been the final chapter—a postscript—in the long-standing clash of urban strategies defined by the battles in the 1950s and 1960s between Robert Moses and Jane Jacobs.

Neither Moses nor Jacobs played a direct role in the Westway saga. Moses was long out of power; Jacobs lived in Toronto by then. But their urban philosophies were central to the argument over Westway.

The idea of massive highways through cities, as we've seen, was heavily promoted by Robert Moses. And while Westway was not Moses's project, it was clearly in keeping with his legacy.[2] In fact, Moses had his own plan to rebuild the West Side Highway, about which he said: "There isn't a project I've been connected with in forty years that would have been built if I had consulted [the public] prior to announcing it."

By the time the Westway fight was engaged, the highway resistance, inspired by Jacobs's victory with the Lower Manhattan Expressway, had strength. Proponents like to attribute the Westway opposition to the total dedication of one woman, Marcy Benstock, an environmental activist most identified as the opposition leader. They like to blame her for Westway's demise. Her vigorous opposition was, in fact, dedicated, formidable, and effective. Clearly, she was the leading public voice. But that opposition was broader and more widespread than recognized or acknowledged. A CBS poll in 1976, for example, found 67 percent of New Yorkers asked wanted the money spent on transit, not a highway.[3] The opposition was, in fact, a diverse but loose alliance: environmentalists, local legislators, transit advocates, community boards, preservationists, fiscal conservatives, and liberals aided by some transportation and environmental officials inside government agencies.

The Westway battle raged during the 1970s and into the 1980s until Mayor Ed Koch and Governor Hugh Carey opted to trade in the federal highway funds in 1985 for a combination of transit and highway investments just as the opportunity for all the states to trade in such funding was about to expire. "There is no question the debate over Westway, in the end, was a plebiscite on mass transit or highways," says Kent Barwick, former president of the Municipal Art Society. "It crystallized the issue and strengthened the resolve of transit advocates. The Lower Manhattan Expressway victory was a mere skirmish in comparison; Westway was the Armageddon of highways in the city." "The real impetus was anticar," adds Albert Butzel, the lead lawyer in the fight against Westway. "It was an opportunity to get rid of a superhighway and to use the money for mass transit. The Lower Manhattan Expressway was the beginning of the end of the automobile fixation; Westway expanded the debate. People realized that the lifeline of the city was mass transit, not highways."

TRANSIT REINVESTMENT WAS HUGE

The defeat of Westway resulted in an enormous reinvestment in the city public transit system, the most in decades. Nationally, trading in highway funds for transit investment was rare. A 1974 federal law first permitted this. Portland, Oregon, was the first to take advantage. Boston traded in highway money to reinvest and reopen some closed suburban rail lines. Later, for the Big Dig, House Speaker Tip O'Neill (D-MA) got a special allocation of four billion dollars. Other cities such as Chicago, San Francisco, Philadelphia, Washington, and Baltimore traded highway for transit funding.

The 1985 trade-in set a pattern for New York trading in highway funds for transit funds that has continued ever since with each five-year Metropolitan Transportation Authority (MTA) capital plan. But it took that significant early trade-in money (only part, but a significant part, of the total funding) to begin to reverse decades of neglect that had accumulated since 1956. In that year, the year of passage of the Federal Highway Act, the building of the Interstate Highway System began, and New York instituted a policy of "deferred maintenance," as Robert Caro points out in *The Power Broker*. "So superbly engineered and maintained had the system been previously (New York had been enormously proud of its subways) that it took years for this systematic neglect to take its toll." By the late 1960s, it had almost reached bottom. "When Robert Moses came to power in 1934," Caro adds, "the city's mass transportation system was probably the best in the world. When he left power in 1968, it was quite possibly the worst."[4]

The first reinvestment was critical to the dramatic turnaround and total upgrade of the citywide system. Today, many users take for granted reasonable subway conditions and find plenty of weaknesses to complain about. But in the mid-1970s, conditions were horrific. Train cars regularly broke down and were taken out of service. Graffiti covered every car. Doors didn't close. The schedule was erratic. The system's infrastructure, invisible to the public, was in terrible shape. Signals and switches failed. Tracks were unsafe. Garbage overflowed station containers. Subway cars and buses were in use well beyond their replacement time. Most stations were deteriorated.

In 2004 the New York Public Interest Research Group Straphangers Campaign mounted an exhibit at the Municipal Art Society titled "The Riders and the Rebirth of City Transit: 25 Years of Advocacy." A companion booklet noted, "It may be hard for many of us to imagine now, but our city's subways and buses were close to collapse in 1979, the year the New York Public Interest Groups founded the Straphangers Campaign. Subway . . . service was so horrendous that a daily commute was enough to make residents question why on earth they chose to live here. The same thoughts occurred to the city's business leaders, who often cited poor transit as the leading reason for moving out of New York."

In 1981 frequent track fires and derailments prompted the National Transportation Safety Board to launch an investigation into the safety of the subway system. Ridership fell to the lowest level since 1917. All of that has been substantially reversed. The station upgrades are particularly visible because the "Percent for Art" policy has meant inclusion of artwork in every renovated station. Nearly 200 stations have been upgraded and artwork installed since 1985 in the 722-mile system, the Works Progress Administration all over again. Sadly, some of the first rebuilt stations are beginning to show their age, primarily for lack of regular cleaning and maintenance. Money for capital projects, with contracts available for the well placed, is always more readily available than the operational funds necessary to maintain the facilities, which requires salaried, union labor.

REINVESTMENT PAYS

Since Westway's demise in 1985, approximately $1.4 billion in Westway trade-in funds have flowed to fix the subways and buses. Additional funds have gone into the regional system. The trade-in for transit funding, what Westway opponents advocated from day one, was the leverage that rebuilt the system. The enormous borrowing the state initiated under MTA chairman Richard Ravitch would not have been possible without it. "It is scary to think what city transit would be like without that support," says Gene Russianoff, staff attorney of the Straphangers Campaign. "Some people remember Westway as a symbol of what couldn't get built, a symbol of how David held off Goliath and saved the subways. The $1.4 billion in trade-in funds was a pittance in terms of need," notes Butzel, "but it came at a critical time at the beginning of the refocusing on transit that that controversy stimulated." The system was in terrible disrepair, Butzel adds, so the trade-in funds were just the beginning. But the beginning of a real turnaround they were.

Today, trains are nearly twenty times more reliable. Graffiti on subway cars is negligible, and transit crime, fires, and derailments have all been dramatically reduced. Every subway car and bus has been either rehabilitated or replaced. The subway fleet has been expanded by four hundred cars and buses by eight hundred in order to meet growing demands. Miles and miles of tracks and antiquated signals have been replaced. Mayor Giuliani's administration slowed that reinvestment when it resumed in 1995 the old pattern by cutting the subway rebuilding program by $625 million over the following five years.[5] In 2004 annual ridership had reached 1.4 billion, the highest since the subway's heyday in the 1950s. In September 2005, the number of daily bus and subway riders reached 7.5 million during weekdays, the highest average daily ridership since June 1971.

The transformation is enormous, but, as historian Mike Wallace points out, "the tangibility of the trade-off" remains elusive. People either forget or downplay the impact of the trade-in money on the subways. "If," Wallace adds, "you could point to a new Second Avenue subway, people would feel differently." Under Mayor Bloomberg, construction of that desperately needed subway line was resumed.

SHOW ME THE MONEY

Mort Downey put it all in perspective probably better than anyone else could. He was with the Federal Department of Transportation from 1977 to 1981, chief financial officer for the MTA from 1981 to 1993, and then back to the federal Department of Transportation as deputy secretary for transportation from 1993 to 2001. Downey remembers this period well, having been in the eye of the storm for more than a decade. "The needs of transit were being debated independent of the Westway issue," says Downy, but they weren't making any headway in gaining new funding from either the governor or the legislature. Politically, however, it became clear to Governor Hugh Carey that in order to get Westway approved, he would have to create the illusion that he was also delivering funds for transit. "He announced publicly that he had applied to Washington for $600 million," remembers Downey. But it was not at all true. When

Washington denied that an application had been made, "Carey, then desperate to save face, persuaded [DOT secretary Neil] Goldschmidt to say that 'it was not beyond the realm of possibility.' But it was all done within the context of getting Westway through."

Then Carey appointed Richard Ravitch as chairman of the MTA in 1980, and everything began to change. Ravitch started talking about the real conditions and needs of the MTA to rebuild the city's transit and the suburban railroads. According to Downey:

> He said a basic minimum capital investment of $1.5 billion a year was needed, when the whole capital budget was holding at $200 million a year and some of that money was being used not for capital but to save the fare. Ravitch was told not to talk about this because they had to get Westway approved, but he basically said, "I have to do the job you appointed me to do."
>
> Ravitch went around the governor, directly to the legislature, to get the first five-year [1982–1986] capital budget of $8 billion, so the time of the trade-in decision [1985] was such that it gave a nice boost to the MTA effort. It was a momentum builder. We would not have gotten the second five-year plan without it. It set the pattern. By 1987, we had the second plan, and by the third, the legislature just knew they had to do it. Ravitch got the debate going, but until he lit the fire under them, they were not supportive of doing both.

By 2007, Downey estimates, $74 billion has been spent rebuilding the system of the subway, buses, and suburban railways.

THE BIG DIG FACTOR

Another significant factor demands consideration. Let's call it the "Big Dig" factor. One disastrous news story follows the next, it seems, about Boston's Big Dig, the tunnel highway that connects the city and Logan International Airport. The tunnel is part of the larger central highway system through Boston. Concrete in the walls of the tunnel seems not to be of required quality and may be giving way. Ceiling panels in the tunnel were discovered to be faulty after one fell on a car and crushed a passenger to death. Other construction defects have been exposed over the years. Overruns have kept costs mounting from an original $2.7 billion estimate to what seems to be probably a $15 billion final cost. Started in 1991, the connector tunnel was opened in 2003 and replaced the elevated highway that had divided the city from the waterfront and the North End. Significantly, it does more than replace; it adds capacity.

Does anyone really believe that Westway's construction would not have gotten the city and state into similar trouble, at least financially? Westway's budget was expected to grow from $2 billion to $4 billion just because of inflation. Downey figures it might have hit $10 billion before completion, less than the Big Dig because the Big Dig may be more complicated, Downey says. It crosses a river and goes through the heart of downtown Boston. Yet Westway was also largely to be an underwater tunnel.

But the much heralded aspect that Westway would have been funded with 90 percent federal and 10 percent state funds would not have lasted the duration of construction. That commitment expired before Westway would have been finished. "Between 1978 and 1981, the picnic was over," Downey says of unbuilt segments of the Interstate Highway System like Westway. "The mood in Congress was 'get it done' and let's move on. The first deadline was set in 1978 and changed in 1981 to 1983, *unless*, as in the New York case, there was litigation." Then it was 1985. The litigation was ongoing. That was the reason Mayor Koch and Governor Cuomo finally agreed to the trade-in that year. There was no guarantee of Westway funds, but the trade-in was secure.

Every other state except New York and Massachusetts had finished their interstate highway segments or were in construction. "There was a total of $6.5 billion to cover trade-ins around the country, not enough for both projects, so those two would have been hanging out there looking for money," Downey explains. New York, like Massachusetts, would be scrambling for money, and mostly it would have to come from the state and city budgets because enough could never again be extracted from Congress that wouldn't take up the transportation budget for the entire state. In fact, Downey adds, subsequent allocations to Massachusetts included a provision guaranteeing that a certain percentage of the money go to projects other than the Big Dig because "it was sucking up so much of the state allocation."

STEEL-WHEEL JOBS VERSUS RUBBER-TIRE JOBS

Westway proponents vociferously argued that Westway was important for the creation of jobs at a time when the New York economy was seriously hurting. Union leader Peter Brennan said on CBS's *Eye On* program in 1976, "Will we build a Westway, and open the doors to jobs, whether it be office buildings or warehouses? . . . Do we talk about getting New York turned around, or do we want to put a China Wall around New York and all die of starvation looking at each other? . . ."

The jobs issue pulls at the heartstrings, but what kind of jobs and for whom were never understood. Jacobs focused on this in our conversation:

> The jobs argument breaks down into a few things. The Lower Manhattan Expressway debate was the first time the question was ever raised as to where are these jobs? Outside or in New York? And the ones that are in New York, how temporary are they? How long do they last? The other thing about jobs is that under this kind of scheme, permanent jobs are eliminated for the sake of temporary jobs in construction.
>
> In fact, this is what New York has been doing for years: it's been cannibalizing itself for the sake of temporary construction jobs. It has lost all kinds of low-cost industrial space. It has driven out—apart from those that want to leave the city for various reasons—businesses and all kinds of jobs, not only for highways but for urban renewal, for public housing, for anything.
>
> It was the expressway that I first saw this issue confronted head-on [at a public hearing], and I had a conversation with Harry Van Arsdale, who was head of the Central Labor Council. In fact, I quoted this somewhere in *Economy of Cities* where a study of how many jobs there were in the SoHo area, before it was SoHo, and how many would be wiped out by the expressway. Van Arsdale was there with a lot of paid construction workers who were given a day's pay, they told us, to come to City Hall and cheer or boo at the right points. They all left promptly before five o'clock.
>
> Van Arsdale was speaking in favor of the expressway, and I said to him, "What about the jobs of all those people that are going to be wiped out by the expressway?" And a lot of those people are blacks and Puerto Ricans who have a very hard time getting work. And he said, "Oh, I can't be concerned about those jobs." And he wasn't. He was concerned with construction only. High-paid construction workers, temporary jobs. To this day, that's the basis on which jobs are talked about for Westway.

This is still true in debates on highways, stadiums, casinos, malls, and similar big projects.

In reality, highways and transit are both job creators, at least for jobs that last the duration of the construction project. The same energy and advocacy never seem to get behind the kind of entrepreneurial investment that creates long-term jobs not in construction.

An important distinction exists, however, in the jobs created by highways and transit. Most of the highway jobs are on-site, with cement, steel, and other supplies coming from distant places. With transit, more meaningful jobs and more of them can be created off-site but within the state.

In 2005 the MTA distributed an eight-page brochure highlighting dozens of subway, bus, and commuter rail parts that are made around New York State. A map of the state showed forty-four locations of parts subcontractors for subway, bus, and railcars. Diagrams of the hybrid buses, subway, and railcars identified the location at which each component is produced. The minimum number of scattered manufacturing sites was ten for hybrid buses produced in Oriskany in central New York; the maximum was twenty-eight for the Kawasaki railcars produced in Yonkers, a city north of New York City. "The economy of the southern tier of the state is very dependent on this work, especially the rebuilding of subway cars," Downey points out. The shells of 660 new subway cars were delivered by ship from Brazil to the Port of Albany, for example, and trucked to an assembly plant with eleven hundred employees in Hornell, in the southwest corner of the state. The Hornell plant is producing the propulsion and gear units. All the parts work, Downey adds, is highly labor intensive. The lighting for new cars comes from Buffalo, the ventilation system from Auburn, and fabricated metal parts from Kingston and Farmingdale. The propulsion system for the new clean-fuel city buses comes from Johnson City and the sheet metal from Utica.

BEYOND TRANSIT: REGENERATION OR REPLACEMENT?

It would be a mistake, however, to evaluate the Westway defeat *only* on the basis of the enormous transit benefit from the trade-in funds. Multiple positive ripple effects are equally significant:

- The Westway corridor from the Battery to Forty-second Street along the Hudson River has been transformed on both sides of the roadway.

9.2 One of those lovely moments with Jane, a martini break in a conversation. *Stephen A. Goldsmith.*

- Neighborhoods around the city experienced tremendous infusions of new residents, lured, in part, by vastly improved transit service.
- A stronger awareness of and interest in the full 575 miles of New York City waterfront evolved or were accelerated after the intense focus on this 5-mile section.
- The regional transit network shared in the new system investments, improving access to the city for local users, commuters, and visitors.

The benefits are not obvious, until one appreciates the critical and beneficial role of transit to urban life and the destructive role of highways. Few New Yorkers living in neighborhoods revitalized in recent decades connect the improved transit benefits they enjoy today to the defeat of Westway. "The Westway trade-in and subway investment made all the difference in my life," reports a longtime resident of Brooklyn's Park Slope. "Before that, you could never count on getting back and forth to Manhattan to make a business meeting on time. You never knew whether your kid's lateness from school was something to worry about. And, you wound up spending a fortune on cabs at night (if you could get them to take you across the bridge), because you never wanted to trust the subway after dark. I'd say the subway improvements maybe doubled the value of my house."

The transformation of the far West Side of Manhattan below Forty-second Street is probably the most visible testimony to the post-Westway change. What Jane said would happen if Westway was killed has, indeed, happened. "There is so much there," she said of the so-called decrepit area. "Plenty of room exists for fill-in development between buildings and on empty lots. Much of that vacant space certainly ought to be developed before you add new landfill at enormous expense, if that's ever necessary. And the new land wouldn't be a success until these fill-ins were done in any case."

During the Westway debate, proponents vigorously argued that the highway and landfill development were absolutely necessary to spur the revival of this stretch of the West Side. Without Westway, the area was doomed, the experts said. They were wrong. This area was certainly "ramshackle." The condition was not debatable; the cause of the condition was. And Westway as the cure was a joke. As Jane said: "What a ridiculous idea that you put in a billion-dollar highway to manicure a place!"

ORGANIC REGENERATION GETS A CHANCE

Anyone who has observed the organic regeneration of urban districts understood how erroneous this notion was. Grand plans, for highways, urban renewal, stadia, and the like, work as impediments to authentic regeneration, and their defeat makes regeneration possible. Regeneration after defeat is not guaranteed; other conditions are necessary.

In the 1970s many properties along the route were turned into sleazy bars and illicit sex spots, supporting the image of extreme deterioration. Owners waited for the big payoff that would come with condemnation. The bars served as a useful, very visual prop for Westway advocates. Mysteriously, all of these places disappeared after Westway's demise.

Something was ready and waiting to happen there, and it did—after Westway's defeat. Now, property along the West Village, Gansvoort Market, and the Chelsea waterfront is among the highest-valued real estate in Manhattan. "The neighborhood is now part of the richest ZIP code in New York City and the 12th richest ZIP code in the country, according to a study by Forbes," the *New York Sun* reported on August 14, 2006.

Many buildings have been renovated, and numerous trendy restaurants and shops opened and new buildings have been built. Too many architecturally distinctive buildings, however, were torn down, viable businesses lost, and residents displaced while the death threat hung over the area and the Landmarks Preservation Commission delayed expansion of the Greenwich Village Historic District. An expansion was passed in May 2006. A small additional district was designated—the omitted remnants of the rich district that existed when the original Greenwich Village Historic District was designated in 1966. But even this time, certain landmark-quality buildings were omitted, enabling developers to replace them with high-rise condos.

Old industrial buildings have been converted to residential lofts in the pattern established in SoHo after the demise of the Lower Manhattan Expressway plan.[6] And although residents complain that the new high-rises are intrusive and out of character, the scale of some of the new buildings—notably the three best known, designed by architect Richard Meier—are only twelve stories. This is modest for the city, especially in contrast to the excessive scale—forty stories plus—permitted in a 2005 zoning change for the industrial neighborhood of Greenpoint-Williamsburg in Brooklyn.

If Westway had been built and the new land created for development, can one imagine zoning for fewer than forty stories, and probably more with incentives? Would a wall of high-rises on a hundred acres at the river be better than what is emerging now? Most people complain about the scale of the apartment towers Donald Trump built along the river between Sixty-fifth and Seventy-second Streets, and they are lower than forty stories. Would the West Side have received zoning less than Greenpoint-Williamsburg's forty stories plus?

THE NEW PARK—BIG IS BIG

The creation of the Hudson River Park along the waterfront puts the lie to the oft-repeated ridiculous belief that nothing big can get done in New York City. Even the *New York Times*, long an ardent advocate of Westway, noted that "this modest park is as big an urban planning success story as anything that has taken place in New York City in 100 years."[7] Modest it may be, but it is still the largest Manhattan park built in more than a century.

Not only is this already a huge accomplishment on its own terms—about three-quarters completed—but it is the largest physical change in the city's waterfront land use since the days when cruise ships and commerce filled a rich assortment of finger piers. The opening of the first segment in Greenwich Village in 2003 marked the beginning of serious city and state efforts to transform for recreational use waterfront areas in neighborhoods throughout the city. New segments seem to open annually.

The first segment—a ten-acre swath in Greenwich Village—included three piers extending a thousand feet offshore with lawns, playing fields, playgrounds, a children's ecology stream, and a display garden, not to mention the spectacular views of the city's skyline from the end of the piers. Users disagree as to how difficult it is to cross the highway. Either way, millions are indeed crossing. Any weekend, people are coming from all parts of the city. Diehard Westway proponents argue that with the highway underground, access to the waterfront would have been better. But there still would be a road to cross, an access road, not much narrower than the present highway.

Only six years since that 2003 opening, one marvels at how much more of the five-mile park already exists, with more constantly under construction. Within some common design elements, like railings, lighting, and comfortable benches, the diversity of uses and potential experiences is remarkable. Boating options range from sailing and kayaking to touring, with more boating opportunities planned. Lawns for picnicking, sunbathing, or socializing are plentiful. Playgrounds, tennis courts, a fabulous historic barge, and more are found along the way. Even a small, protected wildlife sanctuary for migrating birds exists with a variety of plantings and flowers to attract whatever Mother Nature brings.

Protecting the fish was at the heart of the Westway battle, and the new park seems to do this well with a generous assortment of habitat preserves. The areas between the piers are off-limits to filling and platforming and continue to function as they have for years. The piers and pilings slow the river flow and create calmer areas, providing shelter for the fish. Decking has been removed from what used to be piers, creating a series of protected pier ruins—pile fields that are both fish habitat and sculptural reminders of the waterfront's history when piers lined the water's edge, one after another. Their function as habitat is preserved; if more than 30 percent of the pilings in one field is lost, replacement is required. What is sadly missing, however, is any kind of interpretive signage to remind the visitor of some historic events and activity. This waterfront was the incubator of the city's and, in effect, nation's economy in the 1800s. Not a clue is offered.

9.3 The Tribecca boardwalk section of Hudson River Park. *Albert Butzel.*

Nevertheless, born out of the Westway defeat, this is the greatest park development since Central Park and not just because it is the largest park added to the city since then. It is a balanced blend of new park space, recreational uses, city service structures, and nearby new development. The design evolved out of a three-year planning process with definite input from the assorted adjacent neighborhoods. Because the end result reflects that input, Hudson River Park feels more like a string of contiguous but varying parks, some more passive or active than others.

How do you value a five-hundred-acre park attracting people from all over the city? Kayakers, sailors, even swimmers can get into the water, and everyone gets close to the water. It turns out to be an incredibly well-used city park, not the neighborhood park that people expected. The waterfront-park momentum it precipitated spread to Brooklyn's DUMBO, Red Hook, Williamsburg, and elsewhere in the city. The significance of the spread of this momentum is enormous.

Unquestionably, this is a different park from what Westway would have produced. The intention was to create a passive park on the landfill, recalls one Westway defender, who worked on the never-completed design. That meant trees, walkways, and lawns, with ball fields down

9.4 Hudson River Park grassy Pier 45 in Greenwich Village is a popular gathering place. *Albert Butzel.*

around Christopher Street. Some argue that it would never have worked out that way and instead would have been an extension of Battery Park City with a continuation of the same bulkhead and uses. There is nothing wrong with that, but that is not the same as what now exists, with the variety of designs and uses in between rebuilt piers. Being out on the pier, a thousand feet from shore, is a unique experience. "The piers," one planning commissioner commented, "are the best thing to happen to New York in 50 years."

Equally interesting in a diverse, urban way is the variety of residential and commercial development evolving across the West Side Highway on the inland side facing the river. An interesting mix of new and old of reasonable scale, including numerous innovative conversions of unusual commercial buildings, it is a variable stretch that changes from community to community, reflecting both the city's earlier and its recent development history. And talk about serendipitous planning—the celebrated High Line neighborhood, with its own new park paralleling the highway two blocks inland, ties in nicely with the waterside park. In fact, what is evolving along the inland side should be called "Starchitect Row," with buildings by Jean Nouvel, Frank Gehry, Richard Meier, and Robert A. M. Stern. None of them exceeds twenty stories, and happily none overshadows such incomparable landmarks as the Art Moderne Starrett-Lehigh Building. In fact, as a group, the recent new waterfront buildings are among the highest quality of new structures because of high design standards imposed by the City Planning Commission.

None of this would have happened if Westway were built with one hundred acres of solid, continuous park versus piers and one hundred acres of new development that would be towers like Trump's Riverside South above Fifty-ninth Street. None of the inland-side development would have happened as well, or at all, knowing that a wall of towers would be built in front.

The Transportation Debate

Until the mid-1980s, the idea that more and bigger highways solved traffic problems still prevailed. Few observers recognized that highways *through* cities and increased vehicular traffic in cities were inimical to urban life. Few experts understood how crucial public transit was to the functioning of a vibrant city.

Some of this is still true. After all, word usage reflects beliefs. Officials talk about "investing" in highways but "subsidizing" transit. Federal funding for roads and airports is infinitely more generous than for transit. News reporters fail to distinguish between *infrastructure investment* as code words in legislative proposals for highway funding rather than sewers, utilities, streets, and other systems, which used to be—and should still be—what the words connote.

The overwhelming predominance of highway provisions in transportation legislation is accepted as the norm. Some transportation legislation mentions *only* highways and makes little or no attempt to fund transit. The very central concept of mobility is lost. The transportation question should be: mobility for what? Highways are designed to move vehicles; transit is designed to move people. The difference is like night and day. For mobility of people and goods, public transit should be paramount. "Traffic engineers think of moving vehicles from point A to point B," Jane noted in conversation. "But the kind of mobility systems cities need—and once had—link all kinds of places within the city in multiple ways."

Vehicular Domination Still Prevails

The deadest downtowns in cities across America are car dominated. The vibrancy of New York's bustling streets depends on pedestrian, not vehicular, traffic. Unquestionably, New York City has been much more accommodating of vehicular traffic than it was during the 1970s when the City Planning Commission was forced to clamp down on the number of parking spaces in midtown, among other strategies, to discourage driving. This move was a response to a Friends of the Earth air pollution lawsuit in 1977, but the parking-space restriction expired. Garages have not stopped proliferating since. Traffic gets worse. Every new building seems to have another enormous parking garage. The City Planning Commission maintains antiquated standards requiring too much new parking for each new building and residential unit. Curb cuts are granted for private residences on residential blocks where no garages ever existed, allowing one more suburban intrusion to erode vibrant urban streets.[8] Resistance is fierce to tolls on the East River bridges, even by residents in neighborhoods accessible to transit. Tolls, of course, would impose some of the city's costs on commuters and visitors and encourage more transit use. Mayor Bloomberg appropriately and vigorously fought for this to no avail. But he was 100 percent correct to do so.

Delivery trucks get bigger and longer, causing traffic jams at every corner they can't easily turn. Private tourist buses are larger and more numerous than ever and crowd out local buses from public bus stops. For the tourists' convenience, taxpaying residents are inconvenienced. Nothing is done to encourage visitors to use the subway or buses, and hotel doormen only put visitors in taxis, rarely recommending transit. Transit maps should be given to every visitor. And why not a metro card with ten dollars' worth of trips in every hotel room to introduce visitors to transit use? And why not give permit and financial advantages to smaller tour buses with operable windows and no luggage space?

Police, fire, and many other city employees have free workplace parking, even though some of them also get free subway passes and live in transit-accessible neighborhoods. If they don't live near transit, they could park at a transit locale and continue by subway. Imagine the added security if police and firemen took the subway to work like most city residents.

The parking-garage lobby has achieved enormous strength, boldly evidenced after 9/11. To ease the postdisaster traffic congestion, Mayor Bloomberg wisely and firmly required all vehicles coming over the East River bridges to have two passengers. Garages reportedly suffered the loss of business. They were not alone, but they claimed erroneously that people wanting to shop were not coming in because of the limitation. The restriction did not last long. The garage-lobby investment in maximum vehicular traffic was never more clear until its opposition to congestion pricing.

Permit parking for taxpaying residents in neighborhoods burdened by suburban drivers—as is done in Cambridge, New Haven, and other cities—is rejected whenever it is proposed. The city's efficient trolley system and Second and Third Avenue elevated trains—called the El—were eliminated during the Robert Moses era to make more room for cars. As a result, the city has a smaller transit system than it did almost a century ago. But new replacement streetcar lines are dismissed out of hand because it is unthinkable to interfere with street space for cars. New York is way behind European cities, which have extraordinary streetcars, bikeways, and congestion pricing.

So some of the transportation ideas dating from before Westway was killed may still dominate. And some may even be worse. Nevertheless, one should not ignore the differences. The sea change is enormous. Public transit is valued more now than before the Westway fight. New York and the country could have become car-centric without Westway but not without Robert Moses. Yet in small, incremental ways, the public's desire for the return of more mass transit is having an impact as light rail systems are built city by city, section by section, and downtown sections of elevated highways are being dismantled in a number of cities.

Surely, on many levels, the death of Westway marked the end of an era. And, despite dire warnings of gridlock to come if the roadway's capacity was not expanded, traffic flows no worse than twenty years ago, heavy but manageable. And while traffic has increased, adjustments have been made to avenue and crosstown streetlights by the Department of Transportation to assist a smoother traffic flow.

BIG PROJECTS DO GET DONE

Whenever a project like Westway is defeated, the cry is heard: "You can't get anything big done in New York anymore." Every time I hear this lament, I wonder what city they are talking about. Sometimes big proposals—usually for a new overscaled construction project—actually are defeated. But does that mean all big projects are defeated? Evidence indicates otherwise.

Is not the rebuilding during the past twenty years of the city's mass transit big, in fact huge and more complex than any singular building project? The mass transit system is not yet good enough, yet it is on its way. Extension of the Number 7 subway line west along Forty-second Street and downtown to Thirty-fourth Street is under way with an estimated price tag of $2.1 billion, even though the long-proposed Forty-second Street Streetcar would have made more sense. Although it would have been built faster and cheaper, it would have taken minimum surface space away from cars. Horrors!

And what about the ongoing construction of the $6 billion Third Water Tunnel, not due for completion until 2020 and billed as the biggest public works project in America? Planned since 1954 and under construction since 1970, enough progress was made for the city to open a finished 13.5-mile segment, about a quarter of the whole tunnel. This allowed the city to close one of the other two tunnels for repairs. New York was facing a veritable crisis with its old, leaking water infrastructure.

The Third Water Tunnel is as big and ambitious a project imaginable and proceeds with little interference. Funding has varied through six administrations, but under Mayor Michael Bloomberg, even with budget shortages, the city investment in the tunnel was twice the amount of the prior five administrations combined. When finished, New York's water capacity will have been doubled.

One of the largest water-filtration plants in the world is under construction in the Bronx in a ten-story-deep hole blasted out of bedrock. Scheduled for completion in 2012 but already behind schedule and over budget, the plant will be capable of purifying 300 million gallons of water a day. The plant, which will filter water from the Croton watershed, was estimated to cost $660 million when announced in 1998 but by 2008 had reached a projected $3 billion. Considerable opposition to this project occurred because it is under Van Cortlandt Park. The opposition legitimately questioned the selection of the underground Bronx park site when the city owned an alternative site in Westchester where the plant could have been built aboveground. Opponents argued the aboveground site would be cheaper and quicker, which logically makes sense. But the project moved forward, and it will be important to see if the city lives up to its commitment to restore the park better than ever, a commitment that does not seem to be true in the Yankee Stadium neighborhood of the Bronx.

Both Yankee and Shea Stadiums were replaced at the same time. These are enormous undertakings. Stadia have been the favorite big project for cities across the country, even though every economic study has shown they are economic losers. But political and business leaders love their branding and boasting value, even though they exclude fans of modest means. Yankee Stadium is, perhaps, the most egregious in its unfairness to the public, especially the Bronx community. For additional parking garages, a much loved and well-used local park was taken. In return, a less appealing, somewhat distant park space was created. One park is actually located atop the garage and called a replacement. The community will experience the additional vehicular traffic while the Steinbrenners and the Yankees reap the financial profit of the garages. The one good thing that came out of the public debate is the opening of a Metro North train station within walking distance of the stadium. The Steinbrenners always opposed this since it could, it was hoped, get Westchester fans to come by rail instead of car.

A rail link to JFK was built, no small accomplishment given the dissension and debate that preceded its approval. The first proposed route was ludicrous and defeated. A link to La Guardia Airport, however, just as important, doesn't seem to be on anybody's priority list. A connection of the Long Island Railroad to the east side and Grand Central, however, is under construction.

And what about the $200 million restoration of Grand Central Terminal, one of the grandest public spaces and urban gateways almost lost during the era of transit devaluation and lack of interest in historic preservation? It is easy to build from scratch, harder to adjust and revive what exists. But the satisfaction comes with accomplishing what makes urbanistic sense. Grand Central is New York's best face to the visiting and commuting world—a better brand, if you need one, than a stadium—but it does not only benefit the outsider; it is also a destination for New Yorkers. A terrific food market, assorted small local retailers, high-end restaurants, and a food court were added during the restoration, an appropriate diversity of uses bringing in activity of all kinds. This is the best measure of success.

Then there is Central Park, reclaimed and restored to its original Olmsted-Vaux glory over three decades. Its transformation is still ongoing, and Prospect, the Battery, and Riverside Parks are following similarly impressive paths. Central Park's restoration was a big vision accomplished in manageable increments until the large-scale whole was revived by its small-scale components. The park is not big in a build-new way but big in a restorative way. *The revival of Central Park parallels the restoration of the city itself.*

None of these projects is about real estate. Instead, they are about critical infrastructure, of the kind that either makes the city function or adds to the quality of life that makes it a desirable place to live. When one understands the sorry state of the nation's infrastructure, it is nothing short of amazing that New York is proceeding to address some of these crucial infrastructure needs.

Sweeping new gestures in the form of big new real estate projects garner political appeal and grab headlines when proposed, regardless of the legitimacy of their claims; more satisfying and productive gestures are the ones made up of smaller components that are quite complex and stun you in their completion. They don't emerge fresh out of the ground on a huge, cleared site.

GOVERNMENT CAN DO IT BIG AND WELL

One of the most staggering accomplishments achieved primarily by a city agency is the reclamation of the more than a hundred thousand vacant city-owned housing units contained mostly in old tenements and brownstones, the kind Robert Moses invariably demolished when he could.

In the early 1980s conditions were so embarrassing that the Koch administration put trompe l'oeil decals depicting shutters, potted plants, and Venetian blinds to cover windows of city-owned abandoned buildings along the Cross Bronx Expressway. Instead of improving the image of the area and camouflaging the massive problem, it brought more attention to it.

New York was losing thirty-six thousand residential units a year to abandonment. Pushed by community groups looking to occupy and renovate these buildings for affordable units, the city under Koch initiated a number of innovative programs. Grassroots efforts instigated these policies with little public notice. City officials, overwhelmed by the problem, wisely responded to community-based proposals. Mayor David Dinkins aggressively continued the new policies, and momentum was firmly established. Dramatic federal cutbacks under President Reagan pulled the rug out from under these efforts nationwide, and Mayor Giuliani showed no interest in trying to maintain the momentum or look for new creative ways to confront the problem. The momentum slowed. But Mayor Bloomberg recommitted to creating affordable housing. There is some question as to whether the city is losing as many as it is gaining because of gentrification and rent deregulation, according to the *New York Times*.[9]

Developer-built projects seem to dominate, but the renovation trend continues uncelebrated. Community-based efforts that contributed enormously in the past continue the regeneration momentum today.

Local efforts reseeded with modest resources the neighborhoods by the late 1980s. Developers followed, built new projects with big tax or zoning incentives or on low-cost city-owned land, gained the attention of the media, and eventually took credit for scores of neighborhood turnarounds, especially in the South Bronx and Brooklyn.

Low-Density Mistakes Still Happen in a Big Way

Unfortunately, what was built on vacant lots was mostly low-density, suburban housing, instead of the traditional two-family or more row houses containing the density needed for well-functioning urban neighborhoods. Vacant land is now scarce for badly needed affordable housing. Many neighborhoods now lack the density appropriate for their infrastructure or to attract new local convenience stores and small businesses. In contrast, the New York City Housing Authority is now wisely offering parking lots at some public housing sites for development of new moderate- and low-income apartments. This is an important new infill initiative. In fact, other infill potential exists in public housing sites for more than just housing.

Re-creating density where it's been lost is critical. Every recently built single-family home should be allowed to expand or build its unit into a two-family dwelling immediately, even to have the ability to add another floor or two. Many already function as two-family, sometimes three-family, homes illegally. If legalized, health and safety regulations can be instituted and monitored.

Owner-occupied two- and three-family units are a successful, low-scale housing resource in many urban neighborhoods, mixed in with high-density low-rise apartment buildings, creating the population necessary to support local retail, transit, schools, and social institutions—in other words, the components of real communities. The infrastructure already exists to support this. Allowing the expansion of the suburban-style homes is no guarantee it will occur, but permitting it offers new regenerative possibilities. This is the kind of big initiative in small increments that could have a big citywide impact.

One of the bizarre twists in the changes to the city's zoning and building codes is that it has long been illegal to build the city's most successful housing form—the classic brownstone. The four- or five-story brownstone is the perfect structure to serve a single family or as multiple apartments. Easy to reconfigure over time, new brownstones would make infinitely more sense than the single- and two-family suburban housing that has been built in too many neighborhoods over the past twenty years. Between erroneous setback requirements and excessive handicap-access rules that require elevators for more than three floors, the return of the brownstone is stymied. Yet rebuilding brownstones in a big way around the city would go a long way toward adding affordable housing.

MORE BIG THINGS GETTING DONE

Historian Mike Wallace, whose brilliant slim book *New Deal for New York* was published one year after 9/11 and presents a clear and sensible agenda for public actions, goes further. He cites even more big things than I have enumerated, all accomplished by the city but either taken for granted or unrecognized. These are the kind of big projects that matter the most to the overall health and functioning of the city, its neighborhoods, and its economy but never count as "big projects."

Starting with water, Wallace of course cites the tunnel, "fabulously successful and profoundly under-celebrated. The Big Dig is nothing in comparison." He continues: "Great strides have been made with water in general, in controlling pollution, both by private actors and by public agencies, in stopping chemical discharges into our rivers, in instituting critical controls, and in building the North River Pollution Control plant, an astonishing intervention into a massive problem." For years, the Housing Authority has been replacing windows, appliances, and toilets in all public housing units to conserve water and energy.

Wallace also cites the institution of a citywide recycling program, even though not as comprehensive as could be but at least a beginning effort to tackle the enormous garbage problem. And major inroads have been made in controlling air pollution, starting with outlawing the burning of coal in 1966. And in a different direction, he cites the area of policing. Giuliani takes more credit for this than is his due, Wallace says. The intelligent upgrading of technology started before him, under Dinkins. The drop in the crime rate shows the city is capable of responding to big problems. "You can't look at this array of big accomplishments and say the public sector is not able to get big things done," Wallace says.

The big but uncelebrated successes share common threads. None were accomplished by one leader or one developer. None occurred quickly; nothing big ever does. Many responded to citizen pressures or were initiated by individuals. Others responded to new conditions, such as the need to conserve energy and water. Almost all gained public consensus or went ahead without it. None were stopped by the culture of confrontation and contention that interferes only sometimes successfully with the mammoth one-shot, top-down projects that inspire complaints about what can get done in the city. And each in its own way both fortified the connections of the larger city and inspired further efforts, feeding the critical momentum of renewal that produces constant but positive change throughout the city. Authentic regeneration, as already indicated, is a process, not a project. This concept cannot be articulated often enough. Beneficial change is on-going, but it is beneficial because it does not erase or overwhelm a place.

Not to be overlooked in any examination of big things getting done are the projects that have gotten done over time. Battery Park City is in its fifth decade and almost finished. Large waterfront parks are emerging on several sites in Brooklyn. Time-Warner went up overscaled but up nonetheless. After an intense battle with Trump in the initial phase, Riverside South, overlooking the Hudson on the Upper West Side, with its oversized buildings but commendable waterfront park, is two-thirds complete after twenty years and under new ownership.[10] The theater district and Forty-second Street have been totally transformed into a glitzy office park and shopping mall for tourists with restored historic theaters as the only authentic anchors. The district is a classic replacement, not a regeneration. And, of course, huge buildings have gone up all over town.

DEFEAT WITH GOOD REASON

In my experience observing and writing about the New York development scene, big things are defeated because they are too big, inappropriate, and alien to the area for which they are proposed. Less grandiose schemes are accepted after intense and often meaningful public debate and genuine participation. Consensus is key. When achieved, projects go forward, as witness the convention center, Battery Park City, and the train to the plane, all of which were at various points quite controversial.

The death of Westway, and before it the Lower Manhattan Expressway, led to some of the best big new development in the final decades of the twentieth century—big in the overall sense, not big in the sense of one new project or one place. SoHo, of course, and everything it inspired around New York and the country would never have occurred with the Lower Manhattan Expressway built. On the West Side, the Hudson River Park continues to unfold, bit by appealing bit. The Gansvoort Historic District, just north of Greenwich Village, is one of the hottest new real estate markets. Westway would have decimated it. The transformation of the Nabisco Building into the Chelsea Market is a model of small, diverse uses in a huge building with the city's first Whole Foods Market in the ground floor. These are only a few of both the waterfront and the near-inland developments that occurred in the Westway corridor with the defeat of the highway.

Cumulatively, all this adds up to big development, not big development all in one place, at one time. But it is big development nonetheless, in small doses all along the West Side and around the city. The process of authentic regeneration has unfolded in many places, sprouting a potpourri of innovative projects.

Beneficial change is ongoing but never overwhelming. The positive spin-offs are endless and widespread. The geographically varied and diverse nature of the assorted developments cited above are components in the process, not singular projects. That is the kind of change Westway's demise unleashed, adding up to enormous change in the larger city.

Urbanism at its best.

CONCLUSION
Their Shadows Still Hover

> Dull, inert cities, it is true, do contain the seeds of
> their own destruction and little else. But lively, diverse,
> intense cities contain the seeds of their own regenera-
> tion, with energy enough to carry over for problems
> and needs outside themselves.
>
> JANE JACOBS,
> conclusion of *The Death and Life of
> Great American Cities*

But how do you recognize the seeds?

I have tried to identify in this book some of the seeds, the precursors, of the regeneration process. I have tried to show that these often
modest efforts requiring little public investment but worthy of considerable public respect and encouragement are the real generators of urban
resurgence. They should not be carelessly lost. Precursors contrast completely with the highly promoted, unseemly expensive, oversold big-bang
projects like stadia, casinos, malls, mega mixed-use developments, entertainment complexes, and the like, all erroneously offered as urban anchors and revitalizers.

What makes the seeds illustrated in this book as interesting as they are
effective is the diversity of form they come in, all good examples of Urban
Husbandry: community-based action in defense against erosive change;
new infill construction of varying scales that weaves into the existing fabric

rather than replacing it wholesale; conversion of vacant or underused old buildings whether architecturally distinctive or just solid, irreplaceable quality; historic preservation efforts of community landmarks; multiple small changes in transportation preferences leading to mass-transit improvements and vehicular traffic containment; new people and businesses moving into gritty old neighborhoods that officials label as slums to justify demolition plans; artists seeking cheap space adaptable as work space and residences; farmers' markets, community gardens, infill agriculture, locally improved public spaces, self-organized activities transforming vacant neighborhood spaces; small innovative arts and entertainment activities emerging in quirky, off-beat places far from establishment circles; environmental justice efforts in low-income, racially diverse communities; new and expanding manufacturing companies, including green manufacturing, adding real substance to the city's economy; community organizing to defeat a road widening, a highway exit ramp, or, even still today, a highway through a neighborhood; and coalitions opposing a megadevelopment threatening neighborhood scale, social cohesion, economic networks, and architectural character. All these occurrences reflect local citizens' investment of time, energy, and money to make an area grow and contribute to the larger city. The number and variety are endless. But stakeholders don't care about a place if they don't have a role in the process.

These seemingly small, spontaneous actions preview things to come; they are the precursors to positive, often large-scale, change. More numerous and varied precursors exist than indicated here. The challenge is to recognize them in any form, to permit the gradual process of their maturity to unfold, and to nourish them where possible.

Most critical is not to interfere with the precursors, not to mislabel as a slum the emerging but still shabby neighborhood, not to misjudge as blight the weathered, run-down structures and vacant spaces being slowly upgraded and reoccupied with new uses, not to underestimate the self-organizing capacity of local people to respond appropriately to need. Solutions crafted in response to need are very different from formulaic solutions designed from above or afar and alien to local character. The former advances the urban process and promote resilience; the latter fulfills political and real estate agendas unrelated to the place and stifles authentic growth.

This is where a real understanding of the teachings of Jane Jacobs comes in. "Too many people," she said, "think the most important thing about anything is its size instead of what's happening." This requires the appreciation of the small, the new, the start-up, the oddity, the things that could lead eventually to "the next big thing," she added. When it finally evolves into that "next big thing," having grown organically, its significance will be about substance, not bigness.

New York City—and cities across the country—lost a wealth of socially viable communities and renewable industrial neighborhoods in the Moses era of massive clearance. This was not because those districts lacked precursors with regeneration potential but because recognition of precursors and their regenerative value was lacking. The focus was on the new, the big, the efficient, and the planned.

But in the 1970s, when the excessive gush of federal funds ceased and when Moses and his imitators lost power, everything changed. Money was not available for new megaprojects requiring demolition of precursor-filled existing places. Community resistance to excessive clearance was increasingly successful. New Moses wannabes also lost power and funding sources.

In the face of these reversals, a new ferment took hold. While the powerful forces that interfered earlier were focused elsewhere, the seeds of innovation sprouted in the most derelict neighborhoods, as identified earlier—from the Lower East Side to the South Bronx. Unrecognized and left alone, those seeds of regeneration took hold. And without the big money for sweeping change, fertile neighborhoods were left to emerge organically. As Harry DeRienzo, citizen leader of the revival of the truly blighted, burned-out section of the South Bronx, said: "We could do it because no one cared or was really paying attention and there was no big money to do anything else." Such is no longer the case. Progress has been duly noted, celebrated, and expropriated. In fact, in the past decade especially, developers have been cashing in, building on the citizen efforts, in some ways appropriately and beneficially but in others out of character and out of scale.

The lost lesson is this: what local doers did to repair, heal, and regrow their communities and the larger city was tackle the problems and challenges with what Jacobs called "adaptations, ameliorations, and densifications." Local doers conceived of these "adaptations, ameliorations, and densifications" and made them happen.

Opportunities for this kind of urban resilience are the most important things lost under the bulldozer of large-scale demolition. Nurturing self-organized local efforts is rare. These resilience opportunities are invariably found in the derelict old neighborhoods, not the spiffy new ones. Precursors are difficult, if not impossible, to find in an imposed order, too regimented and costly for the quirky, experimental new. The order that Jacobs argued naturally exists in a vital city comes in the form of a perpetually unfinished, intensely interactive, and informal web of relationships. "Everything interesting happens on the edge of chaos," Jane said.

Today we observe precursors leading the way to positive urban change where they are able to survive, thrive, and mature. Those precursors reflect the enduring strength of the Jacobs legacy. But lest one be deceived to think Jacobs's legacy has triumphed, we also observe precursors crushed under the old Moses-style bulldozer of oversized, urbanistically destructive, excessively dependent on public assistance, and economically unjustified. Both legacies survive.

PART I: THE JACOBS LEGACY

Urban Agriculture, Transportation, and Historic Preservation

One could look in many directions to understand precursors. I have chosen three to focus on here: urban agriculture, transportation, and historic preservation. The differences among them are many, but one singular feature unites them: citizen efforts are central to their function as catalysts for positive change. The precursors in all three areas mature into significant agents of change from the bottom up, not the top down. Policies enhancing the precursors changed at the top in response to the actions initiated below, the best kind of political leadership. The beginnings were modest, scattered, and, yes, God forbid, ad hoc, not "planned." As defined earlier, the smart political leadership and planners recognize the precursors, encourage and nurture them, and allow them the opportunity for full growth. "The cities and the economies we have," Jacobs observed, "have been created by ordinary people who didn't have to have a big plan. It is good to remember in the culture that ordinary people can do these things and still do."

Observation continues to bear this out. All Jacobs's ideas are, after all, based on observation of what is, what works, and what doesn't. So whether we look at the diverse assortment of new industries around the city, the rebirth of divergent neighborhoods, or the small, purpose-driven efforts like urban agriculture, environmental justice, or ethnic food production, at the center of the effort invariably is an individual or group of like-minded citizens. None of these or similar efforts were anticipated in any future-directed official document. If a smart, responsive government official or private funder has signed on as a partner, the initiative gains an often unbeatable strength and new momentum.

Most of the popular bromides for urban rebirth reflect little understanding of the fundamental economic process, the underpinning of any strong city. That process encompasses many individual "doers," many components—often unpredictable—and is always fluid and ongoing. "Those with daring and imagination and no money," Jacobs said, are the pioneers of regeneration.

If the organic process is working, the city will give birth to the creative class—whether new entrepreneurs or artists—and not need to attract it. If the process is working, the city will grow and expand its middle class, not need to attract it. If the process is working, existing businesses will grow and new business formations will increase, not need expensive tax incentives to attract them from afar. If "adaptations, ameliorations, and densifications" are happening organically, a city won't need a new edited version of a city to replace the enduring old one.

It is too easy to oversimplify the revitalization process in response to the public desire to understand that process. Thus come the sound-bite or formulaic solutions like "Technology, Talent, and Tolerance," "Skills, Sun, Sprawl," "Attracting the Creative Class," "Transit-Oriented Development," and "New Urbanism." These can be useful clues to positive change, but they are not reflective of the larger urban process in which many interdependent elements function. None of these solutions, however, puts as much faith in the ordinary local people—the social capital of our society—as Jacobs did.

I've done a little bit of this oversimplification myself. In many question-and-answer sessions following a lecture I've given, I'm asked what are the most important things to do to stimulate urban rebirth. The expectation usually is that I'll get into the stadium versus concert hall versus enclosed mall versus museum debate. But that is only about projects, all of which have only one-shot big-bang impacts and branding value, if they have value at all. A collection of visitor attractions, as I've said elsewhere and can't repeat often enough, does not add up to a real city. Jacobs said it even better, as quoted earlier in this book, about the goslings that don't come from the eggs of the golden goose.

I could answer the question in many ways. I often choose as the most critical first steps investing in public schools and public transit and rebuilding urban density. Provide those, I say, and the rest will take care of itself. That also may seem too facile a response, like other formulaic-sounding responses. Yet without the first, middle-class families won't stay or come; without the second, the suburban dependence on the car prevents genuine urbanization; and without density, none of the features of an urban neighborhood, including local retail, services, and entertainment, will have reason to evolve. A low-density collection of car-dependent destinations and commercial sites functions like a large suburb, even if within a city's borders. A suburbanized city is an oxymoron. Hybrids don't work. Undo what the traffic engineers did after World War II, I often add. None of it respected urbanism.

While I still think this is valid, today I would answer the question another way. The critical first step is to recognize the precursors and then to know what to do about them. Successes offer the best clues to new solutions. And if you accept the centrality of the idea of people being the best engine of change, then what is critical is removing the kind of impediments that thwart the capacity of people.

Agriculture Reborn in Cities

Again Jacobs: "The past is a very good revealer of precursors. Cities, for example, are reinventing agriculture again. Dropping of chemicals for weed and pest control, composting instead of only adding to landfills, and creating mobile kitchens to harvest local gardens are all city inventions leading to new innovations and growth." Jacobs observed this in 2004, two years before her death. Even before and certainly since then, variations of urban agriculture have multiplied exponentially around the country. Each unique occurrence is a precursor of positive change and rebirth. Picking up Jacobs's earlier description of good change and bad change—change that builds up the land versus change that degrades it—these precursors are refertilizing urban neighborhoods, adding strength block by block, community by community.

If ever there was an issue that connects all the others, urban agriculture is it; economics, culture, public health, community strength, and more all feel the impact of the explosive change in food that is heavily rooted in cities. And if ever there was an example of big, in fact enormous, change that comes in small doses, starting locally with citizens, it is the current food revolution.

This is as illustrative as one can be of the self-organizing process that Jacobs describes. And don't underestimate these precursors. "There are decisions that we make every day about what we eat that can really change the way we live our lives and the way the world operates," Alice Waters has said.

I've tried to keep a list of all the inventive new forms I hear or read about and have been unable to keep up. New ones emerge daily. Rooftops, backyards, flower boxes, empty building lots, parking lots, apartment terraces—every conceivable place has become a garden.

The significance of the extraordinary growth of urban agriculture is enormous. It goes far beyond cities themselves. In *The Economy of Cities*, Jacobs goes to great length to demonstrate that agriculture was born in cities. Farm production moved out of the city center, as that center evolved and grew. Farm tools, machinery, and even chemical fertilizers were all invented in cities, all of which helped farms outside of cities grow. The cities provided markets for the farms. The farms fed growing urban populations, became efficient, and eventually were bought up by the corporate farms that dominate today.

The Food Landscape Is Changing

If you absorb what Michael Pollan has been writing in recent years,[1] the state of our food supply, now dominated by agribusiness, is so compromised that it is hard to recognize the food production we once accomplished so well. That is changing, slowly, to be sure, step by small step, starting locally in small increments but expanding exponentially. The food landscape today is not what it was even a few years ago when one almost had to go to Europe to find farm-fresh food not mass produced.

This new landscape is having a most dramatic impact on inner-city neighborhoods where fresh food is the hardest to find, decent supermarkets rarely exist, and food- and environment-related health problems are the highest. But in Brooklyn and the Bronx what is available are patches of city-owned undeveloped land.[2] From East New York to the South Bronx, community- and privately run gardens are increasing, obtaining immeasurable help from city agencies and private groups.[3] Some of the urban farmers are producing more than for personal consumption and selling at local markets. One Jamaica-born couple cultivates four sites in East New York and last year sold more than $3,000 worth of produce at a nearby market. In Red Hook, the high school students who run the Added Value garden on an abandoned three-acre asphalt ball field last year sold more than $25,000 in goods. About 135 students have steady after-school jobs, earning money and free vegetables. More than 5,000 kids have visited with their classes.

This is a national inner-city trend with gardens increasing in number in Detroit, Philadelphia, West Oakland, Milwaukee, and elsewhere. Food from the Hood in South Central Los Angeles is probably the most advanced of all.[4] After the 1992 civic unrest when Crenshaw Boulevard, the commercial spine of South Central L.A., went up in flames, students at the local high school decided to aid the community-healing process by planting a garden at the school. Soon they were selling produce at a local farmers' market and selling a salad dressing made to go with the produce. They used their favorite herbs, parsley and basil, to create their "Straight Out the Garden Creamy Italian Dressing" that grew in popularity, with more than 2,000 stores, including some major supermarket chains, carrying it. More than $250,000 earned goes to support college scholarships for the participating students.

Ten years ago, when I was writing *Cities Back from the Edge*, I devoted a whole chapter to the explosive growth of greenmarkets in cities. I illustrated their value in giving birth to new value-added businesses, some of which filled empty downtown storefronts, attracting more customers and more new businesses, adding new economic and social life to moribund downtowns. I noted then that in the 1970s, fewer than 200 markets existed. From 1994 to 1996 alone, their number increased from 1,775 to 2,400, a 38 percent increase. Today, there are more than 5,200 markets, and more than 25,000 growers depend on them.

When planner Barry Benepe and agricultural specialist Robert Lewis conceived of and started the Greenmarket in Union Square, a primary goal was to save upstate small farms, too many of which were being sold to developers because they were no longer financially viable. Today, many of those farms would not exist without the urban outlets that markets provide.

But more than saving farms, markets are often precursors of larger urban change. This pattern was apparent around the Union Square neighborhood and is also apparent in similar forms in market districts everywhere. Restaurants open nearby, taking advantage of fresh produce direct from the farmer. Run-down, empty, but solid buildings get fixed up and re-occupied. New social relationships develop at the market and, in the process, strengthen neighborhoods. Public space is enlivened, and often created for the first time. Regional family farms are given a new lease on life. Young people once again find reasons either to stay on the family farm or to buy farmland and start anew. Many expand their product offering based on customer requests. Some nearby dormant farms are bought not by subdividing developers but by new farmers producing dairy products once only imported from afar, raising goats, sheep, and even alpacas, or growing a wide assortment of once hard-to-find fruit and vegetables.

In the past decade, beyond farmers' markets, many small and larger things have been happening that from the bottom up are not only changing eating habits, restaurant menus, and supermarket offerings but also neighborhoods and lifestyles. Empty, rubble-strewn lots of all sizes in urban neighborhoods are converted to local gardens. Some have become valuable community gathering places. School districts around the country have initiated "farm-to-school" programs to include local foods in school lunches. Fresh foods are slowly becoming available in poor neighborhoods where processed foods dominate. Poor kids are learning how to farm, where food comes from, and how eating affects health, all having an impact beyond measure, sometimes in neighborhood gardens, other times in school gardens. The "buy local" food movement—"a thousand miles fresher"—of which this is all a part is forcing awareness about transportation choices, environmental conditions, and neighborhood health. An increasing number of students seek to be interns on farms as a way of participating in the sustainable food movement. Food has become the political movement of the day. "Opportunity, not necessity, is the mother of invention," Jane said.

Every imaginable esoteric food-related operation seems to be cropping up in New York. Workshops in kitchen composting are increasingly popular. And Brooklyn, already the city's hippest borough, is a hotbed of locally produced foods—from handmade pickles and chocolate to grainy mustard and exotic cheeses—sold in local shops or the back of trucks. Last May, a Brooklyn Food Conference held more than two dozen workshops under the categories of Food and Economic Development, Access to Food, and Growing Food. Hundreds attended, learning how to start everything from a food co-op to a new farm.

The Precursors Are Maturing

Like never before, our industrialized global food and distribution system is being challenged. The sands are shifting, even if slowly. In the United States the number of farms increased by 4 percent from 2002 and 2007, with most of the new farms being small part-time operations. Today, the number of U.S. farms is between 2 million and 2.5 million, including 100,000 new ones in recent years. Until recently, that number had been diminishing since the number of farms peaked at 6.8 million in 1935. And what is even more encouraging is the diversification of farming and increase in organic farms from 12,000 in 2002 to 18,200 in 2007. Congressman Earl Blumenauer (D-OR) wants to institute small diversions from the agricultural budget to encourage sustainable agriculture, create farmers' markets in every community, develop year-round farmers' markets, and nurture small-scale agriculture in other ways.

Promoting local and sustainable food and healthy eating has become a mission of the first lady, Michelle Obama. Before a state dinner in February 2009, she gave a kitchen tour for reporters and culinary students, as Marian Burros reported in the *New York Times* on February 23, 2009. "The first lady took the opportunity to put in a pitch for local and sustainable food and for healthy eating, a recurring theme of hers during the campaign and since she arrived in Washington. When food is grown locally, she said, 'ofttimes it tastes really good, and when you're dealing with kids, you want to get them to try that carrot. If it tastes like a real carrot, and it's really sweet, they're going to think that it's a piece of candy,' she continued. 'So my kids are more inclined to try different vegetables if they are fresh and local and delicious.'" She is also encouraging serving local foods at soup kitchens.

All these small, seemingly unconnected occurrences are precursors of positive change, gradual growth, and an urban resurgence that is hard to fully appreciate before it is full-blown. Understanding how these issues relate to one another forces one to look at a city holistically. Only then do you understand urbanism as a process, not a series of projects.

For forty years, whenever I extolled the virtues of these kinds of small precursors of change, experts and professionals dismissed them as too ad hoc or inconsequential. How wrong they have all been! Community-based efforts were dismissed as too inconsequential to make a difference citywide. The early establishment of farmers' markets had to be fought for to overcome disbelieving and resistant city officials and professional experts. The observation that more people were moving into downtowns to live was dismissed as of minimum consequence since it was mostly young singles and empty nesters, although a funny thing happens to young singles: they have a habit of getting married and having children. Witness Tribeca, where several schools exist that didn't in the 1970s. All such movements of big change start ad hoc and small.

Recognizing Precursors Is Key

It is not as important to be able to measure, explain, or applaud regeneration after the fact; it's more important to recognize, respect, and nurture it in its earliest stages. This is where professionals and policy makers need to observe and listen more carefully to local citizens, to recognize the value of the precursors, to observe closely and not make judgments from afar. If you look closely at what people are doing or what they are identifying as needed in their community, appropriate corrective measures that are under way and new ones to be initiated reveal themselves.

Citing poet Robert Frost's famous quote that "Nature's first green is gold," Jacobs noted in conversation about the positive value of the urban agriculture trend: "That gold is a different kind of chlorophyll than an infant plant needs to start off. It is a very powerful kind of chlorophyll. Largeness has nothing to do with it. It is a different quality and it permits larger things later, but it doesn't overwhelm the chlorophyll; it's a precursor to it. I began to see this when I realized I was looking at the wrong phase of the business cycle, not at the nature's first green gold part of it." Precursors are important to all areas, she added. "Ecologists have to think of precursors when they study the aftereffects of a fire. They not only have to see what has been destroyed but what is left to regenerate." This was true in the aftermath of the St. Helen's 1980 volcano eruption as well as the 1970s burned-out condition of the South Bronx.

This is the fundamental error—a tragic one, in fact—of Moses's urban philosophy and why, as we will see later, this error keeps getting repeated. Moses mistook precursors—often messy at best and hidden in deteriorated and dormant areas, at least—as blight. Actually, precursors didn't fit *his* vision of what the city should be. He was incapable of recognizing the precursors that stood in the way of his bulldozers, incapable of valuing their rebirth potential, and, worst, incapable of knowing how to deal with them other than through elimination. If even half of what he destroyed were nascent precursors or mature but growing contributors to the social, physical, and economic health of the city, one can begin to understand what the city lost and why it took so long to recover from the damage.

Historic Preservation: A Visually Obvious Precursor

If you look at any revived urban neighborhood today, you would be hard-pressed to find a more potent catalyst for its early regeneration than historic preservation. Historic preservation never starts in a big way. Sometimes the first upgraded building may be ahead of its time. Years may pass before other properties are similarly upgraded. Chances are, however, that things—often, small, creative, and productive things—are occurring in neighboring unrestored buildings of primary importance. Yet occasional and scattered upgrading, whether to official historic preservation standards or not, can be an important clue that precursors to more positive change exist. Wherever there is activity, close observation of its nature is called for to understand future possibilities.

Most people don't even know or remember that such celebrated neighborhoods around the country as the French Quarter and the Garden District in New Orleans, Georgetown in D.C., the Battery in Charleston, Rittenhouse Square in Philadelphia, the Victorian District in Savannah, the King William District in San Antonio, South Beach in Miami, Telegraph Hill in San Francisco, Manhattan's Upper West Side, the North End of Boston, Brooklyn's Park Slope, and many more were at one time considered "slums." And those are just the transformed residential districts. Likewise, many of today's viable former industrial neighborhoods, now popular loft neighborhoods, all over the country were once declared slums. *Slum*, in these instances, meant deteriorated, seemingly empty, occupied by unimportant activity, abandoned, or absentee-owned, properties that owners were thrilled to sell.

But many of the buildings in all of these districts also were occupied either by precursors that went unrecognized or offered an opportunity for new small enterprises and start-ups or by new residents. If such areas survived to grow and thrive while upgrading occurred around them, it was only because no larger replacement agenda existed to threaten them or a replacement plan was thwarted either by civic resistance or by failing economic conditions. Many of the empty buildings had a value often invisible to experts but not to potential buyers looking for affordable space.

Many were scheduled for demolition that hadn't happened yet (remember the Civil War–era piers Gregory O'Connell rescued from demolition plans in Red Hook). The historic nature of the architecture was probably not the first point of appeal, but the quality of the design, construction, and space added up to a good package. Now if the neighborhood was hopeless, if the problems so overwhelming a newcomer would stay away, then one could assume any hidden precursors wouldn't last and no new ones would appear.

Every neighborhood in New York that was once judged hopeless has turned the corner, from Brooklyn's Bushwick (site of terrible riots) to Hunts Point in the South Bronx. The regeneration that started in the 1970s in the South Bronx, Park Slope, Bedford-Stuyvesant, SoHo, Astoria in Queens, and Stapleton on Staten Island has steadily gained momentum, and as each neighborhood gained value, appreciation of the adjacent areas took hold. That is the way the regenerative urban process works when it is allowed to do so. The precursors survived and evolved into full-bloom regeneration. This process was visible across the city in gentle waves.

In each of those neighborhoods, the renovation of historic, often architecturally unbeatable, residential and industrial buildings was early in the process. The uses within the upgraded buildings were often innovative and small, and the local businesses that follow the growing population, whether residential or commercial, are also varied and reflective of that new population.

It is safe to say that any neighborhood in which people are willing to go through the expense and endless headaches to restore old, deteriorated buildings absolutely cannot be reasonably judged "blighted" or a "slum." If a business invests private money in an area, no matter how shabby it appears on a windshield survey, how can such an area be considered dead? In those same neighborhoods, longtime residents and businesses that remain also reinforce the inappropriateness of the "blight" tag. We'll see how that applies in three specific projects later.

While historic preservation is greatly appreciated in contrast to twenty or thirty years ago, the understanding and appreciation of existing buildings are still too narrow. Preservation is not fully recognized as a precursor of broad regeneration. Nor is it valued as a serious contributor to a city's local economy and to the national economy as well, nor as a fundamental building block of environmental conservation. (See the epilogue.)

The Economic Contribution Is Huge

The multiple but invisible economic contributions of historic preservation are buried in assorted statistics that cover more than preservation. The federal government, for example, has a category for all jobs; it is called the SIC code, which stands for Standard Industrial Classification. The individual categories covered do not include specialized preservation work. The masonry category, for example, does not identify as a masonry subset the specialized brick masons required for historic buildings. The plaster group doesn't break out ornamental plaster work. And faux painting or wood graining is not identified as a painting specialty. No measurement exists within the SIC code or any other statistical category to even begin to calculate the enormous impact the historic preservation movement has had on the national economy.

Restoration is not recognized as a big contributor to the national economy. It is not easy to measure collectively and is surely below the radar in conventional analysis. But like the big impact in small doses that preservation has had on the regeneration of cities, it has had a similar impact economically. That impact can be observed in logical ways.

This clearly is not the standard way of measuring impacts, but consider this. In 1967, a tall, already balding man with a twinkle-eye smile named Clem Labine (not the ballplayer) bought a four-story brownstone in Brooklyn's Park Slope when the brownstone movement was just beginning to fuel the renaissance of that borough. "That movement," Labine observes, "was totally grass roots with help from no one and nowhere but it helped build Brooklyn's caché as a wonderful place to live." He started on the restoration of this house, a job that never is totally finished because, he says, "there's always something that needs to be upgraded." Labine knew nothing about old houses or how to restore them. The restoration was "a painful self-learning process," he recalls, but he realized that similar buyers of old houses were in the same boat.

In 1973 Labine started the *Old House Journal* in the basement of that brownstone. A twelve-page offset newsletter, it was a how-to primer for new brownstone owners and quickly expanded to cover owners of old houses across the country. Paint-stripping techniques, wood-window repair, and fixing cracked plaster are all similar in an urban row house or freestanding wood-frame building. Labine printed 1,000 copies to give away at flea markets and preservation meetings. He had no mailing list, but each issue included a coupon to subscribe for twelve dollars. He also created a pamphlet, *Field Guide to Old House Styles*, which was a give-away with a subscription.

By 1985 he had 60,000 subscribers across the country and converted the newsletter to a magazine format. With the new format, Labine started taking advertisements. By the time he sold the publication in 1987, there were 65,000–70,000 subscribers and growing, and it had gone from 25 to 100 advertisers but did not go on newsstands until after he sold it. Now it has 150,000 subscribers plus newsstand sales and is thick with ads for businesses and products, most of which did not exist before the preservation movement emerged.

Then in 1976 Labine published the first *Old House Journal* directory, getting listings from "every artisan and supplier we could find," which totaled 256. The catalog inspired Claude and Donna Jeanloz to start Renovators Supply Company, individually soliciting those artisans and suppliers to carry their products in the catalog or by mail order. When Labine sold the *Old House Journal* directory in 1988, 1,800 preservation-related businesses were listed in the directory. From 256 to 1,800 listings is another reflection of the growth in preservation-related businesses in twelve years.

In 1988, Labine started *Traditional Building Magazine* with about 30 ads and sold it in 2002. At its height, before the Internet and recession intervened, approximately 330 advertisers filled the pages. In 2000 Labine started *Period Homes Magazine* for professionals, starting with 25 advertisers, which went to 250 in no time and from 0 subscriptions to 12,000. "What amused me was the architectural profession," Labine says. "They held their noses at preservation because it wasn't 'creative.' Now the majority of firms all have preservationists on staff. They can't afford not to."[5] The preservation market and the economy it represents are now huge.

Another measure of preservation's growth and impact is reflected in a seemingly minor change in the title of *Sweet's Catalogue*. *Sweet's* is the bible for construction contractors and architects looking for products, building materials, and manufacturers to use in their work. About twelve to fifteen years ago, its publisher, McGraw-Hill, discovered that about half of the work done by its users was renovation, not just new construction. The title was changed to *Sweet's Construction and Renovation Catalogue*. "This was about the same time that architects added preservation to their work categories," Labine observes.

Preservation has also revived a variety of the traditional building arts that were almost lost and, in the process, created a host of new professions. "There is nothing that can't be done today but that wasn't the case only 30 years ago," notes Labine. He cites wood graining, ornamental plaster work, stone carving, slate-roof installation and repair, and faux painting and scagliola (the painting of layers of plaster to imitate marble), to name just a few. Many of these were almost lost arts.

The Transportation Link

In *Death and Life*, Jacobs made clear that increasing accommodation of vehicular traffic in cities was a surefire way to guarantee deterioration, whether in a residential or a downtown district. It was a slow process, she said, made in many small moves that don't always easily reveal themselves as destructive to the urban fabric. "Erosion proceeds as a kind of nibbling, small nibbles at first, but eventually hefty bites. Because of vehicular congestion, a street is widened here, another is straightened there, a wide avenue is converted to one-way flow, staggered-signal systems are installed for faster movement. . . . More and more land goes into parking, to accommodate the ever increasing numbers of vehicles while they are idle. No one step in this process is in itself crucial. But cumulatively the effect is enormous."[6] That was 1961, and although New York did not suffer in this regard as much as many other American cities because of its size, Moses's successes around the city clearly led to the erosion to which Jacobs refers. In the name of improving traffic flow, the streets of American cities were remade street by street to favor vehicular over pedestrian mobility.[7] Couple this with the disinvestments in mass transit and the picture is clear on how New York's decline advanced over time.

Jacobs also outlined the counteraction strategy of "attrition," defined as "action taken to diminish vehicular traffic." Attrition happens, she noted, "by making conditions less convenient for cars. . . . If properly carried out, attrition would decrease the need for cars simultaneously with decreasing convenience for cars."[8] Attrition is now happening across the country and certainly reflects the increased popularity of Jacobs's principles, even if the promulgators of attrition are unaware of her teachings and simply come by their understanding instinctively. Nevertheless, that attrition is occurring in a multitude of ways, some more advanced than others, but all working to reknit the nation's urban fabric piece by piece.

Jacobs's Ideas Happening Big Time

Jacobs's critics like to perpetuate the myth that she was against anything big. She definitely was against big highways for all the reasons elaborated earlier in this book. But she was definitely for big networks of mass transit that move people and freight, instead of cars. Infrastructure that supports cities was certainly something big that Jacobs viewed as critical for government support. The key to the size here is network, a network of different modes of interconnected transportation systems that create the lifeline for moving people and goods.[9]

Mass transit knits a region or a city together. And if dense enough, as it once was, a national rail system knits the country together and facilitates the economically and socially productive movement of people and goods without the excessive polluting and congestion-causing dependency on rubber-tire vehicles of any size. The proliferation of re-created transit routes within cities, from Fort Worth and Sacramento to Denver and New York, definitely reflects the increasing ascendancy of Jacobs's urban values over the previously dominant values of Moses.

Elevated highways are coming down, freeways are giving way to boulevards and avenues, traffic through downtowns and city streets is being calmed, parking capacity is being diminished or at least made less expansive, and even garage-front houses (called "snout houses" in some places), where the garage door is more prominent than the front door (if you can find it), are being zoned out. Zipcar facilities (short-term rentals) are proliferating, easing the need for multiple, if any, car ownership. Bike trails are multiplying exponentially, offering alternative commuting possibilities. And bike lanes in cities are increasing as well. Even the availability of "self-serve" rental bike programs has grown. Paris is the leader in this with more than twenty thousand "Velib" bikes available on the streets all over the city. Any balanced transportation system must include the bicycle. All kinds of isolating forms that separated, segregated, and isolated places and people are also coming down or being reconsidered, such as skywalks that drain life from streets. The car is being tamed, not eliminated. That's an important distinction. Elimination of the car strikes terror in the heart of Americans. No balanced transportation advocate is suggesting such a thing.

I have experienced people terrorized by this fear firsthand. In many forums where I have spoken, I am frequently challenged. "You just want to get rid of the car," accusers have declared. "No, I don't," I respond. "In fact, you can happily keep all three cars. I just want you to be less dependent on them." I also add something that appeals to their self-interest. "You don't have to give up your car," I say, "but wouldn't it be good for you if the guy driving next to you does and leaves more room on the road for you?"

Others ask in a similarly challenging way, "Do you have a car?" "Yes," I say, "but I rarely use it to get around the city, mostly for out-of-town trips." In fact, I'd prefer on many occasions to take the train, but, unlike in Europe, we are not allowed to take a dog on the train in most places in this country.

Then comes the kicker: "That's such a New York point of view." I love this one. "The funny thing is," I say, "people west of the Mississippi think everyone east offers nothing to learn from, and everyone east of the Mississippi thinks no lessons for them exist west, and you're all wrong." Taming the car is a national imperative.

One of the bonuses of the improved New York subway system, in fact, is the increasing number of city dwellers giving up the car. Driving around New York City is to be avoided at all costs. People who do, for reasons other than sheer necessity, get what they deserve. It is too easy to get around this city by subway, bus, or taxi to require a car. As other cities and regions improve their transit infrastructure, car dependency will similarly diminish.

A balanced transportation system has a chance to emerge in the future. In many places, a highway's construction started the decay in a neighborhood. Its removal can jump-start its rebirth.

Remember What Was Lost

It is useful to remember what was lost—and how it was lost—in order to understand what is imperative to re-create in a contemporary way. This is not about going backward and re-creating the past; it is about learning from the past what worked and adapting the lessons for today.

Considerable focus today is on high-speed rail, and the Obama administration is appropriately pushing for the re-creation of a national rail system that more effectively connects both regional and more distant destinations. Among other things, this would relieve the excessive pressure on air travel and diminish the dominance of airlines. But the most important form of transit for the regeneration of urbanism is the modern streetcar or bus rapid transit. This transit mode makes frequent stops, like New York's subway, and is easily accessible, comfortable, and reasonably priced. It must be all those things to compete with the car.

We once had an extensive network of streetcar systems, one of the world's finest. And we didn't lose it naturally. It was destroyed to give automobiles more road room. Bradford Snell, a government researcher, first detailed this sorry tale in a 1974 Senate committee report.[10] The story has been told many times, including in the 1998 film *Who Framed Roger Rabbit?*, but it is always worth telling again to understand future possibilities.

In 1921 General Motors lost sixty-five million dollars. Then GM head Alfred P. Sloan decided to do something to turn that around. Stephen B. Goddard, in his revealing and extraordinarily detailed book, *Getting There*, puts it bluntly: "In the 1920s, General Motors, under the leadership of Alfred P. Sloan, and his fellow automakers decided to do nothing less than reorder society to alter the environment in which automobiles are sold by replacing light rail systems with cars and buses. So in the early 1930s, GM approached railroads and electric utility companies, which owned most urban trolleys, and offered to buy their electric streetcar lines, which GM would then replace with buses."[11]

Resistance was strong. Buses were a hard sell. They jolted, smelled, and were not nearly as comfortable as trolleys. Trolleys were smooth, efficient, and frequent. But they were badly in need of repair after World War II. During the war, all the effort that might have gone into maintenance and upkeep of many things like public transit was directed, instead, to military needs. GM and its cohorts could not even pursue a plan of replacing trolleys with buses until after the war, when manufacturing could switch to a domestic focus.

Sloan was undaunted. If the streetcar systems would not willingly sell, they would be taken over and dismantled. With Greyhound and Yellow Coach bus companies, Standard Oil, Phillips Petroleum, Mack Truck, and Firestone Tire Company as partners, GM secretly formed the National City Lines, which bought up streetcar lines in eighty-three cities. NCL cut services, left repairs undone, raised fares, and took money out of each system instead of rebuilding it. Disinvestment in transit was as devastating nationally as it had been when Moses practiced it in New York. The transit systems that had served dense, functional cities so well were sabotaged. Economic life still depended on proximity, and once that critical infrastructure deteriorated, urban economies faltered as well.

As Snell points out, a 1947 court case later confirmed that this secret partnership had "schemed to create a motor monopoly in nearly four dozen cities across the country, taking over more than 100 electric transit systems in the process." Goddard notes: "Yet for their roles in concocting and perpetrating a criminal conspiracy—which helped change the dominant urban energy from electricity to less-efficient petroleum and to alter American urban life forever—the Court fined the corporations five thousand dollars each and the individuals one dollar."[12] The pattern was set. The momentum was in high gear. The direction was unstoppable. In a stark case of twentieth-century waste, the light rail systems either built today or on the drawing boards in many communities are re-creating the earlier transit systems that were so tragically destroyed.

With streetcars, pedestrian needs were still paramount. Building a fifteen-minute walk from a streetcar was a builder's rule of thumb. This is still visible today in so many surviving and desirable former streetcar neighborhoods nationwide. With automobiles ascendant, building highways and moving vehicles became the priority. Furthermore, streetcar lines were built by private land developers and electric utilities. The Interstate Highway System, however, was and still is the largest public works project ever initiated in this country.

Until this dramatic reshaping of the national landscape for the car, Americans managed well with forty-four thousand miles of passenger rail routes run by twelve hundred companies employing three hundred thousand people who ran fifteen billion annual trips, generating an income of one billion dollars. As Snell reported, "Virtually every city and town in America of more than 2,500 people had its own electric rail system."

So the lessons exist to learn from, if the repair and rejuvenation of cities are serious goals. But it is not all about looking to the past; contemporary success stories also exist, providing confirmation and new lessons.

Highways to Boulevards and Avenues

Former Milwaukee mayor John Norquist is a tall, fair-haired man with the Nordic look reflective of the immigrant history of that region. It took him five years to demolish a segment on the north side of downtown of the never-completed elevated Park East Freeway that divided the city, as had been done by through-the-city highways across the country. It would have cost eighty million dollars to rebuild but thirty million to take down. The area, Brewers' Hill and the Italian neighborhood known as the Lower East Side, was reconnected to downtown. Streets that had been disconnected for decades were reconnected. And with the demolition in 2003, developers scrambled to build mixed-use buildings on a major portion of the reclaimed sixteen acres of city land, filling it in the most productive way. "The traffic nightmare that was predicted never happened," observes Norquist, "because the traffic now goes where it wants to go more efficiently." With highways, he points out, drivers are forced either to overshoot or undershoot their destination since exits are spaced so far apart. The avenue that replaced the freeway segment connects directly into the city grid, giving drivers more routing options and allowing them to go directly where they want to go.[13]

Urban Husbandry at its best.

A highway ramp came down in the Coliseum Square neighborhood of New Orleans, and the neighborhood ruined by it in the 1950s has been vibrantly renewed.

In 1974, Portland, Oregon, closed Harbor Drive and created an appealing waterfront park that draws people year-round, way ahead of most of the country.

San Francisco's creation of a tree-lined boulevard with bike trails, parks, and public exhibits where the Embarcadero Freeway—two levels of elevated concrete—once stood is perhaps best known, probably because, more than ever, the waterfront became a popular and economically productive district, one of the city's greatest attractions for both locals and tourists. Nearby real estate values rose 300 percent.

The 1989 earthquake also damaged Central Freeway, a spur into the city. Designed by the renowned boulevard advocates and designers Allan Jacobs and Elizabeth MacDonald, it was rebuilt smaller, as Octavia Boulevard. A *San Francisco Urban Designer* writer wrote in January 2007 that it "feels like it belongs . . . keeps cars moving while making the neighborhood around it a better place to be." New shops and housing developed on the periphery, and a once highway-destroyed neighborhood was revived.

In such cases, as with the rebuilding of Manhattan's West Side Highway, necessary traffic is managed differently through adjustments to traffic lights and other measures. As first observed in the Washington Square Park Moses road defeat, drivers adjust accordingly, and some traffic simply disappears.

Many more cities are grappling with this issue as the deterioration of original highways, elevated or not, demands increasing attention. Chattanooga has also taken down an elevated highway segment. Toronto,

Seattle, New Haven, Trenton, Baltimore, Buffalo, Syracuse, New Orleans, and Overton in Miami are just a few either already seriously considering such a move or just beginning to do so.

New York took down the elevated West Side Highway, defeated the Westway replacement plan, and is now getting a well-functioning quasi-boulevard replacement. But the state and city are taking years to recognize the similar wisdom of taking down the Sheridan Expressway in the Bronx, the 1.25-mile highway built in 1963 and never completed on the west shore of the Bronx River. The state wants to fix it at about three hundred million dollars (plus overruns, of course). A well-organized community plan developed with the help of planner Joan Byron of the Pratt Center would remove it and create a wealth of new parks and affordable housing opportunities. This citizen-led battle is a clear precursor of the continued revival of the South Bronx.

Streetcars Too

The urban healing process is even more visible in the proliferation of light rail systems in a variety of traditional and contemporary forms. San Diego was first, installing a light rail link to Tijuana, going through mostly commercial districts. It was a hard sell at the time, and none of the residential areas wanted it in their neighborhood, fearful of the intrusion of strangers that it would bring. Once up and running and a great hit, however, everyone wanted it, and the San Diego system has been expanding ever since.

Portland, Oregon, of course, is ahead of everywhere else, having first traded in highway funds decades ago to build the light rail system that goes through the city and beyond. In recent years it added a traditional streetcar imported from the Czech Republic that stops more frequently and is more like the streetcar system we lost but most European cities still have, most efficient for shorter downtown trips.

More than seventy cities have followed since, and more have plans on the books. Cities that have already put in the first leg immediately plan for expansion. The successes persuade even the strongest skeptics. Everywhere, ridership exceeds expectations. Developers and increased retail activity have followed. This should not have come as a surprise to anyone.

Now there is talk of reviving a leg of the once vast Brooklyn streetcar system with a leg from Red Hook to downtown Brooklyn, something citizen advocate Bill Diamond started years ago, stopping only when money was not available.

Converting Car Space to People Space

When Janette Sadik-Khan cut the ribbon with Mayor Bloomberg on the immediately successful Times Square pedestrian plaza created in the spring of 2009 by closing Broadway from Forty-second to Forty-seventh Streets to cars, she was hailed by *New York Magazine* and others as a combination of Jane Jacobs and Robert Moses. Not one inch of what she made happen was out of Robert Moses's file drawer; it was totally Jacobs and, to be sure, William H. Whyte as well, who also advocated more street space for people and transit and less for cars. But what Sadik-Khan was doing, and had been doing all over the city by eliminating lanes of traffic to make room for bike lanes and street plazas, was huge in its impact on the city.

Clearly, the enormity of the scale is what observers thought was out of the Moses file drawer, even though Jacobs clearly was an advocate of big, dense transit systems in cities. Many assume that if it is big, it must be Moses. Surely, this was thinking big but big in small bites and without erasing swaths of urban fabric. Not Moses's style at all. And, as has been noted earlier, size is not the defining issue; substance is. And in substance, what Sadik-Khan had done and was continuing to do was pure Jacobs. "The good news about the Moses legacy," she says, "was that he widened so many streets and created so much pavement, there is much that can be reclaimed for people, bikes, and bus–rapid transit. We're showing that our streets can do more than move cars quickly from point A to point B. For too long, we've looked at the city's six thousand miles of streets from behind the windshield and not at what happens on the street." This is the ultimate undoing of one area of Moses's excesses and of the overzealous transportation engineers who followed him with the automobile-is-everything approach to cities. This is the most dramatic example of the piecing back of the abused and undervalued precincts of our cities.

The pattern is now set for the twenty-first century. If the twentieth century was the Age of the Automobile, the twenty-first is the Age of Mass Transit. All of these trends—highways coming down, boulevards replacing in-city highways, re-created transit lines, and street reclamation for public spaces—are bound to continue expanding in the years to come.

This is stitching back the urban tears with strength renewed for the surrounding fabric. For sure, urban agriculture, transportation, and preservation are only three of many areas on which Jacobs's principles prevail. An observant student of her writing can find many more. But Moses, too, remains with us today in a big way, as the following stories illustrate. Both legacies remain strong.

PART II: THE MOSES LEGACY

Atlantic Yards, Brooklyn: Moses Redux

From day one there was nothing urbanistically right about the proposal to build over and beyond the Atlantic Avenue railroad yards adjacent to downtown Brooklyn. The grandiosity alone would have made Moses blush. The combination of Moses-style elements would have prompted him to say, "I taught you well."

Almost every aspect of this one-developer (Bruce Ratner),[14] one-architect (Frank Gehry), 22-acre scheme (8 acres of rail yards, 14 acres of neighborhood), 16 skyscrapers and a 19,000-seat basketball arena, is a Moses descendant, a clone of the outdated 1960s urban renewal model: clearance only; erasure of precursors of regeneration; gigantic scale; a state authority overriding the city planning and zoning review process; absence of democratic process with public input; threat of eminent domain to take private property for a private development; incalculable public funding of more than an acknowledged $300 million public investment up front, and hundreds of millions more over the years to come; isolating design disconnected from existing urban grid; traffic-choking parking capacity for more than 3,600 cars; destruction of architecturally appealing and functional historic buildings; displacement of 33 businesses, 235 jobs, 169 homes, 334 residents (209 tenants, 125 owners); declaration of "blight" of an area with some vacant buildings and empty lots scattered in the larger regenerating district; constant escalation of private and public costs; and public benefits promised (questionable from the start) diminishing with time.

The list could go on. As with many Moses projects, what could be considered blight (no real standard exists) has mostly been created by purposeful neglect of city-owned or MTA-owned property, or developer-purchased and -created vacant lots. The threat of eminent domain, as we've seen in prior chapters, is the surest way to create blight. In this and other cases, blight is simply the purposeful withholding of new investment. Despite this planned blight, condos were selling directly adjacent for $1.5 million in upgraded industrial buildings and for nearly $1 million within the project footprint itself.

As with most of Moses's projects, the mainstream press supports Atlantic Yards. And, as with some Moses projects like the Cross Bronx Expressway, a viable alternative plan exists that would build an arena and redevelop the areas of the district legitimately needing it without destroying what is viable. This case illustrates why there rarely is a real case of NIMBY (not in my backyard). Only if there is no alternative offered can one accuse a community of NIMBY. Usually, there is a viable alternative, proving once again that the opposition is not against change, just against change that is antithetical and out of scale to the neighborhood. Under the alternative, the many recognizable precursors would have the opportunity to run the course of organic change, involving many private investors and minimum public investment. This is the same framework for change that has positively transformed so many of the city's once forlorn districts since the 1970s, from the far West Village and the South Bronx to the Upper West Side, the Lower East Side, and countless areas of Brooklyn and Queens.

In 1953, Moses was declaring as slums viable neighborhoods with potential for new development and growth:

> If we don't clean out these slums, the central areas are going to rot. And it's all nonsense, for some of the people who are interested in this subject, and doubtless they are sincere, to say that the problem can be solved in rehabilitating and fixing up, slicking up, old-law tenements, by repair jobs. Can't be done. You're simply pouring good money after bad. There are very few cases where genuine slums can be fixed up in any other way than by tearing them down entirely and rebuilding, on a smaller coverage, taller buildings, with light and air and modern conveniences. That problem we've got to face. I'm not disturbed myself about the movement into the outlying sections and into the suburbs, that was bound to happen and it isn't unhealthy at all.

He would most likely have said the same thing about Atlantic Yards. Wrong on both counts. Many districts have revived in exactly the way he said was not possible, as this book has shown. His words ring hollow.

Highlighting the Precursors

The first step in the review process, after the Atlantic Yards proposal by Forest City Ratner was unveiled in December 2003, was for the state to declare the targeted area blighted. The state complied. In reality, this so-called public process was the last step in a privately worked-out deal with a predetermined conclusion. But let's look at the area designated as "blighted."

Near the commercial center of Brooklyn, the project site forms a thin triangle at the intersection of Atlantic and Flatbush Avenues where four neighborhoods come together—Fort Greene, Prospect Heights, Park Slope, and Boerum Hill—around the eight acres occupied by the Long Island Railroad yards. The site is adjacent to Atlantic Terminal, the third-largest transportation hub in the city where nine different subway lines and the Long Island Railroad converge.

In terms of transit access, this is an even better site for a sports facility than either Yankee Stadium or Citi Field, both of which have subway lines going to them. So when Ratner unveiled the proposal with a 19,000-seat basketball arena as its centerpiece, many cheered. After years of expensive, publicly funded sports complexes built around the country were proven to be poor economic engines, little support could be found for any sports facility dependent on public funds that they all inevitably are. But by attaching this one to a huge mix of new residential and commercial development with exaggerated promises of affordable housing, new jobs, and tax revenues, Ratner skillfully steered attention away from a singular sports facility. This is what Jacobs identified in the Lower Manhattan Expressway debate as "changing the subject."

Ironically, this area is directly adjacent to the site that could have kept the Brooklyn Dodgers in New York, if Robert Moses had not refused Dodgers owner Walter O'Malley the request to build a new stadium on the site in the 1950s.[15] This also would have been a perfect place to limit access to mass transit, although team owners (in this case also Bruce Ratner, owner of the Nets) love parking facilities from which they reap big financial gains. Thus, more than 3,600 proposed parking spaces—more than just for the arena—in the most congested traffic section of the borough defies urban-design or transportation-planning logic. Madison Square Garden, for example, has no parking garage and reaps no such benefit. Attendees either come by transit or park in nearby office building garages that empty out at night.

The entire plan alone would lack the urban qualities that could evolve into an authentic and fluid urban place. But even worse, the neighborhoods around the development site reflect perfectly the potential for regeneration

10.1 The Atlantic Arts
Building, formerly 31 high-
end condos, empty since
2005 except for one holdout,
Dan Goldstein, co-founder
of Develop Don't Destroy
Brooklyn, fighting the
project. *Tracy Collins.*

when multiple and varied precursors are undisturbed. Revitalization was
occurring despite the blighted properties owned by either the city or Ratner.

Regeneration Was Already Happening

In the decade from 1990 to 2000 the area within a half-mile radius, according to a thorough study by the Pratt Center for Community Development,
experienced widespread new incremental investment with higher-income,
better-educated, and younger residents moving in from other areas of the
city.[16] It was revitalization despite the proximity of the rail yards. The income for the area rose from 45 to 65 percent of the median income for
Brooklyn. Home ownership increased from 12.8 percent to 24.7 percent.
Row houses and small apartment buildings were renovated. Industrial buildings were converted to expensive condominiums. Modest-scale new luxury
residences were built with million-dollar condos. Rooftop and backyard additions were added to brownstones. New small local businesses and some
chains opened. All of this was happening with the retention of both public
and subsidized housing, and both rent-regulated and unregulated low-
income housing. More than 8,000 residents, or almost 15 percent of the
area's population, live below the poverty level. In other words, precursors to
regeneration were maturing into the real thing. One neighborhood resident
told Charles V. Bagli of the *New York Times* that he had watched his block
"evolve from a strip packed with working man's bars to a desolate eyesore
and back to a thriving street."[17]

A neighborhood door-to-door survey, conducted by local resident and trained researcher Patti Hagan, found 864 people living in the six blocks slated for demolition and 200 jobs. Ratner guessed there were 100 residents. A classic case of regeneration in motion, what Jacobs called "unslumming." In the middle of this is the Atlantic Yards site designated BLIGHTED! I don't think so!

Among the rationalizations for the blight designation, interestingly, was the existence of about 50 percent vacant lots or structures built to only 60 percent of allowable density. Many of the empty lots, as noted, were owned by the city or the developer and kept empty (or made empty through demolition) in anticipation of the new development. What better example of "planners' blight"? As for the buildings built to 60 percent or less of allowable bulk, that refers to brownstones, small retail spaces, modest-scale apartment houses, industrial buildings, the very combination of structures that revived the surrounding districts. In 2007 a nearby four-story double-duplex private house was selling for $2 million.

By the definition of "blight" allowed on this site, most of Brooklyn and a good deal of the rest of the city could be declared blighted—exactly Moses's point. This allows wrongheaded projects to be rationalized anywhere in the city, stopped only by successful civic resistance, financial implosion, or occasional court victories.

Historic Preservation Sacrificed

Preservation and restoration of historic buildings have been, as noted, one of the leading precursors of the area's upgrade in recent decades. But that didn't stop Ratner, with the complicity of the city and the state, from slating for demolition some noteworthy but undesignated landmarks, the kind that have been the star revitalization performers in New York and every city across the country.

The most egregious loss has been the six-story 1911 Ward's Bakery with its white terra-cotta facade and colorful Greco-inspired ornamental arches. The owner was planning to convert it to a hotel until he took a nice profit and sold this and another building to Ratner for $44 million in 2005. Closed in 1995, "this factory helped create a market for mass-produced bread," wrote Sam Goldsmith in the Brooklyn Paper. "Thanks to new machinery and techniques that mechanized the process, the factory turned out 250,000 loaves—a lot in those days—and employed hundreds of employees."[18]

10.2 Ward's Bakery, with its terra cotta façade and large arched windows, would have been a designated landmark on any other site. Now demolished. *Tracy Collins.*

Ward's Bakery was on the footprint of a planned superblock on a corner of the whole twenty-two-acre site. Its preservation would have meant moving the location of the arena. Of course, if preserving the building were a goal to begin with, the site planning might have evolved differently.

Ironically, the bakery had a historic sports connection, too. George S. Ward, bakery president, was vice president of baseball's short-lived Federal League, a failed attempt to create a third professional league from 1913 to 1915. His brother, Robert Ward, owned the Brooklyn Tip-Tops, one of the league's eight teams, named after a Ward's bread brand. They played in Washington Park, in nearby Park Slope, where the Dodgers played until moving to Ebbets Field in 1912.

To add insult to the injury of losing this building, Ratner will get credit under the LEED[19] green building standards for eventually incorporating elements of this needlessly lost landmark into his new structure (if the stored elements even survive). The LEED standards are weighted almost entirely in favor of new construction, despite the fact that, as the now well-known saying goes, "the greenest building is the one already standing."[20]

Public Relations and Politics Win Out

Ratner's public relations effort has been amazingly effective from the start, especially succeeding in focusing the spotlight on the virtues of a new sports facility, the one thing even opponents agree is a legitimate goal, but distracting attention from the enormous public cost required. The arena, noted *Daily News* columnist Jimmy Breslin on January 22, 2004, "would be a nice addition to Brooklyn, if you had it . . . someplace that disturbed no human beings who contribute a lot more to the world than a foul shot." Ratner is also a generous philanthropist, strategically donating money to scores of organizations and institutions that just coincidentally results in minimum public debate.

The arena focus leaves in the shadow the debate over sixteen new glass and steel towers ranging in height from approximately 150 to 500 feet, 15,000 new people, gridlock traffic, overcrowded schools, overwhelming transit usage, and more. As Chris Smith wrote in *New York Magazine* in 2006:

> In his push to make Atlantic Yards a reality, Bruce Ratner has crafted the most sophisticated political campaign the city has seen in a very long time, better than any professional politician has mounted to win elective office, complete with gag orders and aggressive polling. And even if Atlantic Yards was wildly disproportionate to the surrounding neighborhoods, its pillars seemed laudable (the subsidized housing) and potentially cool (Gehry; having the NBA's Nets nearby). The developer, Ratner, seemed downright enlightened: a commissioner of consumer affairs under Ed Koch who'd gone out of his way to hire women and minorities to build his other projects.[21]

Smith might also have noted the deceptiveness of the affordable-housing promise. Not only has the promised number of units shrunk since first announced, as predicted, but the money to construct them would be coming from normal public funding sources, not from Ratner's development coffers. In other words, those units could be built now, elsewhere, without Atlantic Yard's construction. If Ratner really cared about creating affordable housing, he could do it now elsewhere in the city. And if such housing is constructed in the future and those public funds still exist, money used here will not be available for similar housing elsewhere in the city. That funding source is finite. And since any affordable units built here will be more expensive to construct than elsewhere, a disproportionate share of the citywide resource will get used here.

So, since its announcement in December 2003, where does the project stand? In light of the current economic crisis, this is hard to say. Ratner tried and failed to get a bailout from the stimulus package to build the

10.3 Dean Street loft co-ops on the Atlantic Yards site, formerly fully occupied. The building has been empty since 2005 and is scheduled for demolition. *Tracy Collins.*

arena. Mayor Bloomberg has denied any increase in city funds. Court challenges continue. In September 2009, Russian billionaire Mikhail Prokhorov agreed to buy 80 percent of the money-losing basketball team and to invest in the larger project. The details remain unclear. One cannot predict what will finally emerge from this overblown proposal. Cynics could easily observe that building the arena for his own team, the Nets, was Ratner's goal to begin with, the rest being window dressing. If anyone really thought that the Gehry-designed development had a chance of evolving as presented for state and public approval, well, then, I have a bridge to sell them.

Ratner would have undoubtedly sold off parcels to other developers to design as they saw fit within the zoning. He still can. Wrote *New York Times* critic Nicolai Ouroussoff, who had high praise for Gehry's design: "New York has had a terrible track record with large-scale planning in recent years. Look at Battery Park City. The MetroTech Center.[22] Donald Trump's Riverside South. All are blots on the urban environment, as blandly homogeneous in their own way as the Modernist superblocks they were intended to improve on."[23] Ouroussoff points to Rockefeller Center as a prime and glorious example of what this city was once capable of producing. Yet Rockefeller Center evolved. It started as a planned site for an opera house, changed with the times, was designed by thirteen different architects, connected seamlessly to the existing grid (even adding a street), is totally geared to pedestrians and mass transit, not cars, and did not overwhelm the airspace of its site.

The alternative to Ratner's proposal had smaller and more manageable components and relied on more than one developer. This could have produced some notable new buildings. The most critically acclaimed buildings designed and built around the city in recent years are on single infill sites, mostly in historic neighborhoods. The scale of the alternative would be more compatible with the existing urban fabric, even including reasonably tall buildings. The surrounding neighborhoods thus would not be overwhelmed. Viable buildings would not be lost nor current residents and businesses displaced. Development and new growth could have continued as they had in the prior decade, step by step, in modest doses. Transportation and pedestrian connections to its surroundings and to the downtown core would be more reasonable. All of this would add up to the kind of development in small or modest doses that leads to big but appropriate change. The alternative design would have had a better chance of genuine public approval and of getting off the ground. What a missed opportunity.

In fact, one of two Dean Street resident architects who offered alternative plans suggested razing the Atlantic Center mall, a much maligned suburban-style enclosed shopping complex built in the 1990s by Ratner just north of the arena site. (A few government agencies occupy space here. This is a typical way government helps economically challenged developer projects.) "If Mr. Ratner were willing to condemn his own property, he would be able to build his arena without displacing anyone from their homes," architect Karla Rothstein, a Dean Street resident who worked on an alternative development, told *Times* reporter Bagli. "It would be an improvement on the existing mall," she added.

Another important consequence of the alternative should be noted. The city would not lose the taxes, residences, businesses, and jobs of the site for the decades that most of this land will lie fallow, just like so many earlier Robert Moses clearance projects did. The losses on these sites is never calculated, just the promises of the new taxes and jobs to come eventually. Those jobs may not even materialize as promised. Seldom does the city or anyone go back after a project is finished to see if promises have been met. And in how many projects have we seen fewer jobs created than promised and then seen those jobs disappear within a short time after completion? The tax incentives that came with those promises are rarely removed.

Measuring the taxes and jobs is fundamentally the wrong way to evaluate a plan, in any case. One must consider how it affects a wide area, including the whole city, and not just the site. Otherwise, everything will continually be suitable for replacement, no matter how well the site still functions. "Just replacing a dime store with a larger five and ten doesn't benefit the city in the long run," notes Ron Shiffman. "Rather, the point is to enable those facilities, like the dime store, to improve themselves. One is a replacement strategy; the other is how an economy grows by nurturing from within."

What Would Jane Jacobs Say?

Jacobs's name was reportedly invoked in the early presentations of the Atlantic Yards proposal. Apparently, the Jacobs qualities included a web of streets and sidewalks, although winding suburban style and not connected to the city's existing grid; ground-floor retail for some of the towers, something every developer now does because it is good business but is also used to claim a Jacobs imprimatur; and, of course, mixed use, which, as shown earlier in this book, is not the Jacobs definition of mixed use but contrasts with Moses's separation of uses. Since her name was involved, it is appropriate to examine the project against her writing.

First, let's dispose of the idea that Jacobs was against change or against big buildings or, indeed, a sentimentalist. First, go back to her letter to Mayor Bloomberg about Greenpoint-Williamsburg. That is a ringing endorsement for change, just a different kind of change than what the city was proposing. In addition, one can look at her enthusiastic championing of the planning and zoning changes in the old garment center of Toronto known as the King-Spadina area. Toronto city officials consulted with her and followed many of her suggestions there, today considered that city's SoHo equivalent. New innovative uses occupy both old and new buildings. New buildings coexist comfortably with old. Once empty or underused old buildings are now full. This is change in a big way. That Toronto district was in no better shape than our city's so-called derelict old neighborhoods.

And, of course, a true reading of Jacobs's books versus a pseudounderstanding would indicate her disapproval of everything about Atlantic Yards but also her expectation for continued change and growth, just not Ratner's idea of change and growth, any more than a Moses plan. A basic Jacobs precept is complexity: no complexity is possible in a monolithic development of this scale by one developer and designed by one architect.

Another basic Jacobs precept is opposition to "cataclysmic" money and development. Surely, this project qualifies as cataclysmic change. The proposal is so inimical to the character of the district and, in fact, the whole borough of Brooklyn that it is off any chart of Jacobs's principles.

Trying to show how Atlantic Yards contradicts every Jacobs principle can be tiresome. And, in fact, she was too unpredictable for such an exercise. Furthermore, Jacobs was never about how to *develop* or *design* as much as how to *think* about development, how to *observe* and *understand* what works, how to *respect* what exists, how to *scrutinize* plans skeptically, how to *nurture* innovation, new growth, and resilience. That says it all.

As it happens, I had a brief conversation with Jane about Atlantic Yards in one of my last visits with her before her death. The development had only recently been proposed, and she agreed that it was right out of the pages of old, discarded development models derivative of Moses. There was not much to discuss. She shook her head and said, "What a shame."

On to Columbia University

Atlantic Yards may be the poster child for current Moses-style development in New York, but it is not alone. Columbia University on the Upper West Side gained city approval for a second campus north of its historic 110th Street site that would provide 6.8 million square feet in eighteen new academic and research buildings on seventeen acres in West Harlem and an underground network six stories deep for tunnels, two power plants, parking, garbage collection, and loading docks. The site encompasses more than eight blocks north of 125th Street between the phenomenal architectural structures of two elevated trestles for Riverside Drive and the Broadway IRT subway. Though lacking in gates or fences, this second campus will feel separated and segregated from the neighboring city. Under single ownership and patrolled by a private security force, this academic island will undoubtedly feel isolated, even if connected to the actual grid and planned skillfully by an accomplished city planning team under the leadership of Marilyn Taylor of Skidmore, Owings, and Merrill.

Like Atlantic Yards, Columbia targeted a semi-industrial, seemingly derelict neighborhood that to the contrary combined regenerative precursors interspersed with opportunities for infill development of varying scale. And like Atlantic Yards, both Columbia's purchase and emptying of properties along with the threat of eminent domain blighted the area, although new businesses, especially restaurants, kept opening in the neighborhood, despite their location under and within sound impact of both viaducts. In fact, enough new restaurants have opened in reclaimed warehouses along Twelfth Avenue to be dubbed "restaurant row" and "a culinary hot spot" for West Harlem.

Unlike Atlantic Yards, however, Columbia could have achieved 85 percent, if not all, the expansion that it says it needs (predicting future needs is always a guessing game) in the next thirty years without erasing a Harlem neighborhood, once known as Manhattanville. That expansion, however, just would not have happened in the same form, with the same design, and according to the same plan as Columbia insisted on.

Forest City Ratner, a private-sector entity with the purpose of making money, is best known in Brooklyn for its two large suburban-style projects, the Metro Tech office park and the Atlantic Center Mall. That is Ratner's style of development, not an urban vision reflecting a real understanding of how a city—its neighborhoods, economy, and public spaces—really works. But from Columbia University, one of the most prestigious in the country, something different was to be expected. Columbia should not behave like a private developer with a suburban view of the city. This 254-year old institution is home to a highly respected planning program, the first historic preservation program at any university in the country, and an impressive roster of urban experts, such as Mindy Fullilove, mentioned earlier, a professor of clinical psychiatry and public health who has written so extensively about the impacts of the ruptured social bonds in communities decimated by urban renewal.

So when Columbia unveiled its proposed new academic enclave necessitating the total clearance of a neighborhood, Moses style, urbanists were correct to be stunned. The individual glass-covered, almost transparent buildings were designed by the world-renowned architect Renzio Piano. The pattern of enlisting "starchitects" merely for the purpose of advancing otherwise troublesome plans had become familiar in recent decades. Both Atlantic Yards and the Columbia plan are perfect examples of this trend.

Expansion Idea Not Disputed

It is very important to understand that no one was denying Columbia the right to expand. No one was denying that its expansion could be good for the city. No one was even questioning if Columbia would really need eight million additional square feet of space in the next thirty years, although such projections are tricky at best. And no one was opposing change. Once again, quite simply, it was the form of the change that was legitimately challenged, not change itself.

Columbia's well-illustrated material presents the proposal as "a new hub of education and economic opportunity, culture and community—weaving together the urban fabric of West Harlem with a revitalized Hudson River waterfront." Ironically, by the way, the revitalized waterfront is something the community has been fighting for for years. It is finally happening without Columbia. Three new piers along the waterfront have been built by the city and state. Sadly, however, the community that fought for and achieved this will not remain to enjoy it or will have to come from afar to visit. Notes the brochure: "The plan would transform what is now a largely isolated, underutilized streetscape of garage openings, empty ground floors, roll-down metal gates, and chain-link fences in the blocks from West 125th to 133rd Streets into a cohesive, reanimated center for educational, commercial, and community life." These are the conditions Columbia fostered and now wants to repair.

Like Ratner at Atlantic Yards, Columbia started buying property in the area and removing tenants well before the announced proposal, again causing much of the blight it decries. Anyone reading the above description would think the proposal is entirely beneficial. No mention is made of the displacement of 400 residents occupying affordable units, including 160 low-income families, 70-odd businesses, and 1,200 jobs. While areas in the city available for blue-collar work dwindle, it is difficult to estimate how many of the displaced businesses will survive in New York or at all. And considering, as well, the shortage of affordable housing, the relocation of low-income families from here, years before new units are built, only puts more strain on the citywide supply. Columbia's description of the site also fails to mention the removal of 150 artists and their studios, a window manufacturer, several film editing studios for cable TV, a wholesale bakery, a catering business, a pharmacy, a furniture restorer, one framing and gilding business, a stone fabricator, a boilermaker, several electricians and plumbers, assorted restaurants, an architectural ornament fabricator, Tools for Schools (an electronics repair and reuse operation), a few construction companies, moving and storage facilities, auto-body businesses, and two gas stations. Six sizable family-owned businesses were included in this mix.

One family-owned business, Hudson Moving and Storage, housed dozens of small businesses in two buildings, from a woodworker to an electrician to a refinisher. Hudson's multiple interior spaces functioned as an incubator for new and growing businesses. Until Columbia started

10.4 Hudson Moving and Storage, on the Columbia site and purchased by Columbia under threat of eminent domain, had been converted into an assortment of creative small businesses. *Ron Shiffman.*

buying up occupied buildings, the area was home to a veritable agglomeration of small businesses that were both part of the citywide economy and servicing it. The value of this network is beyond measurement. Individually and collectively, they add up to hidden links in the city's supply chain and are almost totally ignored and undervalued.

The diversity of businesses present in this "blighted" area is not quite what Columbia would like the public to believe. Of course, many of these uses began disappearing when Columbia started buying properties.

It is worth repeating: Columbia University's expansion needs are real. No one disputes that. Expansion would be a good thing for the city as a whole. Elements of the proposed design are appealing. One could never judge the architectural plans, however, because the only sure thing about them is that they will change dramatically as the project moves forward. But whatever its design, it could all happen without erasing, Moses style, a viable piece of the city that would have revived economically, socially, and physically if not demolished.

The fundamental flaw preventing a compatible Columbia expansion was the university's insistence on the six-story underground space covering the whole site, known as the bathtub. This enormous, really enormous, underground space will take approximately seven to ten years to build and requires an estimated ninety-eight thousand or more truck trips in and out of the neighborhood, transporting debris to landfills. Underground tunnels, parking, loading, and power plants will fill this space. Its creation requires demolition of everything above it on the street level—except, of course, a few buildings Columbia has chosen to retain for its own use.

Serious technical questions were raised, especially by disaster experts, concerning the environmental safety of this "bathtub." The site is located on a fault line and in an evacuation zone for hurricane surges, and it will include labs that work with biohazards. Experts, including some on the Columbia campus, questioned whether the bathtub space could be constructed with adequate safeguards.

The environmental and economic costs were never clearly addressed. But the point here is not to take issue with a very challenging engineering issue; the point is to indicate, yet again, how an alternative was available. Rockefeller Center, for example, brilliantly created a vast underground space in the 1930s that would permit the requisite underground uses[24] and connections without requiring the same underground scale. The university totally rejected the idea without serious consideration. "Cities are bound to change, you have to accept it," the architect, Renzio Piano, was quoted as saying in one news story. "This area is going to change, and should change in significant ways. You can't embalm a city," Columbia president Lee Bollinger was quoted as saying. Neither comment reflects the reality that, yet again, it was not about stopping change or embalming a city but about what kind of change is appropriate. *Embalm* is a favorite word used in recent years by people whose proposals met stiff public resistance. One had to wonder what city—or, indeed, what planet—they were talking about. New York City, for sure, has been in an almost permanent state of construction and change for years, the most dramatic transformation in decades.

It should be noted that Columbia's plan, even if a Moses-style, nonintegrative, demolition-only one, is a better one than Atlantic Yards in terms of street layout, connections to the surrounding grid, and central open space. Nevertheless, it destroys viable urban assets instead of building on them, claims a green building philosophy while erasing environmentally viable existing buildings, replaces instead of enriches an existing neighborhood, and boasts a community involvement process that permitted tinkerings, not meaningful impact.[25] In both places, the critical web of so-

10.5 Willets Point. Not the view officials want to see when they go to Citi Field. *Norman Mintz.*

cial and economic relationships that reach beyond the immediate borders is shattered. The upheaval in many cases is causing irreparable harm. And like Atlantic Yards, the specter and willingness of Columbia to abuse the potential for eminent domain resulted in a totally undemocratic process.[26] Moses would be pleased.

Willets Point

Willets Point is probably the most challenging site to demonstrate both the existence of regenerative precursors and an alternative to a Moses-style clearance strategy. *Bleak* is a mild term for the appearance of this desolate and isolated thirteen-block triangle directly across from the Shea Stadium replacement, Citi Field, in Queens. Its worst sin, in fact, is that it is a visual offense to city officials who deem it imperative to clean up and sanitize the site directly in the eye path of visiting sports fans. The idea of a view of gritty economic life is apparently unacceptable.

This sixty-one-acre site at the geographic center of the city is surrounded by two highways and a subway line. The area is literally bereft of most city services. No basic infrastructure exists here. No sidewalks, no sewer lines, no paved streets, and no street lights are to be found. Pond-size potholes are everywhere. Huge oil-slick puddles collect after a rainfall. Dust rises from the unpaved roads running past and between the waste transfer stations and recycling facilities. And to add insult to injury, police give tickets for parking on sidewalks even where there are no sidewalks. Many of the ramshackle structures are built in unconventional ways, mostly of corrugated aluminum. They are interspersed with reused manufacturing and warehouse buildings and empty lots. A more dismal piece of New York City real estate is hard to find. A pile of "toxic filth that is the result of the government's failure to provide adequate infrastructure in the first place," wrote economist Sanford Ikeda on his blog critiquing the city demolition plan.

So when the city Economic Development Administration announced in 2006 a plan in which the city would buy out all the property owners to clear the site for future development, one can understand why there was a more muted off-site voice in opposition than for either Atlantic Yards or Columbia's new campus. But this is a real case of more than meets the eye.

The miracle is how anything exists on Willets Point at all! The curious must ask why. What can be observed and learned here? Actually, quite a bit.

A Moses Survivor

Ironically, this was the site of an earlier, rare successful battle against Robert Moses. In the 1960s Moses wanted the site for parkland. A then little-known lawyer but future governor, Mario Cuomo, successfully represented the land and business owners to resist this takeover. A later Donald Trump effort to redevelop the area also failed.

But even as a takeover target for decades, with probably the worst physical conditions of any city site, Willets Point is home to 260 businesses and 1,700 to 1,800 jobs.[27] Little vacant or unused land can be found. Property values are comparable to values in other industrial areas of Brooklyn and Queens. Willets Point businesses—mostly auto parts and recycling related—paid approximately $1.1 million in city real estate taxes in 2005.

Twenty businesses are run by landowners, many second- and third-generation family owned. More than 80 percent of the businesses are renters. Most have been in business more than five years at the same location, an indication of long-term stability. Statistics for Willets Point are more revealing and relevant than in many places because it is so difficult for the average eye to observe true economic and urban value here.

But consider carefully what economist Sanford Ikeda also wrote on his blog, in January 2008:

Old, worn-out buildings (or garages) are often good places to incubate ideas, but you can't build old buildings. Places like Willets Point (and Dharavi in India) offer cheap space for poor entrepreneurs who tend in turn, at least initially, to serve poor patrons. Willets Point is a good, though perhaps not perfect, example of an "unslumming" commercial slum, that is, a slum that is bootstrapping its way to economic development. Okay, it doesn't appear on the surface to be all that innovative. But in among the mostly grungy auto shops are a few shinier and larger establishments. So, the most successful either leave for less-toxic pastures or, if they stay, help to unslum the slum.

The Dharavi reference is an interesting one. Mumbai's sprawling Dharavi is the primary so-called slum depicted in *Slumdog Millionaire* that actually patched together scenes from various slums in that city for the film. Like Willets Point, the reality of Dharavi contradicts the perception. While the largest slum in Mumbai, "Dharavi is probably the most active and lively part of an incredibly industrious city . . . including having set up a highly functional recycling industry that serves the whole city," wrote Matias Echanove and Rahul Srivastava, community activists affiliated with PUKAR,[28] in a *New York Times* op-ed piece. Dharavi, they noted, "is all about resourcefulness. Over 60 years ago, it started off as a small village in the marshlands and grew, with no governmental support, to become a million-dollar economic miracle providing food to Mumbai and exporting crafts and manufactured goods to places as far away as Sweden."[29] Estimates of the number of informal businesses and cottage industries are 5,000 to 15,000, with revenues totaling tens, if not hundreds, of millions of dollars a year.

Economist Edward L. Glaeser agrees. "The defining characteristic of Mumbai is not crime or Bollywood, but entrepreneurship even in the city's slums," he wrote in the *New York Times* Economix Blog, on May 26, 2009. Dharavi, he noted, "is a place of remarkable economic energy where poor people are managing to eke out a living as entrepreneurs."

Willets Point is also all about resourcefulness. It looks like sheer chaos but has its own economic rationale. And like Willets Point, the Indian government is preparing to flatten Dharavi and build high-rise towers and

10.6 Rahul and Matias loved the license plate. *Rahul Srivastava.*

business parks, à la Robert Moses, in the mistaken notion that building an economy on real estate instead of entrepreneurship works.

On their trip to New York last year, I took Matias and Rahul to Willets Point. They were stunned at the similarities with Dharavi, the big difference being that in Dharavi, people live where they work as well. The same lack of infrastructure exists, as does the creative patching together of small buildings with corrugated tin and other materials. Residents role up their mattresses each morning and get to work.

"Here is a slice of urban life that connected New York to other cities around the world in which raw economic necessity and a tougher set of choices shaped the landscape more than the luxury of planned architectural interventions that is otherwise New York's signature," they wrote in a blog report of their visit. "From the outside," they also observed, "you would never guess the immense ferment going on beneath."

Effectively, at Willets Point—like Dharavi—over many decades, poor businesses have congregated for mutual support and networking. This is a fundamental and critical component of genuine economic development, in contrast to a publicly subsidized, developer-driven construction project. What evolved on Willets Point is totally self-organized, cannot be "developed" or "planned for," and is invariably overlooked entirely and undervalued by professionals. Many longtime establishments have been doing very well and serve a low-income community while providing jobs for a

10.7 Artistry and ingenuity not just reserved for cars. *Norman Mintz.*

mostly Spanish-speaking workforce from nearby Corona. Many workers walk to work. Firms here "provide a wide range of auto-related services, have longstanding linkages with one another, and both compete and cooperate with one another," noted the Hunter College study.

In effect, this is a classic agglomeration, a natural concentration of interrelated businesses that cluster organically to gain strength from proximity to each other. New York's fur district, jewelry district, garment district, flower district, financial district, gallery district, computer alley, and meatpacking district are all examples of a similar urban economic process. Such agglomerations cannot be relocated. They only happen naturally. Thus, the impact of dispersal would economically weaken the full network and probably some of the individual components fatally.

It is too easy to dismiss the unglamorous existence of scrap-metal yards, auto-body shops, and other messy concerns (41 percent of the total), as happens usually in the press and official descriptions. But this unappealing description masks an assortment of specialized individual auto businesses, including parts, body, glass, tires, muffler, salvage, sales, and one parts supplier specializing in antique cars. There are even brokers who will direct you to the exact business that specializes in your problem. This is a more complex network of businesses than meets the eye, with a wide range of specializations. And, as the Hunter report notes, "auto parts suppliers in the area make access to parts economical and relatively swift." This is real economic efficiency, the organic urban kind. The report adds: "The relations among the operators of auto-related businesses are often cooperative and mutually supportive, and they form a network that strengthens the attractiveness of the area as a specialized district."

One anomaly exists at Willets Point that happens to be the largest employer. House of Spices is the largest manufacturer and distributor of

Indian foods in the country, with one hundred full-time employees. But there is even more diversity that includes a number of businesses that manufacture or distribute steel products, oil and grease absorbents, utility pipes, safety and surveillance equipment, bakery supplies, and ethnic foods.

Willets Point has served as a classic incubator of new businesses. Many here started small and even with a different business mix. Tully Construction Company, for example, has grown from its 1988 start as a highway contractor into a diverse engineering and construction firm handling a wide range of infrastructure, waste management, and environmental projects in the city.

If one understands the essential, though often hidden, natural process of a vibrant urban economy, one understands why Willets Point businesses are resistant to leaving. Replicating the physical conditions that nourish this increasingly rare and vital network is difficult, if not impossible, as discussed in chapter 6.

Aside from questioning the wisdom of wiping out such an economic concentration, one might also question if the city needs yet another combination of housing, offices, restaurants, shops (i.e., malls), a school, a park, a convention center, and a seven-hundred-room hotel. And, to boot, this is in the flight path of La Guardia Airport! How desirable is it to live under low-flying planes? And because of the highways that encircle the area and serve as barriers now, any new development is going to be auto dependent. One thing is for sure. The city will spend endless public funds now, but the site will remain unbuilt and unproductive until the economy rebounds, or longer. Or the area closest to Citi Field will get force-fed new development to create the pretty face officials want visitors to see.

The bottom line for Willets Point is no different from that for Atlantic Yards and Columbia. This should not be an all-or-nothing Moses-style plan. The wisest strategy, if legitimate urban growth is the goal, would be to install the infrastructure and let the real estate market take care of itself.

First of all, the city's public investment would be a fraction of the cost of buying out all these landowners at great public cost *and* putting in the infrastructure *and* preparing the site (probably toxic) for a private developer. Current annual tax payments and critical jobs would not be lost in the meantime. Owners could sell and move or stay, as they see fit, and decide what is best for the future of their businesses. What new development would then occur would not be the force-fed kind heavily subsidized by the city; it would be the kind that responds to both local and larger city market demands. Logically, with infrastructure installed, this could be a desirable relocation site for some of the small manufacturing businesses pushed out from other areas of the city where upzonings are taking their toll. "This eagerness to build anew, however, brings with it an impatience to clear away impediments or, as Moses infamously put it, 'hack your way with a meat ax,'" wrote Karrie Jacobs in a *Metropolis Magazine* Cityside column, "Demolition Man." She was referring to then Governor Pataki's willingness to "tear down whatever is in the way" of developers' plans and to use eminent domain to clear the way. She pointed out how New York is one of the states most willing to use that power meant for a public purpose to advance a private plan.

Clearly, the redevelopment plan is what Jane Jacobs would call a "manicuring job." The image of the auto-parts store with hubcaps, tires, and decorative items covering the facade is considered an "iconic American image" when embalmed in a Walker Evans photograph (*Cherokee Parts Store—Garage Work*, for one) taken in the South during the Depression. But it is another story when it is real and of today.

As this book goes to press, deals are being struck with the landowners closest to Citi Field, the area of primary official attention. Chances are that land will be rapidly cleared and left empty. At the same time, deals are being struck for businesses, like House of Spices, at the back end of the site to remain, reasonably visually removed from the stadium, or to leave with a generous buyout. How transparent is that?

Lost Precursors

Atlantic Yards, Columbia's new campus, and Willets Point all exemplify the remaining strength of the Moses legacy and the continuing loss of precursors to urban regeneration. In each case, precursors of regeneration went unrecognized, devalued, and destroyed. City officials may argue, as always is done, that all Willets Point businesses, for example, will be relocated. Assuming that promise is even partially fulfilled, scattering such businesses near and far always destroys the efficacy of their clustering location and diminishes their numbers, productivity, and economic contribution to the city, something New York cannot afford to keep losing.

No chance exists in a Moses strategy to demolish selectively. This was the pattern during Urban Renewal and why I argue the city lost so much more under Robert Moses than is yet understood. The Moses approach still prevails too often, even if fewer homes and businesses are being demolished with each project. The many productive individual initiators visible around the city, whether Jacobs inspired or not, get considerable attention and distract the public from the impact of the Moses-style projects. It can be deceptive, seducing people to believe Jacobs's precepts prevail.

The fundamental flaw in the Moses approach is its simplicity. It is a formula-based doctrine that oversimplifies what it takes to create enduring places, requires a clean slate, and ascribes no value to what came before. A city is much too complex, too multilayered, too filled with interwoven threads to be sustained by singular, simplistic, self-contained, homogenizing projects. And while many of Moses's parks and swimming pools were beautifully designed and are much admired today even when totally deteriorated and closed, they are inseparable pieces of a whole Moses vision and strategy that sees the city as a series of physical projects rather than the economic, environmental, historical, social, *and* physical system that it is.

Nor is it correct to say that a Moses is needed to achieve public infrastructure and amenities, since countless cities, including New York, boast similarly important achievements not "done" by him. And many more big ones are currently under construction, as we've seen, without a construction czar to move them forward. Not only has this book shown that big things do get done, but it has also shown that many of the projects that don't get done shouldn't.

The idea of Moses as a model for implementation is a scary one as well. That, too, has simplicity at its core. Top-down, take-no-prisoners, my-way-or-the-highway—this is no way for things to get done in a democratic city.

And while there may be no point replaying the battles of Moses and Jacobs, I would call on the wisdom of former Salt Lake City planning director Stephen A. Goldsmith, who argued instead that "replaying the lessons learned from those battles will serve the public discourse very well indeed. More importantly, these lessons will advance the ideas Jane Jacobs placed in front of us and hopefully save many places from repeating old mistakes."

Throughout this book, we have seen where modest-scale initiatives are making big change citywide. Some are citizen initiated; some are initiated by city officials. There is nothing simple about any of them, other than that they work. They reflect Jacobs's principles even though initiated by people who may never have heard of her. The authentic city changes and grows slowly; it resists acceleration. Authenticity is the common thread of the stories in this book.

Gregory O'Connell's innovative development in Red Hook, David Sweeney's rescue and rehabilitation of former factories for new industrial start-ups and small manufactures, Janette Sadik-Khan's transformation of the streets of the city, Eddie Bautista's leadership in transforming how the city disposes of solid waste, the citywide landmark preservation movement's impact on both designated landmarks and undesignated but recyclable buildings and resultant revitalization spur—all is vintage Jane, *all* big change in small incremental steps.

We've seen the citywide impact of the defeat of Westway and its positive consequence along the Hudson waterfront, on the subway system, and in neighborhoods throughout the city, and Joan Byron's technical assistance work with an energetic coalition of South Bronx organizations that will, hopefully, achieve the same broad healing with the proposed tearing down of the Sheridan Expressway. We've seen the resilience of the local industrial economy reinforcing a basic Jacobs economic principle that local economies drive the growth of cities and ultimately the regional and national economies.

If there is one overarching Jacobsian lesson, it is how complex cities are. Her observations of Greenwich Village only appear simple and are too often misinterpreted as advocating similarly scaled and designed neighborhoods everywhere.[30] Instead, her observations are a fractal for understanding thousands of streets and districts. A fractal is simply something that may look and perform the same at all scales of magnitude. So when Jacobs wrote about Hudson Street and the Village, she wasn't suggesting every community need mirror that singular place. Instead, that Village neighborhood must be understood as a fractal to help observe and understand the components of thousands of streets and neighborhoods everywhere that have the potential to *function* in similarly vibrant ways but have their own local character, context, and unique qualities. In fact, a fractal at a larger dimension can take on a different character and look and perform differently.

Through Jane's local lessons, the greater public has come to understand the components of a particular neighborhood or whole city, and to understand how a city's—or any size community's—streets are the spine of any vital, vibrant city. That same public has come to understand their right and value in being a part of the process that leads to change. This is vintage Jane. Public process, on the other hand, was anathema to Moses.

Greenwich Village, Harlem, Boston, and Manchester and Birmingham, England, were for Jacobs lenses for understanding places and economies around the globe. The socially and economically productive spontaneous order that distinguishes vibrant places arises where Jacobsian principles prevail and Moses-style projects fail. Spontaneous, creative order can't exist in a monoculture. Spontaneous order works; imposed efficiency leads to stagnation.

This book has shown how Jacobs's principles are woven into many aspects of urban life. Often, however, they come only after the battle against yet another Moses-style proposal. Ultimately, cities will thrive where Jacobs's lessons shape both the civic debate and the urban process of growth and change. Only through building on local assets, weaving in the new with the old, pursuing new growth through innovation, only with the success of these paths, will localized efforts, which may or may not be Jacobs inspired, prevail; they will not prevail easily. The good news is that New York City's assets are many; much here exists to build on. Many cities are not so lucky and wastefully, sadly, keep demolishing the diminished number of assets they have.

The Moses impact will not disappear. Projects detailed in this book will emerge in varying forms in cities everywhere. Their defeat depends on a vigilant, successful citizenry; the compromises offered are never even close to adequate to mitigate the damage. Invariably, appropriate alternatives exist to achieve pronounced goals.

Citywide, one could debate which philosophy, Moses or Jacobs, was victorious. Evidence can be found for both, often simultaneously, as shown here, in the same city and, surely, in all American cities. Planners and developers would like us to think they follow most of Jacobs's principles. Observation and scrutiny of their plans and designs reveal a different picture. When one looks at where many city governments' primary attention and investment are directed, when one observes the plans and designs being promoted, when one looks at the cataclysmic scale and enormous cost of many proposals, nobody would be foolish enough to claim that her teachings are settled doctrine. Jacobs-style battles are still being fought, not always with success. But she certainly helped frame today's debate about urban development and change. And that alone is an enormous change from when it was Moses's way or no way.

The shadow of Robert Moses and Jane Jacobs still looms large over New York City and all cities. The battle for Gotham continues through the best of times and the worst of times.

Epilogue

> Can stones speak? Go there and listen. You will hear, I swear, the endless murmur of ten thousand tongues expressing wonder at being alive, wonder at being here, and wonder at being free. History becomes a continuing conversation between past and present and the question is whether we listen.
>
> ──────────────
>
> BILL MOYERS,
> *on the occasion of the hundredth*
> *anniversary of the Eldridge Street Synagogue*

In December 1982 I walked into the profoundly historic but crumbling 1887 Eldridge Street Synagogue on the Lower East Side and unwittingly changed my life. For the next twenty-five years, a good part of my time, energy, and passion was devoted to the rescue and restoration of this iconic landmark.

I never expected it. Once again, I had turned into what I write about, one of those people who work to change something in their community, totally ignorant that they have set their sights on an impossible task. That ignorance—and I do mean ignorance—combined with persistence (I was born stubborn) can make the unimaginable happen. And it did.

My friend Bill Josephson, a tall, thick-maned lawyer with a Wall Street firm, knew of my interest in preservation. We had met while both were involved in the battle to save the historic theaters in the Times Square and Broadway theater district in the early 1980s.[1] None of the theaters was yet a designated landmark. Many were threatened with demolition. Several were on the verge of demolition and were lost. The remaining forty-four historic theaters were designated landmarks.

Bill had discovered the synagogue on a walking tour with New York University professor Gerard Wolf, who highlighted this house of worship in his book *Synagogues of the Lower East Side*. This extraordinary mélange of architectural styles—Gothic, Moorish, Romanesque—was the first synagogue built by the East European Orthodox Jews *as a synagogue* on the Lower East Side. Before then, synagogues on the Lower East Side were established in converted churches, storefronts, or ground floors of tenements. This was the first built from scratch as a synagogue. This is a significant fact.

For hundreds of years, East European Jews worshiped in unprepossessing spaces, vernacular in style, meant to blend in with local buildings so as not to attract undo attention. Most East European Jews had fled pogroms and other life threats to settle here. At first, they worshiped only in little local synagogues, called *shteibeles*. But when they realized they were finally in a place where they could worship openly and freely, they built the Eldridge Street Synagogue, K'Hal Adath Jeshurun with Anche Lubz.

It is grand, embellished, and elegant. The reds, greens, golds, and blues are of different hues in a combination of detailed patterns with the center dome dotted with gold stars on a sky-blue background. Boldly it proclaims its Jewishness. Stars of David are everywhere, a clear statement of "we are here, we are Jewish, we are free."

I have no family roots on the Lower East Side. Both my parents' parents settled in Brooklyn after immigrating from Poland and Lithuania. But when I walked into the synagogue, I felt my history emanating from the walls. What an icon of American Jewish history, New York City history, sacred architecture! I was hooked.

Pigeons roosted in the attic and flew in and out of missing windows. Dust was so thick on the pews that you could carve your initials in it. Water was pouring through one corner of the roof. Prayer books were left strewn about. Little objects that worshipers long ago had left behind, including crystal drinking glasses, were randomly scattered. Pieces of stained glass from broken windows were everywhere. No operable bathroom remained. One electric line, connected probably illegally to the street, was gerrymandered for plug-in heaters.

11.1 Balcony window
and coffer before
restoration. (To view all
these photos in color, go to
www.eldridgestreet.org.)
Kate Milford.

Decades before, congregants had worshiped one day and left the next. The upstairs sanctuary was nailed shut. Sabbath services had shifted to the small *bes hamedrash* in the basement.[2] The synagogue remained nailed shut until Professor Wolf persuaded the *shamos*, Benjamin Markowitz, to reopen it. Markowitz, a short, stocky Polish immigrant who came through Ellis Island and always seemed to be wearing the same jacket he arrived with, greeted tourists on Sundays and collected small donations, enough money to pay for oil to turn the burner on for Friday night and Saturday Sabbath services.

A Flashlight into History

Through the dust, despite the pigeons, and beyond the many broken elements, a haunting beauty came through. Sun rays streamed through windows reflecting on the floating particles of dust like a flashlight into history. But it wasn't just the aesthetic beauty that was so compelling. That beauty is found in many historic houses of worship. And it wasn't just the intact condition of original, irreplaceable decorative elements, never subjected to unfortunate modernization. As one entered the building, one was touched by the ghosts of history.

While sitting in the balcony, for example, I thought of the hard lives so many of the worshipers had led, working in overcrowded sweatshops, living in crowded quarters, walking the teeming streets. What a refuge this must have been, the one place they could feel valued. After all, if one is worthy to pray in such a magnificent place, that means something.

A profound, untold story was screaming out from the ornately painted ceiling and walls, from the balcony where women sat, from the bimah where snuff boxes held the corners with four brass torchères, from the brass chandeliers and sconces that had never been taken by scavengers, from the red-velvet-lined Ark that once held numerous Torahs. It was as if a missing chapter of the rich Lower East Side Jewish immigrant story had been found. It had to be told.

For that story to be told, the building, the story's vessel, had to be saved. "What do you think?" Bill asked. "Is it worth spending the rest of our lives saving?" Little did I realize that it would be my life he was talking about.

UNANTICIPATED CONSEQUENCES

There were actually several things I didn't anticipate. I didn't realize that by shepherding this restoration I would be witness to and participant in the changing field of historic preservation. And while I long viewed preservation as the ultimate form of recycling, I didn't expect we would be a model for green preservation and building a local economy, two critical urban issues of the twenty-first century. Localism, buying goods and services close to home, and recycling are fundamental to green design and building blocks for sustainable development of which green design is only one part. But more on this later. "Why do you want to save an old synagogue in Chinatown?" I was often challenged by people unaware of the touchstones of Jewish history remaining in the area. We created a tour, "From Ellis to Eldridge," when tourist interest was just emerging.

It was clear from the start that if we didn't save this building, we would have to reinvent it. Four-fifths of American Jews had passed through the Lower East Side on their way to elsewhere. For the Lower East Side, the Eldridge Synagogue had been a major center of Jewish life, *the* synagogue among many. No other synagogue remained intact from that era. For so many new arrivals, their story started here. For some, we learned from former congregants, it was an occasional visit. For others, membership was the pride of their family. Sendor Yarmolowsky, president of the first Jewish-owned bank on the Lower East Side two blocks away, was its first president. Isaac Gellis, before he famously went into the salami and other delicatessen specialty business, was the first rabbi.

Coincidentally, this synagogue brought together so many threads of my own life. I was brought up in a secular household, almost ignorant of Judaism. Learning about the synagogue and all aspects of Jewish life while working to save this building was a comfortable form of education for me. It would serve the same purpose for many secular Jews and for non-Jews as well, who subsequently visited or got involved in the rescue.

OBSERVING THE URBAN PROCESS

I had been interested in and written about historic preservation for years, and now here was a call to do something more than write about it. And I was fascinated too with the neighborhood. I was in the middle of writing my first book, *The Living City*, and was between publishers, in fact. But here I was discovering, observing, learning about urbanism in a new way. What a perfect urban laboratory in which to observe dramatic but incremental change! Here was the ultimate urban neighborhood, the cradle of immigration, the gateway for millions of new Americans. Here was an urban fabric very much the same as it was one hundred years earlier. Red-brick tenements now home to mostly Chinese, once home to Jews, Italians, and Germans. Storefronts with similar businesses from a hundred years ago—discount fashions, electronics, household goods, specialty foods—owned by new entrepreneurs who would move on as their predecessors had done. The new arrivals were absorbed, given a chance to adjust, to find work, to start a business, to educate themselves and their children. Wasn't that a fundamental definition of urbanism?

And it was all happening in the very same buildings declared a "slum" by Robert Moses decades earlier. The buildings looked the same. Time had taken its toll. But they were fully occupied by new waves of immigrants, either residents or small entrepreneurs. In fact, I've watched waves of new immigrants come and move on perhaps with greater speed than a century ago. People ignored the Lower East Side for decades, thinking it a slum, a residual identity from urban renewal days. Yet change—positive, creative, enduring change—had swept over this area of the Lower East Side, but the buildings haven't been torn down to make it happen. In fact, the physical fabric of this neighborhood—with its variety of building types—was conducive to that process, fertile ground for adaptation, innovation, and growth. In recent years, new space seekers saw the potential of affordable sites in the unrestored tenements and storefronts—the young, the artists, the small restaurants. Attention had shifted. Block by block, especially during the citywide boom, the Lower East Side has become the place to be.

MANY KINDS OF CHANGE

I watched storefronts become Buddhist temples the way they had become synagogues a century earlier. One by one the Jewish merchants sold to the new arrivals. Grand Street, which was 100 percent Jewish-owned dry goods and assorted retail shops when I first started coming to the neighborhood, became an Asian food market with shoppers flooding in from all over the city. Chinatown was still a few blocks to the west. The Bowery was the boundary. Chinatown has since come several blocks east from its traditional environs. It happened over the course of more than a decade. Urban change unfolded daily before my eyes on the surrounding streets.

The businesses on Eldridge Street, too, were still predominantly Jewish owned. Even some jewelers remained around the corner on Canal, dating from when Canal Street was the city's jewelry center before it moved north to West Forty-seventh, known as the Diamond District since then. Now, too, Eldridge Street, from where it begins under the Manhattan Bridge at Division Street north past Canal and Grand, is 100 percent Asian.

I watched a new local economy evolve to serve the new population. On Eldridge Street one finds a job-placement service, a beauty parlor, a bakery with fabulous almond cookies, clothing stores, and, of course, restaurants. Our Asian neighbors were curious whenever we had events drawing crowds and ever so respectful.

I like to tell visitors to stand in front of the synagogue. I tell them to look up and down the block and look at the store signs. Just blink and in your mind's eye convert those Asian letters on the signs to Hebrew and Yiddish. At that moment, you can see how the urban process has continued unabated. The people, the language, and the signs have changed, but the process, the fundamental urbanism, remains strong. In other areas of the Lower East Side, the transformation has been equally dramatic and economically productive. Today, in fact, some areas are upscale with popular boutiques, restaurants, and high-priced condos.

11.2 Restored façade of the Eldridge Street Synagogue. *Kate Milford.*

11.3 Restored interior with East Wall. The original Rose Window was replaced with glass brick after the 1938 hurricane but has since been replaced with a magnificent contemporary version designed by artist Kiki Smith and architect Deborah Gans. *Kate Milford.*

Neighborhood change is not the only kind of change observed over the course of this twenty-five-year effort. Remember, in the mid-1980s, the city was still emerging out of its lowest point of the 1970s. Past images and feelings die hard. The Lower East Side was far from its increasingly upscale image of today. In fact, I had my handbag grabbed off my shoulder one early evening as I walked to the subway to go home. The city was not out of the woods in street crimes, and the Lower East Side was not a place many uptowners would venture to.

It was difficult in the mid-1980s to lure a few people to join the board of the Eldridge Street Project that was in formation. It was also almost impossible to get people to come down to see it. So we did the next best thing. Brilliant consultants filmmaker Leonard Majzlin and historian Richard Rabinowitz created a short video that we took to living rooms uptown where interested hosts invited friends to come hear about the restoration effort. Fund-raising in this way proceeded ever so slowly and in very small increments, but at least it moved forward,[3] forward enough to hire Jill Gothelf, a sharp, young, and enthusiastic preservation architect,[4] to lead us through a restoration.[5]

PRESERVATION IS GREEN

The restoration of the Eldridge Street Synagogue is the largest of a historic landmark in New York that is not affiliated with an institution, government agency, or private development. Actually, this was a conservation effort. The objective was to conserve all the original fabric of the building. And it is a prime example of green preservation; in fact, it is as green as preservation gets. Localism and recycling are the starting points of genuine green building, not technology, and Eldridge is a star performer on all counts. Eldridge not only embraces green building but rebuilds community and builds on cultural assets, another vital component of authentic sustainable development.

Consider the localism component. Metaphorically speaking, Brooklyn restored the synagogue. Three high-skill firms—one in DUMBO,[6] one on Staten Island, one in Williamsburg—restored the 66 stained-glass windows. A Williamsburg firm with ten to fourteen Brooklyn employees restored the 237 intricately detailed brass fixtures and 75-bulb chandelier. A Manhattan-based firm used forty-five of their mostly Brooklyn-based skilled artisans to conserve and restore the exquisitely detailed interior

11.4 The Eldridge Street Synagogue's luminous restored window. *Kate Milford.*

paint work. A Brooklyn salvage firm provided replacement timbers as needed from demolished buildings. A Long Island City firm restored the 154 benches, and another Long Island City woodworker restored wood window frames and doors. And that was just a start.

The attic insulation is recycled blue jeans, the bathroom stall partitions are recycled plastic milk jugs, and the lobby countertop is recycled glass, mostly soda and beer bottles produced at the Brooklyn Navy Yard. Virtually every material element found in the deteriorated building remains, a fundamental goal from the start of this effort in 1982. Elements that couldn't be restored were replaced in kind with recycled material. Not only did this feed the local economy, but think of all the long-distance truck trips avoided with local supplies and the trips avoided adding construction debris to our already overtaxed waste stream.[7]

Sixty to 70 percent of rehabilitation costs normally goes to labor, primarily local labor; the rest goes to materials, much of which comes from nearby salvage. Locally earned wages stay in the local economy, and these jobs do not get shipped overseas. Ordinarily, new construction is half labor and half materials. Most materials for new construction are transported from afar. A million dollars in new construction generates 30.6 jobs, reports economist Donovan Rypkema. But the same million in rehabilitation creates 35.4 jobs. "Environmentalists cheer when used tires are incorporated into asphalt shingles and recycled newspapers become part of fiberboard," says Rypkema, "but when we reuse an historic build-ing, we're recycling the whole thing."

Restoration of either historic landmarks or renovation of plain but functional old buildings gives more of a boost to a local economy, fulfills the goals of sustainability, and exceeds basic green building standards bet-ter than any new construction. As *Time* noted, "It would take an average of 65 years for the reduced carbon emissions from a new energy efficient home to make up the resources lost by demolishing an old one."[8]

Richard Moe, innovative and articulate president of the National Trust for Historic Preservation, has been speaking and writing on this subject with great passion in recent years. "Preservation is sustainabil-ity," he argues. "Buildings are vast repositories of energy." For a 50,000-square-foot building, he notes, the combined costs of teardown and replacement—hauling away tons of waste, reexcavating, manufacturing new construction materials, operating tools, and installing light and heating and cooling systems—"embody" the equivalent of 640,000 gal-lons of gasoline. Even if a project includes 40 percent recycled materials, he adds, it takes some sixty-five years for a "green-energy-efficient office building" to recover the energy lost in demolishing and replacing an ex-isting building.

Environmentalists have been very slow to recognize the value of the built environment, whether for energy or land conservation.[9] "Green advocates coming from the environmental field come at it with eco-gadgetry—solar, wind, and anything high-tech," says Clem Labine. "Somehow to be green, you need to be high-tech. But old houses are already built from the least-en-ergy-consumptive materials like brick, plaster, timber, concrete. Old houses were sited to incorporate passive solar, natural ventilation, and trees. Town-houses with two long warm party walls you share with your neighbors are energy smart." Nature guided the builder's hand before technology.

THE DENSITY ISSUE

Advocates of new green buildings argue that not all old buildings can be made energy efficient. And they point to the overarching need for re-creating density, particularly in cities. First of all, given where they start from, most old buildings worthy of preservation can be made as energy ef-ficient as necessary to strike a balance between preservation, especially of culture and history, and conservation.

The density issue is more complicated and is often used by those who do not recognize the density already existing in low-rise urban neighborhoods with buildings of varying scale. Brooklyn, for example, is on its own one of the densest cities in the country, and the predominant scale is the brownstone, with most apartment houses under twelve stories. But the urban fabric is tight, varied in height, and stylistically diverse.

And remember that the Lower East Side, where the dominant scale is the tenement, small apartment house, and former-loft manufacturing building, is an area still densely populated and economically vibrant. Next door to the synagogue, as another example, stood a classic five-story nineteenth-century brick row house. It once was owned by the synagogue and for decades had ground floor retail. It had a great backyard on the roof of the first-floor shop that was built the full one-hundred-foot length of the site. Pear and magnolia trees bloomed there magnificently. For years the Chinese owners maintained the trees.

New owners tore down the structure and built a taller new, perhaps upscale, version, including a ground-floor shop. One floor was added, but the apartments were made bigger and the ceilings higher. Thus, less people live there now, but it is bigger. When it comes to density, size can be deceptive.

Brownstone and tenement districts are already dense. One of the brilliant features of urban row houses of brownstone size or tenement is their versatility. Single family-residence, two-family or more, take your pick. They can convert to any configuration and back again, depending on the market and population. If density is appropriate, that four-story can be four apartments or eight, rental, condo, or co-op. In such cases, versatility is the key; density, when called for, can be the result.

As far as the density issue goes, it will be decades before any city in this country need demolish one more existing structure in the name of new density; enough vacant land exists, from prior demolitions for big projects that never happened and parking lots, to accommodate the next hundred million people, to be sure.

I don't think I have seen a city in this country without a parking-lot surplus. Not all of them are as dramatic, perhaps, as Tulsa, but they all share the same disease. Tulsa experienced a building boom in the oil-discovery days of the 1920s and was rich in great Art Deco architecture. Many wonderful downtown specimens remain, but on a visit not long ago, I couldn't understand why the streets around them remain empty of pedestrians. Little street-level retail was apparent. Some of the retail exists in the interior of buildings or at suburban malls, but that is not a sufficient explanation. Then I happened to go to the top floor of one of the city's typically banal newer bank buildings. Looking out at the cityscape gave me an "aha moment." Before me lay a sea of parking lots more numerous than the buildings they were created to serve. What a resource for future density, with parking built underground or unnecessary at all. People living and working in cities need to get used to walking a few blocks to their destination if density is ever to be achieved. Again, that means nibbling in one more way at the car culture.

Even New York, as tightly built and dense as it already is, has a sufficient supply of parking lots to fill a big portion of the so-called anticipated need for the population expansion that is supposed to take place by 2030, although it is not clear how that assumption was arrived at. And certainly, planners' calculations for future needs in all cities did not anticipate the economic collapse, the slowdown in new immigrants looking for jobs, or even the return of some immigrants to their home countries because of the loss of jobs.

If the Empire State Building Can, What Is the Question?

The Empire State Building was already undergoing a $500 million renovation in April 2009 when manager Anthony E. Malkin announced $20 million in additional work to make it more energy efficient.[10] The improvements to this 1931 Art Deco landmark with its 102 stories, 2.6 million square feet, 6,500 windows, and 73 elevators are meant to serve as a model for older skyscrapers everywhere. The building has 302 office tenants, and 13,000 people a day use it, including visitors to the observation tower. The renovation add-ons are expected to reduce the skyscraper's energy use by 38 percent a year by 2013, at an annual savings of $4.4 million. Up-front costs, Malkin noted, are often a deterrent for retrofitting older buildings, but the energy savings are expected to pay back those costs in only three years.

This is an enormous precedent for New York and every city. Seventy-eight percent of New York City's greenhouse gases comes from the city's buildings. Commercial buildings contribute 25 percent of that figure. At a press conference announcing this plan, Mayor Bloomberg said, "They are showing the rest of the city that existing buildings, no matter how tall they are, no matter how old they are, can take steps to significantly reduce their energy consumption." Exactly!

The retrofit includes restoration, not replacement, of the existing double-hung wood windows. Here again, restoration versus replacement is significant. Restoration of wood windows is the least-understood building alteration today. The new windows never last as long as the restored wood windows do, and the vinyl of the new ones is not even recyclable when replacement is necessary in about ten or twenty years.[11] Double-paned glass can be inserted in wood frames, and the result is often better than new.

The Green Building Council, even with some baby steps to improvement, still resists acknowledging the true value of historic preservation. The popular point evaluation system still is skewed heavily in favor of new construction. The resistance is difficult to comprehend, unless it is coming from a construction industry of contractors and suppliers that has not yet embraced the economic potential of preservation.

Environmental and green building movements undervalue preservation. The tension between them and the historic preservation movement is palpable. "A simmering rivalry," Blair Kamen, *Chicago Tribune* architecture critic, called it. This is somewhat illogical, he notes: "Both camps drew inspiration from brilliant women who wrote brilliant books—Jane Jacobs, whose 'Death and Life of Great American Cities' assaulted the conventional wisdom about 'urban renewal'; and Rachel Carson, whose 'Silent Spring' helped give birth to the environmental movement by documenting the harmful effect of pesticides. . . . Whether it was the built environment or the natural environment, these women moved their causes from the fringe to the mainstream. The movements they helped birth would seem to be the equivalent of sisters, or brothers—destined to be allies, not adversaries."[12]

Battles over this issue in the future will be many, and, to be sure, some iconic landmarks may not accommodate any and all energy-saving add-ons. If they can't, that shouldn't mean they are disposable. They may not even need to be mechanically adjusted, if the inherent natural systems are allowed to perform as they were meant to. No building need automatically be eviscerated to increase energy efficiency; competing values must be weighed. Community values count. Balance does not mean 100 percent either way. The essence of sustainability is cultural as well as scientific. And preservation is as much about culture as anything else.

The good news is that both the historic preservation and environmental movements share similar goals, and both reflect the legacy of Jane Jacobs. In her sixth book, *The Economy of Nature*, Jacobs reinforced her early embrace of both the preservation and the environmental movements. The more these two movements can find common ground—and like Jacobs be both preservation environmentalists and environmental preservationists—the more New York and all cities will continue to come out from under the residual shadow of Robert Moses.

Historic preservation, as we saw earlier in this book, is a precursor of urban regeneration. But it is also a precursor to a greener planet. Preservation is good environmentalism; good environmentalism starts with preservation. The Eldridge Street Synagogue is a model of both; when I first walked in in 1982, who would have known that it would be such a good story?

Appendix:
Jacobs's Arrest in Her Own Words

"A very curious thing was occurring. I was used to hearings at the Board of Estimate where the microphone for the speaker faces the people holding the hearing, the ones going to make the decision. The speaker's back was always to the audience. At this hearing, however, the microphone was directed the other way. The state people, engineers and people like that, not elected officials, sitting on the stage, had the speakers address the audience. The speaker's back was to the officials. This was very symbolic. The hearing was being held with the idea that it was necessary for people to let off steam, not that they would have anything that would be instructive or informative for the hearing officers whose minds were plainly made up. So when it was my turn to speak, I drew attention to this, how we weren't talking to the hearing officers; we were just talking to each other. It was a charade. Furthermore, it wouldn't matter if we were talking to these officials, because they were not the people who made the decisions anyway. They were just errand boys, sent from Albany to preside while we let off steam under the guise of a hearing. It was phony as a hearing.

"So I decided that at least I would send them back to Albany with the message that we really didn't like this, and since talk would never be that kind of a message, since they didn't hear anything, I planned to just walk across the stage and let them know that I was not content to remain down there talking to my fellow citizens, that I wanted to give them an immediate message. And I said, anybody who wants to come with me, come along. I addressed them instead of the hearing officers. They had set it up for us to talk to each other, so I was going to do that. And so I started up the stage. And pretty nearly all the audience got up and began to follow me as I walked across the stage. That's all I was going to do, walk across the stage and down the other steps. And this threw them into the most incredible tizzy. [She laughs with obvious enjoyment at the memory.] The idea of unarmed, perfectly gentle human beings just coming up and getting in that close contact with them. You never saw people so frightened. They had a policeman up there on the stage. As I came up on the stage with I guess pretty nearly all the audience coming along too, everything was quiet, absolutely quiet, except the chairman, a state engineer, kept yelling, 'Officer, arrest this woman! Arrest this woman!'

"[The policeman] didn't arrest me at first. He came over to me and he said, 'Mrs. Jacobs, come on over here and sit down.' And so I sat down where he suggested, and the chairman was now standing blocking the way. Nobody knew what to do. The woman with the stenotype had jumped up in alarm—nobody was even making an ugly face—and her tape was all running out, and she grabbed her stenotype. So people began picking up this tape that was all around now and sort of tossed it around. That was all that was happening, and this eerie silence and sort of leisurely kind of confetti, it was really surrealistic, because nobody was tearing it up or doing anything violent, just wafting this paper and the engineer was yelling, 'Arrest this woman! Arrest this woman!' Everybody else was absolutely silent. Nobody knew what to do. The policeman said, 'March down the other side; just make a gesture.' So, I made some derogatory remark to him about these people holding the hearing. I forget what I said; it was pretty plain. Something like, 'They've got their minds made up; they're just trying to do us in, these people.' And he said, 'Aren't they, though.' And so there I sat. This scene went on, and after a while I thought, 'Somebody has to bring this to an end. Nobody knows what to do any more than I do.' So I got up from the chair—all these frightened men went down the other side—and went to the microphone again. I said, 'What's the charge? Why am I being arrested?' The policeman said, 'It's at the request of Mr. Toth [John Toth, chief engineer for the State Department of Transportation]. I wouldn't arrest you except that he has demanded your arrest.' So, I said again, 'What are the charges?' And he said, 'Well, that will be worked out at the station house. But I must arrest you. I'm sorry.' And I said, 'Well, I think they're making a mistake.' And he said, 'I think they are too, but I have no choice.' [laughter]

And at this point, Jacobs might have figured it would do the cause well if she were arrested. She didn't want to be arrested, but she was. The crowd followed her to the station and continued the protest as she was booked. It was the same arresting officer who had been on the stage.

"He was really nice. He was always on my side. I was booked on disorderly conduct. A court date set. When we got to court I waited and waited all morning. My case wasn't called. My arresting officer came down to me at one point and said, 'They're making new charges against you. They're opening up law books they've never opened up before.' Jacobs laughs recalling this and laughs further as she reports that the charges they came up with were 'riot, inciting to riot, criminal mischief, and obstructing government administration. Four years in jail. They'd have liked to put me in for it too. They really would. Then my arresting officer had to take me back to the Tombs, the central police station, to get a mug shot, fingerprints, and get me booked as a serious criminal.

"This took a long time, getting booked as a serious criminal. And my arresting officer explained to the jail matron that she didn't need to put me in the cells where people were yelling and screaming, that I was not going to cause any trouble and it would be nice if I could sit out there with her. [laughter] And you see, he was in a bad spot. Here I was the sort of person he had been trained to protect. This was a terrible upset. Now he was arresting me, and the arrest was getting worse and worse. [laughter]

"My favorite moment with him was when he had me brought back in the paddy wagon, although he hated to do it. Every other time he said to me that if I had enough money for a taxi, we could go in a taxi and it would be dignified. [laughter] I could see that was what he wanted, so we always went in a taxi. But this time we had to get down to the Tombs very fast from police headquarters at Broome Street, or we would be put off to night court and be there late. He was trying to protect my innocence. He said, 'And the type of people who are at night court, frankly, Miss Jacobs, I wouldn't want you to mix with.' [laughter] So we hurried down there in the paddy wagon. A matron had to come along. She has to come with any female prisoner. There were just the three of us and a driver. We went tearing down. The Tombs is behind the courthouse at Foley Square. Well, this time I had to come into the courtroom through the prisoner's entrance, because I was a serious prisoner now, not a disorderly conduct prisoner.

"Then there was the arraignment. They wanted the judge to order that I could not address any meeting or take any part in activities until my trial. We found a lawyer to speak against this. I didn't know exactly what was happening. Nobody was being mean to me, torturing me, or making me make confessions or anything. [laughter] So he argued that such an order was an infringement of free speech and that they couldn't enjoin me not to talk. And if I said something that was illegal I could be punished for that, or did something that was illegal, I could be punished for that, but I couldn't be enjoined from exercising my normal, peaceful civil rights. The judge agreed with this. So they lost that round, and that's what they had wanted most. Oh, they made out what a dangerous character I was: Inciting to riot, I was a menace on the streets. I had to be silenced. If I spoke I was to be put right in jail, because it would probably be incitement to riot.

"The next thing was a pretrial hearing. And they turned up with all kinds of lies about how I had damaged the stenotype machine. That's what the 'criminal mischief was.' Mr. Toth was there, and he gave a horrendous account of how terrifying all this was. I guess it was, to him. I guess he wasn't putting this on, but it sounded ludicrous to me, but he really was terrified. Poor, ignorant jerk [laughter], didn't know when to be scared and when not."

This was all happening during the day, unbeknownst to anyone in Jacobs's family. "Well, Jimmy was away at college, and Ned was at school. I guess Mary was at school and had gone to visit a friend, and Bob was still at work. It was the middle of the afternoon when I got home. And Ned came in, threw down his books, and said, 'Well, how'd things go in court?' And I said, 'Oh, all right, I guess.' And he said, 'Seems to me that for a woman of fifty-two, you lead a very exciting life.' [laughter] And all of a sudden, I felt so much better; it was the greatest thing to say. I felt good all of a sudden. That put a new look on it all. Bless Ned. So my real low point didn't last very long, thank goodness.

"But now I had a very expensive, top-grade lawyer, and we had to hold fund-raisers to pay him. The lawyer's strategy was this: to put it off and put it off, as long as possible, until they cooled down. Because they were furious, and they wanted to really sock it to me. He found that out.

"By the time it came to court, we plea-bargained. I pled guilty. I thought I would get fourteen days in jail because it was a second conviction for disorderly conduct. I'd had one when I was arrested in a war protest downtown. We were all let off then with the warning that next time we'd be sent to jail. So I thought I would get fourteen days in jail. I figured I can stand fourteen days of almost anything, okay. Instead, I was convicted of disorderly conduct and let off with a suspended sentence and ordered to pay for the damage done to the machine. I hadn't done any damage to the machine. The lawyer and I tried to get them to put something in writing. Oh, they had said a whole lot about how it had to be repaired and how much it cost, hundreds of dollars' worth of damage to this valuable machine. This was all made up, a hoax. But, that was all they had to really substantiate anything except my standing around where I wasn't invited. So they minimized what was destroyed of the record. They couldn't make a big thing out of that because it would not have been a valid hearing. And actually, very little of that paper was gone, obviously, because they still had a big transcript."

Repeatedly, Jacobs's lawyer kept asking for a valid receipt from the repairman. "What we wanted to do was get a receipt and then investigate and see what corruption and phoniness there was about this receipt since we knew the machine had not been damaged. She had been clutching it to her bosom very protectively. That's why she was losing all the paper. [laughter] The lawyer got no answer at all about the receipt. He telephoned. They never returned his call. So then I wrote to the judge, saying that I had this judgment to pay. I didn't like this debt hanging over my head. I enclosed a copy of the letter that had been sent, told him about the phone calls, and asked him to please order them to comply with their part of the court order so I could comply with my part. Got no answer. But at least I had the letter on the record, if ever it was said, 'Well, she was ordered to do this, and she didn't.'

The whole thing just stopped there. "I guess they could see the trap that we were hoping they would fall into. We would have had a field day if they had tried to falsify a repair bill."

Notes

Preface

1. A big fight was going on within the city's Democratic Party, and I got involved in the Reform wing.

2. What I did know was totally unrelated. Joe Kahn and Sidney Zion at the *New York Post* had done a thorough investigation on who was getting the contracts and making money on the 1964 World's Fair under the direction of Robert Moses. A multiple-page report that was due for publication in the *Post* was canceled just before the fair opened because of the pressure brought on the publisher by advertisers.

3. The year 1975 was considered the worst economic downturn since the Depression.

Introduction

1. In the six books that followed, Jacobs redefined how to understand urban economies, in *The Economy of Cities*; explored the potential gains of Quebec's independence from Canada in *The Question of Separatism*; taught us how real wealth is generated, in *Cities and the Wealth of Nations*; examined the different values embodied in the separate moral codes of commercial and guardian institutions, in *Systems of Survival*; and then synthesized her strands of thought—economic, social, and environmental—in *The Nature of Economy*. In *Dark Age Ahead*, she tied all these issues together.

2. Not long before she died, I asked Jacobs, "What would you like to say to Corbusier or his followers?" She replied in a typical direct and dismissive manner: "People influenced by him are not interested in how cities function, so what am I going to talk to them about? Accuse them of not being interested in how cities function? No. Ask them what they think is a portrait of a city economy, where it comes from, what it does, where it's going? They don't know, and they don't think about that. I don't have anything to say to these people."

3. Robert Fishman, "Rethinking Public Housing."

4. In 1968 Governor Nelson A. Rockefeller merged the Triborough Bridge and Tunnel Authority (totally controlled by Moses) into the MTA, eliminating Moses's key remaining source of power and funding.

5. Carson had already written three books about environmental conditions in the oceans, starting with *The Sea Around Us* (1951).

6. Daniel Horowitz, *The Anxieties of Affluence: Critiques of American Consumer Culture, 1939–1979*, 151–154.

7. McLuhan would publish *Understanding Media* in 1964 and *The Medium Is the Message* in 1967.

8. Mumford and Jacobs were in total agreement, however, on the damage of new highways to all cities and the country as a whole.

9. Daniel Horowitz, author of *Anxieties of Affluence*, has also written books on Vance Packard and Betty Friedan.

10. Jane Jacobs, *The Death and Life of Great American Cities*, 15.

11. I interviewed Jane Jacobs numerous times over the course of twenty-five years. Any quotes without attribution come from these interviews.

12. *Journal of American Society of Architectural Historians*, 1944.

13. This impact may be lessened by the current economic setback but only temporarily.

14. Matias Echanove and Rahul Srivastava, *What We See: Advancing the Observations of Jane Jacobs*.

15. Opened in April 2008, Omar Freilla was the 2007 winner of the Jane Jacobs Prize, given by the Rockefeller Foundation.

16. I tell the story of regenerating the South Bronx in *The Living City*.

17. The technical and spiritual guiding hand of both groups is an extraordinary, dedicated advocacy planner, Joan Byron, whose formal title is director of the Sustainability and Environmental Justice Initiative of the Pratt Center for Community Development. For years, she has helped all these groups pursue their community-shaped agendas while bridging the gap where necessary between them and government.

18. The late Yolanda Garcia, founder and dynamic leader of Nos Quedamos, first alerted the community to the state DOT plan that she uncovered. If completed originally, the Sheridan Expressway would have gone through the Bronx Zoo.

19. The Southern Bronx River Watershed Alliance's members partially overlap with those of the Bronx River Alliance. The SBRWA is composed of Mothers on the Move, the Point, Sustainable South Bronx, Nos Quedamos, Youth Ministries for Peace and Justice, the Tri-State Transportation Campaign, and the Pratt Center for Community Development. But there are groups in each that aren't in the other, and the missions are quite distinct.

20. See Gratz, "Planned Shrinkage: The Economy of Waste," chap. 9 in *The Living City*.

21. Winner of the 2009 Rome Prize for Landscape Architecture.

22. This is not a net gain, however, since thousands of low-income units have also been lost. A study conducted by the NYU Furman Center reported an overall loss of two hundred thousand affordable to low-income units (*New York Times*, October 15, 2009).

23. This was Jane Jacobs's term as well.

24. Too many privileged parkers still clog the streets, double-parked usually. The biggest offenders seem to be the chauffeured cars. A sense of entitlement pervades certain groups of high-wage earners, and the impact is quite apparent throughout the city.

CHAPTER 1

1. Eventually, he brought in my uncle, who quickly struck out on his own, opening several stores in the East Village and then on Long Island.

2. A Spaldeen, made by Spalding, is a pink rubber ball.

3. For a full treatment of this period of urban stress, see my first book, *The Living City*.

4. For the movie, producers achieved a temporary postponement of the West Side blocks coming down for Lincoln Center in order to use them for film scenes. Look at the

pictures of those blocks now and with a straight face say, "Of course that was an irreparable slum."

5. Yes, the same Mario Cuomo who resisted Moses on behalf of Willets Point property owners during the 1964 World's Fair clearance battle.

6. In contrast, on August 14, 2003, a power failure blacked out New York for twenty-five hours. The city coped easily and peacefully. There were fewer arrests than on a normal August midweek day.

7. David Gonzalez, "Will Gentrification Spoil the Birthplace of Hip-Hop?" *New York Times*, May 21, 2007, focused on the concern by music historians and tenants at 1520 Sedgwick Avenue that Campbell's building could lose its middle- and low-income tenancy. The city eventually stepped in to ensure its continued affordability.

8. Thomas L. Friedman, "The Open-Door Bailout," *New York Times*, February 11, 2009.

9. The City Futures, Inc., journal for the annual gala, 2006.

10. The Pratt Center, led by Ron Shiffman, was the advocacy planning model that similar organizations emulated around the country.

Chapter 2

1. Even critic Lewis Mumford was so pessimistic he commented, "Make the patient as comfortable as possible. His case is hopeless."

2. Those tapes are in the archives of the J. M. Kaplan Fund.

3. The full articles are available online at www.NYPAP.org.

4. The commission is an eleven-member body appointed by the mayor for three-year terms. By law it must include three architects, a historian, a city planner, and a Realtor. All five boroughs must be represented.

5. Norval White and Elliot Willensky, eds., *AIA Guide to New York*, 343, 353, 351.

6. The letter began, former MAS director, Kent Barwick remembers, "Jack loved Grand Central."

7. The Battery Park City School and the Spruce Street School.

Chapter 3

1. For a full story of the Greenmarket's founding and significance, see "To Market, to Market," chap. 9 of *Cities Back from the Edge: New Life for Downtown*, by Roberta Brandes Gratz with Norman Mintz.

2. Landscape architect and Village resident Robert Nichols was the chief designer.

3. Conversation with the author, 1978.

4. A British study in 1998, for example, found that closing roads actually cuts driving trips. The research team analyzed sixty cases around the globe where roads were closed or capacity reduced. On average, 20 percent of the traffic just vanished, and in some cases the reduction was even more dramatic.

5. Charles Grutzner, "Strategy Revamped on Washington Sq.," *New York Times*, March 30, 1958, 58.

6. The terms *blight* and *slum* varied according to the appraiser and local definitions. There were point systems that might include the "lack of community facilities nearby" (undefined), point systems that deducted points for lack of closets, insufficient hot water, dirty toilets and yards, pests, and other problems curable without demolition.

7. Eisner alerted them to slum-clearance standards, such as square footage, number of occupants, kitchen and bathroom facilities, and rent levels. The West Village

Committee's own survey showed that by these standards Greenwich Village was not a slum.

8. The corner stores were designed to be either a residential unit or a store, depending on the market, such a basically smart idea, fundamental flexibility.

9. The details and full significance of this community success story are told in *The Living City*, 168–174.

10. As Jacobs scholar Peter Laurence reports in "The Death and Life of Urban Design: Jane Jacobs, the Rockefeller Foundation, and the New Research in Urbanism, 1955–1965," this Moses project in partnership with Metropolitan Life Insurance Company displaced thirty-one hundred families (eleven thousand people), five hundred viable stores and small factories, three churches, three schools, two theaters, plus a series of gas tanks for which the "Gas Light District" was named. Actually, the gas tanks were long gone by the time this demolition took place, having taken place more than a decade before.

CHAPTER 4

1. Bridge Apartments, four high-rises lined up like dominos over the Cross Bronx Expressway, with four thousand residents.

2. Her complete description of the event and the details of her arrest appear in the appendix and on the Web site centerforthelivingcity.org.

3. Mayor Lindsay declared it "dead for all time" on July 16, 1969. In 1971 Governor Rockefeller removed it from the list of proposals eligible for federal highway funding.

4. For a full treatment of how SoHo's history changed the course of American urban history, see "The SoHo Syndrome," chap. 13 in my book, *Cities Back from the Edge*.

5. Chester Rapkin, *The South Houston Industrial Area*, 282. A plaque honoring Rapkin can be found on a building in SoHo between Prince and Spring Streets.

6. As always when I refer to the planning profession, exceptions existed especially among the progressive advocacy planners. This is true even if I don't specifically call attention to this fact.

7. I labeled this process the SoHo Syndrome in the final chapter of *Cities Back from the Edge*.

CHAPTER 5

1. Robert Caro's meticulously researched book *The Power Broker* outlines in detail both the positive and the negative views of Moses.

2. A visit to some public housing sites today reveals a very interesting social phenomenon. Residents bring their own chairs and *sit in front of the fence* on the sidewalk, often at a point where green grass behind the fence could easily accommodate a bench and the fence be removed.

3. Rogers started her work with the Central Park Task Force in 1975, was appointed Central Park administrator in 1980, founded the Central Park Conservancy with the assistance of parks commissioner Gordon Davis in 1980, and left as president at the end of 1995.

4. Betsy Barlow Rogers, "Robert Moses and the Transformation of Central Park."

5. See "The Mess We Have Made," chap. 2 in my book, *Cities Back from the Edge*.

6. Caro, *Power Broker*, 560.

7. It was recently made into a park.

8. Ibid., 707.

9. Joel Schwartz, *The New York Approach: Robert Moses, Urban Liberals, and Redevelopment of the Inner City*, 31.

10. The 1949 Housing Act was an umbrella for several programs, including FHA mortgage insurance, rural home finance, and Title III for public housing. Title I, probably the best known, created a write-down program for residential redevelopment that amounted to a onetime capital grant to which the federal government contributed two-thirds. It required prompt disposal of redevelopment tracks to private sponsors, helping Taft claim that it was written to subsidize private, middle-rent housing, as distinguished from public housing (ibid., 132).

11. Joseph D. McGoldrick, former Columbia University government professor, city comptroller, and slum-clearance advocate, "as early as 1944, had observed that slum clearance projects were not doing what was expected of them," writing, "Such projects have had no regenerative effect on the areas in which they are in place," notes Peter L. Laurence ("Death and Life of Urban Design").

12. Over twelve years New York got seventy million dollars. Chicago came in second with thirty million dollars.

13. Schwartz, *New York Approach*, 295–296.

14. Gay Talese, "Anger Lingering As Bridge Goes Up," *New York Times*, June 19, 1964.

15. Schwartz, *New York Approach*, 294.

16. Policies were eventually developed to fight arson but not to fight fires when they were occurring.

17. The Wallaces quote a 1976 BBC-TV special, *The Bronx Is Burning*, during which a fire chief notes that forty-four thousand people were covered per engine company in the South Bronx as compared to seventeen thousand on Staten Island.

18. See *The Living City*, in which I deal with "Planned Shrinkage" at length.

19. Loren Hinkle, "Closing Summary."

20. The expressway was built between 1948 and 1963.

21. This was only one mile out of the 130 that went through the city between 1948 and 1963 and destroyed twenty-seven neighborhoods.

22. Caro, *Power Broker*, 1080.

23. Ibid., 218.

24. Eventually, Mumford was a very strong critic of Moses's highway building.

25. Quoted in Joseph P. Cusker, "The World of Tomorrow: Science, Culture, and Commentary at the New York World's Fair," 4.

26. Walter Lippmann, "Today and Tomorrow," 51.

27. Caro, *Power Broker*.

28. Jason Epstein, "Way Uptown," 53.

29. Caro, *Power Broker*, 706.

30. Richard O. Baumbach Jr. and William E. Borah, *The Second Battle of New Orleans: A History of the Vieux Carre Riverfront-Expressway Controversy*.

31. *Faubourg Treme: The Untold Story of Black New Orleans*.

32. Bob Young, "Highway to Hell," *Willamette Week*, March 9, 2005.

33. Lisa Schreibman, "Looking for Land? Try Tearing Down a Highway," 10.

34. Caro, *Power Broker*, 940.

35. Lewis Mumford, *The Highway and the City*, 220; Schwartz, *New York Approach*, xvii.

36. Isaacs tried to ban discrimination in housing and advocated giving neighborhoods a voice in local improvements.

37. Caro, *Power Broker*, 15.

38. Ten subway lines and the Long Island Railroad converge here.

39. Robert Goodman, *After the Planners*, 28.

40. Jacobs, *Death and Life*, 209.

41. This continues nationwide under the Federal Hope VI program that replaces low-income public housing units with a smaller total number of mixed-income units, resulting in an even smaller number of replacement units for the lost public housing.

42. Marshall Berman, *All That Is Solid Melts into Air*.

43. Mindy Thompson Fullilove, M.D., *Root Shock: How Tearing Up City Neighborhoods Hurts America and What We Can Do About It*, 224.

CHAPTER 6

1. The full name did not always fit the width of the *New York Post* column size, so for single-column stories it was Roberta B. Gratz.

2. Ninety-six percent of New York City manufacturers are locally owned small businesses that employ fewer than one hundred people.

3. Donald's father retired in 1976, and his older brother, Bill, who had joined the business five years after Donald, retired in 1995.

4. The study was conducted by the Planning Center of the Municipal Art Society in collaboration with the Industrial Technology Assistance Corporation.

5. I am indebted to Stephen Zacks for his excellent article, "Made in the USA."

6. "In Professor's Model, Diversity = Productivity," *Science Times*, January 8, 2008, F2.

7. Sara P. Garretson, "The Changing Face of Manufacturing in New York City," 2.

8. John A. Loomis, "Manufacturing Communities—Learning from Mixed Use," 4.

9. In the 5–4 decision, Justice Sandra Day O'Connor dissented, bemoaning the possibility of "replacing any Motel 6 with a Ritz-Carlton, any home with a shopping mall, or any farm with a factory."

10. I am indebted to the New York Industrial Retention Network for the basic manufacturing and Long Island City information in this chapter.

11. Catherine Rampell, "How Industries Survive Change, If They Do," *New York Times*, November 15, 2008.

12. Adam Friedman, "Rezone Long Island City to Save Jobs," *Newsday*, January 5, 2001.

13. Robert Fitch, "Explaining New York City's Aberrant Economy," 110.

14. Edgar M. Hoover and Louise P. Lerdau, *One-Tenth of a Nation*.

15. A 2008 report of the city's Economic Development Corporation revealed that more than 100 businesses slashed 4,111 local jobs despite getting more than $91 million in tax breaks and incentives from the city. More than 500 companies received assistance since 1998 "to support investment, job retention and growth," of which 35 required a minimum job-creation requirement. Eight of the 35 failed to create the jobs, but only one company lost any benefits.

16. Jacobs, *The Economy of Cities*, 88–89.

17. Ibid., 50–51.

18. Sandy Ikeda, *What We See: Advancing the Observations of Jane Jacobs*.

19. Jacobs, *The Economy of Cities*, 63.

20. William Yardley wrote a very insightful article, "In Portland, Cultivating a Culture of Two Wheels," in the *New York Times*, November 5, 2007, detailing the growth of this "new work."

21. See the Greenpoint Manufacturing story in my book, *Cities Back from the Edge*, 52.

22. A Chicago study showed that local individual businesses produce bigger economic benefits, 70 percent more of a local economic impact per square foot than chain stores.

23. A 2008 report issued by the office of Manhattan Borough president Scott Stringer indicated that property tax breaks meant to stem an exodus of high-paying jobs to suburbia three decades ago have gone mostly to fast-food restaurants, gas stations, and national chain stores.

24. A 1992 Waterfront Plan adopted by the Planning Commission and a community-developed plan assisted by the Planning Department forbid big box stores in the protected harbor.

25. "Ikea a Mixed Blessing for Red Hook," *Crain's New York Business*, 5.

26. A study released at the same time Ikea opened indicates the city needs at least seven more like the one lost to stay competitive as a port. "Industry experts say it would cost about $1 billion just to replace the 730-foot-long former graving dock that was converted into a parking lot," the *New York Post* reported ("Idea Berth Pangs," June 23, 2008). The *Post* also noted that the study estimates the port will lose $50 million to $150 million in revenues to competitive ports over the next five years because it doesn't have enough docks to meet repair and maintenance needs.

CHAPTER 7

1. Recent new owners have totally restored the building, even putting back a brownstone stoop that had been removed before we owned it. At that time, the idea of restoring a stoop was unthinkable. The skills were hardly available.

2. White and Willensky, *AIA Guide*, 367.

3. "Brownstoning—the How-To," *New York Post Magazine*, 6.

4. Morris Brothers closed in 2008.

5. Caro, *Power Broker*, 1014.

6. Paul Goldberger, "West Side Fixer-Upper: New Ideas for Lincoln Center That Don't Involve Dynamite."

7. Martin Filler, "After 50 Years, Lincoln Center Still Offers Plenty to Criticize," 37.

8. Ibid.

CHAPTER 8

1. That book was completed under editors Jane Isay and Bob Bender at Simon & Schuster.

2. John Oakes of the *New York Times* wrote occasional brilliant op-ed pieces, as did Sidney Schanberg, but they were lonely voices. Peter Freiberg reported regularly on the battle for the *New York Post*.

3. I am enormously grateful to the Samuel H. Kress Foundation for support of transcribing those tapes.

4. That was Marshall McLuhan's term for the automobile.

5. In May 1968 new regulations went into effect that required more stringent studies of highways before they were adopted.

6. For the argument that the federal government was paying the bill, see the next chapter.

7. For an analysis of Starr's Planned Shrinkage policy, see my book *The Living City*, 176–177.

CHAPTER 9

1. Contributing federal funds would have run out, as will be shown.

2. In 1971, Mayor John V. Lindsay and Governor Nelson A. Rockefeller signed an agreement to develop a new highway.

3. Jerry Nachman, "Eye on Westway."

4. Caro, *Power Broker*, 932.

5. I am indebted to Gene Russianoff, head of the Straphangers Campaign, for his help in gathering transit statistics.

6. See "The SoHo Syndrome," chap. 13 in my book, *Cities Back from the Edge*.

7. "A Ghost of Westway Rises Along the Hudson: An Old Idea for the Waterfront, Pared Down, Still Provokes Passions," *New York Times*, March 3, 2002.

8. Historically, most carriage or car owners early in the century owned carriage houses separate from their houses.

9. "As City Gains Housing for Poor, Market Takes It Away," *New York Times*, October 15, 2009.

10. In the spirit of full disclosure, the West Side opposition to Trump's original horrific plan started at my dining room table in the mid-1980s. The current development, no longer owned by Trump but originally negotiated by him, is a totally reconfigured plan that emerged through a complicated negotiated process in which a very large segment of the West Side was involved.

CONCLUSION

1. Michael Pollan, *Omnivore's Dilemma*.

2. Mostly these are small-scale efforts. Some cities are trying to justify demolishing whole sparsely populated neighborhoods, turning them into parks and gardens. Thinning out a city is an invitation to only more of the same. Only a reversal, like in the South Bronx, leads to rebirth.

3. Lisa McLaughlin reported in *Time* (August 4, 2008) that six hundred small-scale farms (which are often large-scale vegetable gardens) exist in New York City.

4. For the full story of Food from the Hood's formation, see my book, *Cities Back from the Edge*, 226–229.

5. A slowdown in the real estate market in the 1990s also prompted many to turn to preservation.

6. Jacobs, *Death and Life*, 349.

7. This is why the first thing to improve a downtown can be to undo what the traffic engineers of that era did.

8. Ibid., 363.

9. Also, she favored big public school systems, libraries, health facilities, and water, sewer, and utility systems.

10. Bradford Snell, "American Ground Transport."

11. Stephen B. Goddard, *Getting There: The Epic Struggle Between Road and Rail in the American Century*, 126.

12. Ibid., 135.

13. The same principle works for pedestrians with short blocks, Jacobs showed in *Death and Life*.

14. Forest City Ratner is the corporate name.

15. Michael Shapiro's book *The Last Good Season: Brooklyn, the Dodgers, and Their Final Pennant Race Together* details this sorry chapter of Moses history. Moses wanted O'Malley to build in far-out, less accessible Brooklyn. O'Malley pleaded for this site and finally left town, a major crush for the borough.

16. The influx of white residents should not be interpreted as a necessary ingredient for neighborhood stability.

17. Charles V. Bagli, "Residents Guarding Their Homes Against the Bulldozer," *New York Times*, January 23, 2004.

18. Sam Goldsmith, "City: Ward's Bakery Is Not a Landmark," *Brooklyn Paper*, March 7, 2007.

19. Leadership in Energy and Environmental Design.

20. First coined by architect Carl Olifant.

21. Chris Smith, "Mr. Ratner's Neighborhood."

22. Also a Ratner project in downtown Brooklyn.

23. Nicolai Ouroussoff, "What Will Be Left of Gehry's Vision for Brooklyn?" *New York Times*, March 21, 2008.

24. Truck deliveries, garbage removal, building infrastructure, parking.

25. Community-impact packages, offering benefits to the area, are put forth while the basic plan remains unchanged.

26. The New York State Court of Appeals ruled in December 2009 that the state could not use eminent domain on behalf of Columbia's expansion plan. The blight designation was "mere sophistry" about a neighborhood already undergoing organic rejuvenation, the court found. "Even a cursory examination of the study reveals the idiocy of considering things like unpainted block walls or loose awning supports as evidence of a blighted neighborhood," the opinion noted. The state hired the same consultant as Columbia for its determination of blight. Also, both city and state agencies, the court found, erroneously claimed a public purpose for the rezoning that paved the way for Columbia to annex the area for an obviously private development. The clear message that no civic purpose was being served by the use of eminent domain could influence future attempts to use this power to condemn and take over private property.

27. I am indebted to Dr. Tom Angotti and his Hunter College research team for their excellent, thorough Willets Point Land Use Study, April 2006. Much of the statistical information included here is drawn from that study that included a door-to-door survey of the site. Research assistants included Diana Marcela Perez and Joan April Suwalsky.

28. PUKAR stands for Partners for Urban Knowledge and Research.

29. Matias Echanove and Rahul Srivastava, "Taking the Slum Out of 'Slumdog,'" *New York Times*, February 21, 2009.

30. The idea that Jane might advocate for a six-story building to be built adjacent to my twenty-one-story apartment house or elsewhere in my neighborhood of twenty- to thirty-story buildings is ludicrous.

Epilogue

1. That long-standing saga is detailed in both of my earlier books.

2. A smaller sanctuary.

3. We had three early benefactors: the late Joy Ungerleider Mayerson, who had led the rejuvenation of the Jewish Museum uptown; Joan K. Davidson, then head of the J. M. Kaplan Fund; and the late Brook Astor, head of the Astor Foundation. Davidson and Astor were the most reliable funders of new, innovative New York City cultural

projects, the venture capitalists of NYC philanthropy. Many of today's organizations were nurtured by them. Mayerson was passionately committed to Jewish and cultural programs.

4. Years after she began this job, Jill joined in partnership with Walter Sedvic. Together, they have been leaders of the now popular techniques of green preservation.

5. Our owner's rep, architect Diane Kaese, and project manager, Terry Higgins, were immensely helpful.

6. Down Under the Manhattan Bridge Overpass.

7. The EPA has noted that demolition and construction debris constitutes around a third of all waste generated in this country, and has projected that more than 27 percent of existing buildings will be replaced between 2000 and 2030. In New York City, 60 percent of the waste stream is demolition and construction debris.

8. Bryan Walsh, "Greening This Old House: Saving Money and the Planet by Upgrading Older Homes."

9. For a fuller discussion of this issue, see my chapter "Jane Jacobs: Environmental Preservationist, Preservation Environmentalist," in *What We See*.

10. Malkin is president of Wien & Malkin, supervisor of the building on behalf of the owners, the Malkin family and the Helmsley estate.

11. Public policy often works against doing the right thing. In New York State, for example, state grants are available to low-income property owners for window *replacement* but not window repair, weatherization, or storm-window installation.

12. Remarks delivered at Michigan Historic Preservation Network, Grand Rapids, May 15, 2009.

Bibliography

Abrams, Charles. *The City Is the Frontier.* New York: Harper and Row, 1965.
———. *Forbidden Neighbors.* New York: Harper and Brothers, 1955.
Anderson, Martin. *The Federal Bulldozer: A Critical Analysis of Urban Renewal, 1949–1962.* Cambridge: MIT Press, 1964.
Ballon, Hillary, and Kenneth T. Jackson, ed. *Robert Moses and the Modern City: The Transformation of New York.* New York: W. W. Norton, 2007.
Baumbach, Richard O., Jr., and William E. Borah. *The Second Battle of New Orleans: A History of the Vieux Carre Riverfront-Expressway Controversy.* Washington, DC: Preservation Press, 1981.
Berman, Marshall. *All That Is Solid Melts into Air: The Experience of Modernity.* New York: Simon and Schuster, 1982.
Brown, Mary Elizabeth. *The Italians of the South Village.* Edited by Rafaele Fierro. New York: Greenwich Village Society for Historic Preservation, 2007.
Caro, Robert. *The Power Broker: Robert Moses and the Fall of New York.* New York: Alfred A. Knopf, 1974.
Committee on Governmental Operations, Hon. Bill Perkins, Chair. *Forty Years of New York City Landmarks Preservation: An Opportunity to Review, Reflect, and Reform.* New York: Council of the City of New York, 2005.
Cusker, Joseph P. "The World of Tomorrow: Science, Culture, and Commentary at the New York World's Fair." In *Dawn of a New Day: The New York World's Fair, 1930–40*, edited by Helen A Harrison. New York: New York University Press, 1980.
Echanove, Matias, and Rahul Srivastava. *What We See: Advancing the Observations of Jane Jacobs.* New York: New Village Press, 2010.
Epstein, Jason. "Way Uptown." *New York Times Magazine*, April 11, 2004.
Fainstein, Susan S. *The City Builders: Property, Politics, and Planning in London and New York.* Cambridge: Blackwell, 1995.
Faubourg Treme: The Untold Story of Black New Orleans. Serendipity Films, 2008.
Filler, Martin. "After 50 Years, Lincoln Center Still Offers Plenty to Criticize." *Architectural Record* (June 2009).
Fishman, Robert. "Rethinking Public Housing." *Places* 16, no. 2 (Spring 2004): 26–33.
Fitch, Robert. "Explaining New York City's Aberrant Economy." *New Left Review* (October 1994).
Florida, Richard. *The Rise of the Creative Class—and How It's Transforming Work, Leisure, Community, and Everyday Life.* New York: Basic Books, 2002.
Frieden, Bernard J., and Lynne B. Sagalyn. *Downtown, Inc.: How America Rebuilds Cities.* Cambridge: MIT Press, 1989.

Fullilove, Mindy Thompson, M.D. *The House of Joshua*. Lincoln: University of Nebraska Press, 1999.

———. *Root Shock: How Tearing Up City Neighborhoods Hurts America and What We Can Do About It*. New York: One World/Ballantine Books, 2004.

Gans, Herbert J. *The Urban Villagers: Group and Class in the Life of Italian-Americans*. New York: Free Press of Glencoe, 1962.

Garretson, Sara P. "The Changing Face of Manufacturing in New York City." *Livable City* 18, no. 2 (Fall 1994).

Goddard, Stephen B. *Getting There: The Epic Struggle Between Road and Rail in the American Century*. New York: Basic Books, 1994.

Goldberger, Paul. "West Side Fixer-Upper: New Ideas for Lincoln Center That Don't Involve Dynamite." *New Yorker*, July 7, 2003.

Goodman, Robert. *After the Planners*. New York: Simon and Schuster, 1971.

Gratz, Roberta Brandes. *The Living City: Thinking Small in a Big Way*. New York: John Wiley and Sons, 1989.

———. *What We See*. New York: New Village Press, 2010.

Gratz, Roberta Brandes, with Norman Mintz. *Cities Back from the Edge: New Life for Downtown*. New York: John Wiley and Sons, 1989.

Hammett, Jerilou, and Kingsley Hammett, eds. *The Suburbanization of New York*. New York: Princeton Architectural Press, 2007.

Harrison, Helen A. "The World of Tomorrow: Science, Culture, and Commentary at the New York World's Fair." In *Dawn of a New Day: The New York World's Fair, 1930–40*, edited by Helen A Harrison. New York: New York University Press, 1980.

Hinkle, Loren. "Closing Summary." In *The Effect of the Man-Made Environment on Health and Behavior*, edited by L. Hinkle and W. Loring. DHEW, Publication no. 77–8318. Washington, DC: Centers for Disease Control, 1977.

Hollander, Kurt, ed. *The Portable Lower East Side* 3, nos. 1–2 (1986).

Hoover, Edgar M., and Louise P. Lerdau. *One-Tenth of a Nation*. Cambridge: Harvard University Press, 1960.

Horowitz, Daniel. *The Anxieties of Affluence: Critiques of American Consumer Culture, 1939–1979*. Amherst: University of Massachusetts Press, 2004.

Ikeda, Sandy. *What We See: Advancing the Observations of Jane Jacobs*. New York: New Village Press, 2010.

Jacobs, Jane. *Cities and the Wealth of Nations*. New York: Vintage Books, 1984.

———. *Dark Age Ahead*. New York: Random House, 2004.

———. *The Death and Life of Great American Cities*. New York: Random House, 1961.

———. *The Economy of Cities*. New York: Random House, 1969.

———. *The Nature of Economy*. New York: Random House, 2000.

———. *The Question of Separatism*. New York: Random House, 1980.

———. *Systems of Survival*. New York: Random House, 1992.

Jonnes, Jill. *South Bronx Rising: The Rise, Fall, and Resurrection of an American City*. New York: Fordham University Press, 2002.

Laurence, Peter L. "The Death and Life of Urban Design: Jane Jacobs, the Rockefeller Foundation, and the New Research in Urbanism, 1955–1965." *Journal of Urban Design* 11 (June 2006): 145–172.

Lippmann, Walter. "Today and Tomorrow." *Current History* 50 (July 1939).

Loomis, John A. "Manufacturing Communities—Learning from Mixed Use." *Livable City* 18, no. 2 (Fall 1994).

Mahler, Jonathan. *Ladies and Gentlemen, the Bronx Is Burning: 1977, Baseball, Politics, and the Battle for the Soul of the City.* New York: Farrar, Straus, and Giroux, 2005.

Miller, Donald L., ed. *The Lewis Mumford Reader.* New York: Pantheon Books, 1986.

Moses, Robert. *Public Works: A Dangerous Trade.* New York: McGraw-Hill, 1970.

———. *Working for the People: Promise and Performance in Public Service.* New York: Harper and Brothers, 1956.

Mumford, Lewis. *The Highway and the City.* New York: Harcourt Brace Jovanovich, 1953.

———. *The Urban Prospect.* New York: Harcourt, Brace, and World, 1968.

Municipal Art Society's Preservation Committee. *Greenpoint-Williamsburg Rezoning Area Historic Resources.* New York: Municipal Art Society, 2005.

Pollan, Michael. *Omnivore's Dilemma.* New York: Penguin, 2006.

Rapkin, Chester. *The South Houston Industrial Area.* New York: City of New York City Planning Commission, Department of City Planning, 1963.

"Road Supply and Traffic in California Urban Areas." *Transportation Research* 31A, no. 3 (1997): 205–218.

Robins, Anthony. "Envisioning a Healthy Urban Habitat." *Hillscapes: A Scrapbook* 15 (July 1999).

Rogers, Betsy Barlow. "Robert Moses and the Transformation of Central Park." *SiteLines* 3, no. 1 (Fall 2007).

Schreibman, Lisa. "Looking for Land? Try Tearing Down a Highway." *Planning Magazine* (January 2001).

Schwartz, Joel. *The New York Approach: Robert Moses, Urban Liberals, and Redevelopment of the Inner City.* Columbus: Ohio State University Press, 1993.

Shapiro, Michael. *The Last Good Season: Brooklyn, the Dodgers, and Their Final Pennant Race Together.* New York: Doubleday, 2005.

Smith, Chris. "Mr. Ratner's Neighborhood." *New York Magazine,* August 14, 2006.

Snell, Bradford. "American Ground Transport." Part 4A of hearings on S. 1167, *The Industrial Reorganization Act,* before the Subcommittee on Antitrust and Monopoly Committee of the Judiciary. U.S. Senate, 93rd Cong., 2nd sess.

"The Society for the Architecture of the City." *Village Views* 6, no. 2 (1990).

Wallace, Deborah, and Rodrick Wallace. *A Plague on Your Houses: How New York Was Burned Down and National Public Health Crumbled.* London and New York: Verso, 1998.

Walsh, Bryan. "Greening This Old House: Saving Money and the Planet by Upgrading Older Homes." *Time,* May 4, 2009.

White, Norval, and Elliot Willensky, eds. *AIA Guide to New York.* New York: Crown Publishing, 2000.

Wood, Anthony C. *Preserving New York: Winning the Right to Protect the City's Landmarks.* Manchester, Vt.: Northshire Books, 2007.

Zacks, Stephen. "Made in the USA." *Metropolis Magazine* (March 2008).

Index

The Center for the Living City

For several years before she died, Jane and I discussed ways in which she would like to see her work carried on. In 2004, in collaboration with her, a small group of her friends established The Center for the Living City, a name she suggested.

In varying ways in the years to come, we will build on her work and seek to expand the already substantial population that observes and advocates on behalf of urban life in her tradition.